The EU's New Borderland

Cross-border relations and regional development

Andrzej Jakubowski, Andrzej Miszczuk, Bogdan Kawałko, Tomasz Komornicki and Roman Szul

Routledge
Taylor & Francis Group
LONDON AND NEW YORK

First published 2017
by Routledge
2 Park Square, Milton Park, Abingdon, Oxon OX14 4RN

and by Routledge
711 Third Avenue, New York, NY 10017

Routledge is an imprint of the Taylor & Francis Group, an informa business

British Library Cataloguing in Publication Data
A catalogue record for this book is available from the British Library.

Library of Congress Cataloging in Publication Data
A catalog record for this book has been requested

ISBN: 978-1-138-65495-2 (hbk)
ISBN: 978-1-315-62287-3 (ebk)

Typeset in Times New Roman
by Sunrise Setting Ltd, Brixham, UK

Contents

Figures

Tables

Acknowledgements

We would first of all like to thank Rob Langham at Routledge, who was the first to be interested in our idea of a publication dedicated to the Polish–Ukrainian borderland. We are also grateful to Elanor Best (at Routledge) for her goodwill and helpfulness, as well as Tim Hyde (at Sunrise Setting) and Sarah Harrison for their excellent work on the proofs. Our special thanks go to Lucy Bindulska, who perfectly translated a great part of the book into English.

Andrzej Jakubowski and Andrzej Miszczuk

Abbreviations

AA	Association Agreement
ATO	Anti-Terrorist Operation
CBC	cross-border cooperation
CCP	cross-border cooperation programme
CEFTA	Central European Free Trade Agreement
CIS	Commonwealth of Independent States
COMECON	The Council for Mutual Economic Assistance
DCFTA	Deep and Comprehensive Free Trade Area
DK	Droga Krajowa (trunk road)
EACU	Eurasian Customs Union
ECPUU	European College of Polish and Ukrainian Universities
EEA	European Economic Area
ENP	European Neighbourhood Policy
ENPI	European Neighbourhood and Partnership Instrument
EP	Eastern Partnership
ERDF	European Regional Development Fund
EU	European Union
FDI	foreign direct investment
GDP	gross domestic product
GUAM	GUAM Organization for Democracy and Economic Development
HDI	human development index
HGV	heavy goods vehicle
ICT	information and communication technologies
IMF	International Monetary Fund
KUL	Katolicki Uniwersytet Lubelski Jana Pawła II (John Paul II Catholic University of Lublin)
LBT	local border traffic
LHS	Linia Hutnicza Szerokotorowa (Broad-gauge Steelworks Line)
NATO	The North Atlantic Treaty Organization
NGO	non-governmental organizations
NIS	New Independent States
NNI	new neighbourhood instrument

NUTS	Nomenclature of Territorial Units for Statistics
NZS	Narodowe Siły Zbrojne (National Armed Forces)
OUN	Orghanizacia Ukrainskykh Nacionalistiv (Organization of Ukrainian Nationalists)
PBU	Poland–Belarus–Ukraine
PCA	Partnership and Cooperation Agreement
PGR	Państwowe Gospodarstwo Rolne (State Agricultural Farm)
PiS	Prawo i Sprawiedliwość (Law and Justice)
PLN	Polish złoty (currency)
PO	Platforma Obywatelska (Civic Platform)
PPS	purchasing power standards
PUWP	Polish United Workers' Party
R&D	research and development
RHDI	regional human development index
SPF	small project fund
TACIS	Technical Assistance to the Commonwealth of Independent States
TEN-T	Trans-European Transport Networks
TRACECA	Transport Corridor Europe–Caucasus–Asia
UMCS	Uniwersytet Marii Curie-Skłodowskiej (Maria Curie-Skłodowska University)
UNDP	United Nations Development Programme
UNESCO MaB	United Nations Educational, Scientific and Cultural Organization Man and Biosphere Programme
UPA	Ukrainska Povstanska Armia (Ukrainian Uprising Army)
USA	United States of America
USSR	Ukrainian Soviet Socialist Republic
WTO	World Trade Organization

Introduction

Andrzej Jakubowski and Andrzej Miszczuk

The rapprochement of Poland and Ukraine that has taken place over the last quarter century is one of the most positive examples of bilateral transformation in post-communist Central and Eastern Europe. Despite their complex and burdensome historical legacy, dominated by the tragic events of World War II and the early post-war years, after the fall of communism Poland and Ukraine managed to develop bilateral cooperation in the institutional dimension and rebuild mutual contacts on a social level. At the same time both nations were linked in a strategic partnership, within which Poland began to perform the role of a promoter and patron of a pro-western orientation in Ukraine's domestic and foreign policy.

The issue of Polish–Ukrainian relations on an interstate and cross-border level gained particular significance at the point of the European Union's enlargement in the east and the launch of the European Neighbourhood Policy in 2004. In view of Poland's socio-economic potential as the largest new member state, emerging as a leader in Central and Eastern Europe, as well as the significance of Ukraine as the largest nation included in the Eastern Partnership programme, it could be said that Poland and Ukraine, and in particular the Polish–Ukrainian borderland, have become a kind of geopolitical keystone, connecting the European Union and Eastern Europe. However, while Poland is regarded as an example of successful political and economic transformation, Ukraine remains a nation of largely unexploited opportunity, drawing the world's attention only at moments of dramatic change, such as the Orange Revolution and the Maidan movement.

The success of official Polish–Ukrainian interstate relations is reflected at regional and local levels in the form of joint economic, cultural, educational and scientific initiatives carried out within the two Euroregions existing in the Polish–Ukrainian borderland: the Bug and Carpathian Euroregions. While official interstate relations have developed well, cross-border cooperation has stumbled against barriers of a diverse nature. An undoubted challenge for the development of Polish–Ukrainian cross-border cooperation was the entry of Poland to the European Union. Besides the many opportunities, numerous threats also appeared affecting the social and economic ties that had previously been formed along with institutional forms of cooperation. Now that ten years have passed since the largest expansion in the history of the EU, it would seem an appropriate moment to conduct the first summary of this period.

The proposed publication deals with a topic of major current importance – cross-border cooperation and ties on the new external border of the EU. Its principal aim is to show how Polish and Ukrainian actors have developed bilateral cooperation, adapting to the changing geopolitical conditions and responding to the challenges they generate.

Further aims of the publication are to perform a multidimensional diagnosis of the circumstances determining the current and future shape of Polish–Ukrainian cross-border cooperation, to describe the Polish–Ukrainian borderland as a social, economic and political space, and to evaluate its socio-economic potential. In doing so, it is worth emphasizing that the area regarded as the Polish–Ukrainian borderland, incorporating four regional units (Lublin and Podkarpackie voivodships in Poland; Lviv and Volhynia oblasts in Ukraine) is an example of a relatively young borderland, as the subsequent state boundaries which form its backbone were not created until after World War II. Previously, the studied region belonged in its entirety to one nation (Bałtowski and Miszczuk 1999).

Equally important from a research point of view are questions concerning perspectives on cross-border cooperation in the context of national and regional strategic documents, Polish–Ukrainian bilateral relations, the evolution of EU policies towards neighbouring states and, above all, the geopolitical transformation in Central and Eastern Europe.

Current events in Ukraine have lent a specific context to the discussion, as we find ourselves at a moment of transition. On the one hand there is renewed hope of a pro-western turn in Ukrainian politics, the implementation of reforms and closer proximity to the EU; while, on the other hand, numerous fears have arisen regarding the security and future of this nation, particularly after the annexation of Crimea by Russia and the continuing conflict in Donbas.

The question of Polish–Ukrainian relations has become the subject of several dozen publications in English, although these are somewhat diverse in nature and only lightly touch upon the issues covered in this study. The history of Polish–Ukrainian relations spanning many centuries is presented in, among others, *Poland and Ukraine: past and present* (Potichnyi 1980); 'Polish–Ukrainian Relations: The Burden of History' (Rudnytsky 1987); *Borderland: A Journey through the History of Ukraine* (Reid 2000); and *Galicia: A Multicultured Land*, dedicated to the history of the southern part of the present-day borderland (Hann and Magocsi 2005). The issue of Polish–Ukrainian relations during World War II has also been fairly well examined, the tone being set by the Polish–Ukrainian debate on the massacre of Poles in Volhynia and Eastern Galicia. Among historical publications that deserve mention include *Genocide and Rescue in Wolyn* (Piotrowski 2000) and *Heroes and the Villains. Creating National History in Contemporary Ukraine* (Marples 2007).

The relations between Poland and Ukraine in the first years after the fall of communism are presented in *Polish–Ukrainian Relations in 1992–1996* (Kamiński and Kozakiewicz 1997). Other valuable contributions include 'The Ukrainian–Polish Strategic Partnership and Central European Geopolitics' (Pavliuk 1999) as well as 'Ukrainian–Polish Relations between 1991–1998: From the Declaratory to the Substantive' (Wolczuk 2000). An additional publication covering this issue is *On the Edge. Ukrainian–Central European–Russian Security Triangle* (Balmaceda 2000).

The question of Polish–Ukrainian relations in the context of European integration is the subject of 'European Union and Ukrainian–Polish Relations' (Dybczyński 2000) and the collective work *Strategic Partnership between Poland and Ukraine* (Podraza and Gizicki 2008). Other works deserving of attention include *Poland and Ukraine: A Strategic partnership in a Changing Europe?* (Wolczuk and Wolczuk 2003a) and *Poland's relations with Ukraine: A challenging strategic partnership* (Wolczuk and Wolczuk 2003b), as well as 'Polish–Ukrainian Relations: A Strategic Relationship Conditioned by Externalities' (Wolczuk 2002). Further works of interest are *More than Neighbours: The Enlarged Europe and Ukraine – new relations* (Boratynski and Gromadzki 2004); 'What Holds Ukraine and Poland Together? On External and Internal Factors of Ukrainian–Polish Relations' (Klymenko 2009) and *Public Opinion and the Making of Foreign Policy in the 'New Europe': A Comparative Study of Poland and Ukraine* (Copsey 2013).

However, these publications concern Polish–Ukrainian relations on an interstate level, overlooking or only touching on their regional and cross-border dimensions. Meanwhile, a number of valuable but fragmentary studies are equally unable to fill the gap in this area. These include 'Conflicts and Potential on Poland's Eastern Borders: the Example of the Polish-Russian and Polish–Ukrainian Border Regions' (Stokłosa 2012), 'The Polish–Ukrainian Interstate Model for Cooperation and Integration: Regional Relations in a Theoretical Context' (Spero 2002) and 'Local and regional cross-border cooperation between Poland and Ukraine' (Krok and Smętkowski 2006).

In reviewing the literature on the subject, it is noticeable that there was a growth in interest on the topic of Polish–Ukrainian relations in the period preceding EU enlargement in 2004 as well as in the first years following the Orange Revolution. Apart from the work by N. Copsey, the studies quickly became outdated as a result of the dynamic changes taking place both in the international environment and in Ukraine's domestic politics. There is no up-to-date contribution taking into account the transition process in Ukraine initiated by the Revolution of Dignity or the new dimension of relations between the European Union (including Poland) and Ukraine based on the European Neighbourhood Policy, the Eastern Partnership and the Association Agreement.

There is also a lack of publications available providing a complex analysis of Polish–Ukrainian cross-border cooperation. This study fills the informational gap in this area. Moreover, owing to its inter-disciplinary character, including issues relating to political geography, international relations and economics, it constitutes a unique and up-to-date work of considerable cognitive, explanatory and prognostic merit. It comprises four chapters. The first, by Roman Szul, presents the wider Polish–Ukrainian context of cross-border cooperation in the historical perspective, highlighting the principal factors determining the current shape and nature of this cooperation. The history of the Polish–Ukrainian borderland is shown in the context of Polish–Ukrainian relations, particularly at the time when two conflicting national projects – Polish and Ukrainian – collided. The issue of geopolitical changes is also discussed, including changes along the border, which in the course of the turbulent twentieth century had either integrational or disintegrational effects on the analysed area, resulting in alternate periods of either making or breaking many functional and spatial ties. Chapter 1 also discusses the various models of political and socio-economic transformation adopted in Poland and in Ukraine.

Chapters 2 and 3 are of an empirical nature, based on analyses of statistical data retrieved from different sources, each of which is discussed in detail. Chapter 2, by Andrzej Jakubowski, shows the potential of Poland–Ukraine in terms of its natural environment, demography and economy. Based on cluster analysis, the author summarizes the position of the study area in the context of European regions.

Meanwhile, Chapter 3, by Tomasz Komornicki and Andrzej Miszczuk, presents a diagnosis of existing cross-border ties and forms of cross-border cooperation in the Polish–Ukrainian borderland. The principal outcomes of and barriers to cross-border cooperation are identified and assessed. Detailed analyses are conducted in the following areas: cooperation in nature conservation, including cross-border protected areas; social contacts (labour and student migration); the main transport corridors and their significance; the state of border infrastructure and the size of border traffic; trade contacts, including foreign and border trade; tourist links; and institutional cooperation between various entities.

Finally, Chapter 4, by Andrzej Jakubowski, Bogdan Kawałko, Andrzej Miszczuk and Roman Szul, discusses the challenges and opportunities that face Polish–Ukrainian cross-border cooperation in the context of national and regional strategic documents, bilateral interstate relations, the evolving EU Eastern Policy and European Neighbourhood Instrument, the new geopolitical choices of Ukraine and the geopolitical transformation occurring in Central and Eastern Europe. The summary of this chapter presents possible scenarios for the development of Polish–Ukrainian cross-border cooperation and indicates the consequences for cross-border cooperation and development in the Polish–Ukrainian borderland.

This publication is directed at readers who are interested in the socio-economic and political situation in the Polish–Ukrainian borderland, the Polish–Ukrainian section of the external EU border, the European Neighbourhood Policy and the geopolitical transformations in Central and Eastern Europe. However, the interdisciplinary nature of this publication, incorporating issues of political geography, history, international relations and economics, as well as the current validity of the topics discussed, means that the range of potential readers is no doubt much wider.

Bibliography

Balmaceda, M. M. (2000) *On the Edge. Ukrainian–Central European–Russian Security Triangle*. Budapest: Central European University Press.

Bałtowski, M. and Miszczuk, A. (1999) Granica polsko-ukraińska w perspektywie nowego europejskiego porządku geopolitycznego. *Przegląd Zachodni* 292/3, pp. 29–40.

Boratynski, J. and Gromadzki, G. (2004) *More than neighbours. The enlarged European Union and Ukraine – new relations*. Warsaw: Stefan Batory Foundation, International Renaissance Foundation.

Copsey, N. (2013) *Public Opinion and the Making of Foreign Policy in the 'New Europe'. A Comparative Study of Poland and Ukraine*. Aldershot: Ashgate.

Dybczyński, A. (2000) European Union and Ukrainian–Polish Relations, in: K. Cordell (ed.) *Poland and the European Union*. London: Routledge, pp. 182–98.

Hann, C. and Magocsi, P. R. (2005) *Galicia: A Multicultured Land*. Toronto: University of Toronto Press.

Kamiński, A. Z. and Kozakiewicz, J. (1997) *Polish–Ukrainian Relations in 1992–1996*. Warsaw: Center for International Relations at the Institute of Public Affairs.

Klymenko, L. (2009) What Holds Ukraine and Poland Together? On External and Internal Factors of Ukrainian–Polish Relations, in: J. Besters-Dilger (ed.) *Ukraine on its Way to Europe. Interim Results of the Orange Revolution*. Frankfurt am Main, Berlin, Bern, Bruxelles, New York, Oxford, Wien: Peter Lang, pp. 253–74.

Krok, K. and Smętkowski, M. (2006) Local and regional cross-border cooperation between Poland and Ukraine, in: J. W. Scott (ed.) *EU Enlargement, Region Building and Shifting Borders of Inclusion and Exclusion*. Aldershot: Ashgate, pp. 177–92.

Marples, D. R. (2007) *Heroes and the Villains. Creating National History in Contemporary Ukraine*. Budapest: Central European University Press.

Pavliuk, O. (1999) The Ukrainian–Polish Strategic Partnership and Central European Geopolitics, in: K. R. Spillmann, A. Wenger and D. Müller (eds) *Between Russia and the West: Foreign and Security Policy of Independent Ukraine*. Bern: Peter Lang, pp. 185–211.

Piotrowski, T. (2000) *Genocide and Rescue in Wolyn: Recollections of the Ukrainian Nationalist Ethnic Cleansing Campaign Against the Poles During World War II*. Jefferson: McFarland.

Podraza, A. and Gizicki, W. (2008) *Strategic Partnership between Poland and Ukraine*. Lublin: The John Paul II Catholic University of Lublin: Lublin Business School Ltd of the KUL Development Foundation.

Potichnyi, P. J. (1980) *Poland and Ukraine: past and present*. Edmonton, Toronto: Canadian Institute of Ukranian Studies Press.

Reid, A. (2000) *Borderland: A Journey through the History of Ukraine*. Boulder: WestView Press.

Rudnytsky, I. (1987) Polish–Ukrainian Relations: The Burden of History, in: I. Rudnytsky (ed.) *Essays in Modern Ukrainian History*. Edmonton: Canadian Institute of Ukrainian Studies, pp. 49–76.

Spero, J. B. (2002) The Polish–Ukrainian Interstate Model for Cooperation and Integration Regional Relations in a Theoretical Context, in: J. D. P. Moroney, T. Kuzio and M. Molchanov (eds) *Ukrainian Foreign and Security Policy: Theoretical and Comparative Perspectives*. Westport, London: Praeger, pp. 155–78.

Stokłosa, K. (2012) Conflicts and Potential on Poland's Eastern Borders: the Example of the Polish–Russian and Polish–Ukrainian Border Regions, in: K. Katajala and M. Lahteenmaki (eds) *Imagined, Negotiated, Remembered. Constructing European Borders and Borderlands*. Munster: Lit Verlag, pp. 187–98.

Wolczuk, K. and Wolczuk, R. (2003a) *Poland and Ukraine: A Strategic Partnership in a Changing Europe?* London: Chatham House.

Wolczuk, K. and Wolczuk, R. (2003b) Poland's relations with Ukraine: A challenging 'strategic partnership', in: J. Smith and C. Jenkins (eds) *Through the Paper Curtain: Insiders and Outsiders in the New Europe*. Oxford: Blackwell Publishing Ltd, pp. 77–93.

Wolczuk, R. (2000) Ukrainian–Polish Relations between 1991–1998: From the Declaratory to the Substantive. *European Security*, 1/9, pp. 127–56.

Wolczuk, R. (2002) Polish–Ukrainian Relations: A Strategic Relationship Conditioned by Externalities. *Defence Studies*, 2/2, pp. 143–50.

1 Poland and Ukraine against the background of changes in Central and Eastern Europe in the twentieth and twenty-first centuries

Roman Szul

Relations between Poland and Ukraine as independent states have a short history, starting in 1991, but the history of Polish–Ukrainian relations is long, dating back to the tenth/eleventh centuries. Until the second half of the nineteenth century, when the contemporary notion of Ukraine and Ukrainian nationalism emerged, these were relations between Poland and Poles, and Ruthenian states and Ruthenians. Over most of this 1,000-year period, owing to Poland's eastern expansion over the fourteenth–sixteenth centuries, smaller or greater parts of present-day Ukraine belonged to Poland or political formations dominated by Poles (the Polish–Lithuanian Commonwealth, Galicia as part of the Habsburg empire). The main differences separating Poles and Ruthenians/Ukrainians were religion (Roman Catholic vs Orthodox or Greek Catholic) and social status (in Ukraine Poles used to be gentry and aristocracy, while Ruthenians were mostly peasants). Contacts between the two groups contributed to their linguistic and cultural rapprochement, but rivalry and periodic outbreaks of conflict produced a considerable distrust and prejudice, leading to Polish–Ukrainian conflicts after World War I and during World War II and directly afterwards. From World War I Poland emerged as an independent state with a numerous Ukrainian minority; World War II and its consequences shifted the Polish eastern border westwards, and ethnic cleansing and migrations practically eliminated minorities on both sides of the border, which became the border between Poland and the Soviet Union. Ukrainian aspirations towards an independent state failed twice, but Ukraine survived as a 'republic' within the USSR. The collapse of the Soviet block in 1989 and of the USSR itself in 1991 gave full independence to Poland and brought about independence to Ukraine, something welcomed by some of its inhabitants but only tolerated by others. Both countries decided to build a democratic political system and a free market economy. However, different internal and international conditions at the starting point and thereafter produced different results. Poland, which was almost homogeneous in terms of culture, language and political desire to join the West, and began with some elements of a market economy and a clear idea how to reform the economic and political system, became, with the support and encouragement of the West, a member of NATO in 1999 and the EU in 2004; it had a relatively stable democracy and a prosperous economy, although not without social and political tensions. Ukraine, torn between its Ukrainian-speaking, nationalistic and pro-European west and its Russian-speaking, nationally indifferent and Russian-orientated east and south, could not decide over its geopolitical course and lacked determination to carry out substantial economic and political reforms. Besides, the protracted economic decline of the 1990s, with only modest recovery after 2000, and the chosen method of privatization, which produced a small number of very rich 'oligarchs' and political corruption, generated a disintegrated and frustrated society. These circumstances were conducive to severe political crises. The last one, in 2013/14, brought about bloodshed, a dramatic change of president, the annexation of Crimea by Russia, revolt in two eastern regions supported by Russia and the war, and also a declared victory of the pro-European orientation. The independence of Ukraine and economic reforms in Poland and Ukraine led to an intensification of cross-border contacts which, however, slowed down after Poland's access to the EU, as the border became less permeable. Since Ukraine's independence in 1991 Polish–Ukrainian political relations have improved. Poland was the first country to recognize Ukraine as an independent state, supporting its pro-European aspirations and 'advocating' for it in the EU. A recent surge of patriotic (nationalistic) sentiments in Ukraine and what is considered in Poland as the glorification of perpetrators of genocide on ethnic Poles during World War II may, however, lead to a deterioration in Polish–Ukrainian relations.

Polish–Ukrainian relations in the twentieth and twenty-first centuries

The present Polish–Ukrainian border, as an international border, exists from the end of World War II (1944, with small corrections in the early 1950s). Initially it was a border between Poland (People's Republic of Poland) and the Soviet Union – or, in another words, between Poland and the Ukrainian Soviet Socialist Republic (Ukrainian SSR) as part of the Union of Soviet Socialist Republics (USSR). With the breakdown of the USSR in 1991 and the emergence of the Ukrainian SSR as an independent state called simply Ukraine,[1] this border became the border between Poland and independent Ukraine (as a matter of fact, Poland was the first country to recognize Ukrainian independence).

Despite the short history of the relations between Poland and Ukraine as two sovereign states, Polish–Ukrainian relations have a much longer, and very complicated, history. This was a history of relations between two ethnic groups (Polish and Ruthenian/Ukrainian) and between a state (Poland) and an ethnic group (Ruthenians/Ukrainians). To understand the nature of Polish–Ukrainian relations in the twentieth and twenty-first centuries it is necessary to look back to more distant events. Probably the first relevant event was the settlement (in ancient or early medieval times) on the territory of present Poland and Ukraine of two groups of the Slavic people – let's call them Western Slavs and Eastern Slavs (or Ruthenians, in their and other languages: *Rusins*). If there were no other factors strengthening this divide, differences between the two groups would have disappeared. These 'other factors' were the establishment of states – Poland (by the Western Slavs) and Kiev Ruthenia or Kiev Rus (by the Eastern Slavs) in the early Middle Ages – and the adoption by them of different varieties of Christianity (western, or Catholic, Christianity in Poland, and eastern, or Orthodox, Christianity in Ruthenia). The border between Poland and Kiev Ruthenia was, by and large, in the present Polish–Ukrainian borderland, although sometimes it was more to the west and sometimes more to the east of the present borderline (see Figure 1.1).

Another event of extraordinary importance was the crisis and disintegration of Kiev Ruthenia in the thirteenth century and the incorporation of a part of it in the fourteenth century by Poland. The eastward expansion of Poland (alone or as the stronger partner in the common Polish–Lithuanian state called the 'Commonwealth of the Two Nations') continued in the fifteenth and sixteenth centuries to encompass most of present-day Ukraine (apart from Crimea and the Donetsk–Luhansk region).

The incorporation of Ruthenian lands into Poland had far-reaching consequences. Perhaps the most important were Polish rule in Ruthenian lands and the Polonization (adoption of the Polish language, Catholic religion and Polish

Figure 1.1 Poland and Ruthenia in the twelfth century

Source: Krzysztof Łoboda, on the basis of IGiPZ PAN (1997).

customs and identity) of the local Ruthenian aristocracy, as well as the immigration of non-Ruthenians (peasants speaking western Slavonic – 'Polish' – dialects and confessing Catholicism, as well as Jews, Germans and others, usually merchants or craftsmen) to Ruthenian lands. As a result of these processes a social structure was formed within Ruthenian lands consisting of peasants speaking eastern Slavonic (Ruthenian) dialects and confessing Orthodox religion at the bottom, and an aristocracy speaking Polish (already a unified prestigious language) and confessing Catholicism at the top, with various groups in the middle (among others, very numerous were Jews). It is important to note that the term 'Polish' (e.g. 'Polish nation') meant 'aristocratic' or 'noble'. Peasants speaking western Slavonic dialects and confessing Catholicism (future 'Poles') had no idea of being 'Polish'. The word 'Ukraine' (in Polish 'ukraina'; a similar word exists in contemporary Russian: 'okraina') at that time meant 'far-away lands', 'distant periphery', as from Krakow, Poznan or Warsaw it really was a distant periphery. In contemporary Polish, as in other Slavonic languages, 'Ukraina' is only the name of a country, 'Ukraine'.

The expansion of Poland in Ruthenian lands took place in several waves. The first significant and lasting expansion was, as mentioned above, in the fourteenth century, and was at the expense of the Principality of Galicia-Volhynia (known also as the Kingdom of Galicia-Volhynia and Kingdom of Ruthenia). This principality emerged at the end of the twelfth century from the disintegration of the Kiev Ruthenia and consisted of territory within the present Polish–Ukrainian borderland. Its capital cities were Halych (which gave the Latin name of the part of the principality – Galicia), now a small town in the Ukrainian Carpathian mountains; Chełm (now a town in Poland); Volodymyr Volynsky or Włodzimierz Wołyński (which gave the other part of the name – Volhynia), now in Ukraine; and Lviv/Lwów/Lemberg, now a large city in western Ukraine. One of rulers of this principality, Danylo or Daniel, was in 1253 crowned by a pope's envoy as 'King of Ruthenia'. It is worth mentioning that in 1256 this ruler founded Lviv, a city that would play an extraordinarily important role in Polish–Ukrainian relations. In its century-and-a-half history Galicia-Volhynia was seldom a fully independent state, being the subject of rivalry between Poland, the (Grand Duchy of) Lithuania, Hungary and the Tatars. It is worth noting that it enjoyed good relations with the Principality of Mazovia, then independent; now its territory (including, for instance, Warsaw) is part of Poland. The last ruler of Galicia-Volhynia, Bolesław Jerzy II, was son of the Mazovian prince Trojden. After the death without issue of the last ruler of Galicia-Volhynia, it was divided between Hungary, Poland (the main part, with Halych and Lviv) and Lithuania (Volhynia). The part incorporated into Poland became known as 'Red Ruthenia' and was a separate territorial administrative unit.

From the point of view of future historical events, some elements of the heritage of Galicia-Volhynia should be stressed. First, the very name 'Ruthenia' and its status as a separate territorial unit facilitated the preservation of the feeling of being something different from the rest of the Kingdom of Poland and thus preserved a separate identity among its Ruthenian inhabitants. It should be stressed, however, that identification with Ruthenia did not always exclude identification with Poland as a larger polity. Second, the memory (continuous or reconstructed) that Lviv was established by a Ruthenian king gave Ruthenians/Ukrainians, during their conflict with Poles in the nineteenth and twentieth centuries, the moral argument to treat this city as theirs. Third, the emperors of Austria, who inherited from the kings of Hungary the claims and the title 'King of Galicia', used this to justify their participation in the partitioning of the Commonwealth of the Two Nations (Poland) at the end of the eighteenth century. To confirm their claims they gave the new territory the historic name 'Kingdom of Galicia and Lodomeria'.

At the time that Poland incorporated Red Ruthenia, the Grand Duchy of Lithuania incorporated the northern part of the Principality of Galicia-Volhynia and expanded further south-eastwards, encompassing many Ruthenian principalities, including Kiev, the capital city of the ancient Kiev Ruthenia. This expansion was alleviated by the fact that the Grand Duchy of Lithuania was regarded as another Ruthenian principality, as its rulers and their administration spoke Ruthenian and used (old-)Ruthenian (in fact, a mixture of living Ruthenian and Church-Slavonic) as a chancellery language, once used in Kiev Ruthenia, and the vast majority of its inhabitants were Ruthenians and Orthodox. On the other hand, incorporation by the Grand Duchy was regarded as a kind of protection against Tatars. In such a way the Grand Duchy of Lithuania in a sense re-established the old Kiev Ruthenia, although now its political centre was far away from Kiev, in Vilnius/Wilno/Wilna. After initial rivalry, Poland and the Grand Duchy of Lithuania established friendly relations and, by the end of the fourteenth century, they established a personal union when a Lithuanian prince, Jagiełło (Jogaila), was offered the Polish throne (beforehand, he was baptized as Christian and Catholic; by his baptism he received the name Władysław); at that time the same rulers were Polish kings and Lithuanian grand dukes. Almost two centuries later, the two countries established a real union called the 'Commonwealth of the Two Nations' (1569) by an act known as the Lublin Union, as it took place in this Polish town. The two parts of the Commonwealth – the Crown of Poland (also simply 'the Crown') and the Grand Duchy (of Lithuania) retained many elements of their legal, economic and political systems, including separate armies.

From the point of view of future Polish–Ukrainian relations, the shift of the border between the Crown of Poland and the Grand Duchy accompanying the Lublin Union was very important. The southern part of the Grand Duchy, including Kiev, was then incorporated into the Crown of Poland. In such a way Ruthenian lands found themselves in two state organisms: Poland in the south and Lithuania in the north (Figure 1.2).

This division gave birth to two contemporary nations: Ukrainians (in Poland) and Byelorussians (in Lithuania).[2] It could be said that the history of the Ukrainian nation begins with the Lublin Union.[3]

One of the results of Poland's eastern expansion was the emergence of a category of gentry and aristocracy that defined itself by the Latin formula (Latin was the symbolic language of the gentry and aristocracy, separating *bene nati* from the commons) 'natione Polonorum, gente Ruthenorum', or belonging to the Polish

Figure 1.2 Commonwealth of the Two Nations (1569)

Source: Krzysztof Łoboda, on the basis of IGiPZ PAN (1997).

nation and Ruthenian people. These were people of Ruthenian origin who combined their Ruthenian identity with a larger identification with Poland or the Commonwealth. This category of people played an extraordinarily important role in the history of Poles and Ukrainians. Its detailed analysis exceeds the scope of this text, but it should be pointed out that the very existence of this category indicated that there was no contradiction between being Polish and Ruthenian, and that Ruthenians were simply a regional or ethnographic variety of Poles. The Polish national movement (the whole or its radical part) stuck to this notion practically until World War II, denying the emergence of the Ukrainian (ethnic) nation within Ruthenian society. This was one of the reasons for severe conflicts between the two nationalisms in the second half of the nineteenth and the first half of the twentieth century, during which people of 'natione Polonorum, gente Ruthenorum' had to decide whether they were Polish or Ruthenian/Ukrainian.

The Lublin Union has been subject of divergent interpretations by the parties engaged and by future national movements. Poles from the very beginning assessed it positively: the union strengthened the position of Poland, the change in the border enlarged Polish territory, and the Commonwealth itself was regarded as an extended Poland, to the point that the two names 'Commonwealth' and 'Poland' became synonyms.[4] This assessment has a material justification: the expansion of Polish language, culture and political influence eastwards. Describing Lithuanian and Belarusian approaches are irrelevant from the point of view of this study. In contrast, modern Ukrainian historiography of the nineteenth and early twentieth centuries assessed the union negatively, for three reasons. First, it was advantageous for Poland and Poles, and therefore it was disadvantageous for Ruthenians, predecessors of Ukrainians. For the young Ukrainian nationalism, which largely emerged in opposition to Poland and to the Polish national movement, everything good for Poland had to be automatically bad for Ukraine. Second, the union was unequal: it was a result of the pressure by the Polish side, and, besides, it put a definite end to the tradition of Kiev Ruthenia. Third, it opened the doors to inflows of foreigners – Poles, Jews, Germans – to Ukraine, who occupied leading social positions, pushing down the local Ruthenian (Ukrainian) population. Subsequently this interpretation was largely overtaken by Soviet Ukrainian historiography, playing on the anti-Polish and anti-western, anti-aristocratic and anti-bourgeois sentiments of Ukrainians. In such a way, 300 years after its conclusion, interpretations of the Lublin Union added to the emergence of Ukrainian nationalism. Nowadays, in independent Ukraine, the union is the subject of re-evaluations. It is pointed out that it was a result of a voluntary agreement of 'the equals with the equals' (and not imposed by the Polish side), that inflows of foreigners brought with them economic and technological progress, and that the position of the Ukrainian population in society was not as bad as it was presented earlier.[5]

Of extraordinary importance were events in the mid-seventeenth century, namely the Cossack uprising and its aftermath. Cossacks[6] were a community of free people (not peasantry) composed of persons from various parts of the Commonwealth, mainly outlaws escaping from serfdom or otherwise being in conflict with the law, living in what is now southern Ukraine, out of reach of justice and royal power. They spoke a local Ruthenian dialect, although they could also speak Polish, and, more importantly, they confessed Orthodox Christianity. They formed a self-governed democratic community headed by elected *ataman* and carried out practically independent foreign policy, although formally their territory belonged to the Commonwealth. Some Cossacks enjoyed the status of nobles awarded by the king of Poland and accepted by Sejm (parliament). In the mid-seventeenth century the Cossacks, headed by ataman Bohdan Khmelnytsky, (or Chmielnicki, in the Polish spelling) rose against royal power for several reasons: to protest against the policy of unification of the local Orthodox church with the Catholic church (which, in fact, meant the subordination of the former to the latter), to demand greater access on the part of Cossacks to the ranks of nobles, and to demand social changes. The Cossack uprising occurred jointly with the Ruthenian peasantry, thus becoming a war of the poor Orthodox Ruthenians against the rich Catholic Poles (as well as against Jews, who were probably the most numerous victims of the uprising). Looking for allies against the Commonwealth, Khmelnytsky cooperated with Tatars, Turkey and Moscow. The agreement with Moscow (reached in Pereyaslav between Khmelnytsky and a Moscow envoy in the name of the Russian tsar Alexei) in fact subordinated territory under Khmelnytsky's control to Moscow (Pereyaslav Agreement, 1654) and changed the history of the whole region of Central and Eastern Europe (and a part of Asia). It was a turning point in the history of the Commonwealth of Poland and Lithuania, initiating its fall, and a turning point in the history of Moscow/Russia, launching its rise as an intercontinental empire.[7] Ukraine was divided between the Commonwealth (Poland) and Moscow (becoming Russia) along the Dnepr river, with Kiev 'temporarily', but, practically, permanently, on the Russian side. On the Polish side the uprising, after heavy and bloody fighting, was suppressed by an army headed by Duke Jarema Wiśniowiecki.

It should be added that Khmelnytsky was not the only Cossack ataman, and that relations between the Commonwealth and Cossacks were not always hostile, while relations between Cossacks and Moscow were not always friendly. In this context it is worth mentioning ataman Ivan Mazepa, who, in alliance with Sweden, fought against Russia at the beginning of the eighteenth century, but was defeated (together with his Swedish allies) by Russian emperor Peter the First (the Great) (battle of Poltava, east of Kiev, 1707). Nevertheless, other personalities and events did not leave so far reaching and lasting an imprint on the fate of Poland and Ukraine as did Khmelnytshy and his Cossacks.

There were several important consequences of the uprising: the loss of one half of Ukraine by Poland and the beginning of expansion of Russia in Ukraine; hostility between the two ethno-religious social groups; and the creation of symbols, sources of inspiration and heroes for the future Polish and Ukrainian nationalist movements of the nineteenth and twentieth centuries (for Poles the hero was Wiśniowiecki; for Ukrainians, Khmelnytsky and his Cossacks). In the nineteenth century, when Ukraine was divided between Austria and Russia and the Ukrainian national movement was emerging, it was the legend of the Cossacks that united both parts of Ukraine.[8] It is also worth noting that, in commemorating the 300th anniversary of Khmelnytsky's uprising and the Pereyaslav agreement in 1954, Ukraine was 'rewarded' by the Ukraine-born Soviet leader Nikita Khrushchev by a gift – the incorporation of Crimea into the Soviet Ukraine. At that time probably nobody imagined that 60 years later, in 2014, Ukraine would be independent from Russia and would be in conflict with Russia over Crimea.

The incorporation of eastern Ukraine into Russia did not stop tensions and conflicts between the two groups: Polish, gentry and Catholic on the one side and Ruthenian, peasant and Orthodox on the other. This conflict was sharpened by the activity of robbers called *hajdamaks* and peasant rebellions, which were brutally suppressed by the authorities. *Hajdamaks* and Ruthenian peasant rebels no less brutally attacked their victims (including Jews). What is important for Polish–Ukrainian relations is that the *hajdamsks* became another element deepening the antagonism between the two groups. *Hajdamaks* were heroes praised in popular poetry and by Taras Shevchenko, the romantic Ukrainian poet considered as one of founding fathers of Ukrainian national identity. One event related to the history of the *hajdamaks* deserves special note: the carnage of Uman/Humań, a town in Ukraine, where in 1768 thousands of its inhabitants and Polish and Jewish refugees from the surrounding area, hoping that in this fortress they would be safe, were brutally killed by *hajdamaks* and by Cossacks who, instead of defending the fortress, joined the *hajdamaks* (Serczyk 1990; Serczyk 1978). For future Polish historians Uman was a harbinger of the events in that area in 1943, known in Poland as the carnage of Volhynia (dealt with later in this chapter). Phenomena such as *hajdamaks* and peasant rebellions were nothing special at that time in Europe (and not only Europe), but what gave *hajdamaks* and Uman special meaning was the ethnic context and the memory-creating potential for three (including Jews) ethnic groups.

Continuous foreign invasions and wars in the seventeenth century (against Cossacks, Moscow, Turkey, Sweden, Tatars and even Hungarians) and other factors (firstly the weakness of central government owing to the system of *liberum veto*, or voting by unanimity, which paralysed the parliament, the highest authority in the Commonwealth) contributed to the final collapse of the Commonwealth by the end of the eighteenth century. The attempt to reform and modernize Poland (Constitution of 3 May 1791) only precipitated foreign (Russian) military intervention and the end of the Commonwealth. Its territory was divided between three powers: Russia, Prussia and Austria in the years 1772, 1793 and 1795.

The bigger part of what is now the Polish–Ukrainian borderland fell to Russia and the smaller to Austria. The Austrian part was called 'Galicia'; its western part was populated overwhelmingly by 'Polish' (Catholic, speaking west Slavonic dialects or standard Polish), while in its eastern part Ruthenian peasantry formed the majority in rural areas and Polish, Jewish, German, and Armenian populations were in the majority in towns and cities. After the Vienna congress (1815) within the Russian empire a semi-autonomous 'Kingdom of Poland' was formed whose eastern border ran along the Bug river, separating majority Polish (and Jewish) areas in the west from mixed Ruthenian–Polish–Jewish territories in the east. The name of the region east of the Bug river is *Volhynia* (*Wołyń*) – as noted above, the location of dramatic events during World War II. The autonomy of the Kingdom of Poland was gradually reduced until, by the end of the nineteenth century, it was finally abolished and the country was renamed '*Privislyansky Krai*' (in Russian: 'Vistula River Borderland').

The division of the analysed area between Russia and Austria was of great importance. In the Austrian part the local Ruthenian population mostly belonged to the aforementioned Greek Catholic (United) Church, while in Russia this church was dissolved (often by force) by Russian authorities and its members had to join the Orthodox Church, subordinated to Russian authorities. In 1867 Galicia achieved autonomy, and within it the Polish ethnic group (Poles dominated among gentry and the urban population, which had some privileges in the political system of Austria and Galicia) assumed power, although the Ruthenian population also received greater freedom in terms of political action and cultural activity.

The nineteenth century, especially its latter half, was a time of national (nationalist) agitation and the spread of the idea of national (ethno-national) belonging. Polish national identity was already strong in the time of the partitioning of Poland (the Commonwealth) by the end of the eighteenth century, but was limited to the gentry and intelligentsia (almost exclusively of gentry origin). In the second half of the nineteenth century, both in the Russian and the Austrian part of the analysed area, Polish national identity was gradually adopted by Roman Catholic (and 'Polish'-speaking) peasantry – faster in Galicia than in the Russian part. Ruthenian (Orthodox or Greek Catholic) peasants were immune to the idea of being Polish, despite attempts to make them so, for instance by Polish schools in Galicia. Among Ruthenians (Rusins) in Galicia three national ideas competed: Ukrainian, old-Ruthenian and new-Ruthenian. The Ukrainian national idea, otherwise born in Russian Ukraine,[9] far to the east of Galicia, renamed Ruthenians (Rusins) as Ukrainians and understood them as an ethnic group rather than a territorial group ('inhabitants of the periphery'). According to this idea, Ukrainians were a separate nation, neither Poles nor Russians. Hostility towards Poles (and somewhat less expressed towards Russia) was an important element of the emerging Ukrainian identity. The old-Ruthenian (old-Rusin) idea identified Ruthenia (Rus) with Russia and thus made Ruthenians Russians – Russian minority in Austria. For followers of the third and weakest idea – the new-Ruthenian one – Ruthenians were a separate ethnic group, neither Ukrainian nor Russian. Competition and contact between the Polish and Ukrainian national movements, especially in Galicia, strengthened both nationalisms; they also imitated each other (especially the Ukrainian imitating the Polish) as regards, for example, ideas and organization forms. Particularly important was the creation of ethnic military formations by both nationalist movements, tolerated by Austrian authorities because of Austria's weakness and in the hope that they could be used in Austrian interests. The Polish military formation, the so-called 'legions', turned out after Austria's defeat and disintegration to be the core of the Polish army, which defeated the Bolsheviks in 1920. In Galicia the competition between the two nationalisms was alleviated or accelerated by the democratization of the Austrian political system: elections to the Austrian parliament in Vienna, to the Galician parliament in Lviv and to local councils provided opportunities for confrontation between the two ethnic groups and forced people to decide on their ethnic belonging, as one of the criteria in voting for individuals and parties was their ethnicity.

Because of the weakness of the Ruthenian gentry and intelligentsia the leaders of Ruthenian/Ukrainian society in Galicia were often drawn from the Greek Catholic clergy. The Greek Catholic church strongly supported the Ukrainian idea, especially after 1900, when Andrey Sheptytsky, born as the Polish Roman Catholic count Roman Szeptycki,[10] became its head: the Metropolitan Archbishop of the Ukrainian Greek Catholic Church. One may suppose that the Ukrainian movement was also supported by Austrian authorities unwilling to have a numerous Russian minority in this area bordering with Russia, and keen to counterbalance the growing influence of the Polish element in Galicia. By the end of the nineteenth century Polish national activists in Galicia, having earlier rejected the idea of Ukrainians as a separate ethnic nation (according to the widespread Polish opinion, Ruthenians were a Polish 'tribe'), recognized Ukrainians as an (ethnic) nation and even wanted to cooperate with them, with the motivation of preventing Ruthenians from becoming Russians and representing a threat to Austria, as Poles in Austria preferred to be Austrian citizens rather than being subject to Russian subjugation. The willingness of Polish national activists in Galicia to recognize and cooperate with Ukrainians did not change the general atmosphere of rivalry, if not hostility, between the two groups; and, in any case, Polish concessions to Ukrainians were too modest to satisfy the latter group. For instance, Polish leaders in Galicia did not consent to establish a Ukrainian-language university or to introduce Ukrainian in Lviv University (since the autonomy of Galicia in 1867 the language of instruction there was Polish). In such circumstances, by the turn of the nineteenth and twentieth centuries, Galicia became the centre of the Ukrainian national movement, although the movement was also present across the whole territory of Ukraine under Russian domination (Darski 1993; Fedoruk 2003; Jagiełło 2000; Rudnyckyj 1995; Serczyk 1990; Barwiński 2013; Sosnowska 2009).

Events during World War I, especially the behaviour of the Russian army during its campaign in Galicia, were a great disappointment to the pro-Russian Ruthenians, and subsequent persecutions by Austrian authorities practically annihilated the old-Ruthenian option; the Ukrainian movement thus emerged as the unquestionable winner in the Ruthenian camp.

The non-Ukrainian identity of Ruthenians did not disappear altogether. In the extreme western part of the Ruthenian ethno-linguistic area, in the Carpathian mountains in the present Polish–Slovak borderland, local Ruthenians on both sides of the border retained their Ruthenian identity. On the Slovak side they called themselves *Rusyn* or *Rusnak*; on the Polish side, *Lemko*. As a matter of fact, in the post-war chaos of 1918–20 *Lemkos* declared the independence of some 'republics', consisting of a few villages and lasting a few months until suppression by the Polish army. Now within the *Lemko* community in Poland there are two competing ideas and groups: one considering *Lemkos* a separate ethnic group, the other considering them a regional group of Ukrainians (Barwiński 1998; Barwiński 2013; Duć-Fajfer 2001).

World War I brought about dramatic changes. Poland emerged as an independent state with territory comprising the whole present Polish–Ukrainian borderland and containing a numerous Ukrainian minority. Attempts to create an independent Ukrainian state, both in Galicia (West Ukrainian People's Republic) and Russia (Ukrainian People's Republic), failed, suppressed by either Polish or Soviet Russian (Bolshevik) forces. Fighting between pro-Polish and pro-Ukrainian forces, especially for Lviv, the capital city of Galicia, in 1918 resulted in victory for Poles, defeat and frustration for Ukrainians, and the creation of national heroes and martyrs on both sides. Hostility between Poles and Ukrainians reached an unprecedented level.

It should be stressed that this hostility relates mostly to relations between Poles and Ukrainians in Galicia. Relations with Ukrainians from the Ukrainian People's Republic (Kiev Ukraine) were less negative, even friendly. In April 1920 Poland (then headed by its military leader Józef Piłsudski) and the Ukrainian People's Republic (then headed by ataman Symon Petliura) reached an agreement (the Warsaw Agreement) on their border (it left former Galicia and Volynia in Poland)

and on military cooperation against Bolshevik Russia. Joint Polish–Ukrainian forces could not, however, stop the Bolshevik offensive on the territory of Kiev Ukraine, partly because of weak support for the independence of Ukraine on the part of local inhabitants and the indecisiveness of Ukrainian leaders. Future Ukrainian activists concluded from this failure that what was necessary to bring independence to Ukraine was determination, sacrifice, heroism and discipline on the part of fighters for independence, and, if necessary, the use of terror to intimidate enemies and the population indifferent to the national cause.

For Piłsudski his cooperation with Ukraine was an element of his strategic plan to create a chain of buffer states between Poland and Bolshevik Russia (or Russia as such) – Lithuania, Belarus and Ukraine, possibly federated with Poland. This plan turned out to be unrealistic, as possible partners were either too weak or vehemently rejected it (as Lithuanians in the present meaning of the word did). Russian Bolshevik forces were stopped and defeated by Polish troops led by Piłsudski near Warsaw in August 1920, and in the autumn of that year Poland and Bolshevik Russia concluded an agreement (the Riga Agreement) ending the war. This agreement left the present Polish–Ukrainian border area, and a vast territory east of it, in Poland, and was tantamount to the withdrawal of Polish recognition for the Ukrainian People's Republic, which had in effect already ceased to exist (Figure 1.3).

After the destruction of the Ukrainian People's Republic the Bolshevik authorities of Soviet Russia organized the Ukrainian Soviet Socialist Republic (Ukrainian SSR) as part of the newly established Union of Soviet Socialist Republics. The Ukrainian SSR, as other Soviet republics, was under full control of the central Soviet authorities. It can be said that the establishment of the Ukrainian SSR served two goals: an internal and an external one. The internal goal was to demonstrate to Ukrainians that Bolsheviks were favourable to the demands of Ukrainians for their own statehood (autonomy) and thus to win their sympathy. To present their 'generosity' to Ukrainians, Bolsheviks included within the Ukrainian SSR territories never previously belonging to Ukraine (as part of the Commonwealth of the Two Nations) and populated by migrants from central Russia after the incorporation of these territories into Russia at the end of the eighteenth or in the nineteenth century. These migrants spoke Russian or Russian dialects that were slightly but discernibly different from local Ukrainian dialects. Furthermore, the Bolsheviks gave the Ukrainian SSR considerable cultural autonomy. The external goal was to make an argument for claims to territories of foreign states – Poland, Romania and Czechoslovakia – in the name of the reunification of the Ukrainian nation within the Ukrainian state. During the initial years after its establishment the Ukrainian SSR did a lot to support Ukrainian identity and culture, helping to develop the Ukrainian standard language (unifying its two varieties, created in Galicia and in Russian Ukraine) and introducing it into the public sphere. The course of policy changed in early 1930, when many achievements of the previous policy were reversed (marginalization of the Ukrainian language and culture) and Ukrainian activists were persecuted or emigrated (Masenko 2004). However, probably for external reasons, the Ukrainian SSR was retained. This change in cultural policy

Figure 1.3 Poland in the interwar period of the twentieth century

Source: Krzysztof Łoboda, on the basis of IGiPZ PAN (1997).

coincided with the great tragedy of Ukrainians in the USSR – the Great Hunger, when millions died as a result of an artificially created famine. Until this change, Soviet Ukraine was very attractive for Ukrainians abroad, especially in Poland, and encouraged them to actions against the Polish state.

In Poland Ukrainians were not granted any territorial autonomy, and their cultural autonomy was limited – for instance, they were not allowed to establish a Ukrainian-language university in Lwów/Lviv. The relationship between Polish authorities and the Ukrainian minority (in fact, a majority in south-eastern regions) was generally tense, with periods of improvement and deterioration. Polish authorities carried out an unstable policy towards Ukrainians, oscillating between attempts to establish a *modus vivendi* with moderate Ukrainian forces without, however, considerable concessions in the socio-economic and political spheres, and harsh police actions against the Ukrainian population. For Polish radical nationalist forces, such as ONR (National-Radical Camp), Ukrainians, together with Jewish and German minorities, were enemies of the Polish state and nation, and no compromise with them was acceptable. Although this organization was outside the political mainstream, it was influential enough to stop far reaching compromises. One of its supporters of this Camp killed the first Polish president, Gabriel Narutowicz, a few days after his election by the parliament (in December 1922) because Narutowicz was too liberal towards national minorities and received support from MPs representing parties of national minorities, particularly the Ukrainian minority. Several high-ranking Polish politicians tried to establish good relations with the Ukrainian minority, such as Kiev-born *wojewoda* (representative of the central government) of Volhynia Henryk Józewski, but except for goodwill they had little to offer, especially after the outbreak of the economic crisis in the early 1930s.

In Ukrainian society in Poland there were both moderate and radical forces. The former was represented by Ukrainian National-Democratic Union (UNDO), a legal parliamentary party which accepted the existence of the Polish state and used parliamentary means of fighting for the national–cultural and socio-economic rights of Ukrainians. It is worth stressing that on the eve of the German invasion of Poland this party appealed to Ukrainians to be loyal to Poland and, during the war, in September 1939, the Ukrainian population did not follow the appeals of radicals to attack the Polish army. As regards the radicals, these were two opposite ideological camps: communists and nationalists. Communists were inspired by the Soviet Ukraine; they were mainly active among Ukrainians living in the areas which used to belong to the Russian Empire before World War I. This camp was represented by the illegal 'Communist Party of Western Ukraine', which was supported by the USSR and demanded the incorporation of the south-eastern regions of Poland, or 'Western Ukraine' in its terminology, to the Ukrainian SSR. This party was more communist than Ukrainian. Its influence started to wane with information on the Great Hunger and the persecution of the Ukrainian Rebirth in the USSR. The other radical group were radical nationalists. This group underwent some organizational changes, unions and splits. The most important was established in Vienna in 1929 but was active mostly in Poland as the illegal formation Organization of Ukrainian Nationalists (OUN). This organization rejected the then geopolitical *status quo* and desired to establish a Ukrainian state encompassing, among other areas, territories of Poland considered as ethnically Ukrainian. Its rejection of the geopolitical post-Versailles system, led it to consider that Nazi Germany was the only force capable of destroying the system. It was also influenced by other elements of Nazi Germany: the rejection of democracy, the cult of the strong leader and intolerance for ethnic minorities, as well as some visual aspects, rituals and behaviours resembling NSDAP and Nazi practices. Such ideologies and practices were quite frequent in the interwar Europe, and OUN was no exception. OUN organized terrorist attacks against Polish authorities and politicians (including moderate ones willing to reach an agreement with moderate

Ukrainian leaders). The Polish authorities responded with the incarceration of OUN activists, the settlement of ethnic Poles in Volhynia, police raids against anti-government protestsm and so on, while the economic crisis of the 1930s aggravated the situation even further. OUN became more and more popular among young Ukrainians (Olszański 1994; Friszke 1991), while a lack of substantial success on the part of the moderate UNDO weakened its influence in Ukrainian society. OUN managed to capitalize on the generalized dissatisfaction of Ukrainian society and also made use of opportunities such as those offered by the liberal policies of *voivod* Józewski to create organizational structures and spread nationalistic propaganda (Homza 2013; Wysocki 2003; Posivnych 2010). Not only did the radical nationalist camp grow stronger but within it emerged a stream that can be classed as a neurotic hatred towards Poles (and Jews), void of realistic thinking and desiring the murdering of Poles and Jews regardless of circumstances.[11]

After the German and Soviet invasion of Poland in September 1939 and the defeat of Poland the occupying powers – Germany and USSR – draw the border line according to the Hitler–Stalin treaty of August 1939, which is by and large the present state border. After the German attack on the Soviet Union in June 1941 the whole territory under consideration was for three years under German occupation.

Under German occupation Ukrainian nationalists from OUN and other 'non-affiliated' nationalists supported Nazi Germany in the hope of its help with an independent Ukraine. On 30 June 1941, a few days after the German army entered Lviv, Ukrainian nationalists proclaimed the establishment of independent Ukrainian state, hoping that it would become another state under the German Nazi protectorate. Germany rejected this declaration. Nevertheless, Ukrainian nationalists continued collaboration with Nazi Germany. They manned an army called SS Galizien fighting on the side of Germany on the eastern front, formed police and various military and paramilitary formations supporting German occupation forces, among other things in the extermination of the Jewish population (see, for instance, investigations by Ukrainian historian Ivan Kachanovsky of the participation of OUN(b) in Nazi mass murders in 1941: Kachanovsky 2013). In the meantime, OUN split into several groups, the biggest being OUN(b), under the leadership of Stepan Bandera, and OUN(m), whose leader was Andriy Melnyk. The Bandera group formed the Ukrainian Insurgent Army (UPA), which withdrew its support for Germany and started independent activities, attacking mostly Soviet troops and the Polish population and armed formations. The Melnyk group formed the above-mentioned formation SS Galizien.

There were also various underground military formations on the Polish side. Although none of them collaborated openly with Nazi Germany, they greatly differed in many respects (to the extent that one may have the impression that they fought more against each other than against German occupation forces). Among them the strongest was the Home Army, nominally subordinated to the Polish government in exile; communist formations; and a military formation called the National Armed Forces (NSZ), established by the above-mentioned National-Radical Camp, which was hostile towards minorities of pre-war Poland, including Ukrainians.

For Polish–Ukrainian relations clashes between armed groups of both sides and the activities of the UPA against Polish civil inhabitants were of particular importance. According to Ukrainian historian Volodymyr Vyatrovych (Vyatrovych 2011), it was the Polish side which first attacked Ukrainians in the area of Chełm in 1942; however, this is denied by Polish historians. In 1943 the UPA started a campaign of ethnic cleansing of Volhynia, which reached its apogee in June of that year. Later the UPA started ethnic cleansing in Eastern Galicia. The aim of these actions was to free the future Ukrainian borderland (first Volhynia) from Poles (Jews, in practice, had already been exterminated). The number of Polish victims of this action, who were predominantly women and children, is estimated at between 50,000–100,000 (there are higher estimates of up to 200,000). There were also victims on the Ukrainian side – some thousands of Ukrainians were killed in fighting against Polish self-defence forces and Soviet partisans, or in retaliation actions by Polish forces in areas where Poles were in the majority. After this action and the following forced emigration the Polish population in Volhynia disappeared; it also almost entirely disappeared from former eastern Galicia. Plans made by the OUN-UPA to create a Ukrainian state under German protection failed as Germany first rejected this idea (and arrested Stepan Bandera) and then was defeated in the war. From that time Volhynia (Polish: Wołyń) has constituted a symbol of Polish national tragedy. What matters is not only the number of victims but also the extraordinarily cruel way of killing Poles adopted by Ukrainian nationalist Banderamen and local 'civil' inhabitants. It should be stressed, however, that those Poles who escaped being killed often owed their lives to their Ukrainian neighbours, who warned them in time of coming Banderamen.

The Volhynia tragedy adumbrates Polish–Ukrainian relations and divides Polish and Ukrainian historians and the general public. As regards historians, the division is not between Polish and Ukrainian historians but between those on both sides who admit the tragedy of the Polish population in Volhynia and try to investigate all aspects of the conflict (e.g. as Grzegorz Motyka does: Motyka 2011) and those on the Ukrainian side who for patriotic reasons want to defend the good name of the national heroes of OUN(b) and Bandera by playing down the number of Polish victims or suggesting that it was a war between equal adversaries, that the killings were a spontaneous action of local peasants and not planned and organized by OUN-UPA, or that the Polish nationalists started the fighting and Ukrainians only responded (see, for example, Vyatrovych 2011).

As a result of World War II and agreements between the winning powers Poland fell into the 'zone of influence' of the USSR, and a new borderline was drawn in 1944 between Poland and the USSR according to desires of the latter. Minorities still lived on both sides of the border. On the Polish side Ukrainian UPA guerrillas survived in the Carpathian mountains until 1948; their leaders hoped that a new war between the western powers and the USSR would start soon and they wanted to stay until that time. To fight Ukrainian underground irredentism and to normalize the situation in the border area Polish and Soviet governments (nominally the government of Poland and of the Ukrainian SSR) reached agreement on a 'mutual exchange of population' – that is, on the transfer of the Polish minority from Ukraine to Poland and of the Ukrainian minority to Ukraine. As for the Polish population in Ukraine, the vast majority of those who survived the deportations to Siberia in 1939–41 by Soviet authorities and the ethnic cleaning of 1943 by Ukrainian nationalists voluntarily migrated to Poland. Only a small Polish community in former Polish territory, mainly in Lviv, remained. As for the Ukrainian population in Poland, some of them migrated voluntarily to Ukraine and some were forced by Polish authorities to do so; the last group was relocated from south-eastern Poland to northern and western regions newly incorporated within Poland. The official explanation of the last action (called 'Operation Vistula') was to extirpate Ukrainian irredentism (after the killing, presumably by the UPA, of a Polish army general in 1948). On the Soviet side Ukrainian nationalists were harshly persecuted by Soviet authorities. Soviet security agents also killed Stepan Bandera in Munich.

After these events the borderland between Poland and Soviet Ukraine was almost entirely deprived of ethnic minorities. The border itself was closed (there was only one double crossing point, on a railway and on a road, and entering the other side of the border was very difficult). No relations existed between local authorities and communities on either side of the border, and there were no direct contacts between Polish central authorities and the authorities of the Ukrainian SSR. There were not only institutional and political obstacles to cross-border cooperation but also no desire for contact, especially on the Polish side, after the atrocities of the ethnic cleaning in Volhynia and elsewhere.

While the general attitude among Poles and Ukrainians to each other until Ukraine's independence remained full of suspicions, if not hostile, there was a change in ways of thinking on Polish–Ukrainian relations among some independent intellectuals, especially those living abroad. Among them was Jerzy Giedroyć, a Polish author and publisher of the monthly journal *Kultura* (edited in Polish), living in Paris. *Kultura* gathered intellectuals from the whole region of Central and Eastern Europe with the aim of overcoming hostilities between nations of this region, and primarily between Poles and Ukrainians, to enable both sides to understand their history and contemporary situation, and the aspirations and fears of the other side. The fundamental assumptions for the Polish–Ukrainian dialogue, according to *Kultura*, were acceptation of the existing Polish–Ukrainian border and that the independence, stability and prosperity of Ukraine was vital for the independence and security of Poland.

These assumptions informed official Polish policy as well as the attitude of the main Polish political parties towards Ukraine after Poland regained full independence in 1989. Poland was the first state to recognize the independence of Ukraine in 1991. In fact, in the period 1989–91 Poland carried out a 'two-track' foreign policy towards the USSR, on the one hand maintaining relations with authorities of the USSR, on the other hand establishing contacts with individual Soviet republics, mainly with the Ukrainian SSR, perceiving the ambitions of the latter to be an autonomous player on the international scene. Attitudes of the leadership of the Ukrainian SSR, especially of its last leader and the future first president of

Ukraine, Leonid Kravchuk, greatly contributed to the dissolution of the Soviet Union, which in turn dramatically changed the map of Europe (Figure 1.4).

As mentioned earlier, Poland was the first country to recognize Ukraine's independence (in fact, it was not a spontaneous act but was negotiated in advance by the two countries) and has consistently been the main (if not the only) 'advocate' of Ukraine in Europe, sometimes to the extent that Poland seemed to be more interested in the independence and prosperity of Ukraine than Ukraine itself. Among the many instances of Polish interest in Ukraine was the so-called 'Orange Revolution' in 2004/05, in which the mediation of the then Polish president Aleksander Kwaśniewski helped to find a solution to the political crisis in Ukraine after controversial presidential elections (repeated elections gave victory to the would-be pro-western 'orange' camp, which irritated Russian authorities). Poland (together with Sweden) also proposed the EU concept of 'Eastern Partnership', according to which the EU helps the six post-Soviet states (Ukraine, Belarus, Moldavia, Georgia, Armenia and Azerbaijan) to build democracy and civil society and thus to increase their capacity to cooperate and integrate with the EU. This does not mean, however, that the whole of Polish society and all political groups backed the idea of unconditional support for Ukraine. There were both individuals and groups (mainly former inhabitants of pre-war eastern Poland and their descendants) remembering Polish–Ukrainian conflicts (the solemn celebration in 2013 of the 70th anniversary of the Volhyn tragedy was evidence of the existence and

Figure 1.4 Central and Eastern Europe in 2000

Source: Krzysztof Łoboda, on the basis of IGiPZ PAN (1997).

strength of such groups) according to whom Ukrainians were not ready for reconciliation with Poland and did not deserve support.

Ukrainian attitudes towards Poland were more complicated and unstable, which was a result of the general differentiation of the Ukrainian society and the political instability and indecisiveness of Ukraine in terms of its relations with both the West and Russia, between Ukraine as a separate nation and Ukraine as a Russian region.[12] Generally speaking, until the recent crisis of 2014, Ukrainian governments tried to balance between the West and Russia in the hope of achieving better conditions from both sides. Attitudes towards Poland were instrumental in achieving some benefits from the EU. To Polish disappointment, Ukrainian governments did not show enough desire to reform the country in such as way that would integrate Ukraine with the West.

The attitude towards Poland among the inhabitants of western Ukraine has been very ambiguous. On the one hand, a strong Ukrainian national consciousness (nationalism) and the desire to defend Ukraine's independence from Russian attempts to regain this territory meant that they saw Poland as their ally on the anti-Russian and pro-European front. On the other hand, the glorification of Ukrainian nationalists – Bandera, OUN-UPA and so on – was hardly acceptable to Poles. The widespread opinion in this part of Ukraine was that Bandera and OUN-UPA militants were fighters for democracy and western choices for Ukraine, and victims of communist Soviet persecutions. People holding this opinion cannot understand Polish objections towards these symbols of Ukrainian national identity.

In the recent crisis (the refusal by President Yanukovych to sign the Association Agreement with the EU in 2013, protests against it in Kiev, bloodshed and the toppling of Yanukovych, Russia's annexation of Crimea, the separatist revolt in eastern Ukraine and Russia's military intervention in eastern Ukraine in 2014/15), the Polish government, the main political parties and the media generally supported Ukraine. Generally they represented the Ukrainian point of view of the crisis and tried to convince partners in the EU to help Ukraine withstand Russian pressure and strengthen democracy and its pro-western options. Only insignificant (but for how long?) groups, mainly affected by problems in trade with Russia, complained about Polish involvement in Ukraine.

Some developments in Ukraine, however, are embarrassing for pro-Ukrainian forces in Poland. Ukraine, in a search for an identity free from Soviet and Russian characteristics, tends to find it in its history of independence movements and heroes. Among them are the above-mentioned organization OUN-UPA, accused in Poland of the Volhynia and other massacres. For instance, on 7 April 2015 the Ukrainian parliament adopted a law that named organizations and movements which contributed to the fight of the Ukrainian people for independence and stated that criticizing them would be regarded as contempt for Ukraine and would be punished. Among these organizations and movements, apart from, for example, the Ukrainian People's Republic, the Western Ukrainian People's Republic and so on, were the OUN and the UPA.[13] This law also granted special social privileges to members of these organizations and their families. Interestingly, this law was voted on a few hours after the speech of Polish president Bronisław Komorowski in the Ukrainian parliament and was submitted by Yuriy Shukhevych, son of Roman Shukhevych, the last leader of the UPA. This law, and the circumstances of its adoption, was embarrassing for the Polish government and the main parties and was met with criticism by some opposition parties, media and organizations, especially those related to former refugees from former eastern Poland. Consequently, events glorifiying the OUN-UPA and their leaders Bandera and Shukhevych became frequent in Ukraine, even including statements by some public figures that the extermination of the Polish (and Jewish) population was justified and necessary for building Ukrainian statehood. Polish leaders and mainstream parties and media ignore these in the geopolitical interests of supporting Ukrainian independence, but in the future they may harm Polish–Ukrainian relations, especially across the common border where on the one side (in Poland) there live descendants of victims of UPA pogroms and those for whom the UPA was a gang of murderers of innocent people, and on the other side (in Ukraine) there live those who most actively glorify the UPA.[14]

The independence of Ukraine in 1991 considerably changed the character of the Polish–Ukrainian border. Firstly, the number of crossing points dramatically increased and conditions for crossing the border improved. Until 1998 cross-border movement was practically free, which, together with differences in wages and prices across the border, resulted in the intense cross-border movement of people and goods. The similarity of the Polish and Ukrainian languages (with, in particular, many in Ukraine quite frequently having a good command of Polish) enabled cross-border contacts. Since 1998, as a result of Polish preparations to join the EU, some regulations required by the EU were introduced (visa requirement for Ukrainians coming to Poland), hindering to some extent this movement. At the same time institutional forms of cross-border contacts and cooperation were established at local and regional levels, such as Euroregions (there are two such Euroregions on the Polish–Ukrainian border).

Borders and geopolitics

The Polish–Ukrainian border can serve as an example of relations between borders and geopolitics. Before analysing the case of this particular border and its relations with geopolitics it seems advisable first to present general characteristics of border–geopolitical relations to put the Polish–Ukrainian case into a broader context.

Relations between borders and geopolitics are twofold: on the one hand the geopolitical environment ('geopolitics') determines the characteristics of the border – its location, the conditions of its crossing ('permeability'), cross-border relations of local communities and inhabitants, and policies towards border areas carried out by the central governments of the two countries concerned and, sometimes, by supranational organizations and so on (Miszczuk 2013;[15] Miszczuk 2008; Rykiel 2006; Passi 2008; Newman and Passi 2001). On the other hand the situation in the border area influences to some extent relations between central governments or supranational organizations in terms of, for example, tensions regarding delimitation of the border, the treatment of ethnic minorities and so on, which may harm mutual relations between the countries concerned.

Relationships between borders and geopolitics largely depend on the characteristics of the bordering territorial units ('countries') and the 'rules of the game' determining the behaviours of these countries. Historically, these rules of the game (that can also be called 'paradigms' or 'codes') are changeable.[16] In Europe four such paradigms, resulting from the nature of power over territorial units (countries), can be distinguished: the feudal system, the Westphalian system, the nation-state system and the post-national system.

In the feudal system (European) territory took the form of a kind of private possession (domains) allowing the formation of a hierarchy of 'ownerships' and 'owners' (kings, dukes, other noblemen) entitled to exploit benefits (first of all taxes) from a given area. The same area could have a number of 'owners'; at the same time, the same person could be 'owner' of various areas, and occupy various levels in the hierarchy (e.g. being king in one area and duke in another one). There were two kinds of division between 'owners': vertical and horizontal. The vertical division determined which kind of benefits were attributed to which level of the hierarchy. The horizontal division determined territorial separation of entitlements of the same hierarchical level. Each 'owner' (suzerain) headed a social group composed of his/her family, servants and dependent vassals. In such a way any territory formed a socio-political unit. From the historical point of view the most important among these units were kingdoms, which in most cases gave birth to future nation states. Given that horizontal divisions separated entitlements to benefits rather than territories themselves, uninhabited and useless territories between domains formed border zones (no man's land, *terra nullius*).

Territorial reach and the boundaries of domains were shaped by two mechanisms: legal (peaceful) and military. The legal mechanism in the case of inhabited territories consisted of rules of heirdom, marriage, purchase (and sale) and lease of the whole or a part of the given territory. As a result, domains were being divided and united, their boundaries were shifting. In the case of uninhabited territories (or territories inhabited by 'barbarians', pagans and other non-Christians as well as heretics) the way of changing borders was colonization, if necessary assisted by use of military force. The military mechanism implied invasions and expropriation (also used as a punishment for disloyalty against suzerains, heresies or other sins). Military invasions and conquests took place within the Christian world without any legal justification, but the necessity to justify such actions in the *Civitas Dei* discouraged them in the time of ripe feudalism. Quite often both mechanisms were used: military force was applied to 'strengthen' arguments in legal disputes, legal claims were used as excuses for military actions. In such a way, the territorial reach of individual feudal lords and dynasties tended to reflect changes in their military, economic, demographic, diplomatic and 'matrimonial' power.

It should be noted that there was no clear link between territory and ethnicity. While at the bottom of the social pyramid, among the peasantry, such a link could be discerned, at higher levels they were rarer, because of the all-European (all-Christian) 'marriage market' of aristocracy and royal families and frequent changes of ownership of domains. It was usual that kings and aristocrats did not speak the language(s) of their subjects.

In terms of Polish–Ukrainian relations, the eastward expansion of Poland in the fourteenth century (the incorporation of the territory of present western Ukraine) was a result of two factors: first, personal claims of the then Polish king Kazimierz Wielki (Kazimir the Great) after the death of the king of Halych ('Galicia' in Latin) and the lack of direct successors to the latter – Kazimierz was grandson of a former king of Galicia (his mother was daughter of that king); second, the then power of the Kingdom of Poland, which won the competition for Galicia against other competitors, primarily Hungary and Lithuania. It is worth noting that at the time when the Polish king was incorporating Halych the Great Duchy of Lithuania continued its gradual conquest of Kiev and some other Ruthenian duchies. It should be stressed that when Lithuanian started their imperial adventure they were a pagan people and were fighting mostly against Mongol-Tatars (Ruthenian duchies usually voluntarily accepted Lithuanian domination), so Christian rules of the game did not affect either Lithuanians or Tatars.

The Westphalian system (named after the peace of Westphalia, 1648, ending the Thirty Years War) can be treated as an intermediary stage between feudal and modern nation state systems. This system introduced the notions of state sovereignty and the legal equality of states and strengthened the role of the border as a line separating territories of sovereign states. It was a step towards the 'depersonalization' of states, towards a system in which states had their rulers instead of rulers possessing their territories. The peace of Westphalia and the preceding religious wars definitely ended the Christian *Civitas Dei*, opening the way for nationalism.

Although the peace of Westphalia did not affect directly Poland (the Commonwealth of the Two Nations), which was not a party to the treaty, this treaty, as noted above, can be regarded as the beginning of the idea of the nation state and of nationalism and competition between states in Western Europe, which had effects on Poland. This competition, together with other factors, strengthened centralistic tendencies in European states, a tendency which bypassed Poland. The divergent tendencies in the Commonwealth of the Two Nations (decentralization and weakening of the central government) and in its neighbours (centralization and a desire for expansion) resulted in the elimination of the former from the map of Europe and the partitioning of its territory between the three neighbours (Russia, Prussia, Austria) by the end of the eighteenth century.

The nation state system, which can be said to have started after the Napoleonic Wars and to have reached its 'perfect' stage in the second half of the nineteenth century, even further strengthened the principle of territoriality in governance, formally equalized inhabitants of states – making them 'citizens' and eliminating the hierarchy of suzerains and vassals – and made rulers (presidents, prime ministers, chancellors, kings, parliaments) more dependent on each country's population (on citizenry). The latter meant that, unlike in the feudal system, one person could no longer rule more than one country. Nationalism, which is strictly linked to the concept of the nation state, inaugurated a novelty of extraordinary importance: a nation understood as the supreme sovereign and a community bound by one culture, language, destiny and identity. Building a nation out of inhabitants by diffusing a chosen 'national' language and a standardized national culture and memory, inculcating a common identity and destiny, and eliminating undesired languages, cultures and identities became the highest priority of nation states.[17] From the point of view of state borders, the idea of the nation state and nationalism in their ideal form implied strictly defined (and often relatively impermeable) borders and homogenization of the population (in terms of language, culture and identity), of economy (in terms of the national currency and perhaps also the system of measures and weights), of law and so on within national boundaries. Thus the border became not only a line on a map but also a barrier to movements of people, goods, ideas and so on, and a line separating different languages, cultures, identities and economies.

The idea of the nation state and nationalism as a unification of cultures, languages and identities within state boundaries, implying the elimination of 'undesired' cultures, languages and identities, generated its counterpart in the form of stateless nationalism aiming at preserving endangered cultures, languages and identities.[18] In the analysed case of Polish–Ukrainian relations, this involved two stateless nationalisms – Polish and Ukrainian, as described earlier – competing with state nationalisms (German, Austrian, Russian) and between themselves.

State borders in this part of Europe at the time of the development of nation states reflected, firstly, states' military and political power. This, in turn, depended on states' economic strength, demographic factor (potential number of soldiers) and ideological cohesion among the population (readiness to fight for the national cause). The period of nation states, which started after the Napoleonic Wars and lasted practically until the present day, can be divided into several sub-periods: 1) from the Vienna Congress (1815) to the outbreak of World War I (1914); 2) from the end of World War I and the related treaties and subsequent wars, firstly the Polish–Soviet war (1920), to the outbreak of World War II (1939); 3) from the end of World War II (1945) to the collapse of the Soviet Union (1991); 4) from the collapse of the USSR and the establishment of an independent Ukraine (1991) to the Ukrainian crisis of 2014; 5) since the outbreak of the Ukrainian crisis and the shift of power in Ukraine in 2014. In the first sub-period the territory of the present Polish–Ukrainian border belonged either to Russia or to Austria, which reflected the political and military situation created by the Napoleonic Wars and confirmed by the Vienna Congress. During the second period this territory belonged to Poland, which was the result of wars between the three parties: Polish, Ukrainian and Soviet-Russian. These wars practically eliminated the independent Ukrainian state and confirmed the independence of Poland and its control over the territory concerned. During the third period (1945–1991) the territory under consideration was divided between the semi-independent Poland (as a member of the Soviet block) and the USSR. The shape of the border was determined by several factors: military (the victory of the USSR in the war, the defeat of Ukrainian military formations fighting against both Poland and the USSR in the 'wrong' coalition with Nazi Germany, the participation of Polish armed forces in the war in the 'right' anti-German coalition, which had some political significance), diplomatic (geopolitical considerations of the winning powers, the USSR, USA and UK) and ethnic (domination of the respective ethnic group on the Polish or Soviet/Ukrainian side, this criterion being used in the form most advantageous for the Soviet-Ukrainian side, as the vast territory of this mixed population could be divided between the two states in various ways).[19] In the fourth (1991–February 2014) and the fifth (since February 2014) periods the shape of the border remained unchanged but its nature changed: it separated a (fully) independent Poland (since 1 May 2004 a member of the EU) and an independent Ukraine.[20] The difference between the fourth and the fifth periods is in the character and geopolitical orientation of Ukraine: in the former period Ukraine tried to balance between its West (Ukrainian-speaking, UPA and Bandera-loving) and its East (Russian-speaking, UPA and Bandera-hating) and between the West (European Union) and Russia, while in the latter period (characterized by the loss of Crimea and the 'far east', and conflict with Russia) Ukraine is shifting towards the West (in both senses).

The 'post-national' system mentioned above is characterized by state borders' (gradual) loss of their barrier characteristic. State borders remain where they were established during the period of nationalism and nation states, but become more and more permeable. This is the case in terms of both internal state borders of the European Union and borders between other states (e.g. between Sweden and Norway, or Switzerland and its EU neighbours). So far it is not the case for the Polish–Ukrainian border, despite some forms of cross-border cooperation.

The case of Polish and Ukrainian borders touches upon the issue of national versus sub-national and supra-national borders. In the interwar period (1920–1939) Polish borders were national borders and were shaped according to the rules described above shaping national borders. At the same time and until 1991 the borders of Ukraine (the Ukrainian SSR), except for that which also formed the national border of the USSR, were sub-national borders of the USSR, shaped according to the then considerations of the central government of the Soviet state (for instance, the inclusion of Crimea and south-eastern regions within Ukraine had no ethnic, linguistic or historical foundations). In the years 1945–91 Polish borders were also to some extent internal borders of a supra-national formation – the Soviet block. Their location and character largely depended on the strength and interests of this block, and particularly on its strongest element, the USSR. It should be stressed, however, that despite being 'internal' border of a block, the Polish–Soviet border was almost impermeable, except for long-distance trade. After the collapse of the block and until the accession of Poland to the EU these borders became fully national Polish borders without changing their geographical location. After the accession to the EU Polish borders with other EU members became internal national EU borders (with all resulting consequences), while borders with non-EU members (including Ukraine) became external EU borders (also with all resulting consequences). The borders of Ukraine with Russia, Belarus and Moldova, which used to be internal borders of the USSR until 1991, became, theoretically without changes in their location, international borders, although the logic that shaped them was already outdated. The first contestation of these borders as national borders happened in the early 1990s, when a part of

Moldova bordering with Ukraine declared independence, becoming a de facto Russian protectorate. Ukrainian borders were contested in 2014 when Russia annexed Crimea; the revolt of Donbas is also a kind of challenging of Ukrainian borders.

The geopolitical status of a border (as a national border of an isolated state, as a sub-national border, as an internal border of a supra-national formation or as an external border of a supra-national formation), together with other factors, tends to determine the functions of the border and impact on its borderland. Sub-national borders and internal national borders of supra-national formations such as the EU or the EEA enable the integration of the two borderlands by the smooth cross-border movement of goods, services, labour and inhabitants, thus levelling cross-border differences in costs, prices, wages, legal regulations and so on. National borders of isolated states and external borders of supra-national formations hinder cross-border movements, thus creating or perpetuating cross-border differences. If such borders are suddenly opened, as was the case with the borders of Poland with its neighbours in 1989, this results in extraordinarily agitated cross-border movements attracted by differences in prices and wages.

Border studies attach great significance to so-called antecedent or subsequent borders (for a detailed discussion see Miszczuk 2013; Rykiel 2006). The former are borders established prior to developing the border area. As a result, the infrastructure (roads, railways, and so on) and settlement network, as well as economic and social relationships on both sides of the border, tend, at least in the first period, to link each side with its respective national centres distant from the border, thus leaving an 'empty' space along the border. The latter border divides the existing linkages, cutting the infrastructure, interrupting relationships and so on. The Polish–Ukrainian border was a subsequent border when it was drawn after World War II, as it cut infrastructure. This border, however, reveals some characteristics of an antecedent border, as the present border area before it was divided by the border was mostly an underdeveloped area with poor infrastructure and weak internal ties. Stronger ties, however, existed in the southern sector of the present Polish–Ukrainian border.

Another important issue related to borders and cross-border relations is the character of the border and the resulting characteristics of cross-border contacts. In this respect, several types of cross-border relations can be distinguished (Martinez 1994; Szul 1999), ranging from no contacts and hostility to a full infrastructural, economic and social integration in which the border is only a line on the map. The evolution of the border area from no contact to full contact can be reversed. Polish–Ukrainian cross-border relations have been through several periods since the establishment of this border after World War II as a result of changing geopolitical circumstances and economic policies and situations (described in the last part of this chapter): 1) in the period 1945–88 this border was nominally a border between two friendly states – Poland and the USSR – but cross-border relations were limited: no infrastructure (there were only two border crossing points), no institutions, no incentives, no interest, no contacts; 2) in the period 1989–91 it was the border between a fully independent Poland, undergoing economic transformation, and the USSR, undergoing political and ideological transformation, and was characterized by intense cross-border shopping (Ukrainians coming to Poland) due to price differences; 3) in the period 1992–7 it was the border between Poland (still outside the European Union) and Ukraine (by then outside the Soviet Union), and was characterized by intense cross-border shopping, the establishment of more stable economic relations, the building of infrastructure (more and better equipped border crossings) and institutions (e.g. the Bug and Carpathian Euroregions, initiated by central governments), growing mutual interest and a liberal border crossing regime (no visa requirement on both sides, enabling contacts); 4) in the period 1998–2014 it was the border between Poland, preparing to join the EU and then a member of the EU and the Schengen area, and Ukraine, outside the EU and Schengen, and was characterized by the introduction of organizational (a visa requirement for Ukrainians) and economic (the requirement for Ukrainians to possess a certain amount of money) obstacles to crossing the border for Ukrainians (Poles enjoy a visa-free regime) and by a reduction in cross-border shopping, although more and more Ukrainians are coming to Poland to work (not in the border area) owing to wage differences; 5) in the period since 2015 the border situation has been one of uncertainty given the developments in Ukraine as regards its relations with the outside world – especially with Poland and the EU (the negotiated liberalization of the visa regime) – its economic situation, and economic and political reforms.

Ethnic changes in the Polish–Ukrainian borderland

Given that ethnic changes in the Polish–Ukrainian borderland are inseparable from the history of Polish–Ukrainian relations described above, and that the ethnic composition of the Polish–Ukrainian borderland will be dealt with in a more detailed way later in this book (Chapter 2), in this chapter only the main turning points will be discussed. As mentioned earlier, the present Polish–Ukrainian borderland has undergone dramatic changes since the early Middle Ages, in some respects returning in the second half of the twentieth century to the starting point. After the settlement of Slavic tribes in this area this territory was populated by two large groups speaking similar and mutually comprehensible dialects – the predecessors of future Poles and Ruthenians/Ukrainians. The decisive factor dividing them from the late tenth century was religion – Western Christianity (Catholic) in the west and Eastern Christianity (Orthodox) in the east. Since that time almost to the present religion has remained the main identity-building and dividing factor. It should be stressed, however, that the relation between religion (or rite) and ethnic belonging was not mechanical and one-way (religion/rite determining ethnicity). There were instances of changing one's religion (rite) to accommodate it to one's feeling of ethnic belonging.

The incorporation of what is now western Ukraine into the Polish state from the fourteenth century produced, until around the end of the nineteenth century, waves of eastward migration of ethnic Poles and other groups (mostly Jews, Germans and Czechs, the latter in the nineteenth century). Within the Polish group two different sub-groups should be distinguished – peasants and gentry/aristocrats, of which the latter group later included assimilated local aristocracy. As a result, a broad belt of an ethnically mixed population emerged, composed mostly of Ruthenians (future Ukrainians), Poles and Jews.

It should be stressed that the mixing of population went very deep: there were not only mixed areas and mixed villages but also mixed families. The latter phenomenon relates first of all to Polish–Ruthenian/Ukrainian families, or, perhaps more accurately, Roman Catholic–Orthodox/Greek Catholic families, as mixed Jewish–non-Jewish families did not tend to exist. Mixed families emerged usually as a result of mixed marriages, and the question of the belonging of the children of such families to one or another confession was traditionally determined so that sons belonged to the father's confession and daughters to the mother's confession. Belonging to a confession was confirmed by the place of baptism: in a Roman Catholic church or a Greek Catholic/Orthodox church. Consequently, one's confession was predetermined by the family of birth or the father's/mother's confession. Until the outbreak of inter-ethnic or inter-confessional conflicts, formal belonging to one or another confession was quite often irrelevant, as people often attended masses not in their Church of baptism, or in both Churches, or in none. In mixed villages it was common practice for the whole village to celebrate religious events such as Christmas and Easter twice, according to the Roman Catholic and the Orthodox/Greek Catholic calendar. The inter-confessional mixing of the population may have been due to the doctrinal vicinity of these Christian confessions; according to a widespread popular interpretation, the God was the same and the differences were in the calendar, liturgical dress of priests and architecture of churches. One could say that the doctrinal distance between the Roman Catholic Church and Eastern Christian Churches was smaller than that between these Churches and Protestantism.

Ethnically mixed families also emerged as a result of mixing cultural traditions or memories in nominally one-confessional families – when, for instance, a person who had changed confession married a partner belonging to his/her new confession. At times when the ties between religion and ethnic/national identity were relaxed, people from such families might choose an identity different from that indicated by their baptism (as was the case with the case of some members of the Szeptycki family, described elsewhere in this chapter).

When analysing the past ethnic composition of the present Polish–Ukrainian borderland, one cannot ignore Germans and people of German origin. They were concentrated mostly in the southern part of this area, in historic Galicia. They came here in various waves, starting from the fourteenth century. Given their relatively small numbers and the small cultural distance between them and the local Christian populations, they used to assimilate into the Polish or Ruthenian, or both, ethnic groups (showed by the emergence of a population revealing German, Polish and Ruthenian cultural characteristics[21]). Despite their small number they played an important role, as they possessed rare skills and tended to be relatively wealthy free farmers (as opposed to peasants) or craftsmen (e.g. blacksmiths), and enjoyed high prestige. In the eighteenth century, with the annexation of Galicia by Austria, a new wave of German people appeared, reflecting the ruling shift of the

Habsburg Empire. Many persons of German origin subsequently played important roles in the cultural and political life of the Polish and Ukrainian nations.

Much more numerous and spread all over the analysed area, and beyond it, was the Jewish population. Because of religious and cultural distance they did not mix ethnically with the local population. However, they played an important role in the socio-economic fabric of this area as intermediaries between the aristocracy/gentry/landlords and peasantry: they tended to be tax collectors (collecting peasant taxes for their landlords), administrators of landlords' goods and publicans (selling alcohol to peasants and sharing profits thereof with landlords), as well as other non-agricultural professions. Their roles as intermediaries between lords and peasants led them to be blamed for the exploitation of peasants, spreading alcoholism and so on. The cultural and religious distance between them and the peasantry was another source of prejudice.

The mixing was even stronger in the sphere of language. Ruthenian dialects were infiltrated by Polish dialectal forms brought by Polish peasant settlers and Polish standard forms brought by intellectuals, the aristocracy, the Roman Catholic Church and so on. At the same time, Polish speakers absorbed words and pronunciation of their Ruthenian neighbours, while some Ruthenian elements also appeared in the Polish standard language, mostly as a result of Polonized aristocrats of Ruthenian origin. As a result a very broad belt of mixed Ruthenian–Polish dialects emerged. As a matter of fact, present-day Ukrainian and Belarusian standard languages stem from these mixed dialects. For a long time language was a social rather than an ethnic marker – it separated the aristocracy/gentry, speaking (standard) Polish ('lords' speech'), from the peasantry, speaking various dialects ('peasant speech').

The second half of the nineteenth and the early twentieth century were marked by the growth of ethnic (national) sentiments among the two main groups, accompanied by a change in the self-definition and name of the Ruthenian group to Ukrainian (to distinguish themselves from other Ruthenians, who were first of all Russians). This wave of nationalism created divisions in mixed local communities and even families, as individuals felt obliged to choose their ethno-national belonging.

The dramatic events of World War II – exterminations, voluntary and forced migrations, and the establishment of the present border between Poland and the Ukrainian SSR as part of the USSR – brought about a dramatic change of the ethnic composition of the area: the Polish side of the border was almost completely dominated by Poles, while Ukrainians dominated similarly on the Ukrainian side, and Jews, Germans and Czechs disappeared. The main concentrations of ethnic Ukrainians in Poland and ethnic Poles in Ukraine were located outside the border area. The Polish ethnic group on the Polish side of the border was highly uniform as regards religion, language and identity. The Ukrainian group was more differentiated: in the northern part of the borderland (in Volhynia) Ukrainians were predominantly Orthodox (or religiously indifferent), while in the southern part (Galicia/Halychyna) they were mostly Greek Catholics. Even greater differences could be seen between inhabitants of western, central and south-eastern Ukraine, but their presentation exceeds the scope of this book.

Cross-border contacts in any borderland depend not only on the ethnic composition of this borderland but also on linguistic and psycho-cultural distances between ethnic groups. The relevance of the linguistic distance depends, in turn, on the kind of contacts. Generally speaking, some contacts require good command of a language concerned (these can be called 'high language-intensive contacts') while for other contacts a basic knowledge of a language can suffice ('low language-intensive contacts'); in yet other cases, no linguistic communication is necessary. The psycho-cultural distance influences the attitudes of one ethnic group towards the other – its willingness to contact the other group, to visit its country and so on.

As regards the linguistic distance in the Polish–Ukrainian borderland, three characteristics of this area should be underlined. First, the linguistic similarities of Polish and Ukrainian enable their speakers to understand simple utterances in the other language. Second, active knowledge of the other language tends to be rather poor; there tends to be better knowledge of Polish on the Ukrainian side than vice versa, and immigrants from the other side of the border (mostly Ukrainians in Poland) do master the local language quite well simply through interpersonal contacts, without the need for special courses, but it takes time. Third, a third common language which would be accepted and in which both sides would be fluent is lacking (Russian does not play such a role because of insufficient command of this language by Poles). For these reasons, low language-intensive cross-border contacts, such as shopping, tourism, attending sports events, non-intellectual jobs and so on, do not encounter linguistic barriers. Language is an obstacle in activities where good command, especially good command of specialist terminology, is necessary. One of the areas where there is no absolute language barrier but language nevertheless is an obstacle is university education: at some Polish universities, mainly in Lublin, Ukrainian students form a considerable part, and are admitted without language tests (it is assumed that their command of Polish is satisfactory), but in practice their lack of fluency in Polish lowers the level of education there, causing some problems to Polish students and professors.[22]

As regards the psycho-cultural distance between the two ethnic groups, it seems to be at least as important as the linguistic distance, and its perception by both groups is unequal and changing. Given that there are no regular investigations of this issue, the discussion is based on the subjective opinion of the author, rather than on objective analysis. Poles, generally, feel greater distance from Ukrainians and consequently are less willing to contact Ukrainians or to be interested in Ukrainian culture, politics and so on, than vice versa. An important reason for this is the different memories and interpretations of the historical past, particularly of the Volhynia tragedy, and the general tendency in Poland to 'look westwards'. On the Ukrainian side of the border, people seem to have washed away the massacres from their collective memories and popular interpretations (e.g. in historical works, Ukrainian Wikipedia, etc.) often present these events as a war between equal adversaries and Ukrainian participants in these events (primarily OUN-UPA) as national heroes, fighters for independence against all enemies and victims of Stalin/Soviet oppression. At the same time, Poland's support of an independent

Ukraine after 1989 gains sympathy for Poland among Ukrainians.[23] Polish memories and interpretations are, obviously, different from Ukrainian ones. The events of Volhynia, still fresh in collective memories, are interpreted as crimes committed by Ukrainian nationalists on innocent Polish populations, and organizations and names such as OUN-UPA and Bandera have definite negative connotations, just as do Nazi organizations and names such as the Gestapo, SS and Hitler. Therefore Poles feel uncomfortable when, for instance, walking along a street named after Stepan Bandera in Ukraine (there are such streets in western Ukraine); it is like walking along Adolf Hitler Strasse in Germany (of course, there are no such streets). The attitudes of Ukrainian society towards the history and its symbols is also differentiated territorially, but from the point of view of cross-border relations opinions and attitudes in the border area are more relevant than those held outside western Ukraine.

It appears that within the border area on both sides (including in large cities such as Lublin or Rzeszów), intellectuals and political leaders are more open to contacts with partners from the other side than 'ordinary' inhabitants are. The present psycho-cultural distance between the two ethnic groups now is obviously much smaller than it was in the 1940s, when the present state and ethnic border was being shaped amid bloodsheds and forced migrations. It does not mean, however, that the distance is diminishing in a linear manner with time passing. From time to time memories of hostilities from the past return, aggravating present attitudes. For instance, commemorations of Stepan Bandera and the UPA by Ukrainians are interpreted by Poles as the glorification of enemies of Poland and of murderers of Poles, and as a reminder of Ukrainian nationalism.

Models of political and economic transformation

Cross-border relations depend, among other things, on the political and economic system on both sides of the border. In the late 1980s and early 1990s Poland and Ukraine embarked on deep transformations of their political and economic systems. Models of their transformation reveal both similarities and differences, which resulted from internal socio-economic and political conditions and from external geopolitical circumstances. In turn, models of transformation influenced both the internal situations and international positions of the two countries.

The main common characteristics were, broadly, national independence, democracy and market economy. Differences are in the starting points and the detailed ways in which these three common characteristics have been fulfilled. Poland, despite being a member of the Soviet block before 1989, was a fully fledged nation state with a complete state apparatus and a population revealing a high degree of identification with this state, speaking one language (Polish) and having, broadly, one national memory. Consequently, when political ties with the Soviet block were broken at the end of the 1980s, Poland did not need to build state apparatus to bolster the national identity of its citizens or to decide which language should be the official state language. The breaking of the ties with the Soviet block was generally understood as the regaining of full independence, as something definitely positive that opened the way for further positive changes for the nation as a whole and for its citizens. The feeling of having regained full independence compensated, to some extent, for hardships resulting from the change in the political and economic system, and made people more patient in waiting for positive changes in their lives. National independence, after a very short period of hesitation directly after the collapse of the Soviet block (the dismantling of the Warsaw Pact and COMECON), was understood by almost the whole of Polish society and by political leaders (including those active in the old socialist system) as representing the freedom to join western institutions (the EU and NATO) and to adopt free market and democratic political forms according to established western rules.

Ukraine, until its unexpected independence in 1991, was a Soviet 'republic', a form of statehood that was lacking many elements of regular states, such as a diplomatic service (and property abroad, as the property of the USSR was inherited by Russia), an army and several institutions dealing with economic policy and so on. Ukraine even lacked one common national language: Ukrainian, declared as the only official state language of Ukraine, was spoken by, at best, half of its citizens, the other half speaking Russian (some of them, however, understood Ukrainian). Ukraine had to build state institutions and teach its citizens the state language, alongside transforming its economy, society and identity. Many of its inhabitants did not know whether to be happy to have regained independence or to be sad or angry about the collapse of the Soviet Union. In Ukraine, unlike Poland, unanimous support for independence and consensus about its implications was lacking. For some Ukrainians Ukraine was just like other independent countries in the world, free to decide on its internal affairs and international relations, but for quite a few Ukrainian citizens Ukraine after 1991 was a kind of renewed Soviet Ukraine with slightly enlarged competences within a renewed Soviet Union renamed as the Commonwealth of Independent States (CIS); many of them did not imagine and did not want Ukraine to be distanced from Russia. Because of these divergent definitions of Ukraine's independence Ukraine did not undertake (at least until the crisis of 2013/2014) steps towards joining western institutions, but also opposed Russian offers to join Russian-led projects of closer integration of the post-Soviet countries. The differences within Ukrainian society as regards the significance and meaning of independence resulted from, among other things, different collective memories and symbols (for instance, different attitudes to World War II, the Red Army, the Ukrainian Insurgent Army and so on) which hampered the building of social cohesion and consensus around many issues of internal and international politics. Differences within Ukrainian society had a clear territorial dimension which made these differences even more problematic for the stability of the state, forcing consecutive governments to balance between regions with different languages, identities, historical memories and attitudes towards the Ukrainian state and its foreign relations. Generally speaking, there were two opposite poles, with a large intermediate area closer to one or another pole. Symbolically, these two poles can be located in Lviv (western pole) and Donetsk (eastern pole). In the western pole people spoke Ukrainian, confessed

Greek Catholicism, had a strong Ukrainian identity (which meant that being Ukrainian excluded being at the same, for instance, Russian), identified with the Ukrainian state and wanted to preserve its independence and territorial integrity, wanted closer integration of Ukraine with the West (especially with the EU); many inhabitants of the western pole considered Stepan Bandera and the UPA as national heroes, the Red Army as enemy and invaders and Lenin (and monuments to him) as a symbol of Russian oppression. In the eastern pole, in contrast, people spoke Russian, confessed Orthodox Christianity or no religion, had an unclear identity (encompassing a Russian identity or a 'Slavic' identity (understood as a community of Russians, Ukrainians and Belarussians), and a regional rather than a national identity (Ukrainians as a regional variety of Russians)), their identification with Ukraine was rather weak (Ukrainian independence was, for many of them, an accident, and for some of them Ukraine was little more than a place of doing business), they preferred closer cooperation with Russia and opposed integration with the West (especially with NATO, but also with the EU), practically all of them (except recent immigrants from western Ukraine) considered Stepan Bandera and the UPA as 'fascists' (the strongest condemnation in the former Soviet Union), the Red Army as a liberator from fascism and Lenin as a positive hero. Particularly important for Ukrainian politics was that the eastern pole was stronger demographically and economically. Many people in Ukraine, especially in its eastern and southern parts, can be classified as 'orphans' of the Soviet Union, considering the USSR as a 'lost paradise' and desiring its revitalization in one or another form, such as the Russian-led reintegration of the post-Soviet space.

Different starting points and other factors influenced differences between Poland and Ukraine in the functioning of their political systems. It should be stressed that, despite the label 'communist' commonly used, especially in Western Europe or America, to describe the political system in countries of the Soviet block, there existed considerable differences among individual countries in this respect.

The political system in Poland, after the Stalinist period (1948–56), can be described as 'quasi-pluralist mutual tolerance of the rulers and the society'. The 'rulers' was the Party (the Polish United Workers' Party (PUWP) – it avoided the name 'communist' as this word was highly offensive in Poland), nominally in coalition with two 'allied' parties (the United People Party and the Democratic Party[24]). In the parliament some small opposition groups were also present ('licensed opposition' to some extent related to the Catholic Church). On the 'society' side there was the highly influential Catholic Church (with clubs of Catholic intelligentsia directly linked to the Church), a half- or entirely free legal press, cultural institutions, universities, political initiatives openly contesting the existing system and so on. As regards the rulers, they were mostly or exclusively pragmatists who accepted the fact that Poland had to be a socialist country and be an 'ally' (or satellite) of the USSR for pragmatic reasons (it was impossible to break out from the Soviet block and only the USSR guaranteed western Polish borders). From 1956 to the political crisis of 1980/81 the rulers and the society obeyed an unwritten '*modus vivendi*' that was broken during that crisis, which led to the declaration of martial law (13 December 1981) and the suppression of the opposition. This crisis, however, revealed weakness in the political system and the need for change. Both sides – the rulers and the society – were aware that the only way out was negotiation and a gradual peaceful transition towards a more democratic (or an entirely democratic) system. By the end of the 1980s, in a changed geopolitical environment (due to *glasnost* and *perestroika* in Gorbachev's USSR), the rulers and representatives of the society and of the Catholic Church started 'round table' negotiations which led to partially democratic elections in June 1989 and then to the taking-over of the government by the non-communist opposition. A significant role in the change of the system was played by persons stemming from the former 'licensed opposition' and by the 'allied' parties. In summary, it can be said that at the starting point in 1989 Poland possessed a quite well-structured political elite, and that this elite generally respected the democratic rules of the political game. The overwhelming consensus regarding the transition towards democracy, free market economics and the integration of Poland with the West (the EU and NATO) facilitated the political life and smooth alternation of governments and presidents over the whole post-1989 period.

In the post-round-table political system in Poland a short but important transition period can be distinguished. The round-table agreement envisaged partially democratic elections to the Sejm (the lower chamber of the parliament) and fully democratic elections to the newly established Senate (the higher chamber). According to this agreement, one-third of the seats in the Sejm were assigned in advance to the PUWP, one-third were assigned to the 'allied parties' and one-third were to be distributed according to the election results. Election to the Senate had to be fully democratic. The agreement also envisaged that the president of Poland would be elected by the National Assembly (Sejm and Senate). All seats assigned for free election in the Sejm were won by the Civic Committee 'Solidarity'; this committee also won 99 (out of 100) seats in the Senate (the remaining seat was won by an independent local businessman). Elections were held at the beginning of June 1989. The results demonstrated both a strong desire in society for systemic change and the PUWP's lack of popularity. The National Assembly elected (by a majority of just one vote) the leader of the PUWP, General Wojciech Jaruzelski, as President of the Republic. However, a representative of the PUWP as prime minister could not form the cabinet as other groups in the Sejm, including the two 'allied' parties, refused to join the government. The solution to this situation was a 'large coalition' of all political forces presented in the parliament, headed by a representative of the Civic Committee, Tadeusz Mazowiecki, as prime minister – the first non-communist prime minister in Central and Eastern Europe after World War II. This government took office in September 1989 (two months before the collapse of the Berlin wall). The subsequent months were crucial for political stability and the success of radical economic reforms, and old and new political forces successfully collaborated in leading Poland through this period. In 1990 the Sejm was dissolved and fully democratic elections were held. At the same time President Jaruzelski resigned and a presidential election was held, this time (and in the future) in the form of a general election. The presidential election was won by Lech Wałęsa, leader of Solidarity.

After the transitory stage the political system was elaborated on an equilibrium between the government, formed by parliamentary majority, and the president, elected in a general election. Current policy is determined by the government (Council of Ministers). The president can veto laws adopted by the parliament (this veto can be rejected by a majority of two-thirds of votes in the Sejm), can send laws to the Constitutional Tribunal (it may accept the law, reject it or demand the parliament make some corrections) and can submit his/her own law proposals. In many respects, especially in the realm of foreign policy, the division of competences between the government (prime minister) and the president is unclear. In such a situation cooperation between the government and the president largely depends on the personal qualities and political affiliations of the two parties. With regard to the parliament, since the mid-1990s election to the Sejm is proportionate (the method of calculating the seats, however, gives some privileges to the most successful parties, as their share in seats is higher than their share of votes), with a 5 per cent threshold being a barrier for small parties and protecting the Sejm from excessive fragmentation (in the first fully free and proportional election to the Sejm, in 1990, 29 parties were present). The 5 per cent threshold does not relate only to parties representing national minorities – if such a party won a seat in a constituency it retains this seat despite not having exceeded the 5 per cent threshold nationwide. Since the beginning only one national minority – the German minority – could win seats in the Sejm; initially it had four seats, and now one. Election to the Sejm is based on the majority system: one constituency–one seat.

Since 1990 there have been four presidents (the fifth is now in office) and several governments formed by various parties. Until 2005 the political scene of Poland was dominated by two camps: one stemming from the old regime (the PUWP took the decision to self-dissolve in 1990) and the other originating from the former anti-communist opposition. The former camp was called the 'Left' and the latter the 'Right'. In practice, there were no significant (if any) differences between the Left and the Right as regards internal economic and social policies or international relations. The main differences were biographies and attitudes towards the past. All governments in that period opted for free market economics, democracy and integration with the EU and NATO, with special reference to the alliance with the United States. One can even say that the 'post-communist' left-wing parties were more determined than the right-wing parties to pursue a liberal economic policy and pro-EU and pro-NATO foreign policy. In that period Poland joined NATO (1999) and the European Union (2004). Since the parliamentary election and the presidential election (the coincidence was accidental) in 2005 the old left–right division became irrelevant, being replaced by the division in the former post-Solidarity camp into the socially minded ('populist'), moderately Eurosceptic and conservative Law and Justice Party (PiS) (headed from the beginning by Jarosław Kaczyński) and the liberal, Europhile Civic Platform (PO) (headed by Donald Tusk). PiS governments ruled in 2005–7 and again from

October 2015 (having won 38 per cent of the votes, it gained more than 50 per cent of seats in the Sejm and formed a one-party government). Also in 2015 a PiS candidate (Andrzej Duda) defeated the incumbent president Bronisław Komorowski, supported by the Civic Platform. The Civic Platform (in coalition with a junior partner, the Polish People Party) ruled in 2007–15 (making it the longest period of same-party rule since 1989). From the round-table until the autumn of 2015 the political system in Poland worked smoothly, despite some tensions (especially in 2007–10, between the PO-led government of Donald Tusk and President Lech Kaczyński, twin brother of PiS leader Jarosław). There were no political street demonstrations (apart from those motivated by measures of economic policy) and political conflicts were being resolved in the parliament or by the Constitutional Tribunal. When analysing the political system in Poland it is worth mentioning that political parties (that overcome the threshold of 3 per cent at parliamentary election; 5 per cent is needed to enter the Sejm) receive subsidies from the state budget and that the financing of political parties by individuals is limited, to avoid political corruption. The situation changed in late 2015, after the PiS government and President Duda took office. The current opposition accuses the government and the president of breaching the Constitution and not respecting rulings of the Constitutional Tribunal. For the first time since 1989 political demonstrations took to the streets 'in defence of democracy'. In addition, the EU (in the form of the European Commission and European Parliament) expressed its concern about the condition of democracy in Poland. To solve the conflict the government invited the Venice Commission of the Council of Europe (a body controlling compliance with the law by member states). The conflict around the Constitutional Tribunal is the most serious political conflict since 1989. It should be stressed, however, that so far nobody has been arrested and nobody was killed or wounded in this conflict.

The starting point of the political system in Ukraine was more difficult than that in Poland, and its functioning was characterized by much more conflict. At independence (1991) Ukraine was deeply fractured by the aforementioned ethno-linguistic, ideological, identity and confessional divisions. During the old communist regime there was no mechanism and no will to overcome these divisions, to negotiate a Ukrainian identity and political future. The ruling communist party either ignored these divisions or simply oppressed expressions of undesired opinions. Victims of this policy were, first, people and ideas related to the western pole of Ukraine (members and supporters of the UPA, defenders of the idea of the independence of Ukraine, activists of the Greek Catholic Church and so on). This situation did not create favourable conditions for balanced reflections on Ukrainian history, especially the history of such organizations and personalities as the OUN-UPA and Stepan Bandera, who were popularly perceived in western Ukraine as anti-communist, anti-Russian heroes, fighters for Ukrainian independence. The situation changed in the mid-1980s with the outbreak of Gorbachev's *glasnost* and *perestroika*. At that time a grass-roots movement called the Movement (in Ukrainian: *Rukh*, headed by Vyacheslav Chornovil) appeared, the first aim of which was to protect the Ukrainian language, followed by demands for democratization of the USSR and Ukraine. *Glasnost* and *perestroika* could not, however, create a political elite, let alone a political climate conducive to discussions and overcoming political and ideological divisions.

While the objective conditions at the starting point of Ukrainian independence were highly unfavourable, the subjective factor – or the characteristics of some personalities – was beneficial for Ukraine. Firstly, Leonid Kravchuk, at the time chairman (president) of the Supreme Council of the Ukrainian SSR, or head of the state, was one of the three persons (together with Russian Boris Yeltsin and Belarussian Stanislav Shushkevich) who dissolved the USSR in December 1991; he was then elected the first president of an independent Ukraine. His determination, political instinct and adherence to the principles of democracy and independence helped to lead Ukraine through the crucial initial period. Perhaps even more than his victory at presidential elections in 1991, his defeat to Leonid Kuchma in 1994 confirmed his quality as a democratic leader. He handed over power to his rival in a ceremony charaterized by its friendly atmosphere. As mentioned earlier, he and his successor tried to keep a balance between the west and east of Ukraine and between pro-Western and pro-Russian foreign policy.

Over time, however, the political situation started to deteriorate as differences began to come to the fore, conflicts started to multiply and sharpen, and society's trust in the government started to dwindle. The reason for this, apart from the above-mentioned objective structural factors, was the method of recruitment of the political and economic elite (largely resulting from the method of privatization), the organization of the parliament and what can be called a 'culture of impatience'. Economic transformation, especially privatization, produced a small number of oligarchs located mostly in the industrial east, while the bulk of the population saw their living standards deteriorate and were hardly able to make ends meet. The wealth of the rich resulted not only from their qualities as entrepreneurs or managers but also, if not overwhelmingly, from connections with the state. The intermingling of oligarchs and the state was enabled, among other things, by the election system, as a lack of budget financing for political parties made them dependent on financing by private persons, including the oligarchs. Besides, the immunity offered to members of parliament allowed businessmen running suspicious businesses a good opportunity to 'buy' a seat in the parliament to avoid problems with justice. An opinion became widespread in Ukrainian society that politicians in power were more concerned with the interests of the oligarchs and their own interests than with the interests of the people and the Ukrainian state. The fact that most oligarchs originated from the eastern, 'less Ukrainian' part of the country only confirmed the opinion that they treated Ukraine as a source of quick profit. Dissatisfaction within Ukrainian society, especially among the poorer and more patriotically minded, and those in the west probably less tolerant of political corruption, was strengthened by the sharp fall in living standards in the 1990s and only slight improvement afterwards. At the same time, the political and cultural liberalization of Ukraine enabled the emergence and spread in western Ukraine of the ideology of the OUN-UPA and the cult of its leader Stepan Bandera. This time this ideology had a clear anti-Russian and anti-Soviet character. This situation created a fertile ground for protests and sharp political conflicts endangering the political stability of the country and even its integrity.

The first such conflict erupted at the end of 2004 during the presidential election. The announcement by the state election commission that the election was won by Viktor Yanukovych (a Russian speaker from Donetsk; his rival was a Ukrainian speaker, Viktor Yushchenko, born in central Ukraine but representing the west Ukrainian mentality) sparked large-scale and violent protests on the part of those who considered the election to be rigged (the so-called 'orange' faction), especially in western Ukraine, and counter-protests by Yanukovych's supporters (the 'blue'), mainly in eastern Ukraine. The centre of the confrontation was Maidan Square of Independence in Kiev (Kyiv), where for several months the 'orange' faction continued a sitting strike. When the confrontation was on the brink of armed conflict, foreign mediation, especially by the then Polish president Aleksander Kwaśniewski, backed by the European Union with the presence of a Russian envoy, helped to solve the crisis. The election was declared invalid and a new election was called, which was won by Yushchenko. This event, known as the 'Orange Revolution', on the one hand confirmed the strength of popular protest against the rulers and, on the other, deepened the antagonism between the western and eastern poles of Ukraine. Two heroes of the 'Orange Revolution' – Viktor Yushchenko and an oligarch–politician Yulia Tymoshenko – occupied the two most important positions in the state, president and prime minister. The following years were a time of continuous conflicts between Yushchenko and Tymoshenko (including scandalous scrimmages between their supporters in parliament that were featured on television). For Ukrainians, this was another disappointment. After the end of Yushchenko's term the following presidential election was won comfortably by Viktor Yanukovych. He, like his predecessors, tried in foreign policy matters to balance between Russia and the West, presumably hoping to win some badly needed concessions from both sides. He embarked on negotiations about association with the EU, but finally, in November 2013, he refused to sign the agreement with the EU, considering EU concessions insufficient and Russian economic offers and warnings more convincing. This refusal provoked angry protests from supporters of the idea of closer integration with the EU, especially in western Ukraine. Ten years after the first 'Maidan', protesters began again to gather in the Square of Independence in Kyiv. Yanukovych's refusal to sign the agreement with the EU was only the immediate, direct cause of the protest; other causes were corruption, low living standards, a lack of hope for improvements and, for some protesters, the dilatory pace (or even retreat) of Ukrainization. This protest was called the 'Revolution of Dignity' or 'Euromaidan'. The community of protesters was variegated, but at its core were radical Ukrainian nationalists from western Ukraine, with the black-and-red flags of the OUN-UPA, concentrated in the so-called 'right sector'. Unlike the 'Orange Revolution', the 'Euromaidan' ended in bloodshed when the Berkut special police troops opened fire on demonstrators, killing more than 100 of them in February 2014; some victims appear in fact to have been on the side of the Berkut. The fighting was stopped by the diplomatic intervention of the ministries of foreign affairs of Poland, Germany and

France, which negotiated an agreement between President Yanukovych and the protesters. Less than 24 hours later the 'right sector' rejected the agreement, demanding the dismissal of President Yanukovych, who left Kyiv. This was interpreted by his opponents as his resignation from the position of president of Ukraine, although he and his followers, and the Russian government, regarded this move as a necessary one to save his life, which was endangered by the protesters. The Ukrainian parliament, in extraordinary circumstances, and under pressure from the Maidan protesters, declared the dismissal of Yanukovich (in a way inconsistent with the constitution of Ukraine) and called for a new presidential election to be held in May of that year. According to the supporters of Yanukovych, including Russia, this was a coup d'etat. The election was won by Petro Poroshenko, an ex-foreign minister and oligarch. It should also be mentioned that a few days after the toppling of Yanukovych the Ukrainian parliament adopted an act making Ukrainian the only language of the public sphere. Although this act was immediately vetoed by the acting president Turchynov, it was regarded by (some or many) ethnic Russians as a declaration of intention by the new Ukrainian leaders to persecute Russian, and as evidence that 'fascists' had taken power in Kiev.

The Euromaidan revolution triggered a series of events whose detailed analysis exceeds the scope of this chapter: the occupation of the Crimean Peninsula by the then stationed Russian troops (in uniforms without distinctions); the declaration of independence by the Crimean parliament and the immediate declaration of reintegration with Russia; the official annexation of Crimea by Russia; anti-government (anti-Ukrainian) revolts in eastern Ukraine (supported by Russia); the occupation by the rebels (or insurgents) of parts of the two easternmost oblasts bordering with Russia (Donetsk and Luhansk); fighting between the rebels (and their supporters from Russia and elsewhere), on the one side, and the Ukrainian army, volunteers (mainly from western Ukraine) and private armies of oligarchs loyal to Ukraine (or considering Ukraine a better place to carry out business than Putin's Russia or the 'People's Republics' of Donetsk and Luhansk) on the other; and the Minsk Protocol (between Ukraine, the rebels and Russia, with the German chancellor and French president as mediators), which temporarily put an end to open fighting and proposed a compromise between Ukraine and the rebels concerning the organization of the Ukrainian state and the status of the territories of the two rebel republics. As of February 2016 the agreement has not been fulfilled: heavy weaponry has been not withdrawn from the frontline and the Ukrainian–Russian state border in the two rebel oblasts is not under Ukraine's control. The reform of the territorial organization of Ukraine will be dealt with later in this chapter.

Events after the Euromaidan revolution demonstrated the viability of the Ukrainian state and nation, as Ukraine defended its existence and territorial integrity (apart from territories lost at the beginning of the crisis). However, Ukraine is still facing serious problems. Despite efforts by the new leaders and assistance from the international community, the endemic causes of popular dissatisfaction and low levels of trust in the political elite over matters of corruption, unsatisfactory living standards, and few signs of improvement are still present, aggravated by the existence of armed militias and individuals.[25]

As far as economic transformation is concerned, the two countries' starting points in 1989–91 were different in terms of both material and ideological aspects. Subsequent events, to a large extent, resulted from these different starting points. From the point of view of the future transformation of the economy and economic performances in Poland, as opposed to Ukraine, the following characteristics of Poland's economy at the beginning of the transformation are particularly important:

1 its relatively limited dependence on trade with the Soviet Union (exports of some military equipment and ships in exchange for oil and natural gas in small quantities; Poland relied heavily on its own coal, iron ore and other raw materials), and relatively developed relations with non-socialist countries,
2 its territorial proximity to Germany (and western Europe), a significant matter from the point of view of foreign investments in Poland, especially of small and medium-sized firms, and from the point of view of Polish exports,
3 the existence of a sizable private sector – which in agriculture accounted for 75 per cent of arable land, and which was also present in small businesses in the sectors of commerce, services, crafts and so on – and, consequently, of an incipient entrepreneurial class; this class grew considerably in the 1980s as a result of economic reforms and freedom to travel, work and do business abroad, which was highly profitable given the enormously high exchange rate of hard currencies in Poland.

Owing to the above characteristics, Poland's economy suffered relatively less from breaking trading relations with the USSR (in practice only from the decline in exports, as imports of Russian raw materials continued almost unchanged), there was no pressing need to privatize agriculture and there was a home-grown entrepreneurial class crucial for the market economy.

As regards ideas on economic transformation in Poland, it should be mentioned that the political elites which took over power in 1989 had undergone a considerable intellectual evolution from discussing various forms of a renewed market socialism and 'third ways' at the beginning of the 1980s to the rejection of 'economic experiments' and the conclusion that there was only one 'real' economy, that practised in the West. This conclusion conformed with the opinion of foreign (western) advisers (the so-called Chicago boys) to the Polish government that took office in September 1989 (as a matter of fact, some radical measures towards the liberalization of the economy were undertaken a few months earlier, at the beginning of 1989, by the old, 'communist' government of Mieczysław Rakowski). The main elements of the economic transformation programme introduced in January 1990 were, first, the liberalization of most prices, which resulted in initial hikes in retail prices and the reaching of market equilibrium; second, the gradual privatization of state-owned property in which home and foreign investors could participate; third, the elimination of most subsidies, which forced enterprises to look for income in the market; fourth, the convertibility of the currency (Polish zloty, now PLN) and the elimination of the state monopoly in foreign trade, which opened up

Polish markets to international competition. Particularly important, especially if compared with the situation in Ukraine, was the method and result of the privatization and commercialization of state-owned firms. This was carried out in the following forms:

1 'small privatization' or selling property to individual bidders via auctions,
2 the selling of firms on the stock exchange (to Polish and foreign investors),
3 the selling of firms or other elements of property to 'strategic investors' (usually West European or American firms),
4 the selling (for a reduced price) of firms to their employees,
5 'coupon privatization' (the distribution to citizens of certificates exchangeable for shares in privatized firms).

It should be stressed that the last two forms played a marginal role. As a result, the ownership of the privatized economy turned out to be highly dispersed and the phenomenon of 'oligarchs', characteristic of Ukraine and Russia, has not appeared.

Poland's economic policy, called 'shock therapy', initially produced both positive and negative results. The main immediate positive result was market equilibrium and the elimination of market shortages and related phenomena (queues in shops, a black market, time wasted in queues, unsatisfied demand and so on). This was greatly appreciated by the vast majority of inhabitants. The negative results were the appearance of unemployment (which in the mid-1990s reached 10 per cent), falling GDP (until mid-1992) and problems in some sectors, such as state-owned agriculture, military industry and firms producing for exports to the USSR and former socialist countries (the transition of trade with these countries from planned contracts to the free market resulted in a sharp decline in trade with these countries, as firms from these countries acted in accordance with market principles and, having to pay in hard currency, preferred to buy better products from elsewhere in the world). This programme was supported by practically the whole political class (including the so-called 'post-communists', or parties which emerged from the defunct PUWP, which ruled Poland under the old system). Negative phenomena were either regarded as a temporary by-products of the reform and were dealt with by social protection measures (e.g. unemployment benefits) or were ignored as something normal in the market economy. In 1992 Poland's economy resumed growth, which, with some fluctuation, has continued until the present. It is worth mentioning that Poland's economy shifted its exports quite quickly and smoothly from the USSR (and other socialist countries) to free market economies, mostly to Germany (one-third of exports) and other West European markets.

After a very short period of hesitation, the Polish government decided in the early 1990s that Poland should join western institutions: primarily, NATO and the EU. In 1991 Poland became an associated member, and in 2004 a full member of the EU, and in 1999 it joined NATO. The decision to join western institutions, which was supported by the overwhelming majority of the society and practically all political parties, influenced internal politics in terms of the adoption of measures enabling the transition to a market economy and liberal democracy. Poland's membership of the EU, along with access to European markets and inflow of foreign investments and European funds, not only helped to build institutions compatible with European market economies but also created favourable conditions for the modernizing of infrastructure and rapid growth. It is worth noting that Poland was one of the few countries with positive growth in GDP during the recession of 2008–10. This does not mean that Poland is free of economic and social problems; unemployment is still rather high (about 10 per cent), especially among young people, despite a substantial amount of emigration (about 2 million Poles are living and working abroad, mostly in West European EU countries), and the labour market situation is aggravated by the widespread phenomenon of precarization. There is a growing gap between the rich and the poor which is translated as better-off metropolitan areas on the one hand and disadvantaged small towns and rural peripheries, especially in eastern Poland, on the other. It is worth noting that areas bordering with Ukraine belong to the poorest in Poland. This situation is a source of growing dissatisfaction among part of society, especially in peripheral rural areas and small towns and, for the first time, among young people. Poland's full independence and integration with the EU no longer compensate for the hardships and insecurity of everyday life. In the autumn of 2015 almost 40 per cent of voters (which gave more than 50 per cent of mandates) trusted the Law and Justice party, which promised an easy and quick improvement of the situation. The future will show if the new government will improve the economy or destroy it.

Conditions, both internal and external, for economic transformation in Ukraine were very different from those in Poland. From the point of view of material factors at the beginning of the transformation three factors should be underlined:

1 much deeper economic ties with (the rest of) the Soviet Union, which, during the disintegration of the USSR and its economy, led to a dramatic recession in the Ukrainian economy,
2 geographical, as well as informational, distance to rich market economies that could serve as sources of capital and markets during the transformation to a market economy (neither the Russian economy nor the economies of Central or Eastern European neighbours could offer Ukraine the types of opportunity that the German economy offered for Poland in the crucial years after 1989–91),
3 the lack of a meaningful private economy and of the related incipient entrepreneurial class; moreover, structural characteristics of the Ukrainian economy – a high share of mining, heavy industries, energy transportation infrastructure and military complex – made it especially unfavourable to privatization.

Unfavourable conditions also existed in the sphere of ideas and politics: an absence of intellectual preparedness for economic reform at the moment of the collapse of the Soviet Union and the Soviet economy, and a lack of general social support for a radical market-orientated reform. This latter factor was related to the lack of a generally accepted vision of the place of Ukraine in the geopolitical setting of Europe. Ukraine was not willing to join western institutions and the West was disinclined to present to Ukraine a perspective to assist its admittance. This was one of the elements discouraging a longer-term economic policy. Ukrainian governments preferred policies consisting of reactions to current issues, to avoid problems rather than to cope with them. Given the dramatic fall in living standards accompanying the fall of the USSR, Ukrainian governments tried to avoid inflicting further hardships on the population which would result from price and costs liberalization, the elimination of subsidies to loss-making enterprises and large-scale privatization. Especially concerning were house rents and prices of gas and electricity for households, which were kept below the cost of production. Having no unanimous social support for market reforms, governments were afraid of social revolt resulting from hikes in rents and prices of natural gas and electricity. In such a situation the internal market could not reach equilibrium for a long time (at least one decade). At the same time cheap energy allowed households and enterprises to avoid rationalizing energy consumption and reducing the high energy use of the Ukrainian economy. Governments were more interested in getting cheap Russian natural gas and oil than in increasing energy efficiency. The overwhelming majority of Russian gas exported outside the former USSR by pipelines went through Ukrainian territory, opening up the possibility of Ukraine being able to bargain for better price conditions. Other pressures placed by Ukraine on Russia were Ukraine's geopolitical position (better prices could be achieved from Russia as a result of rejecting the West, Ukrainian Crimea as a location for the Russian fleet and so on). Besides, prices below the cost of production of many goods meant opportunities for quick and easy profits by buying cheap products at subsidized prices and selling them elsewhere at high market prices, and by direct access to state subsidies. This way of doing business created favourable conditions for corruption, such as strong ties between state and business and a culture in which profits depended more on administrative decisions than on market performances, and militated against improvements in efficiency, innovation and so on. The manner in which privatization was carried out in Ukraine, as in Russia, ended up transferring large parts of the economy into the hands of a few well-connected owners, called 'oligarchs'. A political system in which political parties and individual politicians depended for financing mainly on business, and the fate and prosperity of businesses largely depended on decisions taken by politicians added to conditions favourable for political corruption, the protection of vested interests and the avoidance of reforms that would introduce transparency in relations between business and politics. The Ukrainian economy started to recover in about 2000, but primarily as a result of better prices for Ukrainian exports (hard coal, metallurgy, machinery) rather than improved efficiency in the economy. This phenomenon, however, was temporary. Living standards in Ukraine, once not worse than those of its neighbours, started to fall below those in Poland, Russia (which had increased owing to high oil and gas prices and reforms introduced by President Putin after 2000) and Belarus (which profited from good relations with Russia). This situation fuelled popular dissatisfaction, although opinions about the geopolitical course that Ukraine should take – whether to integrate with the West or with Russia – varied. This resulted in the political crisis of 2013/14 described above, ultimately leading to the election of President Poroshenko, promising market and anti-corruption reforms and a pro-European course in foreign policy.

When analysing cross-border Polish–Ukrainian relations it is important to consider the impacts of the above-discussed economic systems and policies in both countries on these relations. The immediate and most visible impact in the years after 1989/90 was on cross-border trade, as a result of differences in prices and exchange rates. Given that Polish economic reforms started earlier and were more radical that those in Ukraine, the Polish currency (zloty, now PLN) first became convertible and its exchange rate in relation to currencies in Ukraine (Soviet rouble, Ukrainian rouble, hryvnia) grew, making Ukrainian prices very low in comparison with Polish ones. This resulted in a massive inflow of Ukrainian small traders to Poland, who sold their products on bazaars in eastern Poland and in large cities in central Poland. Less often, Polish traders went to Ukraine to buy cheap products. It is worth mentioning that this cross-border trade was made possible by the liberal border-crossing regime. Over time price differences gradually diminished, making the trade less profitable. At the same time Poland, in order to meet its obligations towards the European Union, introduced in 1998 visa requirements for Ukrainians coming to Poland, which further reduced the small cross-border trade. The situation was to a degree reversed after 2000, when some products in Poland became cheaper than in Ukraine owing to the collapse of some sectors of the Ukrainian economy, meaning that their products were either unavailable or very expensive. Interestingly, among these were agricultural products, which is surprising given the better conditions for agriculture in Ukraine than in Poland. At that time Ukrainians made shopping trips to Poland for re-selling purposes. Despite differences in the pace and range of economic reforms the two systems are compatible enough to enable mutual foreign investments. These investments are, however, small (in the case of Polish investment in Ukraine) or far from being success stories, as in the cases of investments of firms from the industrial east of Ukraine in steel works, ship building and the car industry in Poland.

Apart from the economic system and political situation and mechanisms in both countries, cross-border relations depended on the territorial organization of the states concerned, first of all in terms of competences and resources of local and regional governments. In this respect Poland and Ukraine have differed considerably, and it was only recently (in 2015 and 2016) that Ukraine started a programme to bring its territorial organization in line with that in Poland. The main difference was in the competence of local and regional authorities, which was greater in Poland than in Ukraine.

The Polish system of local and regional authorities has undergone significant changes since the beginning of the transformation. In 1989 Poland inherited the old socialist system of state organization. This system was changed several times in the post-war period, but the changes primarily affected the size and number of territorial units, without substantial changes in their competences, their functioning and the recruitment of their authorities. In each unit of territorial organization there were councils and executive bodies. Councils were theoretically elected by inhabitants but practically nominated by the governing party (PUWP) and its 'allied parties'. Executive bodies functioned according to the principle of 'double subordination' – horizontal subordination to the respective council, and vertical subordination to the executive body one level above. The former subordination, theoretically, related to political issues, the latter to technical, including financial issues. In each territorial unit there was a committee of the party, which had informal, but real, power. In some places there also existed committees of the 'allied parties': the United People's Party, also translated in English as the United Peasant Party, and the Democratic Party. Politically, the strongest body was the committee, followed by the executive body and finally the council. In 1975, in another reform of state organization, the institution of the *voivod* (equivalent to the French *préfet*) was introduced to control the legality of actions of local and regional governments, which was rather superfluous given that the governing party had enough instruments to control them. In 1989 there existed two territorial levels of state organization: the *gmina* (in English: *commune*) and the *voivodship*.

The first change after 1989 was the self-dissolution of the PUWP and the related disappearance of party committees. Other steps undertaken in 1990 were the elimination of *voivodship* councils and the transformation of communes into self-governed units (organizing fully democratic elections to commune councils and making local executive bodies responsible to their councils). The institution of *voivod*, which was appointed by the prime minister, was retained. Consequently, democracy in Poland existed on two levels: local and central. Poland's still-closer cooperation with the EU (which, among other things, involved receiving the so-called pre-accession funds) with a view to joining this organization encouraged Polish authorities to introduce a self-governed regional level. The main, if not the only, argument for the reform was that it would make it easier to acquire EU funds after accession, improve the absorption of these funds and make the Polish political system more compatible with that prevailing in EU countries, in line with the widespread belief in the EU that regional self-government improves regional development and accelerates European integration. There was no bottom-up pressure for such a reform in Poland; Poles seemed to be fully satisfied with electing their representatives to the national parliament and to local councils. The new territorial organization, which started in 1999, reduced the number of *voivodships* to 16 (before 1975 their number was 17, with largely the same territories and capital cities) and introduced (or re-introduced) an intermediary level between the commune and *voivodship* called the *powiat* (this level, with the same name, existed before 1975).

Consequently, the organization of the state in Poland consists of three levels – local (communes), sub-regional (*powiat*) and regional (*voivodship*, or as it is now often called in Polish, *region*). Each level is independent from the others, has its own elected representation (councils) and executive bodies, tasks and quite stable sources of financing. In fact, one of the main tasks of the regions (*voivodship*) is managing and distributing European funds. Apart from elected bodies at all levels, there is the institution called the *wojewoda* or *voivod* (one in each of 16 *voivodships*), representing the central government, whose responsibility it is to control the legality of actions by self-governing bodies at all levels as well as intervening in extraordinary situations (natural disasters, public security and so on). *Wojewoda* cannot interfere in activities of self-governing bodies as long as these are in conformity with the law (regardless of their purpose). When he/she considers that the law was breached, he/she presents the contested action to the court and the court takes the final decision. To fulfil their tasks territorial units of state organization may cooperate with other units, forming associations. An important element in the construction of local (regional) government is the relationship between representative bodies (councils) and heads of executives (marshals of *voivodships*, presidents or mayors of cities and towns, *starosta* in *powiat* and *wójt* in communes). At the regional and sub-regional (*powiat*) level heads of executive bodies are elected by the respective councils. At local level, including in large cities, the situation has varied between election by councils or directly by inhabitants. Now in most types of local government heads of executives are elected directly by inhabitants. From the point of view of cross-border or trans-national cooperation of units of territorial self-government, they are free to enter various forms of cooperation in the scope of their competences.

As regards the Ukrainian system of territorial organization, its main characteristic is its centralization. This is a result of both the old Soviet bureaucratic heritage and the new political reality of Ukraine. Ukraine, as it emerged from the Soviet Union, was territorially varied from the point of view of ethnic composition, the degree of national Ukrainian consciousness, loyalty to the Ukrainian state, economic interests and so on. The centralization of state power was, in such conditions, a means to counteract centrifugal tendencies.

From the Soviet system Ukraine inherited quite a complicated system of territorial organization. It consisted of 24 *oblasts*, the Autonomous Republic of Crimea and two cities of special status (Kyiv and Sevastopol) at the highest level, *rayons* (*rayony*) and towns (*misto*) with *rayons* (understood as towns districts) at intermediary level, and towns (*misto*) without *rayons*, *rayons* within towns, villages (*selo*) and townships (*selishche*). What makes this system more complicated is the varying status of units. *Oblasts* and *rayons* are territorial-administrative units, towns, villages and townships are self-governed units, *rayons* in towns are both territorial-administrative and self-governed units, and finally, Crimea had autonomy status. Each territorial unit, regardless of its status and level, has its council (*rada*) with its chairperson. What is especially important is that, parallel to these self-governing bodies, there is a system of state administration, representative of the central authorities and appointed by the president, which has large competences, theoretically playing the role of executive bodies of councils and responsible both 'horizontally' (before councils) and 'vertically' (before the central government). Given that heads of state administration are appointed by the central government, they personally and the whole administration depends on central government. This represents the formal method of centralizing power; besides this, there are informal means of centralization and of reducing the practical significance of territorial self-government.

Until now, formal and real differences in the autonomy of local and regional authorities on both sides of the Polish–Ukrainian border, together with other factors, have been an obstacle to cross-border cooperation. One of the results of this was the fact that cooperative initiatives usually came from above – from the governments of the two countries, rather than from institutions and citizens living in the border area.

As of February 2016 a decentralizating reform of territorial organization of the state is underway,[26] preparation for which started in 2015. It consists of the simplification of the system of territorial units to make three clear-cut levels, giving territorial units more autonomy and stable financing and transforming the heads of state administration into *prefekts* (with their secretariat), equivalent to the Polish *wojewoda*; in fact, the reforms would bring the system of territorial organization very much in line with that of Poland. Unlike in Poland, however, the Ukrainian reform does not imply changes to the number and types of territory at the highest level of state administration. However, retaining the 24 *oblasts* (regions) makes their size and population similar to those of the 16 Polish regions. The aim of the reform is at least twofold: to make Ukraine more compatible with European standards and thus to confirm the 'European choice' of Ukraine, and to make territorial government more efficient. Another aim cannot be excluded: to present the decentralization of the state as an answer to the demands of rebels in eastern Ukraine and of the Russian authorities backing them. They demand independence, or at least wide autonomy and the transformation of Ukraine into a federal state. Ukrainian authorities, however, reject the idea of federalization, offering instead decentralization.

From the point of view of cross-border cooperation between Poland and Ukraine, this reform removes one of the obstacles: the incompatibility of the systems of local and regional government on both sides of the border.

Notes

1 In the USSR, but also in the former Yugoslavia and Czechoslovakia, the term 'republic' was largely understood as synonymous with 'region', or a sub-national unit, like the term 'state' in the USA. Therefore, Ukraine, to stress its independence, removed the word 'republic' from its name. (The other two words – 'Soviet' and 'Socialist', were abandoned because of the change in the political system.)

2 This also gave birth to the confusion concerning the meaning of the name 'Lithuania' and conflicts between the contemporary nationalisms – Lithuanian and Belarusian – over who is 'true Lithuanian' and which country is the 'true' heir to the Grand Duchy of Lithuania. It is worth noting that practically until the first decades of the twentieth century inhabitants of the present Belarus called themselves 'Lithuanians' and many places had the adjective 'Lithuanian' in their names, e.g. 'Lithuanian Minsk', now Minsk, the capital city of Belarus. The adjective 'Lithuanian' was necessary to distinguish this Minsk from another Minsk – Mazovian Minsk near Warsaw.

3 His opinion, common to Polish historians, is also shared by Timothy Snyder, an American historian specializing in the history of Central and Eastern Europe (Snyder 2003).

4 In Polish the word for 'Commonwealth' is 'Rzeczpospolita' (the full name of the Commonwealth of the Two Nations is Rzeczpospolita Obojga Narodów). The word 'Rzeczpospolita' is a literal translation from Latin 'Res Publica'; therefore, its other meaning is 'republic', as in the official name of Poland – Rzeczpospolita Polska. The word 'rzeczpospolita' meaning 'republic' relates nowadays only to Poland. For other cases the word 'republika' is used.

5 For a detailed analysis of alternative interpretations of the Lublin Union in Ukrainian textbooks see an interesting article by Ukrainian historian Tetiana Hoshko (2012). A positive opinion on the Lublin Union is expressed also by Pavlo Magochiy (Magochiy 2007, 140). He reckons that the union was not imposed by the Polish side but was also desired by the Ruthenian aristocracy, who wanted Ruthenia to be incorporated to the Crown.

6 The name comes from Turkish and meant 'robber', as they used to make robbery incursions by boats in Turkey.

7 As Lev Gumilev (also: Lew Gumilow), the contemporary Russian historian and philosopher, representing a 'Euroasian' and anti-Western ideology, admits, Moscow's gain was not only a vast territory and population, but also and most importantly people – educated, skilled, speaking western languages and knowing Europe, invaluable for the rise and expansion of Russia (Gumilow 2004).

8 This legend united two inseparable aspects: social (an anti-gentry movement of oppressed peasants) and ethno-national (an anti-Polish and anti-Catholic movement of Ruthenians). See Fedoruk 2003.

9 It is a tradition to consider that Ukrainian nationalism was born in Austrian Galicia, if not invented by Austrians. Ukrainian–Polish–American scholar Roman Szporluk argues that it started in Russian Ukraine (Szporluk 1997).

10 Szeptycki's family belonged to the above-mentioned category of natione Polonorum gente Ruthenorum. The personality of Metropolitan Andrey Sheptytsky, also known as Count Roman Szeptycki, is very important in Polish–Ukrainian relations. He was Metropolitan of the Greek Catholic Church from 1900 to his (natural) death in 1944, during the very turbulent period spanning autonomous Galicia, World War I, the Polish–Ukrainian war of 1918 for Lwów/Lviv (in which he stood firmly on the Ukrainian side, travelling to Western Europe and America advocating for the establishment of an Ukrainian state), the interwar period of Polish rule in Lwów/Lviv, the first Soviet occupation (1939–41), the German occupation (1941–44) and the second Soviet occupation. He was born into a Polish-speaking Roman Catholic aristocratic family, although his father was of Ruthenian origin. In his youth he changed the rite from Roman to Greek Catholic and accepted the (religious) name Andrey. He also accepted Ukrainian national identity and contributed immensely to creating a Ukrainian national consciousness. Opinions on this personality among contemporary Poles and Ukrainians are divergent: for Ukrainians he is a national hero, while Polish opinions range from vehement condemnation and accusation for encouraging Ukrainian radical nationalism, which was responsible for atrocities committed on Polish (and Jewish) populations during the Nazi occupation and for cooperation with the Nazis, to the view that he was a controversial personality living in very hard times who tried, unsuccessfully, to mitigate radical Ukrainians nationalists and rescued several Jews (Hentosh 2003; Zięba 1994; Szul 2014, 106–8). It is worth mentioning that his brother, General Stanisław Szeptycki, was a Polish national hero, one of those who contributed to the victory of the Polish army in the war against Bolshevik Russia in 1920, and was the first minister of national defence of independent Poland. In summary, three of five adult Szeptycki brothers chose Polish identity and two chose Ukrainian (Szul 2014, 106–8).

11 An example of this kind of thinking is Mykhailo Kolodzins'ky, author of 'Military doctrine of Ukrainian nationalists', written for the OUN in 1935 or 1936 in a training camp of Croatian fascists in Mussolini's Italy. In this doctrine, Kolodzins'ky, among

other things, dreams about a Ukrainian Empire reaching the Tian-Shan Mountains and Ukrainian military parades in conquered Warsaw and Moscow, and appeals to Ukrainian nationalists not to shy from 'murdering, robbing and setting fire' – because it is good for Ukraine and God accepts it because God loves Ukraine – and not to take care of the opinions of foreigners. He rejects any, even tactical, compromise with Poles: 'Poles must be washed away from Ukraine to the last leg'. Ukraine should also be free from Jews: 'the more Jews will be killed during the revolution, the better'. Kolodzins'ky's doctrine was discovered in the OUN archives, and described and published with critical comments by Oleksandr Zaytsev (Zaytsev 2013). Zaytsev rightly puts the question: to what extent was this way of thinking typical for radical nationalists, and to what extent did it prepare the ground for massacres committed by them on Polish and Jewish populations during World War II?

12 An excellent analysis of the dichotomies of Ukraine, as well as other issues related to Ukrainian history, is the book by Ukrainian scholar Mykola Riabchuk (Polish: Riabczuk) suggestively titled *Two Ukraines* (Riabczuk 2004). See also his latest book, which discusses, firstly, Ukrainian–Russian relations, including the recent (third) Maidan revolution of 2013/14 (Riabczuk 2015).

13 The text of his law, in Ukrainian, can be found on the website of the Ukrainian parliament: http://w1.c1.rada.gov.ua/pls/zweb2/webproc4_1?pf3511=54689 (accessed: 14 February 2016).

14 Polish expert Robert Sobkowicz reckons that in Ukraine anti-Polish sentiments and the justification of anti-Polish (and anti-Jewish) genocide committed by the OUN-UPA is getting stronger and that if Ukrainians do not come to their senses Polish society will stop being sensitive to Ukrainian expectations and desires for independence and will force the Polish government to change its attitude towards the government in Kiev. http://naszdziennik.pl/polska-kraj/131739,ukrainski-antypolonizm-przybiera-na-sile.html?d=1 (accessed: 12 February 2016).

15 This work gives an extensive discussion on theories of borders.

16 Polish political geographer Zbigniew Rykiel (Rykiel 2006, 184–225) uses the term 'geopolitical code' to describe what in this text is called the 'geopolitical rules of the game'. He distinguishes and analyses the following 13 codes: antiquity, the Middle Ages, great geographical discoveries, the Westphanian order, the Napoleonic order, the Vienna order, imperialism, the First World War, the Versailles system, the anti-Versailles order, the Yalta–Potsdam system, decolonization and globalization.

17 There is abundant literature and a multiplicity of approaches on the subject of relationships between nation, state and culture, including language. For this author two approaches are the most relevant: 1) constructivism, according to which nations are a modern (nineteenth-century) product (construct) of states, or, more precisely, a deliberate construct of those who hold power in the state, and this construction serves their political and economic interests (for instance, the cultural and ideational homogenization of the population eliminates internal conflicts and stabilizes the political situation, linguistic homogenization enables the smooth functioning of the market, especially the labour market, and the army, etc.); 2) ethno-symbolism, according to which the roots of nations go back much further than the modern period; they are a product of long history, and in the modern period the process of nation-building only accelerated. The two 'founding fathers' are, respectively, Ernest Gellner (see, e.g., Gellner 2006) and his disciple–opponent Anthony D. Smith (see, e.g., Smith 2000; Smith 2009). On various approaches to nationalism see Hearn 2006).

18 The 'classical' author quoted as a specialist in stateless nationalism is the Czech historian Miroslav Hroch (see e.g. Hroch 2003).

19 For a detailed analysis see Eberhardt 1992; Eberhardt 2004. These works present both the real shape of boundaries and theories and political concepts of borders.

20 An excellent analysis of the borders of Central and Eastern Europe in this period is presented by Marek Sobczyński (2013).

21 One such person was Iwan (Ivan) Franko, living in Galicia in the second half of the nineteenth century and the beginning of the twentieth century, a writer and journalist who wrote in three languages: Ukrainian, Polish and German. While his writing in Polish and German fell into oblivion, his writing in Ukrainian became extremely popular, making him the second greatest Ukrainian writer (after Shevchenko). To honour him one of the largest towns in western Ukraine was renamed 'Ivano-Frankivsk' (Szul 2014, 108–11; Hrytsak 2003).

22 I owe this information to Andrzej Miszczuk, professor at a Lublin university.

23 According to a recent investigation of public opinion in Ukraine, 58 per cent have a positive or very positive attitude towards Poland (35 per cent neutral, 5 per cent negative and very negative, 2 per cent have no opinion). Poland is the most popular country for Ukrainians. The second is Belarus, with 53 per cent positive or very positive opinions, followed by the EU (as a whole), Georgia, Lithuania, Canada, etc. Russia is at the bottom, with 16 per cent positive and very positive opinions and 59 per cent negative or very negative opinions (Andusieczko 2016, 12). This investigation has, however, limited relevance for our study, as it relates to Ukrainians in general and not only to those living in the border area.

24 The original Polish names of these two parties were Zjednoczone Stronnictwo Ludowe and Stronnictwo Demokratyczne. In both cases the word 'stronnictwo' is used, which means 'party' in English. In Polish there are two words for 'party': 'partia' and 'stronnictwo'; the former was used in the name of the Polish United Workers' Party (PUWP) and the latter was used in the names of the other two smaller parties, which had to stress the difference between the ruling party and the 'allied' parties. The distribution of seats in the parliament and government among the three parties and other groups was decided in advance, before the election, according to a scheme granting the PUWP the leading position. Elections only confirmed decisions undertaken by the parties as the number of candidates in a list only slightly exceeded the number of seats for this list.

25 Compare an analysis made by *The Economist* in September 2015: 'Only 3% of Ukrainians are satisfied with the pace of reforms. None of the officials who pillaged the country under its prior government and were responsible for the deaths of demonstrators in Kiev has been prosecuted. Despite a few fresh faces in government, the old elite continues to dominate, showing little interest in investigating the scams they once ran – and in many cases still do. (. . .) The biggest threat to Ukraine is now not a Russian invasion, but corruption so pervasive that it long ago ceased to be a disease of the post-Soviet system and became the system itself. Police and prosecutors are in fact commercial structures used to gain wealth and power. And while in Mr Putin's Russia security and law-enforcement agencies are controlled by one clan, in Ukraine the privatised state is divided between several oligarchic groups, providing a measure of pluralism (if not democracy). The attempt by Viktor Yanukovych, the former president, to monopolise corruption was one reason for his overthrow. Although Maidan started as a popular movement against corruption, it was supported by the oligarchs, who put their own politicians on the stage. Getting rid of Mr Yanukovych did not end corruption; it merely decentralised it. (. . .) The population is growing poorer – and more radical. Meanwhile, Ukraine is brimming with weapons and thousands of militiamen, angry with a corrupt and listless government they feel has hijacked the revolution' (*The Economist* 2015, 23, 24). Six months later a similar opinion was expressed by the Krakow-based international English language magazine *New Eastern Europe*: 'The post-Maidan "winner takes it all" approach seems to be the key feature of Ukraine's current state of affairs: (s)elected oligarchs in power, selective justice to keep others at bay, selective reforms where state and individual interests match or when local and western pressure combined is strong, and selective de-oligarchisation. The threat from Russia remains the main reason why such a selective state should be tolerated at home and supported in the West. Those who had high expectations are becoming disillusioned. Even without

Crimea and Donbas, a post-Maidan Ukraine is framed by political impunity, competition of oligarchs' interests, a weak central authority and a disenchanted society' (Jarabik 2016).

26 See http://decentralization.gov.ua/news/item/id/345 (accessed: 21 February 2016).

Bibliography

Andusieczko, P. (2016). Ukraińców zwrot na Zachód. *Gazeta Wyborcza*, January 19, p. 12.

Barwiński, M. (1998). Political conditions of transborder contacts of Lemkos living on both sides of the Carpathian Mountains, in: M. Koter and K. Heffner (eds) *Borderlands or Transborder Regions – Geographical, Social and Political Problems*, 'Region and Regionalism', No. 3. Opole–Łódź: University of Łódź, Silesian Institute in Opole, pp. 233–40.

Barwiński, M. (2013). *Geograficzno-polityczne uwarunkowania sytuacji Ukraińców, Łemków, Białorusinów i Litwinów w Polsce po 1944 roku*. Łódź: Wydawnictwo Uniwersytetu Łódzkiego.

Darski, J. (1993). *Ukraina*. Warszawa: Instytut Polityczny.

Duć-Fajfer, H. (2001). Łemkowie – charakterystyka etniczno-kulturowa. *Języki Obce w Szkole*, 6, pp. 55–64.

Eberhardt, P. (1992). *Polska granica wschodnia*. Warszawa: Spotkania.

Eberhardt, P. (2004). *Polska i jej granice. Z historii polskiej geografii politycznej*. Lublin: Wydawnictwo Uniwersytetu Marii Curie-Skłodowskiej.

Fedoruk, O. (2003). Ukrains'ko-pol's'ki vidnosyny u pertseptsii Panteleymona Kulisha (Kontekst halyts'koho suspil'no-literaturnoho protsesu 60-kh rokiv XIX st.). *Ukraina Moderna*, 8, pp. 73–106.

Friszke, A. (1991). Ukraińskie tradycje polityczne. *Więź*, 11–12, pp. 8–25.

Gellner, E. (2006). *Nations and Nationalism*, 2nd edn. Malden, Oxford, Carlton: Blackwell Publishing.

Gumilow, L. (2004). *Od Rusi do Rosji*. Warszawa: PIW.

Hearn, J. (2006). *Rethinking Nationalism. A Critical Introduction*. Basingstoke: Palgrave-Macmillan.

Hentosh, L. (2003). Postat' mitropolita Sheptytskoho. *Ukraina moderna*, 8, pp. 179–212.

Homza, I. (2013). Katalitychna mobilizatsiya radykal'nykh Ukrainskikh natsionalistiv u dobu II Pol'skoi respubliky: vplyv struktury politychnykh mozhlyvostey. *Ukraina moderna*, 20, pp. 151–70. Online. Available: http://uamoderna.com/images/archiv/2013–20/Gomza.pdf (accessed: 22 January 2016).

Hoshko, T. (2012). Rozdumy navkola odnoho siuzhetu (predstavlennia v shkilnykh pidruchnykakh Liublinskoi unii). *Ukraina Moderna*, 19, pp. 121–47. Online. Available: http://uamoderna.com/images/archiv/19/um_19_hoshko.pdf (accessed: 18 January 2016).

Hroch, M. (2003). *Małe narody Europy*. Wrocław, Warszawa, Kraków: Ossolineum.

Hrytsak, Ya. (2003). Ruslan, Bohdan i Myron: try pryklady konstruyuvannia identychnosti sered halytskykh rutyno-ukraintsiv. *Ukraina moderna*, 8, pp. 25–50.

IGiPZ PAN (1997). *Atlas Rzeczypospolitej Polskiej*. Warszawa: Instytut Geografii i Przestrzennego Zagospodarowania PAN, Główny Geodeta Kraju.

Jagiełło, M. (2000). *Partnerstwo dla przyszłości. Szkice o polityce wschodniej i mniejszościach narodowych*. Warszawa: Wydawnictwo naukowe PWN.

Jarabik, B. (2016). Ukraine and resistance. Ukraine's selective state, *New Eastern Europe*, 20 January 2016. Online. Available: www.neweasterneurope.eu/articles-and-commentary/1867-reform-and-resistance-ukraine-s-selective-state (accessed: 16 January 2016).

Kachanovsky, I. (2013). OUN(b) ta natsysts'ki masovi vbyvstva vlitku 1941 roku na istorychniy Volyni. *Ukraina moderna* 20, pp. 215–44, Online. Available: http://uamoderna.com/images/archiv/2013-20/Kachanovsky.pdf (accessed: 12 January 2016).

Magochiy, P. R. (2007). *Istoriya Ukrainy*. Kiev (translation from English: Magocsi, P. (1996). *A History of Ukraine*. Toronto: University of Toronto Press).

Martinez, O. J. (1994). The dynamics of order interaction: New approaches to order analysis, in: C. H. Schofield (ed.) *Global boundaries, Word boundaries*, vol. I. London: Routledge, pp. 1–15.

Masenko, L. (2004). *Mova i Suspil'stvo. Postkoloniyal'nyy vymir*. Kiev: Vseukrainske tovarysto 'Prosvita' im. Tarasa Shevchenka.

Miszczuk, A. (2008). Wpływ uwarunkowań geopolitycznych na ewolucję podziału terytorialnego Polski w XX wieku, in: P. Eberhardt (ed.) *Problematyka geopolityczna ziem polskich*. Warszawa: IGiPZ PAN, pp. 297–318.

Miszczuk, A. (2013). Geopolityczne uwarunkowania rozwoju regionów przygranicznych, in: P. Eberhardt (ed.) *Studia nad geopolityką XX wieku*. Warszawa: IGiPZ PAN, pp. 117–44.

Motyka, G. (2011). *Od rzezi wołyńskiej do akcji 'Wisła'. Konflikt polsko-ukraiński 1943–1947*. Kraków: Wydawnictwo Literackie.

Newman, D. and Passi, A. (2001). Rethinking Boundaries in Political Geography, in: M. Antonisch, V. Kolossov and M. P. Pagnini (eds) *Europe between political geography and geopolitics*. Rome: Societa Geografica Italiana, pp. 301–16.

Olszański, T. A. (1994). *Historia Ukrainy XX w*. Warszawa: Wolumen.

Passi, A. (2008). Territory, in: J. Agnew, K. Mitchel and G. Toal (eds) *A companion to political Geography*. Malden, Oxford, Carlton: Blackwell Publishing, pp. 109–22.

Posivnych, M. (2010). *Voyenno-politychna diyal'nist' OUN u 1929–1939 rokakh*. Lviv: Tsentr doslidzhen' wyzwol'nogho rukhu, Instytut ukrainoznawstwa im. I. Krypiakewycha NAN Ukrainy.

Riabczuk, M. (2004). *Dwie Ukrainy*. Wrocław: Kolegium Europy Wschodniej (translation from Ukrainian original: *Dvi Ukrainy*).

Riabczuk, M. (2015). *Syndrom postkolonialny*, Wrocław: Kolegium Europy Wschodniej (translation from Ukrainian original: *Postkolonialnyy syndrom*).

Rudnyckyj, Ya. B. (1995). Galicja jako problem kultur w kontakcie-konflikcie, in: Z. Kłak and M. Wyka (eds) *Galicja i jej dziedzictwo*, t. IV. Rzeszów: Wydawnictwo WSP.

Rykiel, Z. (2006). *Podstawy Geografii Politycznej*. Warszawa: Polskie Wydawnictwo Ekonomiczne.

Serczyk, W. A. (1978). *Hajdamacy*. Kraków: Wydawnictwo Literackie.

Serczyk, W. A. (1990). *Historia Ukrainy*. Wrocław, Warszawa, Kraków: Zakład Narodowy im. Ossolińskich.

Smith, A. D. (2000). *The Nation in History. Historiographical Debates about Ethnicity and Nationalism*. Cambridge: Polity Press.

Smith, A. D. (2009). *Ethno-Symbolism and Nationalism. A cultural approach*. London: Routledge.

Snyder, T. (2003). *The Reconstruction of Nations. Poland, Ukraine, Lithuania, Belarus 1569–1999*. New Haven: Yale University Press.

Sobczyński, M. (2013). Zmiany polityczne, terytorialne i spory graniczne w Europie Środkowo-Wschodniej po 1989 r., in: P. Eberhardt (ed.) *Studia nad geopolityką XX wieku*. Warsaw: IGiPZ PAN, pp. 181–234.

Sosnowska, D. (2009). *Inna Galicja*. Warsaw: Elipsa.

Szporluk, R. (1997). Ukraine: From an Imperial Periphery to a Sovereign State. *Daedalus, Journal of the American Academy of Arts and Sciences*, Summer, 126/3, pp. 85–119.

Szul, R. (1999). Rola granicy w gospodarce – próba ujęcia teoretycznego, in: A. Mync and R. Szul (eds) *Rola granicy i współpracy transgranicznej w rozwoju regionalnym i lokalnym*. Warszawa: Europejski Instytut Rozwoju Regionalnego i Lokalnego, Uniwersytet Warszawski, pp. 227–32.

Szul, R. (2014). Losy osób z pograniczy etnicznych w Europie Środkowo-Wschodniej (XIX wiek i pierwsza połowa XX wieku), in: A. Wachowiak B. Górczyńska-Przybyłowicz, S. Jankowiak, I. Skórzyńska and K. Stryjkowski (eds) *Dom Otwarty/Dom Zamknięty? Lekcje pogranicza. Europa Środkowo-Wschodnia (XX/XXI w.)*. Poznań: Wydawnictwo Nauka i Innowacje, pp. 97–112.

The Economist (2015). Rule of law in Ukraine. Mr Saakashvili goes to Odessa, *The Economist*, 26 September, pp. 23, 24. Online. Available: http://www.economist.com/news/europe/21667967-georgian-reformer-tackles-ukraines-real-public-enemy-number-one-corruption-mr-saakashvili-goes (accessed: 31 May 2016).

Vyatrovych, V. (2011). *Druha pol's'ko-ukrains'ka viyna 1942–1947*. Kiev: Kyyevo-Mohylians'ka Akademiya.

Wysocki, R. (2003). *Organizacja Ukraińskich Nacjonalistów w Polsce w latach 1929–1939. Geneza, struktura, program, ideologia*. Lublin: Wydawnictwo Uniwersytetu Marii Curie-Skłodowskiej.

Zaytsev, O. (2013). Voyenna doktryna Mykhila Kolodzins'koho. *Ukraina moderna*, 20, pp. 246–56. Online. Available: http://uamoderna.com/images/archiv/2013–20/Zaitsev.pdf (accessed: 19 January 2016).

Zięba, A. (ed.) (1994). *Metropolita Andrzej Szeptycki*. Kraków: Studia i materiały.

2 The Polish–Ukrainian borderland against the background of European regions

Andrzej Jakubowski

The Polish–Ukrainian borderland forms an area on the contemporary European map which is unique and interesting in many respects. Its stormy history, shifting state borders, complex ethnic and religious structure, and location at the crossroads of western and eastern cultures have shaped the present face of this region, giving it an exceptional character. Meanwhile, the peripheral location of the present borderland area has lent it features of peripherality, in both geographical and socio-economic terms. Thus the principal aim of this chapter is to attempt to describe and show the specific nature of the Polish–Ukrainian borderland in the context of the remaining European regions. To this end, we will analyse its natural environment as well as the action taken to protect it. In further sections we will present the administrative divisions as well as the system of borderland settlement. Special attention will be given to describing the social structure as well as the economic potential of the Polish and Ukrainian border regions. This will allow us to make a multi-dimensional analysis of the diverse potential present in the border regions, and subsequently to capture and present a profile of the cross-border area as a whole. Unless otherwise stated, figures used in the text are from the Central Statistical Office in Warsaw and the State Statistics Service of Ukraine in Kiev.

The natural environment and wildlife conservation

The Polish–Ukrainian borderland is situated in the central part of the European continent, at the eastern edge of the European Union. Its longitudinal extent (between 52°17’ and 48°45’) spans just under 400 kilometres, while its latitudinal range (between 21°08’ and 26°11’) covers around 350 kilometres. To the west a natural border is created over a long stretch by the largest of Poland’s rivers, the Vistula. To the south, the border is defined by the main ridge of the Carpathian mountains. To the east, it lies on the western extremity of the Podolian Uplands – Opole as well as the Gologory and Woroniaky Hills. Further on, the border runs northwards along the River Styr. In the region of Lutsk it veers to the east, where it reaches the River Horyn and runs along the plain of the Polesian Lowland to Pripyat, which marks the northern edge of the Ukrainian borderland. Its subsequent course is marked by the River Bug. At the level of Nemyriv, the border takes a north-westerly course, finishing just below the confluence of the River Wieprz and the Vistula.

The cross-border area is divided by the Polish–Ukrainian state border. It runs from the Ushok Pass in the Bieszczady mountains along the San River, and then onwards in a north-easterly direction, where it reaches the Bug river and continues to run along it. The Polish–Ukrainian borderland area is the meeting point of three major tectonic structures – the Central European Paleozoic platform, the Eastern European Precambrian platform and the alpine ranges, which, in physiographical terms, correspond to three megaregions – Extra-Alpine Central Europe and the Carpathian mountains together with the Subcarpathian mountains (belonging to the Western European area) as well as the Eastern European Plain (in the Eastern European area) (Figure 2.1).

The Polish–Ukrainian borderland features a relatively diverse terrain. In its northern part lowland areas predominate. The north-western area of the Lublin voivodship is taken up by the South Podlasian Lowland, at an altitude of between 100 and 200 metres above sea level, which belongs to the Central Polish Lowland within the Central European Plain. To the east this joins up with Polesia, which belongs to the East Baltic–Belarus Basin. In the Polish–Ukrainian borderland there are two Polesian macro-regions – Western Polesia (the Lublin region) and Volhynian Polesia. Western Polesia is mainly a plain (with an average altitude ranging between 130 and 210 metres above sea level), and its relief is diversified only by a few hills and hummocks resulting from glacial activity. Due to the geology and the level topography, this area features large areas of marshland, with a particularly dense drainage system and numerous peat bogs appearing in its landscape. Another feature typical of Western Polesia is clusters of lakes, smaller on the Polish side (the Łęczna–Włodawa Lake District) and noticeably larger on the Ukrainian side (the Shatskyi Lake District). Situated between the West Polesian Lowland and the more southerly upland belt, Volhynian Polesia features a transitional landscape, mainly undulating plain (wold), with its highest point not exceeding 270 metres above sea level.

Large areas of the central Polish–Ukrainian borderland are covered by upland plains. To the south of the Central Polish Lowland is the Polish Uplands province, which on the borderland encompasses the Lublin Upland and Roztocze, belonging to the Lublin–Lviv Uplands. South of Polesia stretches the Ukrainian Upland belt, which on the borderland encompasses the Volhynian Upland, Little Polesia and Podole, belonging to the Volhynian–Podolian Upland.

The Lublin Upland is a lightly undulating, almost treeless plain, the highest areas of which are just over 300 metres above sea level. More hills and dips can be found in its western part, in an area interspersed by numerous gorges situated near the Vistula valley. Towards the south-west, the Lublin Upland runs into the Roztocze ridge, which stretches for more than 200 kilometres almost to Lviv, crisscrossed by deep valleys and ravines, with its highest hills exceeding 400 metres above sea level. The relatively small area of the Volhynian Upland is carved up by numerous valleys, gorges and ravines, with Karst formations to be found in many places. The average altitude ranges from 220 to 250 metres above sea level, in some places exceeding

Figure 2.1 Physiographical divisions of the Polish–Ukrainian borderland

Source: Andrzej Jakubowski, on the basis of Żuchowski (2005).

300 metres. In the central section of Lviv oblast (East of Lviv) the Podolian Upland begins, stretching in a broad belt to the south-east. Average altitudes reach around 300 metres above sea level, although several separate hills (in the Gologory and Woroniaky ranges) exceed 400 metres above sea level. The western edge of Podolia is formed by Opole – a picturesque landscape crisscrossed by narrow, steep-sided river valleys. It is here that the highest hill in Podolia can be found – Kamula Hill in

the Gologory range, reaching 471 metres above sea level. To the north of the Podolian Upland the land falls steeply away to the flat, barely undulating lowland of Little Polesia (the Pobuzhia Valley), separating it from the Volhynian Upland.

Between the upland zone and the zone of foothills and hills, within the Podkarpackie and Lublin voivodships, and also parts of Lviv oblast, is the Sandomierz Valley – an extensive triangular depression. Its northern part encompasses a plain formed by accumulation, squeezed between the Vistula and San river corridors and Roztocze. To the south stretches a plateau which becomes more hilly in its eastern parts.

The foothill zone is represented by the Central Beskidian Piedmont, situated on the northern slopes of the West Carpathian mountains. This is a ridge of hills several kilometres wide, rising to an altitude of 300 to 600 metres above sea level and divided by numerous valleys and dales. The southern section of Podkarpackie voivodship is taken up by the Lower Beskid mountains, where the highest peaks reach 600 to 850 metres above sea level. At the south-eastern end of Podkarpackie voivodship the Outer Eastern Carpathian range (Wooded Beskids) begins, separated from the Podolia by the San-Dniester Plateau, the Upper Dniester Valley and the Stryj–Sambor Piedmont (Western Subcarpathians). On the Polish side of the borderland the Eastern Carpathians encompass the Western Bieszczady mountains (with the highest peak in the Polish part of the borderland – Mount Tarnica, at an altitude of 1346 metres above sea level), as well as part of the Sanok-Turka Mountains. In the area of the Lviv oblast stretches the Middle Beskids, Skole Beskids and Upper Dniester Beskids Mountains, as well as the Western Bieszczady mountains, along with the highest peak of the Polish–Ukrainian borderland – Mount Pikuj (1408 metres above sea level).

The Polish–Ukrainian borderland is rich in mineral resources, reflecting the complexity of its geological structure. The most important among the fossil fuels is coal. Coal seams stretch in a belt over 200 kilometres long and 20 kilometres wide from the border of Lviv and Volhynia oblasts on the Ukrainian side (the Lviv–Volhynia Coalfield) along the north-western part of Lublin voivodship (the Lubelskie Coalfield). In the Polish borderland area coal deposits lie at a depth of 600–1000 metres in almost horizontal seams 1–2 metres thick. In the Ukrainian area the coal seams are somewhat shallower, lying at a depth of 300–700 metres, with a thickness of 0.5 to 1 metre (Zastawnyi 1994). Indeed, it was partly the presence of coal that motivated the transfer of territory between the Polish People's Republic and the USSR in 1951. In the Ukrainian part of Roztocze and in Podolia there are also small deposits of brown coal, although these do not have any industrial significance.

Conventional deposits of crude oil and natural gas occur in the southern part of the borderland. The exploited crude oil deposits (now largely exhausted) forming the Carpathian Oilfield, one of the oldest excavation sites in the world, are found on the northern slopes of the Carpathians (Zastawnyi 1994). Major gas deposits, besides the Carpathian Field, are also present in the Sandomierz Valley (Podkarpackie voivodship) as well as the north-east section of Lviv oblast, forming the Volhynian–Podolski oil and gas region. To the north of the cross-border area significant quantities of peat, the largest in Volhynia oblast, can also be found.

Much hope has been placed in the natural shale gas deposits, initially estimated in Poland at 5.3 trillion cubic metres (the fourth largest in Europe), and a major part of them are found in Lublin voivodship (US Energy Information Administration 2013). A fall in prices of this resource on the world market, the considerable costs of research, the prolonged legislative work on the Shale gas bill, objections from the local community and unsuccessful first boreholes and fissure trials led to the withdrawal of several large international concerns from exploration and excavation (including ExxonMobil, Talisman and Marathon). Current research is being carried out almost entirely by national enterprises, while in Lublin voivodship the well is still being run by the American enterprise Chevron. However, we must assume that in the event of a price change and initial drilling successes, shale gas will start to be excavated on a commercial scale in the course of the next few years. Potential exploitation of shale gas is equally of major significance on the Ukrainian side of the borderland, since the largest deposits of shale gas in Ukraine are found in the west of the country, in Little Polesia and Podolia.

Among the metal ores, potentially the most significant are the recently discovered copper deposits in Volhynia. In the Carpathian Forelands, near Truskavets, polymetallic ores contain lead, zinc and other metals (Zastawnyj and Kusiński 2003), while in Pobuzhia Valley there are small deposits of chromium. Moreover, in some Bieszczady rocks the presence of uranium has been reported. Among non-metal resources, native sulphur (in its pure form) is the most abundant. One of the largest deposits of this mineral in the world can be found in the north-west of the Podkarpackie voivodship (the Tarnobrzeg Field). Sulphur also occurs in the region of Lubaczów (on the Polish side of the borderland), as well as in numerous deposits stretching along the Dniester River from Yavoriv to Novyi Rozdil. In the Lviv oblast there are also large amounts of potassium salt and rock salt, while on the Ukrainian side of West Polesia are found phosphorite deposits. The mineral resources necessary for cement production (plaster, chalks, limestones, dolomites and marls), of major significance for industry, occur in the western part of the Lublin Upland (Chełm, Rejowiec Fabryczny) as well as in Lviv oblast. It is also worth mentioning the therapeutic mineral waters with different chemical components that occur in the regions of Rymanów Zdrój, Iwonicz Zdrój (Podkarpackie voivodship) and Morshyn, Olesk, Truskavets and Skhidnytsia (Lviv oblast) (Figure 2.2).

The Polish–Ukrainian borderland is situated in a temperate climate zone of a transitional nature. As we move east we can observe an increasingly continental climate, with average temperatures falling in the winter months and rising in the summer months. The average annual rainfall fluctuates between 500–550 millimetres in West Polesia to over 1000 millimetres in the Eastern Carpathians, increasing from north to south. The growing season lasts from 180–190 days in the Carpathians to 210–220 days in the Sandomierz Valley.

Running through the borderland area is the Main European Watershed, dividing the drainage basins feeding the Baltic Sea from those feeding the Black Sea (Kondracki 1998). Nearly the whole of the Polish borderland area belongs to the Vistula catchment area, apart from a small corner in the south-east of

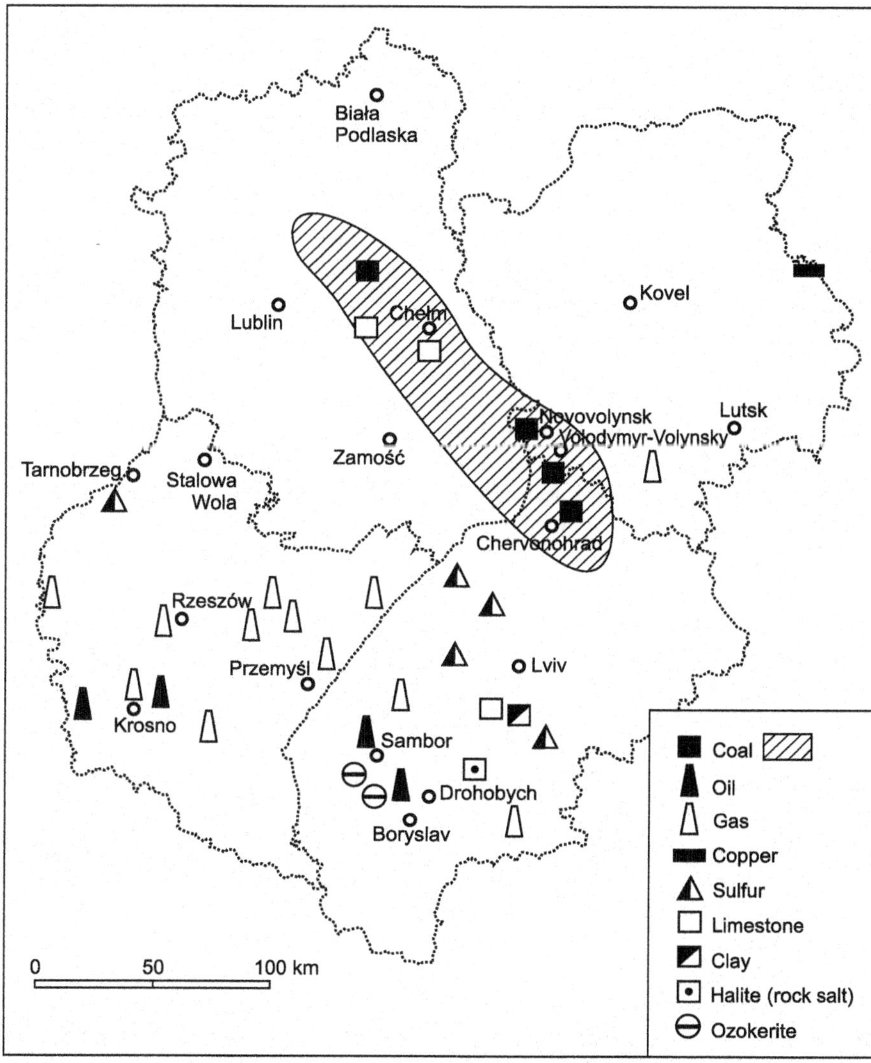

Figure 2.2 Mineral resources

Source: Andrzej Jakubowski, on the basis of Institute of Geography of NAS of Ukraine (2003) and IGiPZ PAN (1997).

Podkarpackie voivodship, which is just within the range of the Dniester river basin. The great majority of Volhynian rivers flow into the Pripyat, which is a tributary of the Dnieper. Only a narrow western fragment of this region feeds the Vistula basin. The greater part of Lviv oblast is incorporated into the drainage system of the second largest river in Ukraine, the Dniester. A smaller area is within the range of the Vistula basin, while rivers feeding the Dnieper basin take up the smallest part of this region, in the north-east (Żuchowski 2005). The largest rivers of the borderland are the Vistula, the Bug, the Pripyat, the Dniester, the Styr, the San and the Wieprz. However, the water resources of the borderland are unevenly distributed and their drainage systems are unusually diversified. The most dense drainage system is found in the mountain and foothill areas of Lviv oblast (the Dniester basin). Abundant water resources also occur in Volhynia and the Podkarpackie region. Meanwhile, the Lublin region drainage basin is particularly sparse, struggling with water shortages (Stanicka 2011). The surface water system is supplemented by lakes. In the Lublin region these are situated mainly in the Łęczna–Włodawa Lake District (West Polesia). However, the majority of lakes are found in Volhynia. The Shatsky Lake District is particularly noteworthy: around 30 lakes of varying size can be found here in a relatively small area, including Lake Svitiaz, one of the largest lakes in Ukraine.

In the border areas of Poland and Ukraine various soil types can be found. According to the classification of the United Nations Food and Agriculture Organization (FAO), cambisols are found in the Lublin Upland, Roztocze and the Carpathians; luvisols in the Lublin and Podkarpackie regions and in Volhynia and Podolia; podzoluvisols in south Volhynia and Subcarpathia; podzols in Podlasie and in the Sandomierz Valley; and chernozems in Podolia, south Volhynia and, here and there, in the Lublin Upland (FAO and UNESCO 1981). This soil diversity is accompanied by diversified usage values, above all in terms of suitability for agriculture. The most fertile soils occur in southern Volhynia, Podolia and the Lublin Upland, while the least suitable for farming are the acidic and excessively wet soils of Polesia (Zastawnyj and Kusiński 2003). The podzols of the Podlasie region and the fork of the rivers Vistula and San are also rather poor. Generally, on the Polish side soils of moderate or low quality predominate. Soils of moderate or good quality can be found more readily on the Ukrainian side of the borderland (FAO and UNESCO 1981).

The diversification of soils is reflected in land use. Over the whole borderland area agriculture predominates: the share of agriculture comes to around 53.6 per cent in the Volhynia oblast, 55.1 per cent in Podkarpackie voivodship and 59.1 per cent in the Lviv oblast, reaching as much as 71.3 per cent in Lublin voivodship. Meanwhile, forests make up barely 23.2 per cent of the Lublin region territory; in the Lviv oblast and Volhynia afforestation amounts to 31.8 per cent and 34.6 per cent respectively, while in Podkarpackie voivodship it exceeds 38.3 per cent. The remaining land use includes built-up areas, water and barren land. In Volhynia there is a particularly high share of wetlands, at 10.7 per cent.

The largest forests of the Polish–Ukrainian borderland are found in its southern and north-eastern extremities – in the Carpathians and in West Polesia. In the case of the latter area, the level of afforestation and above-average natural qualities have led to its inclusion in the Green Lungs of Europe – areas of the greatest natural value in Poland, Russia, Belarus and Ukraine as well as in Lithuania, Latvia and Estonia (Stankiewicz 1993). Moreover, large forest areas lie in the Polish section of the borderland between Lublin and Podkarpackie voivodships, separating the Lublin Upland and the Sandomierz Valley (Janowski Forest and Solska Wilderness).

Both districts of western Ukraine belong to the most densely forested in the country, where the share of forest cover is no more than 18 per cent. Podkarpackie voivodship is also one of the most densely forested regions in Poland. Among the four borderland regions, only Lublin voidvodship has levels of woodland well below the national average (30.0 per cent), owing to the significance of agriculture in land use.

In general, in the borderland area analysed, coniferous trees predominate. On the Polish side pine forests dominate, accounting for over half of the tree stands in Lublin voivodship. The proportion of oak, alder and birch is much lower. Pine also dominates in the forest of Podkarpackie voivodship, although here there is also a proportion of beech and fir (CSO 2015b). In Polesia pinewoods predominate, alongside mixed forests of oak and pine. Black alder and birch are also common (Volyns'ka Oblasna Derzhavna Administraciia 2016). In the Carpathian forests the greatest number of stands are spruce, fir and beech, while in the remaining area of the Lviv oblast beech and oak woods are common (State Statistics Service of Ukraine 2015b). However, these are mainly young forests, without a stable ecology. Older tree stands grow on the Polish side of the cross-border region. The borderland forests are inhabited by a diverse range of animal species, including many rare and protected fauna such as bison, bear, moose, wolf, lynx, golden eagle, lesser-spotted eagle and white-tailed eagle, considered to be the prototype for the Polish emblem.

As a region which exhibits low levels of industrialization, low levels of urbanization and a relatively insignificant human impact on the environment, the Polish–Ukrainian borderland has preserved numerous unique ecosystems of great natural diversity. The most valuable of these have been brought under various kinds of legal protection. However, the system of protected areas in the Polish–Ukrainian borderland has developed rather unevenly (Malska and Molas 2005). The proportions of these areas within the individual cross-border regions vary: there is a greater proportion on the Polish side and visibly less on the Ukrainian side. In Lviv oblast protected areas account for 6.7 per cent of the total land area of the region, in Vohynia oblast 11.0 per cent, in Lublin voivodship 22.7 per cent, while in Podkarpackie voivodship the amount is as much as 44.9 per cent (Figure 2.3).

The most comprehensive conservation of wildlife and landscape value is provided by national parks, encompassing areas of outstanding natural value preserved in their natural or near-natural state (International Union for Conservation of Nature 2016). In the Polish–Ukrainian cross-border area there are 10 parks of this kind. On the Polish side lie four national parks with a total area of 64,900 hectares (along with their buffer zones of 196,000 hectares): Polesia and Roztocze National Parks in Lublin voivodship and the Magura and Bieszczady National Parks in Podkarpackie voivodship. The first of these includes diversified tree stands with numerous protected species in the Central Roztocze area of the upper Wieprz valley, and the second the wetlands of the Łęczna–Włodawa Lake District. The Magura National Park includes typical medium and low mountain landscapes (the Lower Beskids) in which forest ecosystems dominate, while the oldest and the largest of the borderland parks, Bieszczady National Park (established in 1973, with an area of 29,200 hectares), is an alpine landscape including characteristic

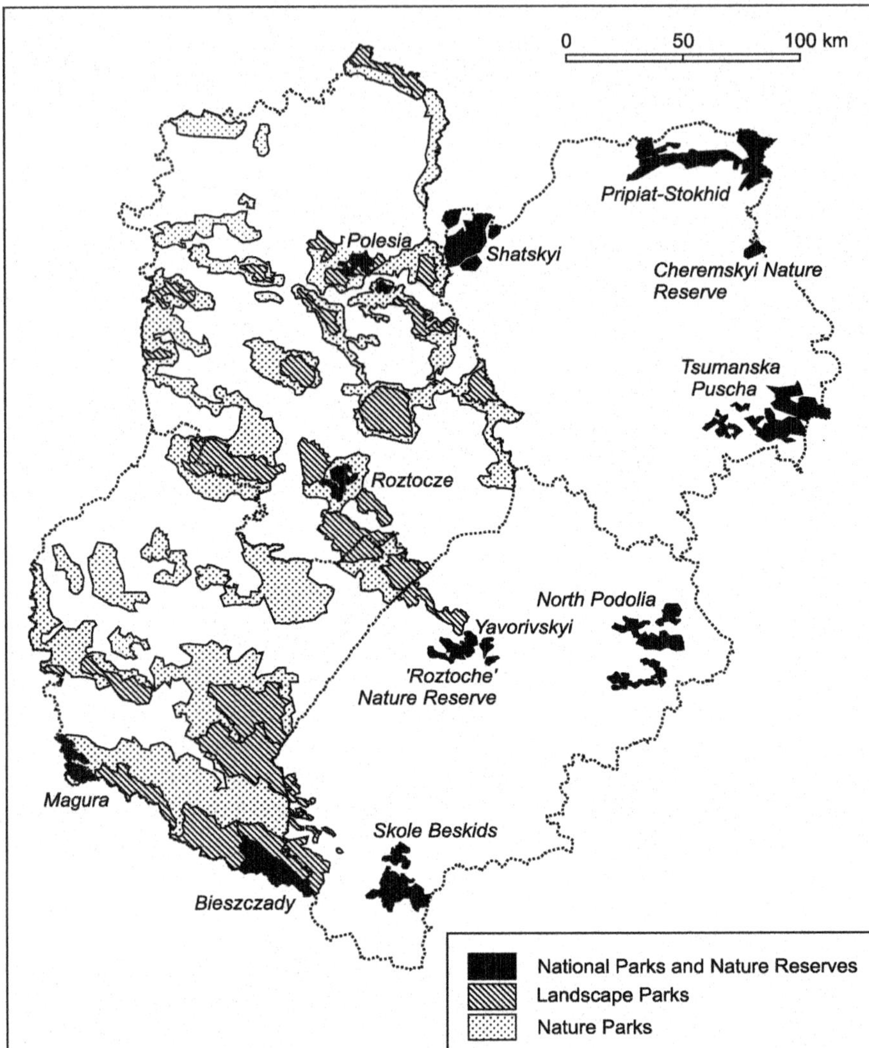

Figure 2.3 Protected areas

Source: Andrzej Jakubowski.

Polonyna – extensive grass pastures above the upper tree line, with numerous species of alpine and subalpine plants. In Podkarpackie voivodship there are plans to create another park, the Turnicki National Park, which would protect the particularly valuable area of the Sanok-Turka Mountains, including beech forests which provide the habitat for lynx, wolves and rich birdlife, including the lesser-spotted eagle, golden eagle and black stork (Baran-Zgłobicka et al. 2011).

On the Ukrainian side of Roztocze (Lviv oblast) Yavorivskiy National Park was established to protect the unique forest-steppe landscape as well as a large beech forest area in the region of the Main European Watershed. The 'North Podolia' National Park, established in 2009, includes the Gologor and Woroniak mountain range, forming the north-western edge of the Podolian Upland. In turn, the 'Skole Beskids' National Park includes the alpine landscapes of the East Bieszczady mountains. The oldest national park on the Ukrainian side of the borderland, the Shatskyi National Park (1983), is tucked away in the far north-western corner of Ukraine and includes a complex of around 30 lakes of varying size. The second Volhynian park, the Pripiat-Stokhid National Park, covers a unique wetland area situated between the rivers Pripiat and Stokhid, whose natural courses are littered with numerous marshes, meanders, braiding and ox-bow lakes and are renowned for their rich birdlife (Procenko 2011). In 2010, in the eastern part of the Volhynia district, the 'Tsumanska Puscha' National Park, encompassing unique wide-leaved deciduous forests forming one of only a few bison habitats, was established. For some time, owing to a lack of funding and the inactivity of the district administration, this park existed only on paper. The matter was taken up again in October 2015 (Ministerstvo Ekologhii ta Pryrodnykh Resursiv Ukrainy 2015). National parks on the Ukrainian side of the borderland cover a total area of 179,700 hectares, with the largest park in terms of area being the Shatskyi National Park, at 49,000 hectares (Derzhavna Sluzhba Statystyky Ukrainy 2014). In Ukraine, besides national parks, an equally high level of protection is provided by nature reserves and biosphere reserves. Situated on the border of the Rivne oblast, the Cheremsky Nature Reserve covers wetland areas consisting of marshes, lakes and forests with unique plant habitats characteristic of Ukrainian Polesia. Meanwhile, the 'Roztoche' Nature Reserve, like the nearby Yavorivskyi National Park, protects a typical forest-steppe ecosystem (Derzhavna Sluzhba Statystyky Ukrainy 2014).

The system of protected areas on the Polish side of the borderlands is supplemented by nature reserves, landscape parks and nature parks, among others. In Lublin voivodship there are 86 nature reserves with a total area of 11,900 hectares, while in Podkarpackie voivodship 95 reserves cover a total area of 11,100 hectares. These encompass natural areas or little disturbed ecosytems, specific plant and animal species, and unique inanimate natural forms. In the Lublin region forest and wetland reserves dominate, while in Podkarpackie forest and landscape reserves are in the majority. In the Polish part of the cross-border area 24 landscape parks with a total area of 525,000 hectares (12.2 per cent of the land area) were established in which areas of particularly high wildlife and landscape value are protected. In Lublin voivodship there are 16 parks of this type (the most in the country) and in Podkarpackie voivodship there are six, while two include territory from both regions. In addition, in Lublin voivodship there are 17 nature parks with a total area of 302,000 hectares (12.0 per cent of the land area). In Podkarpackie voivodship there are 13, although these cover a greater area of 468,600 hectares (26.3 per cent of the voivodship territory). Since Poland's accession to the EU the ecology network Nature 2000 has been operating in Lublin and Podkarpackie regions with the aim of protecting key natural habitats and endangered animal species. Special Protection Areas (SPA) for birdlife cover 19.6 per cent of the land area, while Special Areas of Conservation (SAC) encompass 12.1 per cent of the Polish borderland area.

Protected areas cover almost the entire south-eastern part of Podkarpackie voivodship, including both national parks (Magura and Bieszczady), five landscape parks (Jaśliska, Cisna-Wetlina, the San Valley, Przemyski Hills and Słonne Mountains), and others. In the case of the Lublin voivodship the protected areas are located mainly in the east and south of the region, creating several large, close-set areas, encompassing in the east Polesia National Park and buffer zone, Chełm and Polesia Nature Park and Chełm and Sobibór Landscape Park. The second area, located to the south of Zamość, includes Roztocze National Park and three landscape parks: Krasnobród, Szczebrzeszyn and 'Solska Wilderness'. An important element of the nature conservation system is the forest area situated on the border with Podkarpackie voivodship, which includes the Janów Forests Landscape Park and the Kraśnik and Roztocze Nature Parks (Jakubowski et al. 2013).

The legislative system for nature conservation on the Ukrainian side of the borderland has a somewhat different structure. Besides national parks, nature reserves and biosphere reserves (this form of nature conservation does not in fact apply in the Polish–Ukrainian borderland), protection also includes nature reserves of national significance as well as regional landscape parks and nature reserves of local significance. In Lviv oblast there is a total of 350 protected areas of all types (with a combined area of 157,600 hectares), including five regional landscape parks covering 56,300 hectares, nine reserves of national significance and 34 reserves of local significance (Lvivs'ka Derzhavna Oblasna Administraciia 2015). The nature conservation system in Volhynia oblast includes a total of 379 protected areas covering 222,300 hectares, among which there are 15 reserves of national significance as well as 200 local reserves (Derzhupravvlinnia ohorony navkolyshn'ogho seredovyscha u Volyns'kii oblasti 2012). The greatest concentration of protected areas in Lviv oblast are found in the south, in the Carpathian mountains, as well as in Roztocze. In the case of Volhynia oblast they are concentrated in the north, along the Belarussian border. It is worth adding here that the most valuable borderland areas in terms of wildlife are located near the Polish–Ukrainian border, which provides favourable conditions for creating a cross-border system of nature conservation (Jakubowski et al. 2013).

The natural value of the Polish–Ukrainian borderland can be viewed in terms of its attraction for tourists. There is no question that the diversity of landscapes and natural beauty promotes the development of tourism, including recreational, educational, health and adventure tourism. An obvious asset of the Polish–Ukrainian borderland is the numerous areas which remain in their natural or near-natural state. However, there is another side to the coin: the level of tourist facilities is inadequate, and this, together with foreign tourists' lack of familiarity with the region, difficulty in achieving access and tightly controlled state borders, has resulted in low levels of tourist movement.

Undoubtedly, the legislative system for nature conservation plays an important role, allowing for the preservation of unique ecosystems and enhancing the tourism potential of the border region. On the other hand, the many different forms of protection are often regarded as a barrier to economic development, including attracting investment. It is still the case that nature conservation laws are frequently seen not as an opportunity for sustainable development and sustainable tourism but as a barrier to development and the free use of natural resources. An example could be the unwillingness of the regional authorities in Volhynia to create the 'Tsumanska Pushcha' National Park (ZIK 2012; Volyn' Post 2013).

The presence of extensive unspoilt areas does not mean that the borderland is free from problems of air, water and soil pollution resulting from factories, power plants, residential buildings and vehicles. And although ecologically the territories situated in south-eastern Poland and western Ukraine boast relatively unspoiled natural environments and are generally regarded as clean, certain problem areas can be indicated (Malska and Molas 2005).

The general trend, witnessed on both the Polish and the Ukrainian sides of the borderland since the beginning of the 1990s, is the systematic fall in air pollutant emissions from stationary sources. In 2014 they amounted in the whole cross-border area to 149,000 tonnes, compared with 200,200 tonnes in the year 2000. Carbon dioxide emissions in Lublin voivodship has decreased two and a half times since 1996, and over three times in Podkarpackie voivodship. An even greater reduction has been witnessed in dust emissions. In Podkarpackie there has been a seven-and-a-half-fold reduction, and in Lublin voivodship a tenfold reduction since 1996. This improvement has also been recorded on the Ukrainian side of the borderland. Typical pollution emissions from stationary sources in Volhynia have fallen three and a half times compared with those in 1995. The fall in emissions has been less spectacular in Lviv oblast (having fallen by a quarter since 1995), although, compared with 1990, emissions have decreased threefold. This was partly due to the introduction of more modern equipment, limiting the production of pollutants and improving the efficiency of installations designed to reduce emission levels (currently, 99 per cent of airborne pollutants are neutralized in industrial plants on the Polish side of the borderland). However, the greatest influence was the dramatic reduction in industrial production due to the departure from a planned central economy and the low competitiveness of and loss of markets by industrial plants in border regions.

There is a visible concentration of major stationary sources of air pollution in several latitudinal belts in the cross-border region. The first of these forms a line marked out by Puławy, Lublin, Rejowiec Fabryczny, Chełm, Volodymyr-Volynskyi and Novovolynsk to Lutsk; the second a line from Mielec through Tarnobrzeg, Stalowa Wola and Sokal, Chervonohrad and Kamianka-Buzka. The third belt includes Dębica, Ropczyce, Rzeszów, Łańcut, Przeworsk, Jarosław and Lviv, while the fourth covers Jasło, Krosno, Sanok, Drohobych and Boryslav, as well as Stryi (Wojewódzki Inspektorat Ochrony Środowiska w Lublinie 2015; Wojewódzki Inspektorat Ochrony Środowiska w Rzeszowie 2015).

Currently the most pollution is emitted by factories in Lviv oblast. In 2014 this region was responsible for over two-thirds of emissions (67.3 per cent), with 19.9 per cent from Lublin voivodship, 10.8 per cent from Podkarpackie voivodship and just under 2.9 per cent from Volhynia. However, the border regions' share in the total emissions of Poland and Ukraine is insignificant. Dust pollution from Lublin voivodship amounts to 4.1 per cent of national emissions, while from Podkarpackie voivodship it is 3.0 per cent. The share of gas emissions in these voivodships is even lower, amounting to 2.4 per cent and 1.2 per cent respectively (CSO 2015a). Lviv oblast generates 3.1 per cent of Ukraine's pollution and Volhynia oblast a mere 0.1 per cent (State Statistics Service of Ukraine 2015a). A major threat to the population is the presence of benzo(a)pyrene, a highly carcinogenic compound, the levels of which in the Polish atmosphere well exceed the norm and in fact are the highest in the whole of the European Union (European Environment Agency 2015). It is also worth mentioning that some regions of Volhynia oblast were affected by the nuclear catastrophe at Chernobyl. An area of increased levels of radioactivity spans 163,100 hectares mainly in the Manevychi district (Derzhupravvlinnia ohorony navkolyshn'ogho seredovyscha u Volyns'kii oblasti 2012).

Despite the beneficial changes in terms of air pollution emissions from stationary sources, there are still considerable problems with other types of emission from the most burdensome of low emitters – that is, residential households, many of which are heated by coal-burning stoves. The threat to air purity from vehicles also continues to grow. We need only notice that, in Lublin voivodship alone, the number of cars doubled in the period 2000–2014 from 534,300 to over 1 million, and 78.4 per cent of these were cars of 12 years old or over.

Degradation of the natural environment is also aggravated by water and soil pollution resulting from sewage issuing from both factories and households. The total volume of wastewater in 2014 amounted to 400.4 million cubic metres, including 72.3 million cubic metres in Lublin voivodship (3.4 per cent of national figure) and 69.5 million cubic metres in Podkarpackie voivodship (3.3 per cent of the national figure), and almost all of this was treated (99.3 per cent in Lublin voivodship and 98.3 per cent in Podkarpackie voivodship). In Lviv oblast 215 million cubic metres of sewage was produced, of which 69.6 per cent underwent treatment, while in the Vohynia oblast 43.6 million cubic metres were produced of which 98.6 per cent was treated. Owing to the modernization of sewage treatment plants and the construction of new plants in the borderland, the quality of treated wastewater continues to improve, reducing the load of pollution from water to the land. This affects the quality of water in rivers, which in the last 25 years has undergone a visible improvement, a good example of which is the River Bug (WIOŚ w Lublinie 2015). A major impact on the environment, above all on water quality, is exerted by sewage system investments. Compared with 2003, the total length of the sewage network in the borderland area grew by a third. However, this expansion applied mainly to the Polish side of the borderland, owing to the financing of infrastructure investments through EU funding.

Administrative divisions and settlement structure

The present administrative division of the Polish–Ukrainian borderland has been shaped over centuries of political change. In the past these lands belonged to several states, including Kiev Rus, the Principality of Galicia-Volhynia, the Kingdom of Poland, the Grand Duchy of Lithuania, the First (Polish–Lithuanian Commonwealth) and Second Polish Republic, the Austro-Hungarian Empire, the Russian Empire and the USSR, and today the independent Poland and Ukraine; thus national identities have been changed many times. In each of these states there was a different territorial system and a different form of public administration (Kuczabski and Miszczuk 2005). Moreover, in different historical periods the current borderlands fell either within one single nation (I and II Polish Republic) or were divided up by state borders: from the time of the Polish partitions to the outbreak of World War I on a latitudinal alignment and in the present day on a near longitudinal alignment.

The first administrative unit with its capital in Lviv was established in 1272. At that time the city became the capital of the Principality of Galicia-Volhynia. In 1434, under the First Polish Republic, Rus voivodship was created with its capital in Lviv and existed until 1772. In the period 1772–1918 the city functioned as the capital of the Kingdom of Galicia and Lodomeria, which was part of the Austro-Hungarian Empire, while in the years 1920–39 the Lviv voivodship was part of the Second Polish Republic. The Lublin voivodship, then much smaller in area than today, was established in 1474. In the period of the Polish partitions this region existed as the Lublin Governerate. The general shape of the present-day Lublin voivodship was not recovered until after World War I. In turn, the origin of Volhynia goes back to 1566, when the Volhynia voivodship with its capital in Lutsk was created, although already in medieval times the city was the capital of the sovereign Principality of Lutsk, which was a part of the Principality of Volyhna and then of the Principality of Galicia-Volhynia. Volhynia voivodship also existed in the years 1920–39, encompassing the areas of today's Volhynia and Rivne oblasts. It is worth adding that, in the period 1462–1793, Lublin, Rus (Ruthenian) and Volhynia voivodships bordered the small Belz voivodship, with its seat in Belz, to whose tradition the modern Podkarpackie voivodship is linked, and whose symbol of a silver griffin is used on the regional emblem. Of the borderland regions, it is Podkarpackie voivodship that has the shortest history. It was established after World War II as Rzeszów voivodship, in a similar shape to that of today, covering the western lands of pre-war Lviv voivodship and the eastern lands of Cracow voivodship.

The administrative division of Poland in the Polish–Ukrainian borderland devised in 1945 included Lublin and Rzeszów voivodships, divided into districts (*powiat*) and communes (*gmina*). As a result of the administrative reforms introduced in 1975, removing district (*powiat*) divisions and increasing the number of voivodships from 17 to 49, there were five voivodships on the border with Ukraine – Bialskopodlaskie, Chełmskie, Zamojskie, Przemyskie and Krośnieńskie. The current administrative division of Poland was formed on 1 January 1999 on the strength of reforms in public administration that brought back the three-tiered administrative division of Poland into communes (*gminy*), districts (*powiaty*), including cities with district status, and provinces (voivodships), which were reduced in number to 16.

The administrative division of present-day Ukraine was devised after World War II (Figure 2.4). Despite numerous ideas for state territorial reform, the same divisions were maintained after regaining independence in 1991. There have thus

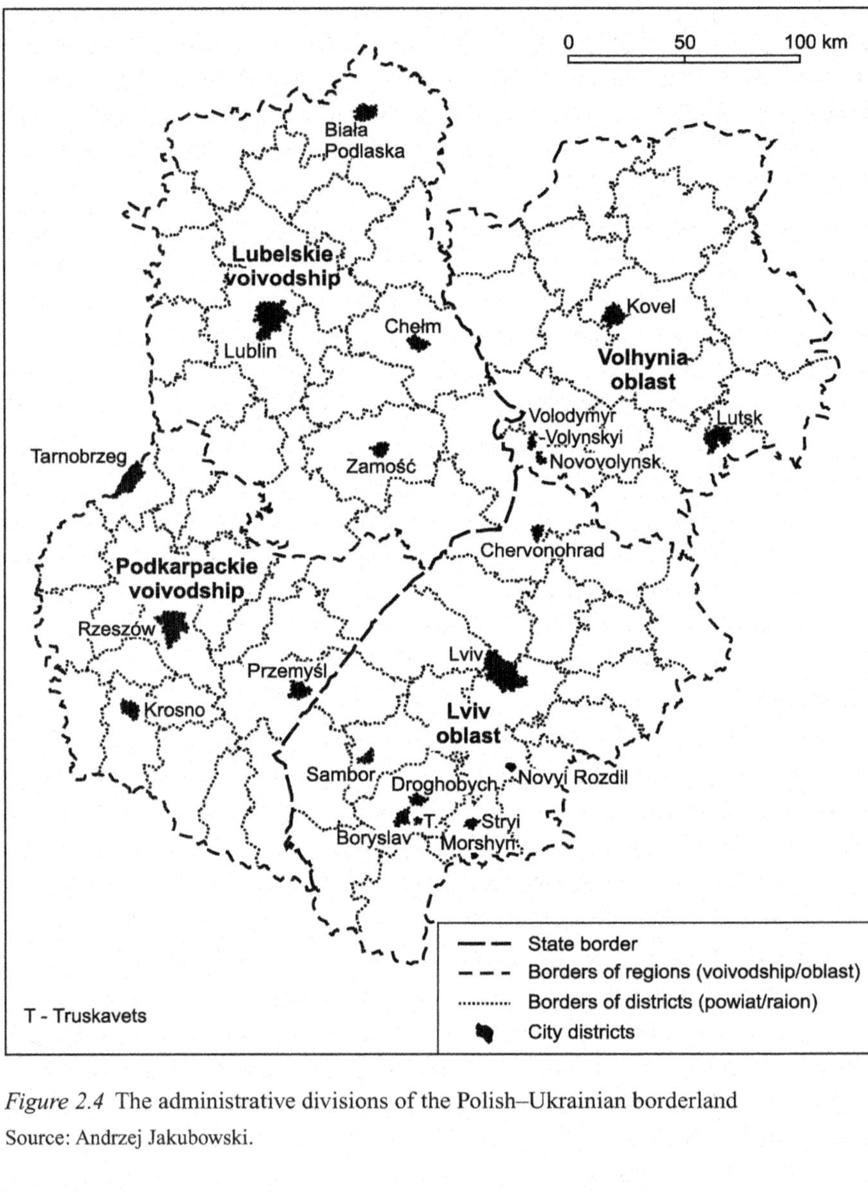

Figure 2.4 The administrative divisions of the Polish–Ukrainian borderland

Source: Andrzej Jakubowski.

been seventy years of stability, and the only major changes in this period were made back in the 1950s, involving the incorporation of Crimea, the joining of Odessa and Ismail oblasts and, in the Polish–Ukrainian borderland, the merging of Lviv and Drohobych oblasts. As in Poland, in Ukraine there is a three-tier system of administration. The regional level includes 24 regions (oblasts), the Autonomous Republic of Crimea (as of 2014 recognized as temporarily occupied by the Russian Federation) and cities with regional status (Kiev and Sevastopol). On the level of sub-regions are districts and cities with regional significance. However, the local level is more diversified, and includes urban councils, urban-type councils and rural councils.

In evaluating both systems of territorial division in terms of the degree of decentralization and the level of self-government, it can be said that in Poland on every level the territorial self-government has clearly defined competencies and disposes of its own revenue and budget, while the autonomy of individual units is subject to legal protection according to the provisions of the European Charter of Local Self-Government. These features are largely lacking in the administrative division of Ukraine, which still resembles that of the soviet era and has not been modified to the needs of the present time in terms either of the undefined competencies or the lack of financial resources, which are unsuited to the needs of a decentralized government and leave the local self-governments at the mercy of the central government administration (Kuczabski and Miszczuk 2005; Kovbasiuk 2014). Thus, from the moment of Ukraine regaining independence the development of self-government has occurred almost entirely at the level of city councils with regional (oblast) status (*Koncepciia reformuvannia miscevogho samovriaduvanniata terytorial'noi orghanizacii vlady v Ukraini* 2014).

In 2014 in Ukraine work began on constitutional reform, the key element of which was administrative reform, prepared on the basis of Polish experiences. Owing to financial and organizational difficulties, including legal obstacles (the need to change the constitution) to making whatever changes are necessary in the number and size of territorial units, the key element of the first stage of reforms is providing self-governing units with funds by guaranteeing them revenues from certain taxes. Action has also been taken to merge the smallest rural settlements. Some of these number only 500 inhabitants, which makes them completely inefficient from a socio-economic point of view. It seems that the main obstacle to reforming the territorial system in Ukraine is not only the civil war (referred to as an Anti-Terrorist Operation) in the east of the country and fears of decentralization (which present a potential threat to unitary government, especially in the light of the federalist demands put forward by Donbas and supported by the Russians), but also the lack of a self-governing tradition, including a lack of understanding of the idea of self-government by a large part of Ukrainian society (Skorupska and Kościński 2015).

Four borderland territorial units at regional level (NUTS 2) – i.e. Lublin voivodship and Podkarpackie voivodship on the Polish side, and Volhynia oblast and Lviv oblast on the Ukrainian side – cover a total area of 84,900 square kilometres, of which 43,000 square kilometres lies on the Polish side (that is, 50.6 per cent of the borderland area and 13.8 per cent of Polish territory), and 42,000 square kilometres on the Ukrainian side (that is, 49.4 per cent of the borderland area and 6.9 per cent of Ukrainian territory). The biggest of these administrative regions is the Lublin voivodship, covering 25,100 square kilometres. Lviv oblast covers an area of 21,800 square kilometres, Volhynia oblast covers 20,100 square kilometres, and Podkarpackie voivodship, the smallest region of the Polish–Ukrainian borderland, covers 17,800 square kilometres.

By analysing their size in the context of other European regions, it is noticeable that they are generally large, with surface areas comparable with the administrative regions of Germany, France or Sweden. Their population potential is also significant (with the exception of Volhynia oblast), being comparable with the average populations of French and Spanish regions, although lower than the average populations of German and Italian regions.

Lublin voivodship is divided into 24 districts (*powiaty*) and Podkarpackie voivodship into 25. Most of these districts – 20 in Lublin voivodship and 21 in Podkarpackie voivodship – are so-called 'landed' districts, being formed of a concentration of communes (*gminy*), while eight (four in each voivodship) possess city district status: that is, they are administrative units with a dual character, being in reality communes possessing and realizing all the competencies and functions of districts (cities with *powiat* rights). Within Lviv oblast are 20 districts (*raiony*) and nine cities with regional significance, while in Volhynia oblast there are 16 districts (*raiony*) and four cities of regional significance. The size of the Polish districts (*powiaty*) and Ukrainian districts (*raiony*) is to a large degree dependent on the potential and sphere of influence of the urban centres which are their seats (Table 2.1). Units at the sub-regional level (on the Polish side without city districts, while on the Ukrainian side without cities of regional significance) have comparable average areas, covering 1251.3 square kilometres in Volhynia oblast, 1243.0 square kilometres in the Lublin voivodship and 1074.6 kilometres^2

Table 2.1 A profile of the administrative divisions of the Polish–Ukrainian borderland in 2015

	Lublin voivodship	*Podkarpackie voivodship*	*Lviv oblast*	*Wolhynia oblast*
Districts (*powiaty/raiony*)*	20	21	20	16
Cities	43	51	44	11
of which city districts/ cities of regional significance	4	4	9	4
Urban-type settlements	–	–	34	22
Communes (*gminy*)	213	160	–	–
Rural councils	–	–	633	379
Rural settlements	1664	4045	1850	1054

*Without city districts/cities of regional significance

Source: Own study, on the basis of Central Statistical Office of Poland and State Statistics Service of Ukraine data.

in Lviv oblast. The average size of the *powiats* in Podkarpackie voivodship is somewhat smaller (835.9 square kilometres). The populations also come within a similar range, with an average of 87,300 in the Polish part and 73,100 in the Ukrainian part. Thus *powiats* and *raions* are units which display many similarities, both in spatial terms and demographic criteria. In the European context, however, we can point to certain weaknesses at the intermediate level of Polish and Ukrainian administrative structures that are visible in both the dimensions mentioned.

The basic unit of administrative division in Poland is the commune (*gmina*). Lublin voivodship is divided into 213 units of this type (including 20 urban, 170 rural and 23 urban–rural units), while Podkarpackie is divided into 160 (including 16 urban, 109 rural and 35 urban–rural units). The average *gmina* covers an area of 115.2 square kilometres and numbers around 11,500 inhabitants. The structure of local administrative units in Ukraine differs. In Lviv oblast there is a total of 711 councils (44 urban, 34 urban-type and 633 rural) and in Volhynia oblast 412 (11 urban, 22 urban-type and 379 rural). The average area of each council is 37.3 square kilometres, and the number of inhabitants does not exceed 3,200. These are also much smaller than *gminy* in terms of structure. While on the Polish side of the borderland nearly 16 settlements, on average, fall within one administrative unit, in the western oblasts of Ukraine it is fewer than three. All this contributes to the fact that on the Ukrainian side of the borderland basic units are much smaller and as a result weaker and less efficient in socio-economic terms than are *gminy*. This presents a certain barrier to local development, although in Europe basic administrative units of a similar size exist in, for example, Switzerland, Germany, Austria and Luxembourg.

The settlement structure of the Polish–Ukrainian borderland has been shaped by changing conditions. Differences between settlements within individual regions have been determined above all by natural conditions, while similarities result from their common history. Finally, the post-war period had a major impact on settlement processes in the analysed area, involving, on the one hand, rapid centralized industrialization and urbanization processes and, on the other, changes in ownership, the consolidation of arable land and the creation of large-scale farms and farming cooperatives, while these processes took place at different rates and on different scales in Poland and in the Soviet Union.

In 2015 the settlement system in the Polish–Ukrainian borderland consisted of 149 towns (including 21 city districts or cities of regional significance), 56 urban-type settlements and 8,787 rural settlements. The dominant role in the settlement structure was played by urban centres, as the units with the widest catalogue of social and economic functions. The towns of the Polish–Ukrainian borderland are rather unevenly distributed. The urban network is much denser in the south than the north, or, more precisely, the north-east. The uneven spread of urban centres is fully reflected in the average area serviced by one city, which spans around 350 square kilometres in Podkarpackie voivodship and over 1830 square kilometres in Volhynia oblast.

The level of urbanization in the analysed cross-border area stands at 50.5 per cent, and thus about the same number of people live in towns as in the country.

Lviv oblast has the highest percentage of urban dwellers (61.0 per cent). The urban population just prevails in Volhynia (52.3 per cent). However, in Lublin and Podkarpackie voivodships, and thus in the Polish borderland area, the majority of the population are rural dwellers (urban inhabitants account for only 46.2 per cent and 41.3 per cent respectively). It is worth noting that in the case of each of the analysed regions the scale of urbanization is much lower than in the country as a whole: in Ukraine this reaches 69.0 per cent and in Poland 60.4 per cent.

Although almost two-thirds of urban centres fall on the Polish side of the borderland, eastern Poland has a much lower urban density than the west of the country, which is the result of historical processes of urban diffusion that in Poland (and in Central and Eastern Europe in general) ran from west to east (Smętkowski 2010). A similar situation is apparent in Ukraine, where the urban network of Lviv oblast is among the most developed in the country. From around 149 cities located in the cross-border area as many as 112 (that is, over three-quarters) are small towns numbering fewer than 20,000 inhabitants, and the majority of these are very small towns with populations of no more than 10,000. Only 33 towns are classified as medium-sized (from 20,000 to 100,000 inhabitants) and a mere four as large towns (over 100,000).

The largest towns in the borderland are Lviv (759,100 inhabitants), Lublin (341,700 inhabitants), Lutsk (217,100 inhabitants) and Rzeszów (185,100 inhabitants), each of them acting as a regional capital. Remaining urban centres with over 50,000 inhabitants include: Drohobych, Chervonohrad, Kovel, Zamość, Chełm, Stalowa Wola, Biała Podlaska, Stryj and Novovolynsk. Without doubt the only borderland town with a metropolitan character is Lviv. This status is held by neither Lutsk or any of the towns situated on the Polish side of the borderland. In the opinion of M. Smętkowski (2010), none of the Polish borderland towns can be called a metropolis (he points to the existence of a mere seven metropolitan centres in Poland), although in the light of the National Spatial Development Concept 2030 – the most important strategic document relating to spatial planning policy – this status is also assigned to Lublin (MR 2011). Although Smętkowski acknowledges Lublin as the most important centre in the class A category of regional towns, he points out that it falls short of towns of the first group in many respects. Meanwhile, he considers Rzeszów to be a regional class B centre. This does not change the fact that the local government authorities in both towns aspire to metropolitan status, demonstrated by their membership of the Union of Polish Metropolises and life membership of the European association of metropolitan cities, 'Eurocities' (to which Lviv also belongs as an associate member, as one of four Ukrainian cities, alongside Kiev, Odessa and Kharkiv). This does not mean, however, that cities such as Lublin, Lutsk and Rzeszów do not perform an important regional function (or even a supra-regional function, in the case of Lublin), thus forming centres of extensive functional systems inhabited by large numbers of people. For instance, the Lublin Metropolitan Area, designated by the Lublin authorities, and several surrounding districts (*powiaty*) are inhabited by 712,100 people.

Evaluating the degree of urban network ties on the Polish–Ukrainian borderland, it should be noted that the period during which the border was impenetrable (1945–91) led to a severance of numerous spatial and functional ties linking both parts of the current cross-border region, at the same time leading to the peripherialization and marginalization of towns, especially those in the borderland (Miszczuk 2015), not only in geographical terms but also economically. A particularly vivid example of this peripheralization of borderland towns is the city of Belz, located close to the state border. Once the seat of the medieval Duchy of Belz, and in the period 1462–1772 the capital of Belz voivodship under the First Polish Republic, it is currently a small provincial settlement, numbering barely more than 2,000 inhabitants, several times fewer than before the outbreak of World War II. Marginalization is also evident in the cases of Hrubieszów, today a peripheral town pushed into the easternmost corner of Poland with just 18,000 inhabitants, having once been the second largest centre (after Lublin) of the Lublin Governerate, and Przemyśl, located ten kilometres from the border, which before World War II was the second largest town in what was then Lviv voivodship.

It is worth adding that many of these towns are historical centres, having witnessed the complex events of the borderland. The concentration of numerous historic monuments makes them attractive for the development of tourism. Two centres in particular are listed as UNESCO world heritage sites: Lviv, which contains the largest concentration of historic monuments in Ukraine, and Zamość, the Renaissance 'ideal town'. Besides Zamość, the historic old town complex of Lublin has also been designated a Polish National Historic Monument. However, not only large and medium-sized towns but also numerous small towns scattered over the whole borderland area, whose heydays have long since passed, are attractive in terms of tourism. Many of them were once the seats of great magnates in whose hands lay extensive landed estates. Among these, particularly noteworthy are the estates of Łańcut, Baranów Sandomierski, Krasiczyn, Kozłówka, Zhovkva, Pochaiv and Ostrogh. Some places are also health spas, including Nałęczów and Truskavets, which were already well-known resorts of this type back in the nineteenth century.

On the Polish side of the borderland, in order to enhance the urban network, the designation of 'city rights' has been given to settlements which once held this status but lost it owing to a decline in importance and depopulation in the nineteenth century or the first half of the twentieth century, or – in the case of some towns in the Lublin voivodship – to the Tsarist repression following the failed anti-Russian January Uprising in the years 1863–4. In recent years city status has been granted to six towns in Podkarpackie voivodship and five towns in Lublin voivodship. Today this process is initiated from the bottom up by local authorities, treating the regained status as a mark of prestige that increases the chances of development and sometimes also historical justice. It comes as no surprise that these aspirations are declared by a whole series of town authorities. However, this designation is unlikely to effectively remedy the weak urban network, since in recent years city status was regained mainly by small or very small towns. Within this group only Boguchwała numbers a little over 5,000 inhabitants, while the rest are inhabited by around 1,000–3,000 people. The lack of urban functions and inhabitants was the reason why the Council of Minsters rejected the request for city status by the towns of Końskowla and Skierbieszów, while Lubycza Królewska regained it only on the third attempt.

On the Ukrainian side of the borderland the network of towns is supplemented with so-called urban-type settlements. Although they do not hold formal town status they do possess certain urban features – mostly poorly diversified – including an economic base structure dominated by one or two functions of an industrial, administrative, transportation, social–cultural or health resort nature (Zastawnyj and Kusiński 2003). In the same way their status can be defined as midway between town and village. In 2015 there were on the Ukrainian side of the borderland 56 settlements in this category, including 34 in Lviv oblast and 22 in Volhynia. In 2014 216,400 people were living in urban-type settlements, with 113,500 in Lviv oblast and 102,900 in Volhynia. The average settlement in this category numbered just under 4,000 inhabitants, although they were bigger in Volhynia oblast (averaging 4,700 inhabitants) than Lviv oblast (3,300 inhabitants). The largest of them all – Maniewicz and Ratne in Volhynia oblast – numbered around 10,000 inhabitants, and performed the function of regional capital, while the smallest – Novi Strilyshcha in Lviv oblast – numbered only 900 inhabitants.

A predominant part of the borderland area is rural. It is inhabited by almost 4 million people and typified by a great diversity of settlements in terms of size and density as well as generic types. This diversity is influenced by historical and economic factors, as well as natural features such as soil quality, relief and degree of afforestation. The intensity of land use and spatial diversity are quite well reflected in rural population density. Similar intensities of rural settlement can be seen in Podkarpackie and Lublin voivodships, and in Lviv oblast (almost 50 inhabitants per square kilometre in rural areas), while in Volhynia oblast densities are around half. Also noticeable is the greater density of rural populations in areas on the outskirts of large and medium-sized towns, which is tied to ongoing suburbanization processes. Nearly half (over 4,000 of 8,700) of rural settlements can be found in the Lublin voivodship. In this region they are smaller, however, with an average number of inhabitants not exceeding 300, compared with around 500 in both west Ukraine oblasts and over 700 in Podkarpackie voivodship.

In Podkarpackie voivodship, in the Ukrainian Carpathians and in Polesia it is common to come across linear villages, often with a two-row arrangement of smallholdings. Carpathian mountain villages are often stretched out in long 'chains' running along rivers and streams; individual homesteads may be scattered some distance apart across a hillside. Meanwhile, villages in Polesia were affected by the difficult geographical conditions, including large areas of bogs and marshy ground, forcing settlements to be located on small hills; as a result West Polesia is dominated by isolated villages (Zastawnyj and Kusiński 2003). The rural landscape of the Lublin Upland is typified by compact settlements in a dense network including numerous chains of houses, often stretching for several kilometres along roadways. This type of settlement also dominates in the Sandomierz Valley.

Meanwhile, in the north-western part of Lublin voivodship, rural settlements are accompanied by numerous hamlets – clusters of farmsteads situated away from the main settlement, but still an integral part of the village (Wesołowska 2012). On the Ukrainian side of the borderland there remain a few examples of *khutor* – villages made up of single farmsteads scattered over a wide area. This village system grew up in the area of today's Ukraine as a result of the Tsarist Russian agricultural reforms (the so-called Stolypin reforms), although, owing to the liquidation of villages deemed non-viable in the Soviet period, few have remained (Zastawnyj and Kusiński 2003). These diverse generic settlement types present potential opportunities for socio-economic development in rural areas. Such opportunities are even greater where large settlements with close-knit forms dominate, and are less in the case of small, loose-knit villages of a dispersed nature (Wesołowska 2012).

In assessing settlement patterns in the Polish–Ukrainian borderland, several similarities can be identified. Above all, this area is predominantly rural, with relatively low levels of urbanization. The urban network is weak, especially in the northern part of the macro-region, evident in not only the low density of towns but also their low populations. Small and medium-sized settlements prevail, with few large towns. Each of the analysed parts of the cross-border area is situated in a peripheral part of the nation, far away from the most important national centres. This is significant, as in modern economies a key role is played by large, multi-functional cities that concentrate intellectual, economic and technological capital and thereby become the main beneficiaries of the rapidity and scale of development. In each borderland region, it is also noticeable that one city dominates as an administrative, economic, cultural, educational or scientific research centre, distancing medium-sized centres, which are equally important for creating conditions for sustainable development (Bronisz et al. 2011). The diversified distribution of inhabitants in the Polish–Ukrainian borderland is reflected in population density patterns. The most densely populated areas are the former Galicia, particularly in the central and western parts of Podkarpackie voivodship (averaging 119 inhabitants per square kilometre) and the central and southern parts of Lviv oblast. This latter region is one of the most densely populated in Ukraine (116 inhabitants per square kilometre, compared with 75 inhabitants per square kilometre in the country as a whole). A much sparser population density is found in the north-western part of the cross-border area – in some districts (*raion*) of Volhynia oblast situated near the Ukrainian–Belarussian border the average population density only just exceeds 20 inhabitants per square kilometre (Figure 2.5).

Society

Without a doubt, one of the principal factors determining socio-economic development is demographic potential. However, Polish and Ukrainian experiences prove that socio-economic transformation can in fact have a great impact on demographic processes. The period of systemic and structural transformation, which began in

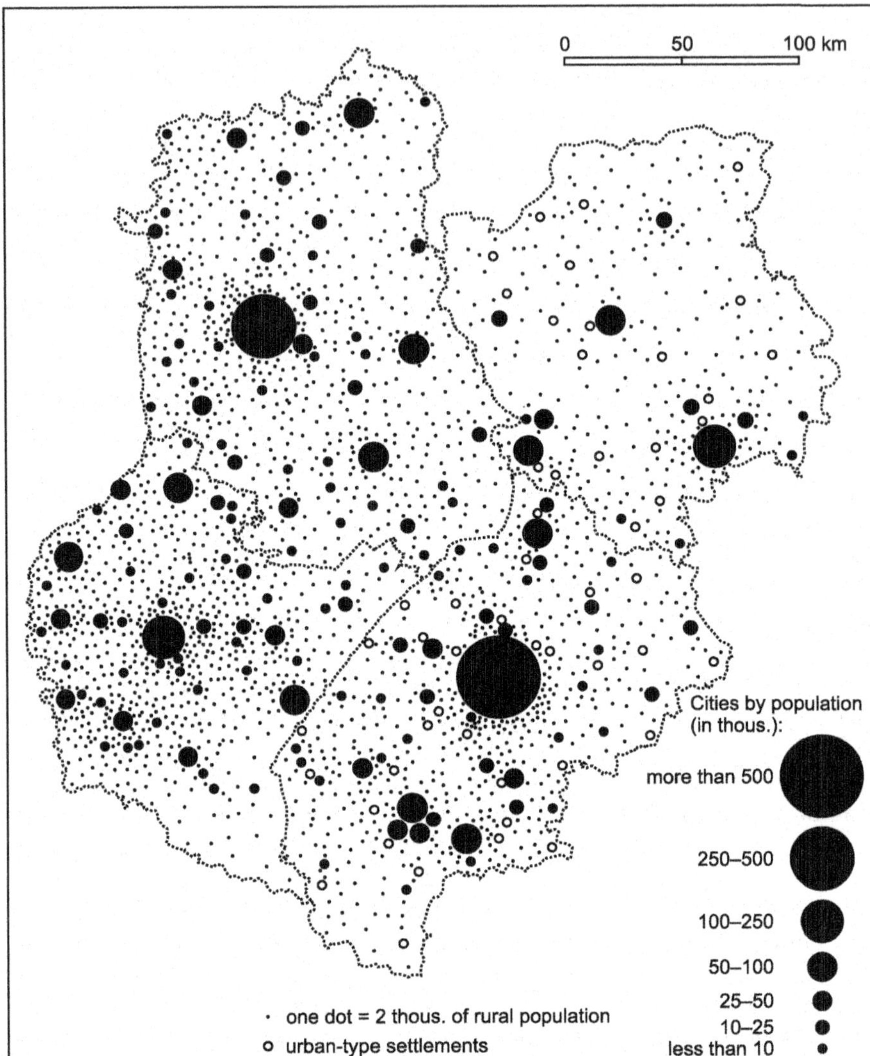

Figure 2.5 Population density

Source: Andrzej Jakubowski, on the basis of Central Statistical Office of Poland and State Statistics Service of Ukraine.

Poland in 1989 and in Ukraine in 1991, had a visible demographic dimension, evidenced in a fall in the number and rate of births, a fall in the number of marriages, an increased number of births outside of marriage and an increase in the average age of first-time mothers. These changes also included growth in migratory movements, shown by increased outflows of people abroad due to greater ease of movement on an international scale, as well as continued high levels of internal migration owing to difficulties in finding work (Szymańczak 2000).

Over the past 25 years Poland and Ukraine have recorded a number of negative demographic trends. Following a demographic boom in the 1970s and 1980s, in the subsequent decade these nations entered a phase of demographic decline. A particularly steep drop in population was recorded in Ukraine. From 1993 to 2014 the number of inhabitants of this country fell by 6.8 million people – that is, 13.1 per cent – from 52.2 million to 45.4 million. In Poland too, in the years 1997–2007 annual estimates suggest that the number of inhabitants fell by 158,000 (0.4 per cent), although the national census records of 2011 gave a figure higher than expected, thereby making it impossible to assess the real scale of decline in the years 1997–2014.

Although there is no question that foreign migration had a significant impact on this phenomenon, the fall in populations of both countries was due above all to the drop in birth rates and, in the case of Ukraine, a rise in the death rate, as a result of which these countries have experienced negative population growth since independence. At the same time, in both countries a process of population ageing became evident – not so much because of longer lifespans, which in Ukraine are still among the lowest in Europe, but above all owing to declining numbers in the youngest age groups. The trends described above were, and still are, observable in the borderland regions, although in different time periods and on varying scales.

The dramatic fall in Ukraine's population was the consequence of the onset of unfavourable socio-economic phenomena in this country. Population decline affected both towns and rural areas, and the main cause of depopulation was the drastic fall in the birth rate combined with increased emigration. The decline in the birth rate was due above all to fewer births, and this was influenced by low family incomes, a fall in the number of marriages (which in the analysed area remains the institution accepted as creating the best conditions for raising children), the recurring phenomenon of female infertility (most often due to abortion) and the poor health of mothers (Flaga 2006). Meanwhile, in the 1990s there was also a significant rise in the second contributor to demographic decline in Ukraine – the mortality rate. A rise in the death rate can be linked to worsening economic conditions, which led to increased levels of illness and shortened lifespans. While in the second half of the 1980s the lifespan of Ukrainian men was on average 66.5 years, and that of women 75.2 years, at the start of the following decade it was reduced to 62.4 years for men and 73.6 years for women. Ukraine also witnessed a severe drop in the number of marriages, an increase in births out of wedlock, a growth in the number of divorces and a particularly high number of abortions, which in the 1990s became the main method of birth control (Flaga 2006). These unfavourable demographic processes showed no signs of diminishing in the following decade. While in the years 1991–2000 the number of inhabitants fell by 2.5 million (4.8 per cent), in the years 2001–10 they dropped by a further 3 million (6.0 per cent). It was not until more recently (2011–14) that a slow-down in the pace of population decline was recorded, amounting to 350,000 people over four years.

It should be underlined, however, that these negative trends were less pronounced in the western oblasts of Ukraine than in the country as a whole, and the ensuing demographic processes were quite different. The specific nature of this area was determined above all by a lower intensity of the negative factors which largely contributed to the demographic decline in Ukraine as a whole. For example, the number of abortions per 1,000 women here was almost half the national rate, and the case was similar for births outside marriage. In western Ukraine there were also lower levels of pathological phenomena (alcoholism, drug abuse, suicide) which in the 1990s visibly contributed to increased death rates in the country. In the regions of western Ukraine the ratio of marriages remained relatively high, and the birth rate, although reduced, was better than in other regions. The mortality rate was also markedly lower than in the country as a whole. In western Ukraine a certain delay in demographic processes could be seen relative to the rest of the country. At the time when other regions were entering the 'second stage' of demographic transition, the western regions still remained in the 'first stage' (Flaga 2006).

Equally, the rate of demographic change taking place over the past 25 years on the Polish side of the borderland should be viewed in terms of demographic transition theory. Poland, as with other countries of Central and Eastern Europe, witnessed from the beginning of the 1990s a dramatic drop in fertility rates caused by far reaching changes relating to family creation and breakdown as well as changes in the area of procreation and fertility patterns, which can be linked to political and economic transformation processes. And although changes in fertility patterns occurred much later than in western Europe, the transformation took place over a much shorter space of time (Kotowska and Chłoń-Domińczak 2012). As a result of these processes, in the years 1995–2014 the number of inhabitants in the country was reduced by 130,800. The scale of transformation was unevenly spread, something which is reflected on both sides of the border. While in the last twenty years the number of inhabitants of Lublin voivodship fell by 96,900 people (in absolute values, a greater decline was noted only in Śląskie and Łódzkie voivodships), in Podkarpackie the number of inhabitants rose slightly (by 23,600 people). By comparison, in the period 1995–2014 the population of Lviv oblast fell by 232,500 people – more than 8 per cent. In the same period in Vohynia oblast there was a drop in population of 35,400 people (3.3 per cent) (Figure 2.6).

At the beginning of 2015 the Ukrainian part of the borderland was inhabited by 3.5 million people (2.5 million in Lviv oblast and 1 million in Volhynia, which represented almost 8 per cent of the population of Ukraine and 45.6 per cent of the cross-border population). In 1991–2014 the share of the population of both western Ukraine oblasts in the overall population of the country experienced slight growth. Meanwhile, in the Polish part of the borderland there lived just over 4 million people, including just over 2 million in both Lublin voivodship and Podkarpackie. The whole borderland area at the turn of 2014 and 2015 was inhabited by almost 8 million people – that is, more or less, the size of the population of Israel or Switzerland (Table 2.2).

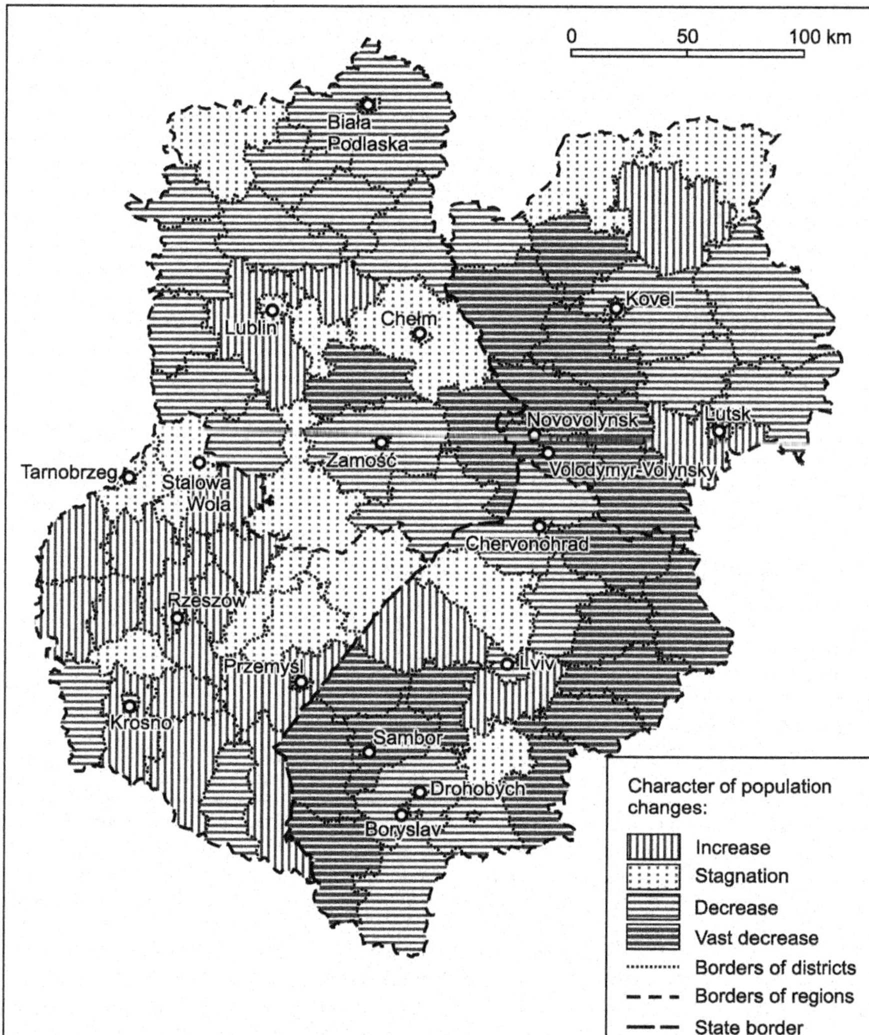

Figure 2.6 Changes in the number of inhabitants by districts in the years 1988/1989*–2014**

* Data for Polish part comes from Population Census held in 1988, data for Ukrainian part from Population Census held in 1989.

** Data for Polish part as of 31 December 2014, for Ukrainian part as of 1 January 2015.

Source: Krzysztof Łoboda, on the basis of Central Statistical Office of Poland and State Statistics Service of Ukraine.

Among the general populace in the Polish–Ukrainian borderland, women predominate. The feminization index in 2014 was 105 in the Polish borderland and over 111 on the Ukrainian side. The higher proportion of women in the Ukrainian area has several causes, partly historical (Flaga 2006). Currently, however, the

Table 2.2 A demographic profile of the Polish–Ukrainian borderland in 2014

	Lublin voivodship	*Podkarpackie voivodship*	*Lviv Oblast*	*Volhynia oblast*
Population (in 000s)	2147.7	2129.2	2537.8	1042.9
per 1 km^2	85	119	116	52
males (in 000s)	1041.0	1042.7	1193.3	490.3
females (in 000s)	1106.8	1086.5	1326.1	549.9
per 100 males	106	104	111	112
Urban areas (in 000s)	992.8	880.3	1547.0	545.4
in % of total population	46.2	41.3	61.0	52.3
Rural areas (in 000s)	1155.0	1248.9	990.8	497.5
in % of total population	53.8	58.7	39.0	47.7
At age: (in % of total population)				
0–14	14.8	15.4	16.1	19.4
15–64	69.3	70.2	69.5	67.8
65 and more	15.9	14.5	14.4	12.8
Live births	19828	19953	30270	14668
per 1000 population	9.2	9.4	11.9	14.1
Deaths	22107	18361	32450	13748
per 1000 population	10.3	8.6	12.8	13.2
Natural increase	−2279	1592	−2180	920
per 1000 population	−1.1	0.7	−0.9	0.9
Immigration	20104	19025	28130	14229
Emigration	25864	21274	26587	13604
Net migration	−5760	−2249	1543	695
per 1000 population	−2.7	−1.1	0.6	0.6
Actual increase	−8039	−657	−637	1615
per 1000 population	−3.7	−0.3	0.3	1.5

Source: Own study, on the basis of Central Statistical Office of Poland and State Statistics Service of Ukraine data.

main reason for this is the high mortality of men of reproductive age as a consequence of increased levels of cardiovascular disease and higher levels of pathology (such as alcoholism and drug abuse), which are common in countries arising after the collapse of the USSR (Eberhardt 2003). However, in rural areas a particular problem is in fact a surplus of men of marriageable age (i.e. 20–29 years old). This phenomena is influenced by migration processes, leading to the over-representation of women in cities. In a majority of rural communes of Lublin voivodship the feminization index in this age group is less than 90 per cent. A similar phenomenon can be witnessed in western Ukraine, where the ratio of women to men in cities has been continually rising since the mid-1990s, while in rural areas it has been falling since the beginning of the decade.

A particularly important problem is the ageing population, involving changes in the age structure which lead to a lower proportion of younger age groups and a growing proportion of older people. It should be noticed that this trend is prevalent throughout Europe, but takes on certain characteristic features in depopulated areas, to which – as a whole – the analysed region belongs. The population ageing process is mainly the consequence of the lengthening of average lifespans, improved living standards and better medical care, as well as falling birth rates, changes in the family model and its role, later marriage, a delay in the typical age of child-bearing and a decline in large families with multiple offspring (Miszczuk et al. 2010). Although the age structure of the borderland population shows some signs of gradual change towards falling numbers of young people in the pre-productive age group (0–14 years old) as well as growing numbers of people in the productive age group (15–64 years old) and the post-productive age group (65 years old or over), these changes for the time being do not give cause for concern. The negative trends in the age structure of the population are reflected in the youth index, calculated as the proportion of people in the pre-productive age group in relation to the overall population. In the last decade there has been a fall in this index (the greatest in Lublin voivodship), but, apart from this region, it is still at a higher level than the national and EU averages. The ageing process of society is not shown by the demographic burden index, which is calculated as the ratio of people in the post-productive age group to the number of people of productive age. This value in the Polish–Ukrainian borderland has declined, above all owing to the significant growth in the numbers of people of productive age. At the same time, the value of this index in the cross-border area is at a much lower level than the average for EU countries. Analysis of the spatial distribution of indices for youth, old age and the demographic burden show that the most favourable (i.e. the youngest) age structure is found in Volhynia oblast and Podkarpackie voivodship, while the current problem of an ageing society is most visible in Lublin region. Although the Polish–Ukrainian borderland currently has large numbers of people of productive age, in the near future we are likely to observe the gradual shift of consecutive population cohorts towards the post-productive age. In this respect the borderland area will not be an exception. The problem of an ageing population is current in the whole of Europe, but the degree of its advancement in the Polish–Ukrainian borderland is presently much lower than the EU average.

As mentioned previously, there are many factors which contribute to this process. One of them is the growth in average life expectancy, which in Podkarpackie is one of the highest in the country, at 75.1 years for men and nearly 82.8 for women. The lives of inhabitants of Lublin voivodship are a little shorter. In recent years there has been marked progress in this respect on the Ukrainian side of the borderland. Although the average life expectancy in Ukraine belongs to the lowest among European nations, in 2014 in Lviv oblast it was at last higher than the national average, reaching 73.1 years (68.2 for men and 77.9 for women).

The second factor influencing the shape of the population age structure is natural movement. In the last decade the majority of borderland regions (with the exception of Lublin voivodship) recorded a gradual increase in the birth rate index, which together with the fall in mortality rates led – after several years of decline – to the appearance in 2009 of natural growth (although exclusively in Volhynia oblast and Podkarpackie voivodship). The improvement in the natural movement index has been equally visible in Lviv oblast and Lublin voivodship, although until the present time there have been no records of excess births over deaths.

In assessing the birth rate intensity it is also necessary to look at the total fertility rate. This measure provides a synthesis of population reproduction processes, and a value of 2.1 guarantees the replacement of generations. Low fertility is indicated when the total fertility index falls within the range 1.35–1.5, while very low fertility is indicated when it does not exceed 1.35 (Kotowska and Chłoń-Domińczak 2012). The highest total fertility index is recorded in Volhynia oblast (1.856 in 2013), and a fairly favourable situation is presented in Lviv oblast (1.552 in the year 2013). A particularly negative situation in this respect is apparent on the Polish side of the borderland, where in 2014 the index hit record low levels: 1.212 in Podkarpackie and 1.245 in Lublin voivodship.

Migration processes also have a major impact on population levels in the borderland, directly affecting the population numbers and structure, and indirectly shaping natural movement. They are dependent on a wide range of 'pull' factors – that is, the general attractiveness of a given area – and 'push' factors – mainly connected with difficulties in the job market. Areas experiencing are large urban centres and their environs, while outflow is from peripheral areas or places that are lagging economically. In analysing data on population movements it is important to be aware that they do not relate so much to real flows but to registered data, reflecting the number of notifications of changes in address, and this applies to both Polish and Ukrainian data (Jakubowski 2015).

For years Lublin and Podkarpackie voivodships have experienced the greatest population outflow. In the period 2004–14 92,400 people left Lublin voivodship to take up permanent residence in other Polish voivodships (above all Mazovia), and the migration balance amounted to −53,000 people. The scale of migration in Podkarpackie was a little less, although here too in the last decade the overall migration balance is negative, numbering −22,000 people. This means that regions making up the Polish–Ukrainian borderland are generally areas of out-migration, although it is only in the Polish part that the negative balance of inter-regional migration can be translated into real population movements.

No less important in terms of shaping demographic potential is foreign migration, and in this respect the borderland regions also exhibit out-migration. However, the scale of registered emigration of a permanent nature is small, partly due to the method of collecting data and exacerbated by the fact that people are unwilling to definitively and permanently break ties with their homeland in official records. For this reason more reliable information can be gleaned from analysing temporary migration, particularly work-related, which in many cases is extended, thus becoming *de facto* permanent emigration.

According to the estimates of the Central Statistical Office of Poland (GUS 2015), at the end of 2014 more than 2 million inhabitants were temporarily living outside the country, which is the most since Poland joined the European Union in 2004, when around 1 million Poles were living abroad. In 2014, around 2 million people were living temporarily in Europe, the majority – just under 2 million – in EU member states. Among EU countries, most people emigrated to Great Britain (685,000), Germany (614,000) and Ireland (113,000) as well as the Netherlands (109,000) and Italy (96,000). However, these data do not give us information on the region from which people migrated. For this purpose it is possible to use data from the National Census conducted in 2011, which revealed that just over 2 million Polish inhabitants were temporarily residing abroad. In this group there were 178,600 people from Podkarpackie voivodship (8.9 per cent of total temporary emigrants) and 112,200 people from Lublin voivodship (5.6 per cent). Both these voivodships belong to the group of Polish regions with the highest number of emigrants. Among the inhabitants of Lublin voivodship, the most common foreign migration destination was Great Britain (41,800 people), and there were also a significant number (11,200) residing in Germany, Italy (11,100, mostly women) and the United States (10,500). Meanwhile, inhabitants of Podkarpackie voivodship, apart from Great Britain (51,100 people), most often emigrated to the United States (40,900), this being the traditional destination for emigration from Podkarpackie since the second half of the nineteenth century. In the case of this voivodship, a sizeable proportion emigrated to France (16,500), Italy (14,600) and Germany (11,400). Without doubt, a major role was played by so-called migration networks, providing, above all, information about the experiences of friends and relatives, and this makes it possible to observe certain patterns – for example, Italy and the Netherlands are particularly popular among inhabitants of the east and south-east of Lublin voivodship, Germany among those from the west of Lublin region and Ireland among those from the region around Łuków.

Owing to geographical proximity and familiarity with the language, many inhabitants of Ukraine still choose to emigrate to the Russian Federation. According to the statistics of Rosstat in the period 1997–2014, just over 1 million Ukrainian citizens settled in Russia, and this number has significantly increased in recent times as a result of the conflict in Donbas (Rosstat 2015). A more precise analysis of the scale and direction of labour migration among the inhabitants of western Ukraine can be gleaned from the results of research conducted in 2008 and 2012 by the Ukrainian State Statistics Committee. Based on these results, the number of emigrants residing temporarily abroad in 2012 can be estimated at around 1.2 million people, compared to around 1.5 million in 2008. The main destination was still Russia (511,000 people), while the number of emigrants from Ukraine in this country fell over four years by about 200,000 people. Other places chosen were: Poland (168,400), Italy (156,000), the Czech Republic (153,000), Spain (52,600) and Germany (27,800). In both rounds of research the largest group of emigrants were inhabitants of west Ukraine – 847,300 people in 2008 and 846,100 people four years later. In 2012 the most popular emigration destinations for inhabitants of this region were Russia (282,100 people), Poland (158,000 people), the Czech Republic (142,700 people), Italy (133,400 people) and Spain (41,300 people) (Chebanova 2009; MOP 2013). In many instances transfers of funds generated by working emigrants from Poland and Ukraine constitute the main source of income for households in the country of origin, although in the case of Poland their size is continually diminishing (Chmielewska 2015), which is influenced by whole families moving to the destination country as well as the gradual weakening of ties with the home country.

As a result of mass movements of people, as well as ethnic cleansing carried out in the borderland during World War II and in the early post-war period, the current borderland on both the Polish and Ukrainian sides features considerable homogeneity in terms of nationality (Eberhardt 2011). This situation was exacerbated over time, as shown in consecutive census records. According to national census records conducted in Poland in 2011 (during which it was possible to declare two national-ethnic identities), the number of inhabitants in Podkarpackie voivodship who declared their nationality to be other than Polish (under the first or second identity) amounted to 12,000 people, including 4,100 representatives of the Ukrainian minority. The figure for ethnic minorities in Lublin voivodship was even smaller (10,200 people), of whom 2,200 were Ukrainians. In total, the number of people who declared Ukrainian identity in these two voivodships was 12.4 per cent, out of 51,000 members of the Ukrainian minority in Poland. At the same time only 2,500 inhabitants of Podkarpackie voivodship and 800 inhabitants of Lublin voivodship declared their native language to be Ukrainian.

While Poland is generally speaking homogeneous in terms of nationality, Ukraine is an example of a multi-ethnic country in which, according to the last census of 2001, ethnic minorities amounted to 10.7 million people – that is, 22.2 per cent of the overall population. The largest minority group in Ukraine is Russians (17.3 per cent of the total population). In 2001 the number of Polish nationals amounted to 144,100 people, indicating a reduction of 75,000 compared with 1989 figures, mostly due to emigration (Yevtukh et al. 2004). More information on the topic of ethnic change in Ukraine will no doubt be revealed in the next census, due in 2016.

Set against the diversified ethnic structure of this nation, the two western Ukrainian regions appear almost mono-ethnic, with a clear prevalence of Ukrainian people. In 2001 Ukrainians constituted 94.8 per cent of the population of Lviv oblast. Among minorities, most numerous were Russians, at 92,600 (3.6 per cent). The next largest groups were Poles (18,900 people (0.7 per cent)) and Jews (5,400 people (0.2 per cent)). An even greater homogeneity is exhibited in the ethnic structure of Volhynia oblast, in which Ukrainians make up 96.9 per cent of the population, Russians 2.4 per cent (25,100 people), Belarussians 0.5 per cent (3,200 people) and Poles 0.2 per cent (800 people), making Volhynia the region with the fewest Polish people of all the former eastern lands of the Second Republic of Poland. Moreover, most of them came here after the war from the east (Rąkowski 2005), especially from exile in Siberia or Kazakhstan.

While a large portion of Ukrainian society lacks a clear and well-formed linguistic and cultural identity (Riabczuk 2004; Wilson 2002), this is certainly not the case when it comes to the inhabitants of west Ukraine, where the importance and influence of the Ukrainian culture and language has been undisrupted throughout the soviet period, and russification processes were the least advanced. This is reflected both in the census records, according to which 97.3 per cent of inhabitants in Volhynia oblast and 95.3 per cent in Lviv oblast spoke Ukrainian. Interestingly, Poles in Ukraine are one of the most Ukrainianized minority groups – over two-thirds (71 per cent) declared Ukrainian to be their native language.

As shown in the last chapter, the borderland area featured great cultural and ethnic diversity at every stage in its history. Even more complex in this respect was – and to a large extent still is today – the religious and ethno-religious situation. While the Polish population living in the borderland area was and is predominantly single-faith, and belonging to the Roman Catholic Church was commonly regarded as a mark of Polishness, the Ukrainian population, owing to its complex turns of fate, belonged at different periods of history to the Russian Orthodox Church or the Greek Orthodox Church, which acknowledges the primacy of the pope by virtue of the Union of Brest concluded in 1596. And while the Russian Orthodox Church became a tool for the russification of people living in the Volhynia region, the Greek Orthodox Church which developed in the area of east Galicia gradually became the exclusive religion of the Ukrainian people and a sign of their Ukrainian ethnicity.

At the time of the Soviet Union, as a result of the liquidation of the Ukrainian Autocephalous Church in 1930 and the Greek Orthodox Church following the annexing of east Galicia into the Ukrainian Soviet Socialist Republic in 1946, the official monopoly was held by the Russian Orthodox Church of the Moscow Patriarchate, although its activity was subjected to far-reaching restrictions. After regaining independence the idea of an autonomous Church arose in Ukraine, and in 1990 the Ukrainian faction of the Russian Orthodox Church reformed as the Ukrainian Orthodox Church (from 1992, the Ukrainian Orthodox Church of the Kiev Patriarchate). The Greek Catholic Church was legalized in December 1989 and a special Ukrainian council was called in Kiev to decide on the re-establishment of the Ukrainian Autocephalous Orthodox Church, which for several decades had functioned as a church of the Ukrainian diaspora. Thus currently in Ukraine four influential church organizations function side by side – three (among seventeen in the world) orthodox Churches and the Greek Orthodox Church (Wilson 2002).

This complexity is fully reflected in the Ukrainian part of the borderland. While the population of the northern cross-border area – Volhynia – is predominantly orthodox, remaining within the sphere of influence of the Moscow Patriarchate (to which nearly half of the total 1,472 parishes belong), in Lviv oblast the Greek Catholic Church is noticeably dominant (to which over half of the 2,821 parishes belong) (Centr Razumkova 2011).

As already mentioned, the Polish part of the borderland is currently mono-ethnic and, in the religious sphere, dominated by the Roman Catholic community. According to the census of 2011, only 21,300 inhabitants of Lublin voivodship and 10,300 inhabitants of Podkarpackie voivodship professed a religion other than Catholicism (ISKK 2015; GUS 2014). The orthodox community today mainly inhabits the north-eastern parts of Lublin voivodship (Polesia) as well as its south-western parts (the Zamość region), while the Greek Catholic community resides in the area of former Galicia, south of Hrubieszów (Czerwonka 2007). According to data from the Statistical Institute of the Catholic Church (ISKK 2015), Catholics constituted 96.6 per cent of the Przemyśl diocese, 96.5 of the Rzeszów diocese and 93.3 per cent of the Lublin diocese. Meanwhile, in the light of data from the Central Statistical Office of Poland, the Orthodox community in Podkarpackie voivodship today numbers 20,200 people, while in Lublin voivodship it is 12,500.

Although the Polish part of the borderland has to a large extent lost its multi-faith character, the church structures still exist here, providing for the religious needs of minority groups, above all the Ukrainian community. In this area two orthodox dioceses operate – the Lublin–Chełm diocese, with its seat in Lublin, which covers the Lublin voivodship as well as part of Mazovia voivodship, and the Przemyśl–Nowy Sącz diocese, with its seat in Sanok, covering Podkarpacke voivodship as well as the eastern part of Małopolskie voivodship. The first diocese includes 31 parishes and 48 places of worship, concentrated mainly in the north-eastern and south-eastern parts of Lublin voivodship, as well as two monasteries (in Kostomłoty and Turkowice) (Prawosławna Diecezja Lubelsko-Chełmska 2016). Meanwhile, the Przemyśl–Nowy Sącz diocese numbers 17 parishes, of which nine are located in Podkarpackie voivodship. The Greek Catholic Church has a somewhat weaker structure, with the seat of the Przemyśl–Warsaw diocese in Przemyśl. In the borderland area it includes a total of 32 parishes, of which 29 are located in Podkarpackie voivodship and three in the Lublin voivodship (ISKK 2015). While the Greek Catholic Church in Polish territory has a noticeably Ukrainian character, in the light of census records it appears that we are mistaken in thinking that the orthodox religion is linked only to Ukrainian and Belarussian people, since the majority of its followers emphasize their Polish ethnicity (Czerwonka 2007).

A feature of the whole borderland region is the generally higher levels of religious participation in comparison with the rest of the country. The share of people attending Sunday Holy Mass in 2014 was 64.6 per cent in the Rzeszów diocese and 59.6 per cent in the Przemyśl diocese, these being the highest levels out of all the dioceses in the country (with the exception of Tarnów), with the Polish average amounting to 39.1 per cent (ISKK, GUS 2014). Meanwhile, according to the results of studies conducted by the Razumkov Centre, the percentage of people professing to be 'religious' was 89.2 per cent in west Ukraine (compared to 71.4 per cent in the whole country), while the percentage of affirmative responses to the question 'Were you raised in a religious faith?' was 78.9 per cent among inhabitants of west Ukraine compared to an average 36.5 per cent in the country as a whole (Centr Razumkova 2011).

This religious diversity in the borderland region appears to have a much wider context. In the opinion of S. Huntington, the ideological division into two blocs during the Cold War has been replaced in the present day by an even deeper civilizational divide in which religion plays a key role. In his opinion, the historical borders between the western and orthodox civilizations, dividing the European continent into Western (Latin) and Eastern (Byzantine) parts, is defined by the line of the reach of western Christianity from the beginning of the sixteenth century, running more or less through the territory of both west Ukrainian oblasts (Huntington 1993). According to this view, the whole Polish–Ukrainian borderland territory lies in a peripheral zone of one civilizational and cultural sphere.

However, this definition of the 'eastern boundary of western civilization' is disputed by P. Eberhardt (Eberhardt 2004). In his opinion, the true cultural dividing line of Europe runs much closer to the present-day Polish border, and partly corresponds to it exactly (Bański 2008). According to his conception, the border between western Christian civilization and Byzantine civilization divides the Polish–Ukrainian borderland territory, bringing the Lviv oblast within the range of western civilization while leaving the Volhynian territory in the sphere of influence of eastern culture (Eberhardt 2004). Leaving this question aside, it seems indisputable that this is an area where eastern and western cultures merge, although, in contrast to Huntington's theories, the representatives of different religions have, over the years, achieved a means of peaceful coexistence.

The multicultural character of the region is also made visible in the numerous historic monuments which provide a material testament of past eras, particularly with respect to the diverse religious buildings – Catholic, Orthodox, Greek Catholic, Armenian churches and monasteries, Jewish synagogues (called here *bożnica*) and Protestant places of worship. A good example is metropolitan Lviv, which is the seat of five Christian bishops – the Roman Catholic and Greek Catholic Archdiocese, the Eparchies of the Ukrainian Orthodox Church of the Moscow Patriarchate, the Ukrainian Orthodox Church of the Kiev Patriarchate and the Arch-eparchy of the Armenian Catholic Church. A similar concentration of churches, including metropolitan churches of various faiths, can be seen in Przemyśl, Lutsk and Lublin. Meanwhile, a perfect example of a multicultural provincial borderland town is Włodawa, known as the town of three cultures, in which the Roman Catholic church, Orthodox church and Jewish synagogue exist side by side.

An important measure of the human capital and professional expertise of a population is the level of education. One of the best measures in this field is the share of the population in higher education. Although this does not provide information on the human capital resources possessed and is not fully comparable for Poland and Ukrainian areas,[1] it does make it possible to draw certain general conclusions. The overall value of this indicator for Polish and Ukrainian borderland regions is lower than the average for the 28 countries of the European Union, where in 2014 higher education was held by 29.3 per cent of people aged 15–64. The percentage of the population in this age category with a higher education in Lublin voivodship came to 26.9 per cent, while in Podkarpackie it was 23.8 per cent (Eurostat 2015). The value of this indicator for inhabitants of Lviv oblast aged 6 and above in 2015 was 25.6 per cent, while in Volhynia it was 18.2 per cent, in comparison with a national average of 23.0 per cent. Bearing in mind the varying age categories, we can deduce that the share of people with a higher education is slightly higher in the Ukrainian part of the borderland. While in both regions of eastern Poland the value is lower than the national average (27.0 per cent), it is here that human capital has undergone the greatest improvement in recent years. We need only remember that, in 2000, the share of graduates from higher education institutions in both eastern voivodships barely exceeded 10 per cent of the population. A similar transformation has taken place in the Ukrainian part of the borderland. According to the census records of 2001, 11.9 per cent of inhabitants of both Ukrainian borderland regions possessed a higher education in a comparable age group.

Without doubt this improvement was spurred by the development of academic centres in the borderland, contributing to the rapid development of higher education (including private institutions) that was witnessed in Poland and Ukraine from the early 1990s. Of course, the current academic tradition of the Polish–Ukrainian borderland stretches back much further, to the end of the sixteenth century, and is tied to the founding of the Zamojski Academy in Zamość by Jan Zamojski in 1591, which was the first private and the third – after Cracow (1364) and Vilnius (1578) – university of the Commonwealth, rapidly becoming one of the main centres of scientific learning in Poland. In 1661 King Jan Kazimierz Waza opened the Lviv Academy in Lviv – a university whose complex history is reflected in the manifold names which it has borne in the past (including the Lvov Academy, Josephine University, Franciscan University, Jan Kazimierz University and finally the Ivan Franko National University of Lviv), where the languages of instruction at different periods in history were Latin, Polish, German and Ukrainian. Today, the university occupies a special place among Ukrainian higher education institutions as one of the oldest (the Kiev-Mohylańska Academy in Kiev was founded just three years earlier) and the most distinguished in the development of science in Eastern Europe.

There are currently 63 schools of higher education in the cross-border area, forming an important element of the socio-economic potential of the region. In the academic year 2014/15 a total of 298,400 students were receiving a higher education here. The most important academic centres of the borderland and one of the largest in Ukraine is Lviv, in which there are 21 higher education institutions educating 122,000 students, including the above-mentioned Ivan Franko National University of Lviv, Lviv Polytechnic, Lviv Academy of Foreign Trade, Lviv Agricultural Academy, Danylo Halytsky Lviv National Medical University, Lviv Academy of Fine Arts and the M. Lysenko National Academy of Music. The second largest academic centre of the borderland (and the seventh in Poland) is Lublin, which has 69,700 students. This city is the seat of nine higher education institutions, including four universities (only Warsaw and Poznań boast more): the Marie Curie-Skłodowska University (UMCS), the John Paul II Catholic University of Lublin (KUL), the University of Life Sciences and Medical University and Lublin Polytechnic. Among the largest academic centres of the borderland is Rzeszów, where there are four higher education institutions (including Rzeszów University and Rzeszów Polytechnic) educating 45,800 students. The remaining academic centres in the area are of much lesser importance – in regional and local terms – and these include Lutsk, Drohobycz, Biała Podlaska, Jarosław, Krosno, Chełm and Zamość. The widest educational offering is available in the two largest academic centres of the borderland. In Lviv students of social sciences, economics, law and engineering/technical disciplines predominate, while in Lublin the greatest numbers study economics, administration and medicine. At the same time both centres are rapidly expanding their doctoral study programmes, which in the academic year 2014/2015 educated 3,100 post-graduates in Lublin and 2,400 in Lviv.

In assessing the significance of academic centres in the Polish–Ukrainian borderland, it needs to be stressed that, among the group of higher education institutions located here, only Lviv Polytechnic and Lviv University belong to the strict elite, holding high positions in the national rankings of higher education institutions. According to the ranking 'Top-200 Ukraine 2015' they came in 6th and 9th place (EuroOsvita 2015). In 2015, in a similar ranking performed annually by the monthly journal *Perspektywy*, the best higher education schools in the Polish part of the borderland came some way down the list in 25th place (Medical University), 26th place (UMCS) and 32nd place (KUL), (Perspektywy 2015). An additional problem among higher education schools is the falling number of students, which is particularly hard-felt in the Polish part of the borderland, where in the last decade student numbers have fallen by over 20 per cent.

An interesting question from a sociological point of view is the electoral preferences of borderland inhabitants, which define to some extent their social character. From the moments when Poland and Ukraine regained independence (in 1989 and 1991 respectively), and thus in the period when elections in these countries became free and democratic, the preferences of inhabitants were noticeably different in both parts of the cross-border area in comparison with the remaining regions of Poland and Ukraine. In both the Polish and the Ukrainian parts of the borderland right-wing parties have dominated for many years – conservative in axiological terms, although favouring greater state intervention in socio-economic areas – and even nationalist parties, although in the Lublin region the agrarian party maintains a traditionally strong influence.

According to electoral studies in Poland and Ukraine conducted by I. Kavetskyy (2010), in the years 1997–2007 in the Polish part of the borderland (which is similar to the whole of eastern Poland) the traditionalist–interventionist option dominated; however, in western Ukraine the traditionalist–liberal option dominated, with traditionalist–interventionist options having growing influence. These observations are confirmed by the results of the elections in Poland and Ukraine in recent years, although it would appear that in the socio-political divisions of the Ukrainian political scene a key role is currently being played by attitudes towards political reform and European integration, and not the classic right–left divide.

The winner of the early presidential elections in Ukraine, brought about by the removal of Viktor Yanukovych, was Petro Poroshenko, who gained 69.9 per cent of the votes in Lviv oblast, the most in all the Ukrainian regions. In the proportional parliamentary elections conducted in 2014, the three biggest parties supporting European integration (The People's Front of Arseniy Yatsenyuk, the Poroshenko bloc 'Solidarity' and the 'Self-Reliance' party of the mayor of Lviv, Andriy Sadovyi) together gained 72.2 per cent of the votes in Lviv oblast and 61.6 per cent in Volhynia oblast, compared to 54.9 per cent on a national scale (TVK 2015). This indicates that the electoral mood in west Ukraine is much more pro-independence, pro-reform, pro-European and anti-Russian than in other regions of the country. Meanwhile, the major influence of the nationalist movement in this area is confirmed by the electoral results of the nationalist party 'All-Ukrainian Union Svoboda' (Freedom), led by Oleh Tyahnybok, which in the 2012 elections won a victory in Lviv oblast with 38.1 per cent of the votes, and came second in Volhynia oblast with 18.0 per cent of the votes. Svoboda achieved similar success in the local elections in 2010, gaining 34.5 per cent of the votes in Lviv oblast. Although in recent parliamentary elections it did not repeat its earlier success, it is still an important force in regional politics (TVK 2015).

The electoral preferences of eastern voivodships in Poland are revealed in the results of the presidential and parliamentary elections conducted in 2015. The winner of the presidential elections was Andrzej Duda, the candidate from the conservative (and at one time regarded as Eurosceptic) 'Law and Justice' party, gaining 51.55 per cent of the votes in the second round, with the greatest support won in the voivodships of Podkarpackie (71.39 per cent) and Lublin (66.37 per cent). Similarly, in the parliamentary elections won by the 'Law and Justice' party with 37.58 per cent of the votes, the highest result was in the eastern voivodships of Poland – 55.09 per cent in Podkarpackie and 47.76 per cent in Lublin voivodship[2] (PKW 2015).

An important factor determining opportunities for the development of cross-border co-operation is the attitudes of inhabitants in each part of the borderland area to each other. Research by the Ukrainian 'Rating' Sociological Group, performed in 2015, commissioned by the International Republican Institute and conducted on a representative sample of 1,800 respondents, showed that Poland is a nation for whom Ukrainians have the greatest liking, with 58 per cent describing their relations with their western neighbour as warm or very warm, and only 5 per cent describing them as cold or very cold (Reiting 2015). The results of a similar study conducted in April 2014 showed that Poles enjoy the greatest liking in west Ukraine, with as many as 79 per cent of respondents from that region describing relations with Poland as warm or very warm and negative feelings being expressed by only 2 per cent (Debata 2014). The attitude of Poles to Ukraine and Ukrainians is less clear-cut. On the one hand a positive attitude and liking towards Ukrainians was expressed by roughly one-third of those studied (36 per cent), but the percentage expressing a negative opinion was also significant. Ukrainians, alongside Germans, are among the nations that provoke the most emotion, very seldom meeting with an indifferent response. At the same time it is worth emphasizing that the relations of Poles and Ukrainians have improved the most over recent years among all the nationalities included in the study, and the percentage of people declaring sympathy towards them rose in the years 1994–2015 by 27 percentage points (from 9 per cent to 36 per cent) (CBOS 2015).

Economy

Poland appears to be an example of successful transformation and economic achievement and this is the verdict presented by western economists and media (*The Economist* 2015; Schüssel 2015; Kowalczyk 2014). Despite considerable economic and social costs, such as increased unemployment and the collapse of numerous non-viable businesses, it is generally accepted that the transformation in this country has brought positive effects. However, as O. Subtelny (2000) wrote, in Ukraine the economy is the sphere which in the period of transformation provoked the most frustration, overriding all other issues, problems and achievements that Ukraine experienced from the beginnings of its independence. Between 1991 and 2000 Ukraine's economy shrank by 63 per cent, which was one of the worst results among post-soviet countries. Uncompetitive factories vegetated, production being discontinued in many of them, trade collapsed, unsafe mines became unprofitable and collective farms – mainly owing to the growing costs of production – were not able to maintain themselves (Subtelny 2000). At the beginning of the 1990s this country found itself on the brink of economic disaster as GDP had fallen each year in the last decade of the previous millenium, the inflation rate reached 5,371 per cent, 5 million jobs were lost in industry and nearly 70 per cent of society lived on the verge of poverty (Wilson 2002). Although the economy of the USSR had become more and more inefficient and its collapse, together with the inevitable consequences, was only a question of time – and this was also expected in Ukraine – the costs of independence, freeing themselves from the Russian economy and transforming into a market enconomy turned out to be, in the case of Ukraine, exceptionally high (Subtelny 2000). While in 1989 the GDP per capita in Poland and in Ukraine was at a similar level (and in Ukraine was even a little higher), today in Ukraine it is three times lower than that of its western neighbour.

Over the course of the past 20 years, three main periods can be distinguished in the Ukrainian economy. The first, called the transition period (1991–9), involved a drastic drop in GDP and widespread economic crisis. It was not until the end of the decade that the first signs of improvement appeared, and the first regions to experience GDP growth were Lviv and Volhynia oblasts. In the second stage (2000–2007) there was visible economic recovery. One of the economic city leaders was Lviv, while Vohynia oblast recorded a more than two-fold increase in GDP compared with 1999, which was the second best result in the country (after the capital, Kiev). The third period, which began in 2008, was the period of world crisis, which affected Ukraine more keenly than it did other post-socialist countries (Kabinet Ministriv Ukrainy 2014).

In analysing the economic potential of both western oblasts of Ukraine it is necessary to be aware that in the Second Polish Republic this area – like both borderland Polish voivodships – was counted among the so-called Poland 'B' category, with a predominantly agricultural profile and a particularly weak industrial sector. After World War II the Volhynia and Lviv oblasts functioned for almost half a century as a periphery of the soviet empire. Although they experienced accelerated industrialization from the 1950s, the scale of the investments made here cannot be compared with those in other areas of the country.

The Polish part of the borderland area also shows severe economic lag. In the period between the wars there were attempts to remedy this by creating the Central Industrial Region, one of the biggest projects of the Second Polish Republic, encompassing the area of today's Podkarpackie, Lublin and Świętokrzyskie voivodships. Despite the implementation of numerous investments following World War II, this area was unable to make up the disparity in development, which was not helped by the proximity of the 'closed' border with the Soviet Union. Today, owing to the deep-set structural lag, poor use of local assets (such as infrastructure, or technological and innovation potential) and low labour efficiency, this area comes within the poorly developed 'eastern Poland', this term carrying a perjorative connotation. Of course, this situation is reflected in economic indicators. In the years 1995–2004 all three sub-regions situated along the border with Ukraine (Bialski, Chełm-Zamość and Krosno-Przemyśl) were in a state of long-term stagnation, with the lowest results in the country (Gorzelak 2007a), and in the period 1998–2003 recorded a relentless drop in GDP, despite visible growth in its value on a national scale (by 15.1 per cent) (Gorzelak 2007b).

The situation of both borderland voivodships underwent some improvement after 2004, and the absorption of EU funds provided the impulse for positive change. However, bearing in mind that, in the last financial perspective, both Lublin voivodship and Podkarpackie voivodship were the biggest beneficiaries, receiving aid under three programmes (the Regional Operational Programme, the voivodship component of the Social Fund and the Eastern Poland Development Programme) totalling the equivalent of 2.1 per cent of their cumulative GDP from the years 2007–13 (only Warmińsko-Mazurskie and Podlaskie voivodships received more),[3] the development outcome achieved (including impact on GDP growth) was only modest. This was determined, above all, by the poor direction of EU aid, inefficient infrastructural investments and a lack of supply effects (Misiąg et al. 2013). The funds utilized brought mainly demand effects, and without question led also to improved living conditions for the inhabitants of eastern Poland, but did not remedy the severe development lags compared with the rest of the country. It is worth mentioning that under the EU financial perspective of 2014–20 both voivodships of eastern Poland are to receive, relatively, the most financial aid, which under the Regional Operational Programmes alone (and thus without participating in nationwide programmes or special eastern Poland programmes) will amount to €2.23 billion in Lublin region and €2.10 billion in Podkarpackie region, which corresponds to 14.2 per cent and 13.5 per cent of GDP in both voivodships in 2013.[4]

The GDP generated in the Polish–Ukrainian borderland in 2013 was €38914.5 million (Table 2.3). Around 40 per cent of this value was generated in the Lublin and Podkarpackie voivodships and 15 per cent in Lviv oblast, but less than 5 per cent in Volhynia oblast. These values show the disproportionate nature of the Polish and Ukrainian parts of the borderland in terms of their economic potential. At the same time we should be aware that the share of Lublin and Podkarpackie voivodships in Polish GDP in 2013 came to 4.0 per cent and 3.9 per cent, which can be deemed fairly low, considering the fact that the population potential of both regions comes to about 5.5 per cent. A similar situation is present in both western Ukrainian regions. The share of Lviv oblast in Ukraine's GDP comes to 4.2 per cent, and that of Volhynia 1.4 per cent, while their respective demographic potentials are 5.6 per cent and 2.3 per cent of the Ukrainian population.

Table 2.3 Gross domestic product in 2013

	GDP (in mill €)	*GDP per capita (in €)*
POLAND	394479.4	10245.78
Lublin voivodship	15656.4	7246.59
Podkarpackie voivodship	15501.6	7282.31
UKRAINE	140683.2	3092.68
Lviv oblast	5851.2	1830.96
Volhynia oblast	1905.3	2304.01

Source: Own estimation, on the basis of Central Statistical Office of Poland, State Statistics Service of Ukraine, Eurostat and World Bank data.

At the same time the Polish–Ukrainian borderland regions have shown a diversified development rate in recent years. In constant prices the estimated annual average growth in GDP in the Lublin voivodship year-on-year was 3.4 per cent and in Podkarpackie was 4.1 per cent, compared with an average 4.0 per cent in Poland, which indicates a slight tendency towards divergence in these regions. Similar GDP growth rates were recorded in Volhynia (average 4.0 per cent), and lower in Lviv (average 1.8 per cent), although these values in recent years were close to or slightly higher than those in Ukraine as a whole. For example, in the years 2010–13 GDP in Lviv oblast grew on average by 3.0 per cent year-on-year, while in Volhynia oblast it grew by 2.4 per cent – that is, the same as in the country as a whole (Table 2.4).

In all the borderland regions the economic indicator of GDP calculated per inhabitant was distinctly lower than the average values for Poland and Ukraine. In 2013 the value of this indicator in Podkarpackie voivodship was €7282.3, while in Lublin voivodship it was €7246.6, corresponding respectively to 71.1 per cent and 70.7 per cent of the national level (€10245.8), giving these regions the last two places in the country. The GDP per capita in the Lviv oblast came to €2304.0 (that is, 74.5 per cent of the national average), while in the Volhynia oblast it was €1831.0 (that is, 59.2 per cent of the Ukrainian average). In this respect these units came 13th and 22nd out of a total of 27 Ukrainian regions.

In all the borderland regions the greatest share of Gross Value Added (GVA) was generated by services. Their share in the GVA structure ranged from 64.9 per cent in Volhynia oblast to 75.3 per cent in Lublin oblast, while in the remaining regions it slightly exceeded 70.0 per cent. The share of industry in generating GVA in the regions was highest in Podkarpackie voivodship (27.1 per cent), was similar in Lublin voivodship and Lviv oblast (20.4 per cent and 20.3 per cent respectively) and lowest in Volhynia oblast (18.3 per cent). At the same time, 16.8 per cent of GVA in this region was generated by agriculture. Half that amount (8.6 per cent) came from farming in Lviv oblast. Meanwhile, in Lublin and Podkarpackie voivodships the agricultural sector generated 5.9 per cent and 1.9 per cent GVA respectively. The structure of GVA creation in the borderland regions differed from that of the countries as a whole. Despite the fact that the significance of agriculture in the economic structure of the borderland regions is

Table 2.4 Gross domestic product growth rates in the years 2004–13

	2004	*2005*	*2006*	*2007*	*2008*	*2009*	*2010*	*2011*	*2012*	*2013*	*Annual average growth (2004–13)*
POLAND	105.1	103.5	106.2	107.2	103.9	102.6	103.7	105.0	101.6	101.3	104.0
Lublin voivodship	102.6	101.9	104.7	106.4	104.8	100.8	103.7	105.5	101.7	101.6	103.4
Podkarpackie voivodship	105.5	105.7	105.6	105.1	105.3	101.3	103.6	105.8	100.6	102.3	104.1
UKRAINE	112.1	102.7	107.3	107.9	102.3	85.2	104.1	105.2	100.2	100.0	102.7
Lviv oblast	105.2	98.1	108.3	105.8	100.7	88.3	102.3	108.7	102	98.8	101.8
Wolhynia oblast	119.0	103.7	103.5	112.1	106.1	86.0	100.2	105.3	104.8	99.3	104.0

Source: Own study, on the basis of Central Statistical Office of Poland and State Statistics Service of Ukraine data.

diminishing, in the case of Lviv oblast and Lublin voivodship its share was still nearly twice the average in either Ukraine or Poland. At the same time, the significance of industry and construction was visibly less than the national average in the economic structure of all the borderland regions with the exception of Podkarpackie voivodship.

The adverse structure of GVA is further impeded by low work efficiency. This is apparent in every region of the Polish–Ukrainian borderland, and in every form of activity. The GVA calculated per worker in Poland was €34,900, while in Lublin and Podkarpackie voivodships it was one-third lower, amounting to €24,000 and €23,600 respectively. A particularly adverse influence on this state of affairs was the situation in agriculture. Bearing in mind its semi-subsistence character and its large share in the employment structure (38.5 per cent in Lublin voivodship and 32.8 per cent in Podkarpackie voivodship), the GVA per worker in Lublin region was half that in the nation as a whole and in Podkarpackie as much as four times lower. This negative disparity, though less pronounced, was also displayed in productivity in industry and services. Work efficiency also significantly deviated from the national average in both western Ukrainian oblasts. For example, in Lviv oblast the GVA generated by one worker both in industry and in agriculture was around 40 per cent below the national level. Poor work efficiency in the Polish–Ukrainian borderland area thus results both from the specific nature of the economy in regions of the macro-region (with an above-average share of farming and a below-average share of industry) and the below-average productivity of individual sectors.

This economic structure is reflected in the labour market. In the employment structure (Table 2.5) a noticeably low share of people work in industry and a significantly higher share work in farming, which relates to the above-mentioned features of the economic structure of the borderland region. Owing to the particular significance of farming in Polish and Ukrainian borderland regions it is worth taking a closer look at this sector. In the 1990s Poland and Ukraine adopted different development models in the farming sector. In Poland, collective farms

Table 2.5 Structure of employment by economic sectors in 2014

	Economic sector			
	Agriculture	*Industry*	*Construction*	*Services*
	in %			
POLAND	16.4	20.3	5.6	57.7
Lublin voivodship	38.1	13.0	4.2	44.7
Podkarpackie voivodship	32.3	19.7	4.6	43.4
UKRAINE	17.1	16.0	4.1	62.8
Lviv oblast	18.2	14.9	6.5	60.4
Wolhynia oblast	23.4	12.8	2.8	61.0

Source: Own study, on the basis of Central Statistical Office of Poland and State Statistics Service of Ukraine data.

(State Farms – so-called *PGR*) were liquidated, and the majority of agricultural land was transferred into the ownership of individual farmers. In Ukraine, however, a largely unsuccessful attempt was made to reform the collective farms, as a result of which so-called farming industries operate there alongside individual farms (Lerman et al. 2007). However, what distinguishes both the western regions of Ukraine from the rest of the country is the above-average share of farmland owned by private individuals, amounting to 70.9 per cent in Volhynia and 74.9 per cent in Lviv oblast, compared with just 43.6 per cent in the whole country.

Certain socio-economic features have become characteristic in the agricultural practices of the Polish and Ukrainian borderland, such as the functioning of small farms based on dual occupations. In many cases there is a tendency to limit farm production and focus on subsistence, thereby not participating in the agricultural market, which is particularly inefficient (Górz 2005). This situation is not helped by the fragmentation of farms. Although over several years their average size has grown, the area of almost half of the farms in Lublin voivodship is not more than five hectares. Even greater fragmentation prevails in Podkarpackie voivodship, in which as many as 81 per cent of farms belong to the above category. At the same time, the high percentage of those employed in farming should come as no surprise. As B. Górz (2005) points out, in the east and south-east of Poland farming has become the 'stabilizing factor in the difficult conditions of the local labour market, acting as a kind of "storage space" for the large numbers of unemployed' – people who take up temporary work, often abroad, for whom the farm provides some kind of economic base, guaranteeing 'minimal subsistence in the form of home produce and providing a sense of social security thanks to the farm insurance system'. For both the Polish and the Ukrainian sides of the borderland it is justifiable to claim that the percentage of farm workers testifies to the continuing phenomenon of 'hidden unemployment', reflecting the difficult situation in the labour market.

A good indicator of the condition of the labour market is the level of employment among people of productive age, which in both Polish voivodships amounted to 50 per cent and was not much below the national level. This indicator reached higher levels than in Ukraine as a whole but lower levels than in the two oblasts of western Ukraine: 54.9 per cent in Volhynia oblast and 55.3 per cent in Lviv oblast. With the exception of Lviv oblast (8.6 per cent), all the borderland regions showed higher than average unemployment (according to the International Labour Organization), which in 2014 amounted to 14.0 per cent in Podkarpackie voivodship and 9.9 per cent in Lublin voivodship (compared with 9.0 per cent in Poland) as well as 9.9 per cent in Volhynia oblast (compared with national levels of 9.3 per cent). The average monthly salary was significantly lower on the Ukrainian side of the borderland. In Volhynia oblast this was €145 and in Lviv oblast €158, representing respectively 78.2 per cent and 81.1 per cent of the average salary in Ukraine. The average salary in both Polish regions was lower than national levels but several times greater than in the Ukrainian part of the borderland. In 2014 it was €862 in Lublin voivodship and €816 in Podkarpackie voivodship; that is, 90.0 per cent and 85.2 per cent of the Polish average.

The main industries in Volhynia oblast are the agri-food industry (e.g. the Torczyn production plant), the wood industry and the machine industry, concentrated in urban centres such as Lutsk, Kovel, Novovolynsk and Volodymyr-Volynskyi. In Volhynia oblast coal mining is also of major significance. A better situation in terms of industrial development can be seen in Lviv oblast. However, the multiple industries of this region are mainly concentrated in the capital. The industrial plants found here include those related to metallurgy and machinery, electro-technology, chemicals, textiles and food production. The remaining industrial centres are connected with mining and processing natural resources. This is the case in Drohobych, Boryslav and Stryi in the south of the region, where crude oil is extracted and refined, Sokal and Chervonohrad in the north, where coalmining takes place, and the regions of Yavoriv and Zhydachiv, where sulphur is mined. As M. Flaga observes (2006), in the period of economic transformation the industrial complex present in the area became not an aid but an burden, and was the cause of many problems.

A similar challenge is presented by the share of industry on the Polish side of the borderland. In many towns of this region there was, almost until the end of the twentieth century, some kind of industrial monoculture. Plants such as WSK Rzeszów, WSK-PZL Mielec, WSK-PZL Świdnik, WSK Gorzyce (aircraft industry), Stalowa Wola Steelworks (arms industry), the furniture factories of Sokołów Małopolski and Kolbuszowa (furniture industry), Stomil in Dębica, the chemical plant in Nowa Sarzyna, the Azoty chemical plant in Puławy (chemical industry), URSUS and the truck factory in Lublin, the FŁK-Kraśnik bearings factory and the construction equipment factory in Janów Lubelski (automotive and machinery industry) employed several thousand workers and displayed low efficiency, low innovativeness and limited trade links. Some of them underwent successful restructuring, often falling into the hands of foreign investors (Kozaczka 2010). An example of skilful adjustment to changing business conditions in the mining sector is the Bogdanka coal mine, which stands out as a positive landmark on the map of unprofitable industries of this type in Poland.

Because lack of capital was an important barrier to regional development in the Polish–Ukrainian borderland – including the industrial sector – high hopes were placed in foreign direct investment. In the years 2007–10 the annual average inflow of investment to the Polish–Ukrainian cross-border area was €209 million in Podkarpackie voivodship, €188.8 million in Lviv oblast, €132.8 million in Lublin voivodship and €43.6 million in Volhynia oblast. The inflow of foreign direct investment to borderland regions in reference to nationwide values was insignificant, however, which testifies to the Polish–Ukrainian borderland's low attractiveness for investment. The share of Lviv and Volhynia oblasts in the inflow of foreign direct investment to Ukraine was 3.4 per cent and 0.8 per cent respectively, while the share of Podkarpackie and Lublin voivodships in the inflow of foreign direct investment to Poland was 1.9 per cent and 1.2 per cent respectively.

In order to attract foreign capital to the borderland region several Special Economic Zones were created. The aim of their activities is to encourage investment and stimulate economic development by, among other things, developing specific business areas, creating jobs, developing brownfield assets and increasing the competitiveness of products and services. The first unit of this type in Poland was created in Podkarpackie voivodship. In September 1995 the Special Economic Zone Euro-Park Mielec was created as a 20-year pilot zone. The positive experience of its operation encouraged authorities to create further areas of this type, including the Tarnobrzeg Special Economic Zone Euro-park WISŁOSAN (in 1997) and the 'Starachowice' Special Economic Zone, each with sub-zones in the Polish part of the Polish–Ukrainian borderland. They quite quickly became centres of growth and economic development in the region (Kozaczka 2010). And although the idea of Special Economic Zones has attracted widespread criticism, the benefits derived from their activity have provided the argument for extending their operation to 2026.

Similarly, in Ukraine in the years 1996–2000 12 Special Economic Zones were created, of which three were located in the Polish–Ukrainian borderland. The first, 'Javoriv' Special Economic Zone, is situated barely more than a dozen kilometres west of Lviv, near the Polish border. An important argument in favour of this location was the proximity of the border crossing 'Krakovets', which it was hoped would support the development of infrastructure relating to storage facilities, transport services and production. An important motive for creating the Zones was also the drive to save jobs, which were under threat in the region owing to reductions in mining and the production of sulphur (*Zakon Ukrainy Pro special'nu ekonomichnu zonu 'Yavoriv'* 1999). The second zone created in the Lviv oblast, 'Kurortopolis Truskavets' presents a different picture. This was intended to stimulate investment and innovation targeted at maintaining and utilizing the natural therapeutic resources of the Carpathian resort of Truskavets (*Zakon Ukrainy O special'noi ekonomicheskoi zone turistsko-rekreacionnogo tipa 'Kurortopolis Truskavets'* 1999). The third economic zone, 'Interport Kovel', situated in Volhynia oblast and covering an area of around 57 hectares, was set up with a view to utilizing the potential offered by its location on the Gdańsk–Odessa international transport corridor, developing international links and developing the transport and production infrastructure (President of Ukraine 1999). Moreover, in Ukraine, nine so-called Priority Development Areas were set up, one of which was located in Volhynia oblast (the city of Novovolynsk and the urban-type settlement Zhovtneve). These were set up for a period of 20 years, and in conformance with the Act on Special Economic Zones they were granted relief – primarily, lower income tax rates and reduced land charges.

The Special Economic Zones in Ukraine still exist officially, although in 2005 the Tymoshenko government ended the tax relief, allegedly in order to eliminate abuse of the law and tax evasion. Thus the SEZs present in Ukraine today do not actually have the same status and should be regarded as examples of Priority Development Zones (Shutova 2013). The intentions of the Azarov government for these zones was supposed to be so-called Industrial Parks, targeted at stimulating economic growth through drawing investment (including foreign investment) into the field of industrial production or scientific research activity. Their essence is therefore similar to SEZs. In line with the Supreme Council of Justice Act of 2012 on Industrial Parks, investors can count on specified forms of relief and preferential rates, including financial support in the form of interest-free loans and exemption from duty on goods intended for equipping a given industrial park and on goods used for certain activities. This development has been upheld by the new A. Yatsenyuk government. Following the adoption of the bill, 12 industrial parks were created, of which only four actually began to function. This group includes the Lviv Industrial Park 'Riasne 2', in which authorities are conducting intensive talks with potential investors, although, owing to the existing legal ambiguities, they have not yet managed to come to any binding agreements (UNIAN 2015).

The state of the cross-border economy is largely determined by conditions for conducting business. These conditions can be assessed using the research findings of international institutions, including the World Bank. According to the findings of the report 'Doing Business 2015', showing the level of ease of running a business in 2014, Poland occupied 32nd place and Ukraine 96th out of nearly 200 countries in the study. It is worth stressing that both nations are among the leaders in terms of the greatest improvement in conditions for doing business in recent years. These changes are reflected in the advances that Poland and Ukraine have made in the general classification in the space of just two years – in this period Poland advanced by 23 places (from 55th place in 2013) and Ukraine by 41 places (from 137th place in 2013) (World Bank 2015). The ease of conducting business is also shown by the Index of Economic Freedom, prepared by *The Wall Street Journal* and Heritage Foundation. In the table for 2016 Poland was in 39th place (18th in Europe), a significant advance, and was first among the group of countries that are classified as 'partly free' (even so, this is a worse result than most Central European countries), while Ukraine found itself in 162nd place out of 178 countries classified, occupying the last place out of all European countries. Poland was positively rated for its 'lawful government' and its relatively low levels of corruption, while negative ratings were given for its excessive fiscalism and overgrown bureaucracy. Meanwhile, with reference to Ukraine, particularly negative ratings were given in respect of ownership rights, low market-openness and ubiquitous corruption (Miller and Kim 2016). The problem of corruption in Ukraine has been highlighted for many years by Transparency International. In the most recent ranking, 'Corruption Perceptions Index 2015', Poland is in 30th place, while Ukraine comes in 130th place (Transparency International 2015). A further problem is the share of the informal economy. According to various sources, the share of the shadow economy in the GDP of Ukraine reached between 20 and 50 per cent (Bochi and Povoroznyk 2014). According to the findings of F. Schneider, its share in the Ukrainian economy at the beginning of the millennium was the highest of all European countries (Schneider and Klinglmair 2004). The problem of the shadow economy also affects Poland, although on a much smaller scale than in Ukraine, and is estimated by the Central Statistical Office of Poland at around 19.1 per cent.

One of the most important factors shaping socio-economic development is communication and transport infrastructure. Communication routes which provide access to an area increase its value, contributing to growth in the competitiveness of a given area, in terms of both attracting investment (and thus the possibility of gaining outside growth factors) and increasing export opportunities.

The Polish–Ukrainian borderland is located on the pan-European corridor, which makes it a relatively important transit area on the European and even the inter-continental scale (Figure 2.7). Its situation close to the most important European transport routes could turn out to be a major factor mitigating the negative consequences of its peripheral position in the macro-region (Kawałko 2005). In view of the importance of road freight and passenger transport, a key role is played

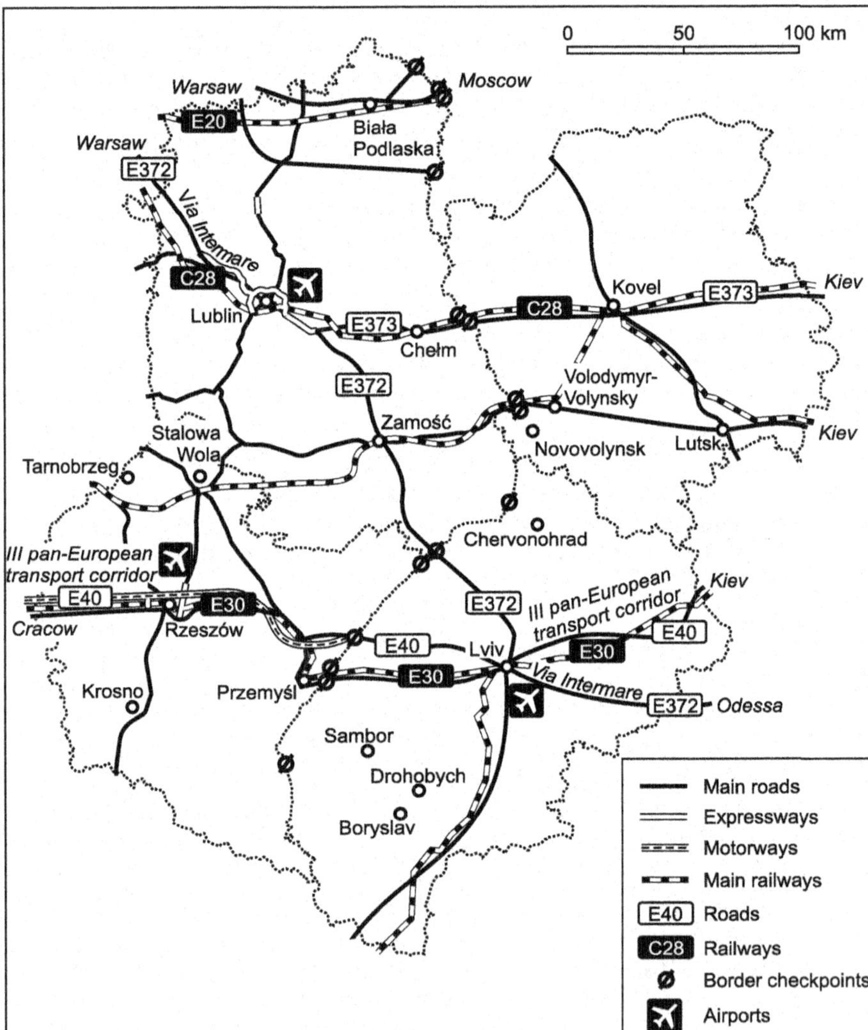

Figure 2.7 Main transport corridors on Polish–Ukrainian borderland

Source: Andrzej Jakubowski.

here by access to road infrastructure. In the east–west network the most important route is the E40 European route, the longest in Europe (over 8,000 kilometres), which lies on the III pan-European transport corridor,[5] leading from Calais, on the English Channel, through Brussels (Belgium), Cologne, Dresden (Germany), Wrocław, Cracow and Rzeszów (Poland). Via the border crossing at Korczowa-Krakovets it links Poland and Ukraine, leading on towards the east through Lviv, Kiev, Kharkiv (Ukraine), Volgograd, Astrakhan (Russia), Tashkent (Uzbekistan), Bishkek (Kirgistan) and Almaty (Kazakhstan) and becoming the bridge between eastern Europe and central Asia. This route ends in Kazakhstan, not far from the Chinese border. In the area of the Polish–Ukrainian borderland it is served by the Polish A4 motorway (of which the last remaining section, from Rzeszów to Jarosław, is due to be completed in 2016), and by the M11 and M6 on the Ukrainian side. This is one of the most extensive transport options on the Europe–Asia axis, although its potential is not sufficiently utilized – this route takes only 1 per cent of road transit from Europe to the east (Lipińska-Słota 2010).

Of less significance on the European scale, but important in terms of Polish–Ukrainian cross-border links, are the international routes E372 and E373. The first of these, connecting Warsaw and Lviv via Lublin and Zamość, lies along the planned transport corridor *Via Intermare*, creating the shortest link between Gdańsk (on the Baltic coast) and Odessa (on the Black Sea). The second links Lublin and Kiev via Chełm, Kovel and Korosten, creating the shortest link between the capital of Ukraine and western Europe. It is worth mentioning the national highway S19, which does not have a Polish–Ukrainian cross-border dimension but is an important part of the regional transport network, providing not only a backbone to eastern Poland but potentially an important transit route connecting the Baltic states (Klaipeda in Lithuania) with the Balkans. At one time Poland attempted to have the above-mentioned route (as a *Via Carpathian* route) incorporated into the Trans-European Transport Network (TEN-T) as one of the priorities of EU transport infrastructure policy to 2030, but this was turned down by the European Commission.

No less important in terms of access, especially in terms of freight transport, is the railway infrastructure. This form of transport accounts for over half, and in Poland around 13 per cent, of freight transport. In the trans-European dimension the railway line connecting Poland and Ukraine is the E30/C-E30 line on the route from Berlin to Moscow via Dresden, Zgorzelec, Wrocław, Cracow, Rzeszów, Medyka/Shehyni, Lviv and Kiev. From an international and transnational point of view the railway line C28 is also very important, being the shortest connection between Warsaw and Kiev, with a short section of broad-gauge track on Polish territory, leading from Zawadówka to the state border.

The differing gauges of rail track are the main barrier to rail transport development between Poland (and therefore western Europe) and Ukraine. The differing track gauges in Poland (1435 millimetre) and Ukraine (1520 millimetre) necessitate changing the truck chassis, which significantly prolongs the time taken to cross the border, negatively affecting the efficiency of this form of transport. This is why the Broad-gauge Steelworks Line, built back in the 1970s, has such potential. It was constructed to import iron ore from Kryvyi Rih in Ukraine and export Polish coal and sulphur to the USSR. Linking the Ukrainian broad-gauge rail network with Upper Silesia (terminating in Sławków), it is the most western-reaching railway line with a track gauge of 1520 millimetres. It allows the transport of freight from Ukraine and thus also from Russia, central Asia and even the Far East without the need for time-consuming transhipment at the border. For some years plans have been in existence to make wider use of the Broad-gauge Steelworks Line infrastructure for rail freight transport from Far Eastern countries to Western Europe. This means of transport is not only cheaper but many days faster than the alternative sea route.

A major threat to the route that lies on the Polish–Ukrainian cross-border region is the growing significance of alternative routes, including two routes included in the TEN-T: *Rhine–Danube*, an offshoot of which leads from Munich through Prague and through Slovenian territory to the Ukrainian border, and the *Mediterranean*, leading to Ukraine through Hungary (*Infrastructure – TEN-T – Connecting Europe*). In terms of rail transport, a competing route is the international railway line E20/C-E20, belonging to the II Pan-European Transport Corridor joining Berlin with Moscow, especially in the context of the concept presented in 2013 by the Chinese leader Xi Jinping of a 'New Silk Road' – a network of infrastructure connections (mainly land and sea transport corridors) connecting China with western Europe (Kaczmarski 2015).

Despite its favourable proximity to an international transport corridor, the Polish–Ukrainian borderland features weak road and rail infrastructure density, which determines access to and the internal coherence of the macro-region. The density of the surfaced road network calculated per 100 square kilometres is 28.5 kilometres in Volhynia oblast and 91.1 kilometres in Podkarpackie (in comparison, the density of the German road network is 180 kilometres). Particularly troublesome is the insufficient network of fast roads, such as motorways and expressways. Other problems are the relatively poor quality of existing roads and the bad state of their surfaces, which compromise safety, and the lack of bypasses, which means transit traffic often has to go through built-up areas.

However, much progress has been made in recent years in the area of transport infrastructure. On the Polish side of the borderland the last missing section of the A4 motorway between Rzeszów and Jarosław (part of the E40 corridor) is nearing completion. This investment was originally planned for completion in 2012, as part of preparations for the Euro 2012 Football Championships, organized jointly by Poland and Ukraine. This event prompted the resurfacing of roads on the E373 and E40 routes in Ukraine, although this work was not aimed at converting these roads to motorway standards. There are also no plans in the near future to extend the E372 and E373 roads on the Polish side to the Ukrainian border, and the expressway that was begun in 2015 along the above routes covers only the section from Warsaw to Piaski, a few kilometres to the south-east of Lublin.

An opportunity to transform the peripheral nature of the region in communication terms is the wider use of air transport. In the Polish–Ukrainian borderland there are three civilian international airports – Lviv, Świdnik, near Lublin, and Jasionka, near Rzeszów. In terms of passenger volume, the largest is Rzeszów

International Airport, which served 645,200 passengers in 2015 (Rzeszów International Airport 2016). The Danilo Halitskyi International Airport in Lviv, with a modern terminal building completed in 2012 (on the eve of Euro 2012), served nearly 570,600 passengers in 2015 (making it the fourth largest in Ukraine), flying to 11 destinations (Danylo Halytskyi International Airport 'Lviv' 2016). The youngest airport of the borderland and one of the youngest regional airports in Poland is Lublin Świdnik Airport, which opened in December 2012. In 2015 it served 265,000 passengers, and recently its flight network has been greatly expanded (Lublin Airport 2016). However, the volume of passenger traffic at this airport is somewhat lower than was expected.

The socio-economic situation in the Polish–Ukrainian borderland against the background of European regions

The processes of integration taking place in Europe are shaping a certain common space in which we can distinguish centres as well as peripheral areas. Naturally, the phenomenon of peripherality is relative and can be viewed from a number of perspectives: geographical–communication, economic, socio-demographic and cultural, political–administrative, and spatial (Miszczuk 2013). This does not change the fact that these areas remain dependent on the centres (core areas), only copying innovations and being unable to generate their own growth factors. In analysing the European space, R. Domański (2002) sees the western part of Europe, including the territories of France, Germany, Austria, Switzerland, Belgium, the Netherlands, Luxembourg, the greater part of Great Britain, the north of Italy as well as part of Spain, Denmark and the Czech Republic, as the core area (the so-called Pentagon). Meanwhile, he counted the Polish–Ukrainian borderland within the Central-Eastern and Eastern European Peripheries (Figure 2.8).

Some idea of the potential of the Polish–Ukrainian borderland can be gained by comparing the basic characteristics of the region with the European Union. The four regions of the Polish–Ukrainian cross-border area occupy an area roughly equal to 1.9 per cent of the area of the EU and their population accounts for 1.6 per cent of EU demographic potential, while in 2013 they generated a cumulative GDP equal to 0.3 per cent of EU GDP. It is this last value that shows most distinctly the relative weakness of the Polish–Ukrainian borderland in the EU setting.

There is no doubt that both borderland voivodships belong to the least developed regions both in Poland and in the whole European Union (Figure 2.9). It is worth mentioning that, in the years 2004–7 – and thus up until the accession of Bulgaria and Romania – the GDP (per capita in Purchasing Power Standards (PPS)) in both voivodships was the lowest among all the regions of the united Europe. The GDP per inhabitant in Lublin and Podkarpackie voivodships in 2013 came to 70.7 per cent and 71.1 per cent of the Polish average, respectively. The purchasing power of the population in both voivodships was half the EU average (Poland – 68 per cent of the EU average). And, although they belong to the least developed regions of the European Union, this level of development appears

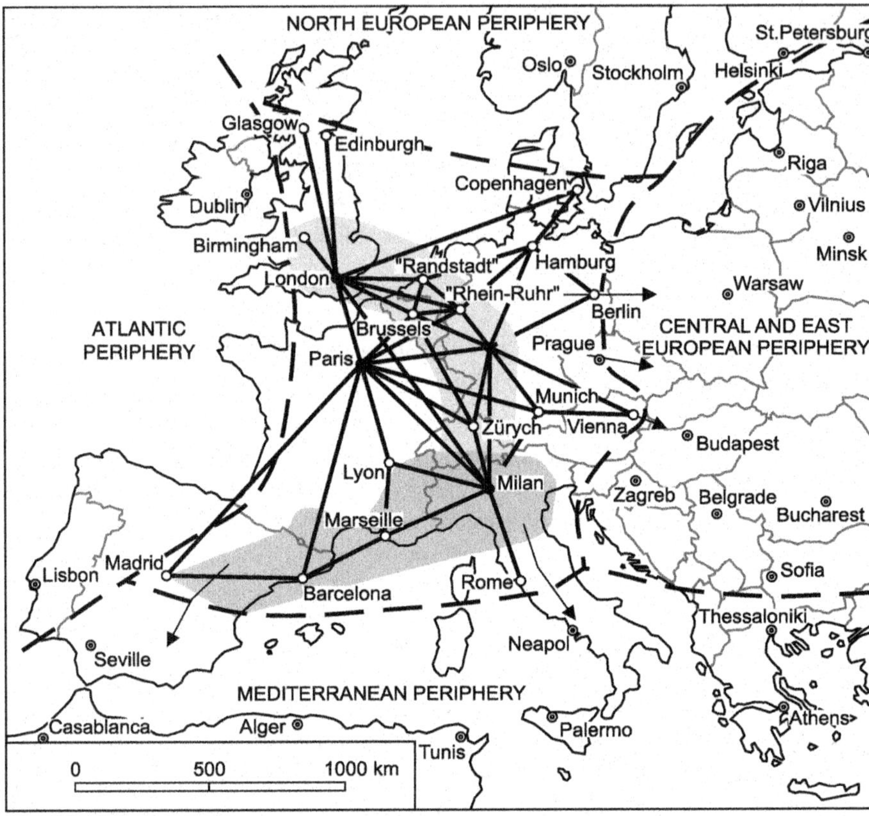

Figure 2.8 Central and peripheral areas in Europe

Source: Domański (2002).

relatively favourable in comparison with the areas on the other side of the border. Allowing for purchasing power, the GDP per capita in Lviv oblast was around 18.9 per cent of the EU average, while in Volhynia oblast it was 15.0 per cent (Ukraine – 25.4 per cent).[6] In the general classification, including 296 statistical units at European Union regional level (NUTS2) as well as all the Ukrainian oblasts, Podkarpackie voivodship came in 255th place in terms of GDP at purchasing power parity per inhabitant, Lublin voivodship one place below it, Lviv oblast in 282nd place and Volhynia oblast in 291st.

The analysed administrative units thus belong to the least developed regions in Europe, as well as within their respective countries, bearing clear traits of peripherality in a geographical as well as an economic sense. Moreover, the development of the regions situated on each side of the border is marked by considerable asymmetry to the detriment of the Ukrainian side, which, considering the geopolitical conditions pertaining until the present, only intensifies the difficulties in

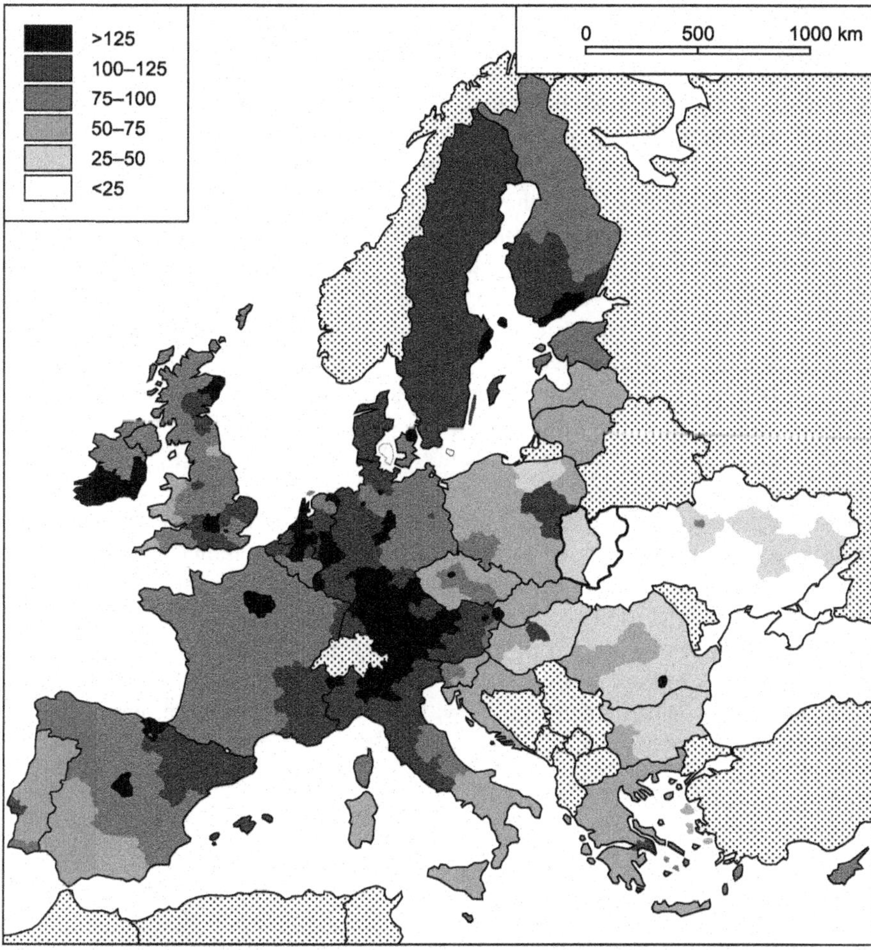

Figure 2.9 Gross Domestic Product (per capita in PPS) by region at NUTS2 level in 2013

Source: Krzysztof Łoboda, on the basis of Eurostat and State Statistics Service of Ukraine.

developing advanced forms of cross-border co-operation and increasing the cohesion of the Polish–Ukrainian borderland region.

However, GDP per capita is an imperfect measure, and takes only the economic dimension into account. In response to the limitations of this indicator, other measures have been considered, including the Human Development Index (HDI) elaborated by the United Nations Development Programme (UNDP), which focuses on the three essential elements of human life: life expectancy (health), knowledge (education) and a level of income which allows a decent living. The GDP per capita is thereby taken into consideration, but is treated as just one of several indicators for performing analysis.

In the original methodology used by the UNDP the level of social development at country level is compared by assessing not only GDP per capita but also data on the average life expectancy at birth and two indices relating to knowledge – the mean years of schooling and the expected years of schooling (UNDP 2015). Meanwhile, for many years there have been attempts to use the HDI index for making comparisons at a regional level. In the Country Report on Social Development Poland 2012, elaborated by the Project Office of UNDP (2012), the HDI ranking methodology was applied with the aim of assessing the level of development in regional and local administrative units at NUTS2 and NUTS3 levels. In this report the health indicator was represented by the index of life expectancy at birth and the aggregated mortality rate due to cancer and heart disease, the educational dimension by the percentage of children in preschool education (in the 3–4 year age group) and the average secondary school exam results (at 16 years old, for maths and science subjects) and the economic dimension by the level of declared income in tax returns. Attempts to adapt the methodology of the HDI index for regional analyses were made by M. Kowerski and S. Matkowski (Kowerski and Matkowski 2005). For the purposes of their Modified HDI, they adopted a formula incorporating the GDP index, the life expectancy index and the education index, calculated as the number of students per 1,000 inhabitants.

In order to show the level of social development in the regions of the Polish–Ukrainian borderland in the context of European Union regions in 2013, a modified model of HDI was used, incorporating comparative indices representative of three key spheres of human life – health, education and affluence – to construct a Regional Human Development Index with the following formula, based on the geometric mean:

$$RHDI = \sqrt[3]{\left(I_{Health} \times I_{Education} \times I_{Income}\right)}$$

Where:

I_{Health} – life expectancy;

$I_{\text{Education}}$ – students in tertiary education as a percentage of the population aged 20–24 years;

I_{Income} – regional gross domestic product (PPS per inhabitant).

The data for individual regional units of the EU and Ukraine were standardized, with extreme values taken to be:

- For life expectancy: 20 and 85 years (in line with UNDP methodology);
- Education levels: 3 (minimum value of the analogical index for the Seychelles according to the World Bank) and 100;
- For GDP (per capita in PPS): €73.57 (which equates to a minimal value of $100, in line with the HDI methodology) and €86,400.00 (the level for the Inner London region). In addition, in the case of the last index a logarithmic operation was performed to reflect the non-linear growth of real incomes (Kowerski and Matkowski 2005).

The results obtained fall within the interval 0 to 1. In order to make the results more readable, the UNDP categorization system was adopted, which defines the following sub-intervals:

- a result < 0.550 indicates a low level of human development;
- a result in the interval 0.550–0.699 indicates a medium level of human development;
- a result in the interval 0.700–0.799 indicates a high level of human development;
- a result > 0.800 indicates a very high level of human development.

According to the findings, Lublin voivodship (0.748) and Lviv oblast (0.717) exhibit a high level of human development, Podkarpackie voivodship (0.654) a medium level and Volhynia oblast (0.549) a low level. However, it should be emphasized that the values achieved by this last region were only slightly below the lowest sub-interval value for countries with a medium level (by 0.001). Meanwhile, Lublin voivodship and Lviv oblasts recorded higher values than the country level (0.733 for Poland and 0.693 for Ukraine), while Podkarpackie voivodship and Volhynia oblast recorded lower values (Figure 2.10).

The best result in the 296 territorial units was achieved in the Région de Bruxelles-Capitale/Brussels Hoofdstedelijk Gewest in Belgium, while the lowest was Severozapaden in Bulgaria (0.257). Among borderland regions in the general classification, Lublin voivodship came highest, in 125th place, followed by Lviv oblast in 163rd place, Podkarpackie voivodship in 235th place and finally Volhynia oblast in 272nd place. In conclusion, it is worth emphasizing that each of the regions of the Polish–Ukrainian borderland features relatively higher levels of human development, measured by the RHDI index, in comparison with other European regions, than levels of economic development, measured exclusively by means of GDP (per capita in PPS).

Analysis of GDP per capita and RHDI revealed significant diversification in the sphere of economic and human potential in the European space as well as their relatively low levels in the case of the Polish–Ukrainian borderland. However, owing to their broadly defined socio-economic potential and level of development it is worth performing some kind of typology of regional units, taking into account their differing characteristics, including structural features. In order to achieve such a typology, effective use can be made of multi-dimensional analysis methods to distinguish reasonably homogeneous groups of units (subsets) that are alike in terms of the statistical sets of diagnostic traits adopted in the analysis. As a result we are able to obtain, from one diversified group, several homogeneous subsets which meet the criterion of separability and completeness (Mirkin 2005).

The cluster analysis method performed in this study using the k-mean algorithm is a type of non-hierarchical method. It requires formulating an a priori assumption regarding the group size that is to be achieved by means of the analysis. For each of the sets, defined in advance, one element is chosen to act as its 'representative'. The division of the remaining elements of the set is based on finding those which are least removed from these 'representatives'. An unquestionable advantage of the k-mean method is the guarantee of obtaining clusters

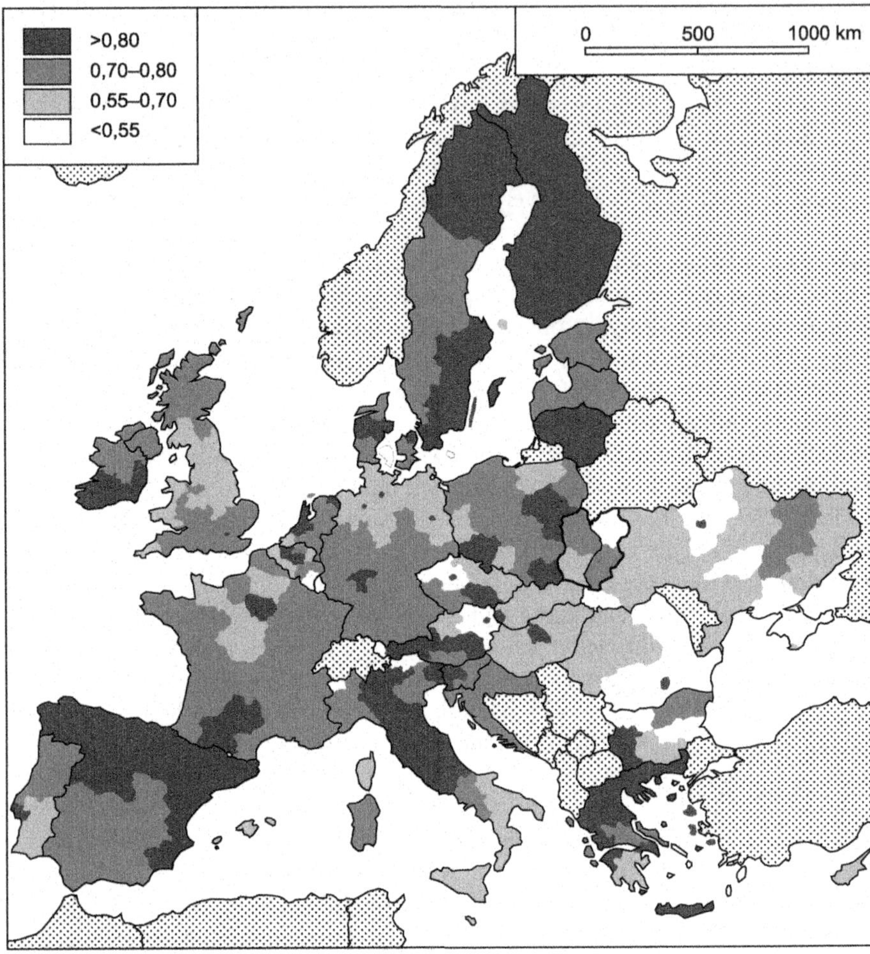

Figure 2.10 HDI by regions at NUTS2 level in 2013

Source: Krzysztof Łoboda, on the basis of Eurostat and State Statistics Service of Ukraine.

that differ from one another to the greatest possible extent. This results from the assumptions of the method themselves, placing objects in different clusters leading to a distribution which simultaneously ensures their maximum internal homogeneity as well as maximum heterogeneity between clusters. It is worth underlining that this method seems to be the most effective means of grouping when analysing a large number of objects.

To achieve the fullest possible profile of the issue in question, bearing in mind the availability of comparative data at NUTS2 level for the 296 regions of the European Union and Ukraine in the same year (2013), the following set of diagnostic traits were used to analyse the socio-economic diversification of the European space.

These diagnostic traits describe to the widest possible extent the multi-faceted nature of the analysed phenomenon:

1 Regional gross domestic product (PPS per inhabitant) – stimulant
2 Economic activity rate – stimulant
3 Unemployment rate (according to MOP methodology) – de-stimulant
4 Share of population at ages 15–64 employed in agriculture, forestry and fishing – de-stimulant
5 Total intramural R&D expenditure (GERD) (€ per inhabitant) – stimulant
6 Crude net migration rate – stimulant
7 Life expectancy – stimulant
8 Students in tertiary education (ISCED 5–6) – as a percentage of the population aged 20–24 years – stimulant.

The above diagnostic traits were verified through a coefficient of variation analysis as well as the degree of correlation of each pair of variables, and then normalized in order to homogenize the variables.[7] The initial grouping made using the Ward method, one of the hierarchical methods, showed the possibility of creating from three to six clusters, and thus the analysed units were divided up for each of these variants.[8] Based on an accuracy assessment of the classification results for each grouping performed using the coefficient of homogeneity (allowing an assessment of cohesion within the clusters), the coefficient of heterogeneity (allowing an assessment of diversification between clusters) and the coefficient of accuracy (the quotient of both the above measures), four groups of European regions were distinguished as being the most accurate groupings in terms of variation in socio-economic potential.[9] At the same time, using the set of values presented below for the arithmetic mean of the diagnostic features exhibited by each cluster, they were graded and ordered into classes: A, B, C and D.

Firstly, the most numerous cluster (Class A) included 112 of the most developed regions of Western Europe, situated mainly in the territories of Germany, Austria, the Netherlands, Belgium, Sweden and northern Italy and including almost all the metropolitan regions (such as Inner London, Ile de France, Noord Holland, Stockholm, Hamburg, Bremen, Stuttgart, Vienna, Prague, Bratislavský kraj). These are units which we can call ‘development leaders’, featuring high and very high values in all analysed indices. The second cluster (B) included 85 territorial units featuring average GDP (per capita in PPS), relatively low levels of unemployment and a low share of people employed in farming, but also low index values in the spheres of health and education. This group incorporated regions situated primarily in France, Italy and Great Britain, as well as parts of the better-developed regions of central Europe, including four Polish voivodships (Mazowieckie, Małopolskie, Wielkopolskie and Pomorskie), as well as Kiev. The third cluster (C), featuring average GDP (per capita in PPS), high levels of unemployment, a significant share of persons employed in farming and relatively high index values representing social development, included regions in Greece, Italy and Spain. Finally, in the fourth cluster (D), there were 61 of the least developed

European regions, featuring the lowest values in all indices, reflecting the level of their socio-economic development. This group consisted of Lithuania, Latvia, five regions in Bulgaria, six in Hungary, eight in Romania, two in Portugal, 12 in Poland – including both voivodships of the Polish–Ukrainian borderland, Lublin and Podkarpackie – and 26 regions of Ukraine (all except Kiev).

The spatial diversification of the study results are shown in Figure 2.11. The multi-dimensional comparative analysis performed enabled the classification of European and Ukrainian regions in terms of their socio-economic potential. At the same time, it was possible to highlight the disproportionate development in core and periphery areas on the continental scale. The expanse of regions assigned to

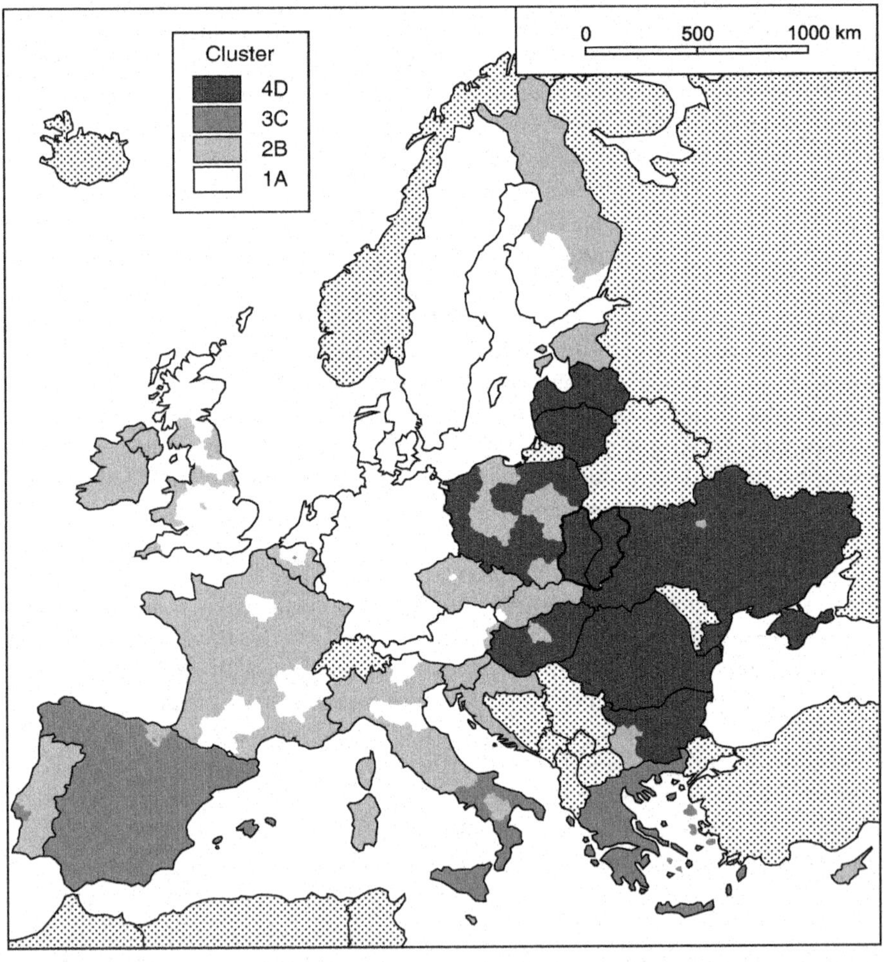

Figure 2.11 Spatial diversification of regions at NUTS2 level in 2013 in terms of classes of socio-economic potential

Source: Krzysztof Łoboda, on the basis of Eurostat and State Statistics Service of Ukraine.

Class A coincides with the central European area, while regions assigned to classes B, C and D mark the European periphery (see Figure 2.8).

The deliberations entered into in this chapter have made it possible to capture the specific nature of the Polish–Ukrainian borderland. This is, without doubt, an area of considerable asymmetry, particularly visible in the disproportionate economic development, which is the consequence of, among other factors, the different models of economic development as well as the different geopolitical vectors adopted in the last 25 years by Poland and Ukraine. This is manifested in the level of GDP per capita (both in real values and at purchasing power parity) as well as incomes, both of which are several times higher on the Polish side of the borderland. In this respect the axis of the Polish–Ukrainian borderland runs longitudinally, along the state border. In contrast, the dividing line in terms of the settlement system and economic structure runs latitudinally. The northern area of the borderland incorporates regions that are generally poorly populated, with a sparse urban network and significant farming sector, while the southern part is densely populated with a relatively better developed industrial sector. To a certain extent, there are perceptible differences that are a legacy from the period of partitions and the dependence of the borderland regions on the Russian and Austro-Hungarian empires. However, the diversification presents itself quite differently when it comes to demographics. Volhynia oblast and Podkarpackie voivodship can be regarded as active regions in demographic terms, as shown in their relatively favourable age structure and positive phenomena and processes of natural movement. In contrast, Lublin voivodship and Lviv oblast show overall depopulation, and the demographic structure appears to be ageing. Meanwhile, the dividing line of the borderland in terms of human and intellectual capital, measured by education levels, runs in quite the opposite direction. In this respect the most favourable situation is enjoyed by Lublin voivodship and Lviv oblast, where two major academic centres are located.

However, if we look at the Polish–Ukrainian borderland from a different perspective – national or even European – it appears that its constituent regions are alike in many respects. They are, after all, typical peripheral areas (in spatial as well as socio-economic terms), and this applies both to the Polish and the Ukrainian territories, but this feature is even more pronounced on a continental scale. All four of the analysed cross-border regions exhibit major structural backwardness in their economies, manifested in the considerable share of people employed in the least productive and lowest-paid farming sector, in the poorly developed industry and in low levels of innovation.

Notes

1 Eurostat data for the European Union, including Poland, relates to people aged 15–64, while data for Ukraine comes from research into living conditions in households and includes people from age 6 and over. For the purposes of comparison data was also used from the Census records of 2001 for the same age group (persons aged 6 and over).

2 A slightly higher result than in Lublin voivodship was gained by the Law and Justice Party in Małopolskie voivodship – 48.18 per cent.

3 Author's calculation. Data relating to the cumulative size of GDP according to the Central Statistical Office (GUS). Data concerning the level of funding according to the Ministry of Regional Development. Conversion of EUR to PLN according to the average exchange rate at the end of the period 2007–13 according to the European Commission.
4 Author's calculation. Sources of data as above.
5 The Pan-European transport corridor creates a coherent transport system in the European space. It was defined at the II Pan-European Transport Conference in Crete in 1994, and expanded at the III Pan-European Transport Conference in Helsinki in 1997.
6 Author's elaboration based on data from the Central Statistical Office of Poland, the State Statistical Committee of Ukraine and EUROSTAT. PPS calculated according to the World Bank.
7 Analysis of the correlation coefficient for each pair of variables (the critical value of the correlation coefficient was set at 0.75) did not lead to exclusion of any of the traits. The selected variables, expressed in the form of indices, were classified depending on their nature into two groups: factors with a positive impact (stimulants) and a negative impact (de-stimulants) on socio-economic potential.
8 Research conducted using Statistica 10.0.
9 There are at least several measures of the homogeneity and heterogeneity of clusters, based mainly on standard measures of central trends. The simplest of these and the most commonly used is the method based on the coefficient of variation. This method was also used in this study. Calculations were made using MS Excel.

Bibliography

Bański, J. (2008). Polska i Europa Środkowo-Wschodna w koncepcjach podziału Europy, in: P. Eberhardt (ed.) *Problematyka geopolityczna ziem polskich*. Warsaw: IGiPZ PAN, pp. 121–34.

Baran-Zgłobicka, B. et al. (2011). *Mapa zamierzeń inwestycyjnych na terenie polskiej części pogranicza polsko-ukraińskiego*. Lublin: Uniwersytet Marii Curie-Skłodowskiej.

Bochi, A. and Povoroznyk, V. (2014). *Shadow economy in Ukraine: Causes and Solutions*. Kiev: International Centre for Policy Studies.

Bronisz, U. et al. (2011). *Potencjał ekonomiczny miast w województwie lubelskim w latach 2000–2010*. Lublin: Urząd Statystyczny w Lublinie.

CBOS (2015). *Stosunek do innych narodów*. Online. Available: http://www.cbos.pl/SPISKOM.POL/2015/K_014_15.PDF (accessed: 11 February 2016).

Centr Razumkova (2011). *Relighia i vlada v Ukraini: problemy vzaemovydnosyn*. Kiev: Centr Razumkova.

Chebanova, V. (2009). *Zovnishnia trudova mighraciia naselennia Ukrainy*. Kiev: Ukrains'kyj Centr Social'nykh Reform, Derzhavnyi Komitet Statystyky Ukrainy.

Chmielewska, I. (2015). Transfery z tytułu pracy Polaków za granicą w świetle badań Narodowego Banku Polskiego. *Materiały i Studia*, 314. Online. Available: https://www.nbp.pl/publikacje/materialy_i_studia/ms314.pdf (accessed: 1 February 2016).

CSO (2015a). *Environment 2015*. Warsaw: Central Statistical Office.

CSO (2015b). *Forestry 2015*. Warsaw: Central Statistical Office.

Czerwonka, A. (2007). Relations Between Christians of Different Denominations in the Eastern Borderland of Poland on the Basis of Lubelskie Voivodship, in: W. Janicki (ed.) *European Multiculturalism as a Challenge – Policies, Successes and Failures*. Lublin: Maria Curie-Skłodowska University in Lublin, Polish Geographical Society, pp. 269–80.

Danylo Halytskyi International Airport 'Lviv' (2016). Online. Available: http://lwo.aero/en (accessed: 20 January 2016).

Debata (2014). Online. Available: http://www.debata.olsztyn.pl/wiadomoci/polska/3255–79-proc-ukraincow-w-zach-ukrainie-lubi-polakow.html (accessed: 22 January 2015).

Derzhavna Sluzhba Statystyky Ukrainy (2014). *Zapovidnyky ta nacional'ni pryrodni parky Ukrainy u 2013 roci*. Kiev: Derzhavna Sluzhba Statystyky Ukrainy.

Derzhupravvlinnia ohorony navkolyshn'ogho seredovyscha u Volyns'kii oblasti (2012). *Ekologhichnyi passport. Volyns'ka oblast'*. Online. Available: http://ecology.volyn.net/?p=environment (accessed: 3 February 2016).

Diecezja Przemysko-Warszawska Kościoła Greckokatolickiego (2016). *Diecezja Przemysko-Warszawska Kościoła Greckokatolickiego w Polsce*. Online. Available: http://cerkiew.org/ (accessed: 23 January 2016).

Domański, R. (2002). *Gospodarka przestrzenna*. Warszawa: Wydawnictwo Naukowe PWN.

Eberhardt, P. (2003). Przemiany demograficzno-narodowościowe na Ukrainie 1989–2001. *Przegląd Wschodni*, 8 (z. 3), pp. 741–58.

Eberhardt, P. (2004). Koncepcja granicy między cywilizacją zachodniego chrześcijaństwa a bizantyjską na kontynencie europejskim. *Przegląd Geograficzny*, 76/2, pp. 169–88.

Eberhardt, P. (2011). *Political migrations on Polish Territories (1939–1950)*. Warsaw: Polish Academy of Sciences.

EuroOsvita (2015). *Reitingh universitetiv Ukrainy III–IV rivniv akredytacii TOP-200 Ukraina u 2015 roci*. Online. Available: http://www.euroosvita.net/index.php/?category=1andid=4068 (accessed: 29 January 2016).

European Environment Agency (2015). *Air quality in Europe – 2015 report*. Online. Available: http://www.eea.europa.eu/publications/air-quality-in-europe-2015 (accessed: 28 January 2016).

Eurostat (2015). *Database*. Online. Available: http://ec.europa.eu/eurostat/data/database (accessed: 1 February 2016).

FAO and UNESCO (1981). *Soil Map of the World*. Paris: UNESCO.

Flaga, M. (2006). *Procesy demograficzne oraz ich uwarunkowania w zachodnich obwodach Ukrainy w okresie przemian ustrojowych*. Lublin: Wydawnictwo Uniwersytetu Marii Curie-Skłodowskiej.

Górz, B. (2005). Rolnictwo Polski południowo-wschodniej (uwarunkowania rozwoju i współczesny stan), in: B. Głębocki (ed.) *Struktura przestrzenna rolnictwa Polski u progu XXI wieku*. Poznań: Bogucki Wydawnictwo Naukowe, pp. 311–56.

Gorzelak, G. (2007a). Rozwój - region - polityka, in: G. Gorzelak and A. Tucholska (eds) *Rozwój - region - przestrzeń*. Warszawa: Ministerstwo Rozwoju Regionalnego.

Gorzelak, G. (2007b). Rozwój polskich regionów a polityka spójności Unii Europejskiej, in: G. Gorzelak (ed.) *Polska regionalna i lokalna w świetle badań EUROREG-u*. Warszawa: Wydawnictwo Naukowe SCHOLAR, pp. 12–34.

GUS (2014). *Kościół katolicki w Polsce 1991–2011*. Warszawa: Głowny Urząd Statystyczny.

GUS (2015). *Informacja o rozmiarach i kierunkach czasowej emigracji z Polski w latach 2004–2014*. Warszawa: Główny Urząd Statystyczny.

Huntington, S. (1993). The Clash of Civilizations? *Foreign Affairs*, Summer, pp. 22–49.

IGiPZ PAN (1997). *Atlas Rzeczypospolitej Polskiej*. Warszawa: Instytut Geografii i Przestrzennego Zagospodarowania PAN, Główny Geodeta Kraju.

Institute of Geography of NAS of Ukraine (2003). *Atlas. Ukraine. Industry and Investment Activity*. Kiev: State Scientific and Production Enterprise 'Kartographia'.

ISKK, GUS (2014) *Rocznik statystyczny. Kościół katolicki w Polsce 1991–2011*. Warszawa: Instytut Statystyki Kościoła Katolickiego SAC; Główny Urząd Statystyczny.

International Union for Conservation of Nature (2016). *Global Protected Areas Programme*. Online. Available: http://www.iucn.org/about/work/programmes/gpap_home/gpap_quality/gpap_pacategories/gpap_pacategory2/ (accessed: 12 January 2016).

ISKK (2015). *Annuarium Statisticum Ecclesiae in Polonia*. Warszawa: ISKK.
Jakubowski, A. (2015). *Przemiany demograficzne na obszarze Euroregionu Bug w latach 2003–2013*. Lublin: Urząd Statystyczny w Lublinie.
Jakubowski, A., Bronisz, U. and Dziaduch, S. (2013). *Diagnoza sytuacji społeczno-ekonomicznej na obszarze województwa lubelskiego, obwodu brzeskiego, obwodu wołyńskiego oraz obwodu lwowskiego*. Lublin: Urząd Statystyczny w Lublinie.
Kabinet Ministriv Ukrainy (2014). *Derzhavna strateghia reghional'nogho rozvytku na period do 2020 roku*. Kiev: Kabinet Ministriv Ukrainy.
Kaczmarski, M. (2015). *The New Silk Road: a versatile instrument in China's policy*. Warsaw: Centre for Eastern Studies.
Kavetskyy, I. (2010). *Przestrzeń wyborcza Polski i Ukrainy. Ujęcie porównawcze*. Szczecin: Wydawnictwo Naukowe Uniwersytetu Szczecińskiego.
Kawałko, B. (2005). Infrastruktura komunikacyjna, in: B. Kawałko and A. Miszczuk (eds) *Pogranicze polsko-ukraińskie. Środowisko. Społeczeństwo. Gospodarka*. Zamość: Wyższa Szkoła Zarządzania i Administracji w Zamościu, pp. 173–7.
Koncepciia reformuvannia miscevogho samovriaduvanniata terytorial'noi orghanizacii vlady v Ukraini (2014). Kabinet Ministriv Ukrainy.
Kondracki, J. (1998). *Geografia regionalna Polski*. Warszawa: Wyd. Naukowe PWN.
Kotowska, I. and Chłoń-Domińczak, A. (2012). Zarządzanie finansami publicznymi w kontekście zmiany demograficznej. *Studia ekonomiczne*, 72/1, pp. 7–24.
Kovbasiuk, J. W. (2014). *Misceve samovriaduvannia v Ukraini: suchasnyi stan ta osnovni napriamy modernizacii*. Kiev: Nacional'na Akademiia Derzhavnoho Upravlinnia pry Prezydentovi Ukrainy.
Kowalczyk, H. A. (2014). *Ukraine – the World Is Watching*. Online. Available: http://www.huffingtonpost.com/henryk-a-kowalczyk/ukraine-the-world-is-watc_b_5756578.html (accessed: 10 February 2016).
Kowerski, M. and Matkowski, S. (2005). Gospodarka, in: B. Kawałko and A. Miszczuk (eds) *Pogranicze polsko-ukraińskie. Środowisko. Społeczeństwo. Gospodarka*. Zamość: Wyższa Szkoła Zarządzania i Administracji w Zamościu, pp. 105–30.
Kozaczka, M. (2010). Rola specjalnych stref ekonomicznych w rozwoju województwa podkarpackiego, in: D. Błaszczuk and M. Stefański (eds) *Strategiczna problematyka rozwoju Polski Wschodniej*. Lublin: Wyższa Szkoła Ekonomii i Innowacji w Lublinie, pp. 363–74.
Kuczabski, A. and Miszczuk, A. (2005). Podział administracyjny, in: B. Kawałko and A. Miszczuk (eds) *Pogranicze polsko-ukraińskie. Środowisko. Społeczeństwo. Gospodarka*. Zamość: Wyższa Szkoła Zarządzania i Administracji w Zamościu, pp. 67–76.
Lerman, Z., Sedik, D., Pugachov, N. and Goncharuk, A. (2007). *Rethinking agricultural reform in Ukraine*. Halle: Leibniz-Institut für Agrarentwicklung in Mittel- und Osteuropa (IAMO).
Lipińska-Słota, A. (2010). Korytarze transportowe w kontekście powiązań UE i Polski – analiza obciążenia i perspektywy rozwoju. *Prace Naukowe Politechniki Warszawskiej*, 76, pp. 93–102.
Lublin Airport (2016). Online. Available at: http://www.airport.lublin.pl/en/ (accessed: 20 January 2016).
Lvivs'ka Derzhavna Oblasna Administraciia (2015). *Ekologhichnyi passport L'vivs'koi oblasti*. Online. Available: http://www.ekologia.lviv.ua/file/monitoring/ekopasport_2015.pdf (accessed: 1 February 2016).
Malska, M. and Molas, W. (2005). Ochrona Środowiska, in: B. Kawałko and A. Miszczuk (eds) *Pogranicze polsko-ukraińskie. Środowisko. Społeczeństwo. Gospodarka*. Zamość: Wyższa Szkoła Zarządzania i Administracji w Zamościu, pp. 51–65.

Miller, T. and Kim, A. B. et al. (2016). *2016 Index of Economic Freedom. Promoting Economic Opportunity and Prosperity*. Washington, New York: The Heritage Foundation, The Wall Street Journal. Online. Available: http://www.heritage.org/index/pdf/2016/book/index_2016.pdf (accessed: 12 February 2016).

Ministerstvo Ekologhii ta Pryrodnykh Resursiv Ukrainy (2015). *Kivercivs'kyj Natsional'nyi Pryrodnyi Park 'Cumans'ka Puscha' rozpochav svoiu diial'nist'!* Online. Available: http://www.menr.gov.ua/press-center/news/125-news3/4277-kivertsivskyi-natsionalnyi-pryrodnyi-park-tsumanska-pushcha-rozpochav-svoiu-diialnist (accessed: 2 February 2016).

Mirkin, B. (2005). *Clustering for Data Mining. A. Data Recovery Approach*. Boca Raton: Chapman and Hall/CRC, Taylor and Francis Group LCC.

Misiąg, J., Misiąg, W. and Tomalak, M. (2013). *Ocena efektywności wykorzystania pomocy finansowej Unii Europejskiej jako instrumentu polityki spójności społeczno-gospodarczej oraz poprawy warunków życia*. Rzeszów: WSIiZ.

Miszczuk, A. (2013). *Uwarunkowania peryferyjności regionu przygranicznego*. Lublin: Norbertinum.

Miszczuk, A. (2015). Directions of Development of Tourism in the Polish–Ukrainian Cross-Border Area in the New European Union Programming Period (2014–2020) in the Context of Regional Planning Documents. *Barometr Regionalny*, 13/3, pp. 49–59.

Miszczuk, A., Smętkowski, M., Płoszaj, A. and Celińska-Janowicz, D. (2010). Aktualne problemy demograficzne regionu Polski wschodniej. *Raporty i analizy EUROREG*, 5/2010, p. 65.

MOP (2013). *Zvit schodo metodologhii pracy, orghanizacii provedennia ta rezul'tativ modul'nogho vybirkovogho obstezhennia z pytan' trudovoi mighracii v Ukraini*. Kiev: Mizhnarodna Orghanizacia Praci, Derzhavna Sluzhba Statystyky Ukrainy, Instytut Demoghrafii ta social'nykh doslidzhen' im. M. V. Ptukhy Nacional'noi Akademii Nauk Ukrainy.

MR (2011). *Koncepcja przestrzennego zagospodarowania kraju 2030*. Online. Available: https://www.mr.gov.pl/strony/zadania/polityka-rozwoju-kraju/zarzadzanie-rozwojem-kraju/koncepcja-przestrzennego-zagospodarowania-kraju/ (accessed: 1 February 2016).

Perspektywy (2015). *Ranking szkół wyższych 'Perspektywy'*. Online. Available: http://www.perspektywy.pl/RSW2015/ranking-uczelni-akademickich (accessed: 29 January 2016).

PKW (2015). *Państwowa komisja Wyborcza*. Online. Available: http://www.pkw.gov.pl (accessed: 29 January 2016).

Prawosławna Diecezja Lubelsko-Chełmska (2016). *Prawosławna Diecezja Lubelsko-Chełmska*. Online. Available: http://www.lublin.cerkiew.pl/ (accessed: 2 February 2016).

President of Ukraine (1999). *Ukaz prezydenta Ukrainy Pro special'nu ekonomichnu zonu 'Interport Kovel'*. 22 chervnya 1999 roku, N 702/99.

Procenko, L. D. (ed.) (2011). *Shmaraghdova merezha v Ukraini*. Kiev: Khimdzhest.

Rąkowski, G. (2005). *Wołyń. Przewodnik krajoznawczo-historyczny po Ukrainie Zachodniej*. Pruszków: Oficyna Wydawnicza 'Rewasz'.

Reiting, S. G. (2015). *Dynamika suspil'no-politychnykh pogliadiv v Ukraini*, Kiev: Center for Insights in Survey Research.

Riabczuk, M. (2004). *Dwie Ukrainy*. Wrocław: Kolegium Europy Wschodniej im. Jana Nowaka-Jeziorańskiego.

Rosstat (2015). *Mezhdunarodnaia migraciia*. Online. Available: http://www.gks.ru/wps/wcm/connect/rosstat_main/rosstat/ru/statistics/population/demography/# (accessed: 1 February 2016).

Rzeszów International Airport (2016). Online. Available: http://www.rzeszowairport.pl/ (accessed: 20 January 2016).

Schneider, F. and Klinglmair, R. (2004). *Shadow Economies Around the World: What do We Know?* Basel: Center for Research in Economics, Management and the Arts.

Schüssel, W. (2015). *Polish Lessons for the Ukrainian Economy*. Online. Available: http://www.theglobalist.com/polish-lessons-for-the-ukrainian-economy/ (accessed: 11 February 2016).

Shutova, O. S. (2013). Vil'ni ekonomichni zony yak roznovyd terytorial'nykh podatkowykh zvil'nen'. *Chasopys Kyivskogo Universytetu Prava*, 1, pp. 157–61.

Skorupska, A. and Kościński, P. (2015). Ukraina: reforma samorządowa przyśpiesza powoli. *Biuletyn PISM*, 16/1253, pp. 1–2.

Smętkowski, M. (2010). Miasta i sytem osadniczy Polski w perspektywie europejskiej, in: A. Tucholska (ed.) *Europejskie wyzwania dla Polski i jej regionów*. Warszawa: Ministerstwo Rozwoju Regionalnego, pp. 183–99.

Stanicka, M. (2011). Warunki naturalne, in: W. Janicki (ed.) *Województwo lubelskie. Środowisko - społeczeństwo - gospodarka*. Lublin: Norbertinum, pp. 46–54.

Stankiewicz, D. (1993). *Zielone Płuca Europy – wspólna inicjatywa państw dorzecza Morza Bałtyckiego*, Warszawa: Biuro Studiów i Ekspertyz.

State Statistics Service of Ukraine (2015a) *Social and Demographic Characteristics of Households in Ukraine*. Kiev: State Statistics Service of Ukraine.

State Statistics Service of Ukraine (2015b) *Statistical Yearbook Environment of Ukraine 2014*. Kiev: State Statistics Service of Ukraine.

Subtelny, O. (2000). *Ukraine: A History*, 4th edn. Toronto: University of Toronto Press.

Szymańczak, J. (2000). Zmiany demograficzne. *Informacja Biura Studiów i Ekspertyz*, 735, pp. 8–17.

The Economist (2015). Ukraine. The other battleground. Online. Available: http://www.economist.com/news/leaders/21651819-west-should-do-much-more-help-ukraines-economy-other-battleground (accessed: 10 February 2016).

Transparency International (2015). *Corruption Perceptions Index*. Online. Available: http://www.transparency.org/cpi2015#downloads (accessed: 2 February 2016).

TVK (2015). *Tsentra'lna Vyborcha Komisiia*. Online. Available: http://cvk.gov.ua/ (accessed: 10 February 2016).

UNDP (2012). *Krajowy Raport o Rozwoju Społecznym Polska 2012. Rozwój regionalny i lokalny*. Warsaw: Biuro Projektowe UNDP w Polsce.

UNDP (2015). *Human Development Report 2015. Work for Human Development*. New York: United Nations Development Programme.

UNIAN (2015). *Industrial'ni parky w Ukraini: bez ekonomychnoho dyva*. Online. Available: http://economics.unian.ua/industry/1124071-industrialni-parki-v-ukrajini-bez-ekonomichnogo-diva.html (accessed: 2 February 2016).

US Energy Information Administration (2013). *Technically Recoverable Shale Oil and Shale Gas Resources: An Assessment of 137 Shale Formations in 41 Countries Outside the United States*, Washington: US Department of Energy.

Volyn' Post (2013). *Chomu na Volyni dosi ne stvoryly nacinal'nyi park 'Cuman'ska Puscha'*. Online. Available: http://www.volynpost.com/news/10950-chomu-na-volyni-dosi-ne-stvoryly-nacionalnyj-park-cumanska-puscha (accessed: 6 February 2016).

Volyns'ka Oblasna Derzhavna Administraciia (2016). *Pryrodni resursy oblasti*. Online. Available: http://voladm.gov.ua/prirodni-resursi-oblasti/ (accessed: 2 February 2016).

Wesołowska, M. (2012). Wsie zanikające w województwie lubelskim, in: J. Plit and J. Nita (eds) *Źródła kartograficzne w badaniach krajobrazu kulturowego*. Prace Komisji Krajobrazu Kulturowego. Sosnowiec, pp. 229–40.

Wilson, A. (2002). *Ukraińcy*. Warszawa: Świat Książki.

WIOŚ w Lublinie (2015). *Raport o jakości wód rzeki Bug oraz jej dopływów w latach 2005–2014*, Lublin: Wojewódzki Inspektorat Ochrony Środowiska w Lublinie.

Wojewódzki Inspektorat Ochrony Środowiska w Lublinie (2015) *Raport o stanie środowiska województwa lubelskiego w 2014 r.* Online. Available: http://www.wios.lublin.pl/srodowisko/raporty-o-stanie-srodowiska/raport-o-stanie-srodowiska-2014–2/ (accessed: 1 February 2016).

Wojewódzki Inspektorat Ochrony Środowiska w Rzeszowie (2015). *Raport o stanie środowiska w województwie podkarpackim w 2014 r.* Online. Available: http://www.wios.rzeszow.pl/publikacje/publikacje-o-stanie-srodowiska/raporty-o-stanie-srodowiska-w-woj-podkarpackim/raport-za-rok-2014/ (accessed: 5 February 2016).

World Bank (2015). *Doing Business 2015. Going Beyond Efficiency*. Washington: World Bank Group.

Yevtukh, V. B., Troshchyns'kyi, V. P., Halushko, K.Y. and Chernova, K. O. (2004). *Etnonacional'na struktura ukrains'koho suspil'stva. Dovidnyk*. Kiev: Naykova Dumka.

Zakon Ukrainy O special'noi ekonomicheskoi zone turistsko-rekreacionnogo tipa 'Kurortopolis Truskavets' (1999, N 18, st. 139) Vedomosti Verkhovnoi Rady (VVR).

Zakon Ukrainy Pro special'nu ekonomichnu zonu 'Yavoriv' (1999, N 15, st.82) Vedomosti Verkhovnoi Rady Ukrainy (VVR).

Zastawnyi, F. (1994). *Geografiia Ukrainy*. L'viv: Wydawnyctwo 'Svit'.

Zastawnyj, F. and Kusiński, W. (2003). *Ukraina. Przyroda - Ludność – Gospodarka*. Warszawa: Wydawnictwo Akademickie DIALOG.

ZIK (2012). *Volyns'kii vladi ne dozvolyly likviduvaty 'Cumans'ku Puschu'*. Online. Available: http://zik.ua/news/2012/01/16/328810 (accessed: 6 February 2016).

Żuchowski, W. (2005). Środowisko geograficzne, in: B. Kawałko and A. Miszczuk (eds) *Pogranicze polsko-ukraińskie. Środowisko. Społeczeństwo. Gospodarka*. Zamość: Wyższa Szkoła Zarządzania i Administracji w Zamościu, pp. 29–49.

3 Cross-border relations in the Polish–Ukrainian borderland

Tomasz Komornicki and Andrzej Miszczuk

The real existence of cross-border areas is not determined merely by the potentials of borderland regions described as a set of diverse features. The areas exist due to multiple links beyond borders, the intensity and character of which are obviously dependent on the aforementioned potentials. Therefore, the purpose of this chapter is to analyse the Polish–Ukrainian borderland in terms of cross-border cooperation on environmental protection, the development of border infrastructure and transport accessibility, border traffic, social relations, labour and student migration, economic relations including local borderland trade, foreign trade between border regions, tourist traffic and institutional cooperation: bilateral between regional and local authorities, euro-regional and partnerships arising through the implementation of cross-border projects.

In analysing cross-border interactions, the basic historical conditions of Ukrainian–Polish border operation should be taken into account. This is a classic subsequent border (founded after the establishment of basic spatial development elements; Hartshorne 1936). The Polish–Ukrainian border cuts through the area that was a part of Poland before World War II. On the Ukrainian side, almost complete resettlement of the Polish population took place, either during the war (deportations into the Soviet Union), or after 1945 (moving the Polish population to areas which did not remain in the Soviet Union). Additionally, in the following years, the Ukrainian population living on the Polish side of the borderland was also resettled (initially to the Ukrainian side and later, in the so-called 'Operation Vistula', to areas recovered from Germany). Migration movements and the establishment of a sealed border caused the interruption of functional social links and the limitation of serious economic interactions. The result of these activities stunted the development of some cross-border towns. Lviv in Ukraine (at the regional level) and Przemyśl in Poland (at the local level) are examples of towns cut off from their influence zones by the border. In addition, certain elements of the transport infrastructure lost their significance and were closed or began to function merely locally. This concerned, primarily, the east–west railway infrastructure (Komornicki 2014).

During the period of the Polish People's Republic (1945–89) the entire border with the Soviet Union, including the current Polish–Ukrainian border, was characterized by a very low level of permeability. It represented a kind of 'second iron curtain' separating the socialist countries of Central Europe from their 'Big Brother' (Komornicki and Miszczuk 2010). In time, the restrictions on passenger border traffic became even greater than for journeys to Western Europe. Instead of the 63 road and rail routes crossing the subsequent border with the Soviet Union in 1939, in the early 1980s the People's Republic of Poland was linked with the Soviet Union (the border length 1310 kilometres) by only two road border crossings and three rail border crossings. Goods and army transportations were checked at a few other rail border crossings. At the Polish–Ukrainian border all rail lines were closed for passenger traffic except for the Rzeszów–Lviv route. Until the end of the 1980s only one border checkpoint was open at Medyka. It was, except for lorry transportation, used mainly as a transit route from Poland to Romania and Bulgaria (Komornicki 2014).

The transformation period after 1989 was characterized by the dynamic growth of spontaneous social and economic interactions across the Ukrainian border (described below). Following the enlargement of the European Union in 2004 this trend weakened. The number and length of border sections between the EU and third countries dramatically increased. Meanwhile, the intermediate zone that had existed for 15 states (except the Balkans) earlier associated with the EU (including Poland) almost completely disappeared. This process has resulted in the polarization of the European system of border regimes. Two types of border began to dominate: poorly formalized (or virtually non-existent – the Schengen area) borders within the EU and formal (usually with a visa regime for immediate neighbours) borders on EU external borders. As a result, the Polish–Ukrainian border has become one of the few examples of borders where in less than 20 years the border has spectacularly opened, only to be resealed, playing an increased role as a formal and legal barrier. Moreover, in 2014–15 this situation coincided with new geopolitical factors related to the war in eastern Ukraine and mass migration at the external borders of the European Union.

The analysis included in the chapter makes use of the authors' own studies, published and unpublished data and studies by various institutions: the Border Guard Headquarters' data on cross-border traffic, the Ministry of Labour and Social Policy's data on migration of foreigners seeking to achieve a legal work status in Poland, the Educational Foundation's 'Perspektywy' study on foreign students, the Central Statistical Office and the Statistical Office of Rzeszów's survey results on cross-border trade and the Customs Department of the Ministry of Finance's data on foreign trade. Data on exports by region are actual data from INTRASTAT statements and customs declarations. Unless otherwise stated, figures used in the text are from the Central Statistical Office in Warsaw.

Most of the presented relations have been described on the basis of spatial data from Polish territory and the Polish part of the borderland. This is due to the lack of comparable data on the Ukrainian side.

Environmental protection and management

The protection and management of the natural environment are activities which tend not to be willingly undertaken as cross-border activities. Many countries believe environmental issues to come under their 'national' competence. However, they reserve the right to intervene in a situation of environmental hazard from a neighbouring country (Ricq 2006). Currently, the need for the joint management of border areas in order to protect borderland environmental assets is more often perceived, however. This involves counteracting air and water pollution and soil degradation. Instruments for this kind of management may include, among others (Ricq 2006):

- scientific studies on environmental pollution and methods of eliminating it,
- creating a system for monitoring environmental hazards,
- establishing a system for the notification of hazards and devising cooperation plans if they occur,
- developing joint cross-border databases on the environment,
- establishing cross-border forms of environmental protection (parks and reserves).

The Polish–Ukrainian borderland, as outlined in Chapter 2, is a cross-border system of physiographic units conducive to joint protection activities. One such initiative was the idea developed by G. Rąkowski (2000) of the Institute of Environmental Protection, which involved the development of cross-border protected areas understood as ecological links between the system of protected areas in Poland and that in neighbouring countries. Their aim was, on the one hand, to protect the most valuable areas, in terms of nature, landscape and culture, divided by Poland's eastern border, and on the other to develop sustainable tourism (including at an international level) in these areas. In the case of the Polish–Ukrainian borderland, three cross-border protected areas have been identified (Figure 3.1):

- Western Polesia – an area of approximately 325,000 ha of which the Polish part is approximately 225,000 ha and the Ukrainian part approximately 100,000 ha
- Roztocze – an area of approximately 200,000 ha of which the Polish part is approximately 130,000 ha and the Ukrainian part – approximately 70,000 ha
- Eastern Beskids – an area of over 300,000 ha of which the Polish part is approximately 109,500 ha, the Ukrainian part approximately 150,000 ha and the Slovakian part approximately 40,800 ha.

The transboundary protected area of Western Polesia is located on both sides of the River Bug border and includes the Łęczna–Włodawa Lake District on the Polish side, comprising more than 60 lakes, the largest of which is Białe Włodawskie Lake, covering an area of 106.4 ha. In summer, approximately 40,000 tourists spend time by this lake. On the Ukrainian side Western Polesia includes Shatsky Lake District, located in the interfluve of the rivers Pripyat and Bug. It consists of more than 30 lakes much larger than the lakes on the Polish side. In the 1990s the Polesia National Park was established in the Polish part, as well as three

Figure 3.1 Transboundary protected areas in the Polish–Ukrainian borderland

Source: Rąkowski (2000).

landscape parks: Łęczna Lake District, Sobibór and Chełm parks. Part of the Shatsky Lake District also belongs to the Shatsky National Park, set up in 1983. On the Ukrainian side there are also three wetland reserves in which water tourism and cycling are the preferred types of tourism. In order for them to be more cross-border in nature there is a need to construct a border ferry checkpoint on the River Bug. Currently, the potential of the river for tourism is completely untapped, despite its being an axis of the Polish–Belarusian and Polish–Ukrainian (Figure 3.2) borderlands as well as part of the state border. Many years of research and monitoring indicate that the primary hazard to the waters of the River Bug is biogenic pollution along its entire length (Kawałko and Miszczuk 2008). According to the Polish classification, the whole border section of the River Bug contains excessively polluted waters, causing their disqualification both in terms of utility (water supply) and recreation (Figure 3.3). The reason for this state of affairs is primarily a lack of comprehensive solutions in the field of water and wastewater management in Lviv, Ukraine and Brest, Belarus.

The River Bug has a great potential for development and water tourism. In order to make this happen, the river should be prepared for this function in terms of infrastructure by, for example, the construction of river marinas, the provision

Figure 3.2 The cross-border nature of the Bug River Basin

Source: Kawałko and Miszczuk (2008).

of equipment hire and the organization of accommodation and catering facilities, as well as the maintenance of the river's status as a place allowing sailing. Attractions for tourists could also be developed by restoring old canals to link up Shatsky Lake District with the River Pripyat as well as by constructing border crossing checkpoints.

The planned cross-border protected area 'Roztocze' comprises an upland ridge extending over a length of 180 kilometres and a width of 20 kilometres. It is a watershed separating the rivers Vistula and Dniester. A large part of it is covered by various forms of protection. On the Polish side these include the Roztocze National Park, established in 1974, and four landscape parks – Szczebrzeszyn,

Figure 3.3 The purity of the River Bug Basin

Source: As Figure 3.2.

Krasnobród, South Roztocze and Solska Ancient Woodland – and on the Ukrainian side Yavorivskyi National Park, established in 1998, and Roztocze Reserve. The cultural attractions of the area are clustered in three cities: Lviv, Zamość and Zhovkva. The preferred types of tourism here are hiking, nature tourism, health spa tourism, cycling and agro-tourism.

The last of the cross-border protected areas in the Polish and Ukrainian borderland is the Eastern Beskidy Mountains, which also includes the Polish–Slovakian borderland. It consists of long parallel mountain ranges of a height not exceeding 1,500 metres above sea level. The main ridge of the Eastern Beskidy Mountains is the watershed dividing the basin of the Rivers San, Stryj and Tisza. Most of the area is protected in the form of the Bieszczady National Park, established in 1973, and two landscape parks – Cisna-Wetlina and San Valley – on the Polish side, Uzhanskyi National Park and Nadsanskyi Landscape Park on the Ukrainian side, and the National Park 'Poloniny' on the Slovak side. As a result of post-war resettlements of the Ukrainian population, the area on the Polish side is also now sparsely populated and is characterized by a very low level of socio-economic development. The preferred types of tourism here are hiking, biking, water tourism and skiing.

Referring to the concept of cross-border protected areas, the Polish Committee for UNESCO – Man and the Biosphere Programme (MaB) initiated the creation of international biosphere reserves in the eastern borderland of Poland. Biosphere Reserves are established around areas protected by a certain country's law in order to protect their biodiversity but also to promote principles of sustainable development in local communities. Therefore, a Biosphere Reserve, in contrast to a national park, is characterized by zoning. Zone A (core) is a tightly protected central zone. Zone B (buffer) includes areas with lower protection status, where extensive economic activities are allowed. Zone C (temporary, transit) denotes regions of economic activity within which, however, recommendations for sustainable management of the environment are implemented owing to their proximity to zone A (Breymeyer 2011).

In the Polish–Ukrainian borderland there are now two UNESCO MaB Biosphere Reserves (Figure 3.4). These are:

- The East Carpathian International Biosphere Reserve, established in 1992 and expanded in 1998, which covers: Bieszczady National Park, Cisna-Wetlina Landscape Park and San Valley Landscape Park (Podkarpackie Voivodship) on the Polish side, Nadsanskyi Landscape Park (Lviv oblast) and Uzhanskyi National Park (Zakarpattia oblast) on the Ukrainian side and the Slovak National Park 'Poloniny'
- The 'Western Polesia' Transboundary Biosphere Reserve, established in 2002 and expanded in 2012, which covers, on the Polish side, Polesia National Park and Sobibór Landscape Park (Lublin voivodship), on the Ukrainian side, Shatsky National Park (Volhynia oblast), and the Belarusian Biosphere Reserve 'Pribuzhskoye Polesye' (Brest oblast).

Extensive activities have been undertaken to establish a third Biosphere Reserve, 'Roztocze', covering, on the Polish side, Roztocze National Park and the landscape parks South Roztocze, Krasnobród, Szczebrzeszyn, Solska ancient woodland and Janów Forests (Lublin voivodship), and, on the Ukrainian side, Yavorivskyi National Park, Ravske Roztochchia landscape park and Roztochchia reserve (Lviv oblast).

The establishment and operation of the International Biosphere Reserves is based on a model of multi-entity management and is a modern example of cross-border cooperation that implements the knowledge and experience of neighbouring countries and regions.

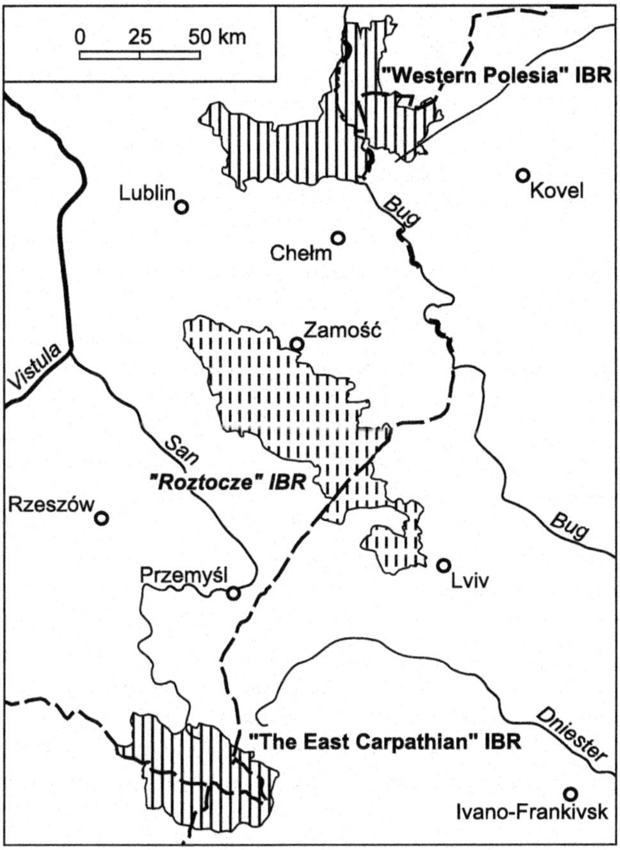

Figure 3.4 UNESCO MaB Biosphere Reserves

Source: As Figure 3.2.

Communication, border infrastructure and border traffic

The road and railway network of the Polish–Ukrainian borderland is sparser than the national average (see Figure 2.7). This is partly due to the lower population density (particularly in the vicinity of the southern Carpathian section of the border). The borderland road service is provided by corridors which run towards the major Polish metropolises. These are primarily the latitudinal corridors from Lviv via Rzeszów towards Cracow (one of the so-called trans-European corridors), encompassing the A4 motorway, the national road DK94 and the rail line E30, as well as the diagonal corridor from Warsaw via Lublin to Kiev and Lviv (often referred to as *Via Intermare*), which is envisaged as eventually providing links between Gdańsk in Poland and Odessa in Ukraine), encompassing national roads DK17 and DK12 and corresponding railway lines. Moreover, towards the border there are several other national and regional roads, including the road DK74 towards Zamość and Hrubieszów and the DK28 in the Carpathian corridor (Krosno via Sanok to Przemyśl). In the vicinity of Hrubieszów, towards the border, is the LHS – a railway line of the Eastern European gauge leading from the terminal in Sławków, near the Upper Silesian Industrial District. The condition of the regional and local road infrastructure is very diverse. Some routes were renovated in the funding period of the Regional Operational Programmes of 2007–13, or earlier, under the Integrated Regional Development Programme 2004–6. The regional railway lines play a very limited role and many have suspended passenger services. In the Podkarpackie voivodship an above-average role (compared with the national situation) is played by the public bus service as a result of the polycentric labour market system and scattered settlement patterns.

The airports situated closest to the borderland, in Rzeszów and Lublin, have been operating since 2012. According to research into the market areas of Polish airports (Komornicki and Śleszyński 2011), Podkarpackie voivodship and the southern parts of Lublin voivodship are located entirely within the zone of influence of these facilities. However, the actual air access to the region depends mostly on the flight connections offered, not the mere existence of an airport or even recorded traffic. The airports in Lublin and Rzeszów are characterized by low-level traffic focused mainly on migration routes (low cost travel to the United Kingdom, Germany and Norway) or holidays (charter flight to Mediterranean countries). This prevents efficient communication with the major European cities and thus does not allow for the inflow of foreign tourists by air. The closest airports with a more diverse flight network are Cracow and Warsaw. Potentially, such a role could also be played by Lviv airport, which is located at a relatively close distance. Chapter 2 presents a more detailed description of the borderland transport situation.

To conclude, in terms of communications, the specific nature of the Polish–Ukrainian borderland can be described as follows:

- a a peripheral location as regards major transport hubs and investment in Poland and Ukraine;
- b located in the vicinity of a poorly permeable external border of the European Union;
- c characterized by heavy transit traffic from Ukraine to Western Europe;
- d poorly equipped with modern transport infrastructure;
- e has relatively large areas subject to different forms of protection, thus inhibiting investment in transport;
- f has an underdeveloped settlement network (due to historical factors), the support of which is one of the major objectives of Poland's regional policy in the area.

Owing to these factors, access to entities located in the borderland or in the vicinity is difficult (compared with other parts of the country and even with other areas in eastern Poland; see Komornicki et al. 2008, Komornicki et al. 2010;

Komornicki et al. 2015). However, a period of major investment co-financed by the European Union is gradually changing this situation. The first significant result is the completion of the A4 motorway in 2016 along the entire section from the German border to the Ukrainian border. This significantly improves access to the borderland in the northern Podkarpackie section and southern Lublin section (Figure 3.5). However, change in areas in the Carpathian mountains and in the central Lublin region is not spectacular. Thus the significant road investments made as a result of the inflow of EU funds and EU cohesion policy has improved the Ukrainian borderland transport infrastructure in a spatially selective way. Furthermore, the density of border crossings (see below) is fairly low, resulting in the formation of 'access channels' to the border on the roads leading to check-points (Komornicki et al. 2008). Other recent investments in the area or in the vicinity of the borderland are the modernization of the national road DK74 and the construction of the Hrubieszow bypass. The current UE financial perspective

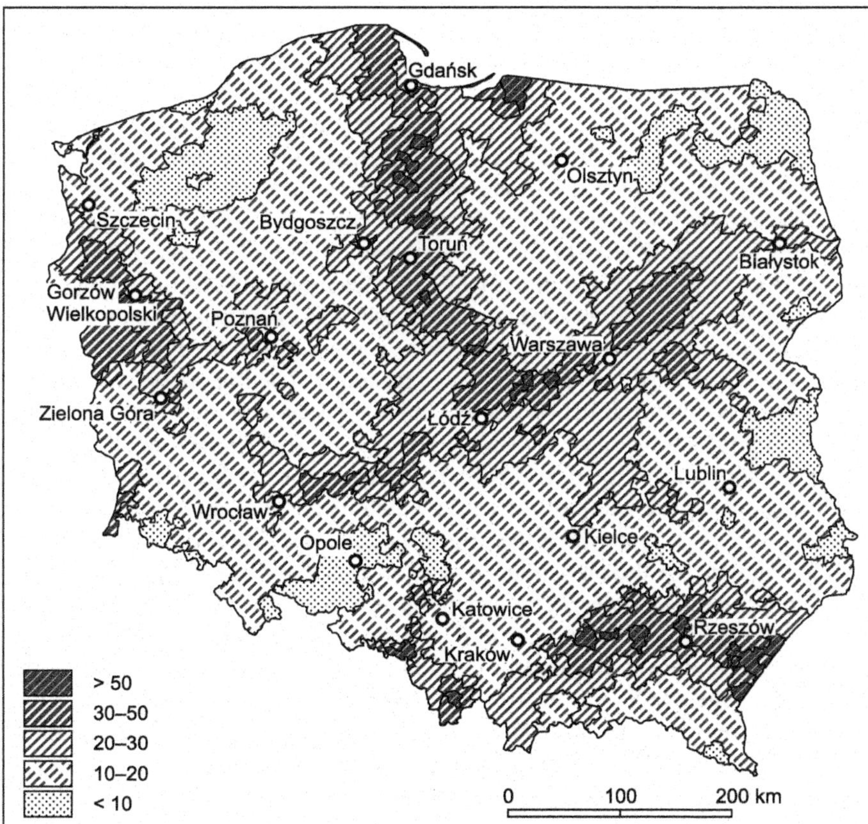

Figure 3.5 Changes to potential transport access resulting from road investments 2007–15

Source: Sławomir Goliszek, Krzysztof Łoboda, on the basis of Komornicki et al. (2015).

(2014–20) does not anticipate much improvement in access at the border with Ukraine in Podkarpackie voivodship. However, the completion of the S17 Warsaw–Lublin express road and a section of the S19 Lublin–Rzeszów road will improve communications between the Lublin section of the borderland and the rest of the country and Western Europe. Currently, a bypass around Sanok, in the vicinity of the border, has been completed and a call for tenders has been made for bypasses around Tomaszów Lubelski, on the national DK17 road section.

In rail transport, the largest recent investment that has improved access to the Polish–Ukrainian borderland was the modernization of sections of the E30 railway line from Cracow to Rzeszów and towards Medyka. Borderland rail access in Lublin voivodship remains weak.

Throughout the whole transition period (especially in the 1990s) the number of border crossings in Poland rapidly increased. However, this trend was somewhat less dynamic on the eastern border, including the border with Ukraine. Following 1989, when crossings were opened on major routes, subsequent checkpoints were launched less and less often, and the borders are still intersected by hard-surfaced roads where there are no border checks. At the time of the Schengen area enlargement (December 2007) 14 public road crossings were in operation on the Polish section of the European Union external border, six of which were on the Ukrainian border. Four Polish–Ukrainian border crossings serviced heavy freight road transport without any restrictions. In subsequent years, two local checkpoints were launched: in Budomierz, near Lubaczów, and in Dołhobyczów. There are still no road or tourist border checkpoints in the Bieszczady Mountains in the vicinity of the East Carpathian International Biosphere Reserve. Owing to the potential environmental impact, traffic is not allowed from Ustrzyki Górne directly into the Zakarpattia oblast in Ukraine.

Out of seven railway lines crossing the Polish–Ukrainian border, only two (the Dorohusk line on the Warsaw–Lublin–Kiev route and the Medyka line on the Cracow–Lviv route) service regular passenger traffic. The importance of railways in two-way passenger traffic between Poland and Ukraine in the transition period quickly diminished. Its relatively stronger status was maintained only because of the very poor permeability of road border checkpoints. Crossing the border by rail involves changing the width of the track, which means the handling of freight in so-called ‘dry ports’ (of which the largest is Żurawica–Medyka near Przemyśl) and the changing of the chassis in passenger transport (which entails a stop of several hours at the border). The exception is the line from Ustrzyki Dolne to Khyriv, where rail connections use the European track gauge. However, passenger traffic on this route was suspended. In addition, the borderland is intersected by the broad gauge (1520 millimetre) LHS line (Broad-gauge Steelworks Line; No. 65) running from the Ukrainian border (in the region of Hrubieszów) westward (see Figure 2.7). Attempts made in the 1990s to organize international passenger transport crossing points in Hrubieszów (1990–2000) and Hrebenne finally ended in failure. The standard gauge line in the direction of Lviv (as proposed in the early 1990s; cf. Lijewski 1994) was also not reactivated. An important factor inhibiting the development of railway transport was the scale of petty trade and smuggling, control of which via road traffic proved to be much easier.

Transport infrastructure, however, is not the main element affecting border permeability and the development of bilateral interaction. The key role is still played by the very intensive nature of border formalities. The waiting time for border control is very long – border queues of several hours apply to both trucks and cars – not because of an insufficient number of border checkpoints, but owing to detailed control procedures which are carried out separately by Polish and Ukrainian border guards. The level of control is necessary partly because of the intensity of petty smuggling of alcohol and tobacco. The queues on the Ukrainian side also stem from corruption. With the exception of the border checkpoint in Medyka, pedestrian traffic at all other border crossings along the Polish–Ukrainian border is prohibited (a European phenomenon).

Investigations showed that the waiting time of passenger vehicles in 2011, at all border checkpoints on the Polish–Ukrainian border, rarely fell below two hours (Rosik 2012). It is worth noting that times recorded by the border guard relate only to the wait before starting the inspection. The inspection itself also takes around one to two hours for passenger vehicles. A long waiting time, typically about six hours in 2011, is common at Hrebenne, situated on the route from Lviv to Lublin and Warsaw. Many Ukrainian citizens working in the Lublin region and in the Mazowieckie voivodship travel on this route. The waiting times recorded for freight transport tend to be several times longer. The average values are not as high as those recorded in the 1990s (up to 24 hours' average waiting time; Komornicki 1999), but they still testify to the significant transaction costs associated with crossing the border. All border checkpoints record occasional 'critical days', on which the waiting time increases to up to 20–30 hours. The most difficult situation was recorded quite consistently at Dorohusk (road traffic between Kiev and Warsaw; Rosik 2012).

Before 1989 the Polish–Soviet agreement on visa-free travel was officially in force. In practice, in order to cross the border, it was necessary to show a certified invitation or be a member of an officially organized tour. In the 1980s an agreement on so-called simplified traffic was signed and several border checkpoints designated for local communities were launched. After 1989 the interpretation of the Polish–Soviet agreement on visa-free traffic changed. A voucher confirming the purchase of tourist services could be issued even by a small private company. As a result, this document was widely available and its use did not necessarily relate to tourist services. Thus, the border became *de facto* fully permeable for Polish citizens and all countries once belonging to the Soviet Union. A decade of rapid increase in traffic and cross-border trade began. In 1995 the Polish–Ukrainian agreement on visa-free travel was signed. However, in October 2003 Poland terminated it owing to its obligations towards the European Union. Nevertheless, Ukraine waived the introduction of a visa regime for Poles. In December 2007 Poland and Lithuania joined the Schengen area, and the border with Russia, Belarus and Ukraine became the boundary of that area. Following Poland's accession to the European Union the former agreement on simplified traffic also ceased to apply and such traffic no longer took place. Efforts were launched to come to an agreement, as authorized by the Schengen principles, on local border traffic.

Finally, an agreement was concluded and has been in force since 2009. Visa-free traffic applies to people residing in the borderland area.

Border traffic on the Polish–Ukrainian border has undergone major changes since the beginning of socio-economic transformation in 1989 (Figure 3.6). The direct causes of these changes in the first period were (Komornicki 1999):

- the final liberalization of Polish passport regulations;
- passport facilitation in the former Soviet Union;
- the decentralization and privatization of road transport and foreign trade;
- the impoverishment of former Soviet Union societies (motivating trips to Poland to resell poor-quality goods) and part of Polish society (creating demand for the above goods);
- the competitiveness of goods produced by some branches of Polish industry on the markets of its eastern neighbours;
- high customs duty and excise tax on alcoholic beverages, tobacco and fuel in Poland, encouraging petty smuggling from the eastern border.

Many of these factors were short-term and unstable in nature, resulting in fluctuations in the intensity of border traffic. The first drop in growth occurred in 1992–3 and was related to the fact that the mass arrival of people selling goods in cross-border trade (retailers) was replaced by the arrival of buyers (wholesalers; Komornicki 1995). The greatest drop took place during the Russian crisis of 1998.

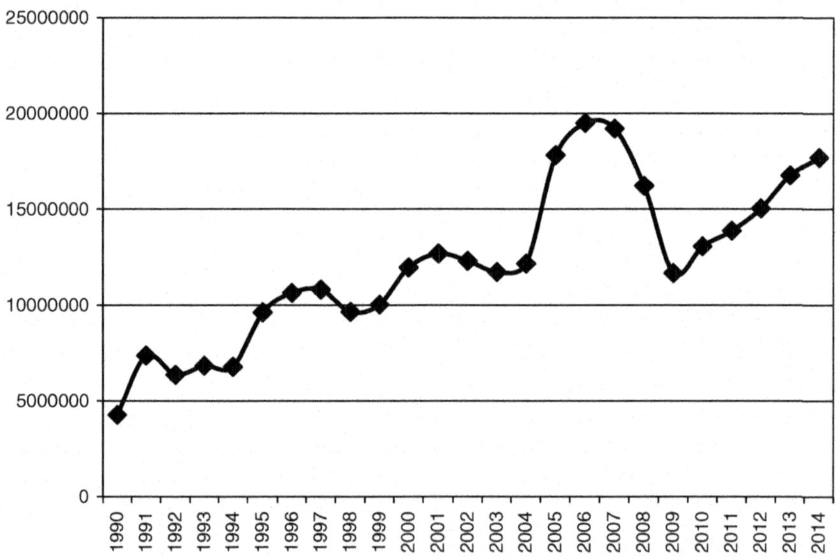

Figure 3.6 Movement of people crossing the Polish–Ukrainian border 1990–2014

Source: Own study, on the basis of Border Guard data.

It was, however, temporary and in 1999–2001 a revival of petty trade and traffic had already occured.

A factor that permanently influenced the situation on the Polish eastern border was the introduction by Poland in October 2003 (immediately before accession to the European Union) of visas for Ukrainian citizens. Nevertheless, traffic with Ukraine increased again with time because Ukraine did not introduce retaliatory measures. In subsequent years the intensity of traffic has increased, presumably as the result of the implementation of agreements on local border traffic. These trends continued in 2014, despite the geopolitical changes taking place. In comparison with 2013, traffic with Ukraine has increased by about 1 million people. In 2014 the border was crossed by local border traffic in the order of about 8.4 million Ukrainians (in both directions).

The heaviest passenger traffic is at the road checkpoint in Medyka (4.6 million people in 2014: Table 3.1). This is the only border crossing on the entire eastern border allowing pedestrian traffic. A previous reduction in traffic, following the Schengen regulations, occurred primarily at major Polish–Ukrainian border crossings (especially in Medyka and Dorohusk), while local checkpoints (Zosin, Krościenko) recorded an increase. This related to changes in the traffic structure (during this period in favour of Poles). Ukrainian citizens who commuted or were in transit frequently chose main routes into Poland. Poles travelling to Ukraine to purchase excised goods were mainly residents of the immediate border area, and they chose the closest border checkpoints. In 2014 changes in the opposite direction can be observed (in comparison to the reference year of 2010). There has been a sharp increase in traffic in Dorohusk and Korczowa – that is, on major transit routes. Meanwhile, Polish–Ukrainian local border checkpoints show stasis or even a significant decrease in pedestrian traffic.

Table 3.1 The busiest Polish–Ukraine border crossings (more than 1 million travellers) in 2014

Border crossing	*Route; transport corridor*	*Persons crossing the border in 2007*	*Persons crossing the border in 2010*	*Persons crossing the border in 2014*	*Change 2010–14*	*Share of Poles 2014 in %*
Medyka	Cracow–Lviv	6266902	4534861	4614020	102	8.9
Dorohusk	Warsaw–Kiev	3387317	2567212	3268078	127	10.5
Korczowa	Cracow–Lviv	2623034	2454531	3065987	125	7.5
Hrebenne	Warsaw–Lviv	2562824	2926041	2692102	92	11.5
Zosin	Zamość–Łuck	1680903	1966501	1962056	100	8.9
Krościenko	Sanok–Khyriv	2131639	2425271	1422898	59	33.7

Source: Own study, on the basis of Border Guard data; Komornicki (forthcoming).

Throughout the period of transition, the trend in the structure of border traffic as regards the share of Polish citizens and foreigners was also variable. In the period 1991–2003 the volume was completely determined by the arrival of foreigners (mainly Ukrainians). The movement of Poles was negligible. However, the introduction of visas and Poland's accession to the European Union led to a spectacular increase in the number of Poles crossing the border, mainly to purchase excise goods. Meanwhile, the Polish–Belarusian traffic was dominated by foreigners. In 2014 a drastic change in the structure of traffic on the Ukrainian border occurred. Once more, Poles constituted only 11.3 per cent of all travellers. In comparison with 2010, the absolute number of Poles crossing the border with Ukraine (in both directions) halved, and in comparison with 2013 there was a decrease of about 300,000. However, we should be cautious in linking this trend with the geopolitical situation. The greatest changes occurred in 2010–12, and thus it should be assumed that their cause was the restriction on the import of excise goods or the regaining of the border market by Ukrainian citizens (as a result of the local border traffic agreement). The dominance of Ukrainian citizens was lowest at the Krościenko border checkpoint (see Table 3.1). This can be explained by the existence of permanent connections from tourist resorts in the Bieszczady Mountains to Lviv. In absolute values, the number of Poles travelling (one way) by overland routes to Ukraine decreased from 2.1 million in 2010 to just 1.0 million in 2014.

The structure of incoming traffic to Poland via the bilateral border is clearly dominated by Ukrainian citizens (Table 3.2). Out of almost 8 million foreigners crossing the border in 2014, up to 7.8 million were Ukrainian citizens. The second largest group constitutes Germans in transit heading for Ukraine through Poland. Currently, citizens of Romania and Moldova are also among the major groups travelling through Ukraine to Poland. Previously, it was the Russians who dominated.

Table 3.2 Citizens by selected countries entering Poland via the border with Ukraine in 2014

Nationality	*Entries to Poland in 2014*	*Probable transit route*
Ukraine	7,780,711	Movement to Poland and further to the whole of Western Europe
Germany	41,755	Transit from Ukraine via Poland
Romania	21,941	Transit to Poland and other EU countries via Ukraine
Moldova	16,947	
Russia	10,405	
Czech Republic	9,784	Transit from Ukraine via Poland
Lithuania	8,410	
Latvia	5,376	
Refugee (Art. 1 of the 1951 Convention.)	292	Inflow to EU
Total	**7,952,084**	**XXX**

Source: Own study, on the basis of Border Guard data.

It is characteristic that in 2013–14 the number of Russians crossing the Polish–Ukrainian border decreased four-fold (despite the fact that in 2013 numbers were already low, at approximately 40,000; Komornicki forthcoming). This must be related to the escalating conflict in Donbas. There is also minimal transit from Belarus and Bulgaria. Moreover, in 2014 only 292 refugees (within the meaning of Article 1 of the 1951 Convention) were recorded at the Polish–Ukrainian border. The border between the two countries did not, therefore, experience high migration pressure from third countries. It should be noted that the total number of foreigners entering Poland via the Polish–Ukrainian border in 2014 amounted to 7,952,000, while the number of people departing the same way was only 7,745,000. This means that there were more than 200,000 people who 'did not come back' to Ukraine. Some of them, certainly, could have travelled back by a different route (or by air), but the same could also occur in the case of arrivals to Poland. Such a deficiency was not recorded in other sections of the Polish eastern border with Belarus and Russia. At the border of Belarus there was a surplus (about 100,000 people). Even if we assume that these are the same travellers returning by a circular route (although there is no direct evidence), it can still be assumed that about 100,000 incoming crossings in 2014 in fact represent emigration, or long-term departure from Ukraine, to Poland or other European Union countries. Regardless of these numbers, in 2014 82,000 Ukrainians arrived in Poland by air.

A lack of data on traffic at other Polish borders (especially with Germany) makes it difficult to estimate the numbers of Ukrainians in transit through Poland, heading for other countries. The last estimate of the kind comes from 2007 (before Poland's accession to the Schengen area); apparently 13 per cent of Ukrainian citizens checked at the bilateral border were travelling to other countries (Komornicki and Miszczuk 2011).

The whole period after 1990 was characterized by a generally upward trend in HGV traffic across the Ukrainian border (Figure 3.7). Polish membership of the EU and the Schengen area did not substantially affect this trend. In 2009, however, a drop in traffic could be observed, clearly related to the global economic crisis. Nevertheless, in the years 2010–13 there was a renewed increase in HGV traffic, although this, too, was interrupted by the events of 2014. The largest drop (in comparison with other sections of the eastern Polish border) occurred on the border with Ukraine, where the number of vehicles recorded at border checkpoints decreased from 748,000 to 611,000, which can tentatively be put down to the geopolitical turmoil. However, it has to be remembered that the number of crossings at the border was still significantly higher in 2014 than that recorded in 2009. The decrease in goods exchange does not therefore mean a return to the situation witnessed in the first wave of the global economic crisis.

In the years 2010–14 there was a decrease in HGV traffic at all bilateral border crossings except Dorohusk (Table 3.3). In previous years, this traffic moved to border checkpoints at Medyka and Korczowa. The causes were found to lie in the development of the road infrastructure in Poland (here, progress in the construction of the A4 motorway). Current data indicate that transit traffic from Ukraine is once again using the route via Lublin and Warsaw to Berlin. Possible reasons for this

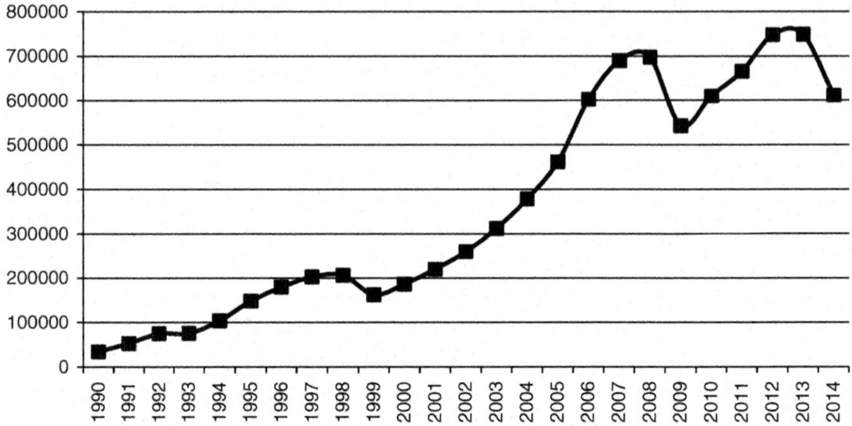

Figure 3.7 HGV traffic across the Polish–Ukrainian border in the period 1990–2014

Source: Own study, on the basis of Border Guard data.

Table 3.3 HGV traffic at the main Polish–Ukrainian border checkpoints in 2014

Border crossing	*Route; transport corridor*	*HGV traffic in 2003*	*HGV traffic in 2010*	*HGV traffic in 2013*	*HGV traffic in 2014*	*Change 2010–14*	*Change 2013–14*
Dorohusk	Warsaw–Kiev	158828	265527	343449	302133	114	88
Korczowa	Cracow–Lviv	52204	159208	177135	147418	93	83
Hrebenne	Warsaw–Lviv	70265	98047	125296	94542	96	75
Medyka	Cracow–Lviv	30845	84700	102015	66962	79	66

Source: Own study, on the basis of Border Guard data.

situation include road investments in the region of the capital (A2) and Lublin (S17). In 2013–14 heavy goods vehicle traffic decreased at almost all Polish eastern border checkpoints, with the most significant decrease at Medyka and Hrebenne.

The analysis of cross-border traffic of people and vehicles has made it possible to draw some general conclusions and make some recommendations. It has been shown that the movement of goods is significantly influenced by geopolitical and macroeconomic situations, while the size and directions of movements of people are decided mainly by the formal situation (e.g. agreements on local border traffic) as well as the border trade situation. Moreover, events in Ukraine resulted in an increase rather than a decrease in traffic, although this was largely local border traffic. This can be associated with the deteriorating economic situation, which resulted in the search for additional sources of income (petty trade or work in Poland).

At the same time, the difference in the number of foreigners arriving and departing may indirectly indicate migratory movement from Ukraine, Poland and the European Union. Heavy traffic from Ukraine entered Poland directly, rather than through Belarus, and gradually moved once again to the route through Warsaw and the A2 motorway. It can be assumed that infrastructure factors determined the Ukrainian transit routes in Poland.

Changing trends regarding the concentration of traffic, especially freight, have been observed over a long period of time. Initially a tendency towards de-concentration dominated, associated with the opening of new border checkpoints and their initial low capacity, leading to a preference for more distant, but less congested checkpoints. Recently, the situation has visibly reversed, and people and freight are once more concentrating on main road routes. An important factor is probably the development of the Polish network of motorways and expressways.

Social relations

An important manifestation of the social cross-border ties existing between Poland and Ukraine is the flow of workers. This mainly consists of an inflow of Ukrainians to Poland owing to the significant differences in income levels. For many years a phenomenon of cross-border labour migration was the so-called grey market, which came about as a result of complex procedures which discouraged people from legalizing employment. Thus, it is difficult to make reliable estimates about the influx of workers from across the eastern Polish border.

Until 2008 the only means of legalizing employment for Ukrainian citizens was to obtain a work permit, and this form of employment continues today, alongside another method based on a statement of intention to employ a foreigner. In order to obtain a work permit, a foreigner should have a visa (Schengen or national) or a temporary residence permit allowing them to take up employment in Poland. The employer requests a work permit from the relevant voivodship governor corresponding to the head office of the company. Certain occupations require a so-called labour market test, involving the presentation by the district governor of information on job-seekers with similar qualifications as the foreigners registered in the District Labour Office. Moreover, some occupations in Poland are regulated (including, among others, architects, lawyers and doctors), which means that, in order to pursue them, the recognition of a person's professional qualifications is necessary.

In principle, a work permit is issued for a period of three years, with the possibility of extension. There are various types of permit, depending on whether a foreigner is employed in a Polish company, performs a management role in a foreign or Polish company in Poland, or has been delegated by a foreign employer. Any change in the place of employment (employer) requires a new work permit. Data on the number of work permits for Ukrainians (by selected employee group) in the years 2010 and 2014 are presented in Table 3.4.

Ukrainians were the largest and fastest-growing ethnic group among applicants for work permits in Poland in 2010–14. This phenomenon was undoubtedly influenced by the events destabilizing the political and socio-economic situation in

Table 3.4 Work permits for Ukrainians in 2010–14

	2010	*2014*	*2010 = 100,0*
POLAND			
Total number of work permits for foreigners in absolute numbers	36622	43663	119.2
– work permits for Ukrainians in absolute numbers	12894	26315	204.1
– work permits for Ukrainians in % (number of permits for foreigners = 100.0)	35.2	60.3	–
Work permits for Ukrainians by employee groups (in %)	100.0	100.0	204.1
– managers, consultants, experts	3.2	2.8	176.3
– skilled workers	27.5	34.9	258.9
– unskilled workers	26.3	18.0	139.7
LUBLIN VOIVODSHIP			
Total number of work permits for foreigners in absolute numbers	619	1380	222.9
– work permits for Ukrainians in absolute numbers	283	870	307.4
– work permits for Ukrainians in % (number of permits for foreigners = 100.0)	45.7	63.0	–
Work permits for Ukrainians by employee groups (in %)	100.0	100.0	307.4
– managers, consultants, experts	4.2	0.9	66.7
– skilled workers	30.7	54.3	542.5
– unskilled workers	1.8	1.8	320.0
PODKARPACKIE VOIVODSHIP			
Total number of work permits for foreigners in absolute numbers	389	670	172.2
– work permits for Ukrainians in absolute numbers	230	569	247.4
– work permits for Ukrainians in % (number of permits for foreigners = 100.0)	59.1	84.9	–
Work permits for Ukrainians by employee groups (in %)	100.0	100.0	247.4
– managers, consultants, experts	10.0	4.9	121.7
– skilled workers	45.7	55.0	298.1
– unskilled workers	3.0	12.0	971.4
POLISH–UKRAINIAN BORDERLAND (Polish part)			
Total number of work permits for foreigners in absolute numbers	1008	2050	203.4
– work permits for Ukrainians in absolute numbers	513	1439	280.5
– work permits for Ukrainians in % (number of permits for foreigners = 100.0)	50.9	70.2	–
Work permits for Ukrainians by employee groups (in %)	100.0	100.0	280.5
– managers, consultants, experts	6.8	2.5	102.9
– skilled workers	37.4	54.6	408.9
– unskilled workers	2.3	5.8	700.0

Source: Own study, on the basis of data from the Ministry of Labour and Social Policy of the Republic of Poland.

Ukraine (as detailed in Chapter 1). However, it should also be emphasized that the volume of work permits issued for foreigners (including Ukrainians) in 2014 was small in comparison to the number of people working in Poland – 14.2 million legally and 711,000 thousand on the ‘grey market’ (*Praca nierejestrowana w Polsce w 2014 roku* 2015). The largest densities of Ukrainians employed with work permits were recorded in the following voivodships: Mazowieckie (52.7 per cent of total work permits), Wielkopolskie (6.9 per cent), Małopolskie (6.6 per cent), Pomorskie (5.4 per cent), Lubuskie (4.7 per cent), Kujawsko-Pomorskie (4.0 per cent) and Lower Silesia (3.7 per cent). Against this background, Lublin and Podkarpackie voivodships, constituting part of the Polish–Ukrainian borderland, displayed quite low results, with 3.3 per cent and 2.2 per cent respectively (Figure 3.8). However, these voivodships showed a higher growth rate in work permits for Ukrainians than the national average. Ukrainian skilled workers also dominated to a much larger extent in these voivodships.

In terms of the gender structure, Ukrainian women constituted on average in Poland around one-third of those receiving work permits, while in Lublin and Podkarpackie voivodships the percentage did not even exceed 20 per cent. This dominance of Ukrainian men seeking to legalize their work in Poland, may, in the long term, result in the migration of their families.

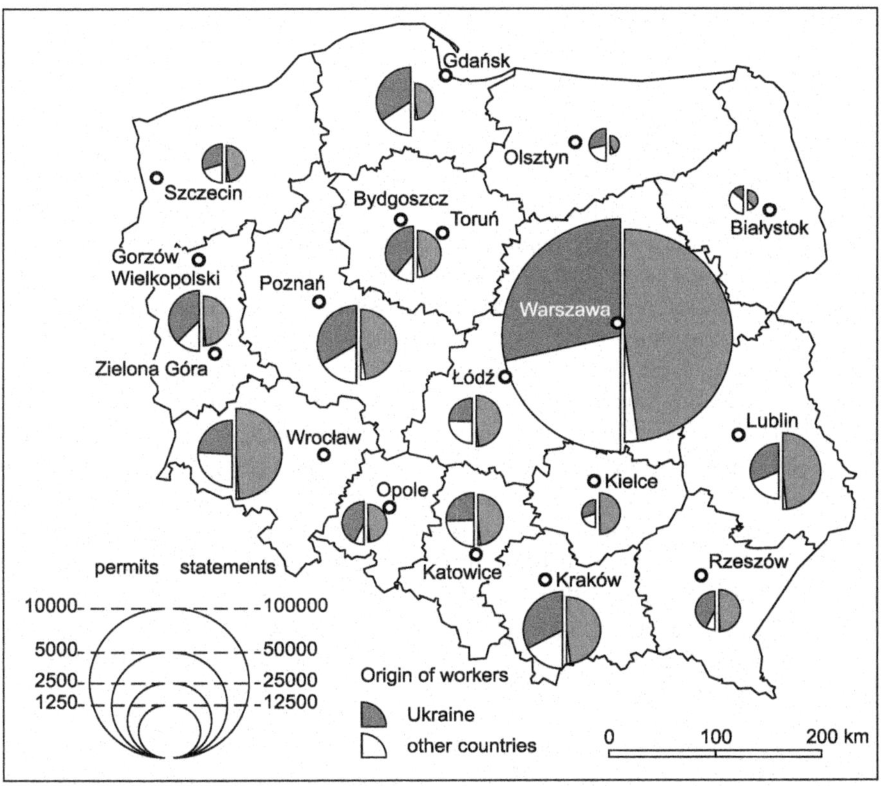

Figure 3.8 Work permits and statements of intention to employ a foreigner for Ukrainians in 2014

Source: Krzysztof Łoboda, on the basis of data from the Ministry of Labour and Social Policy of the Republic of Poland.

As far as sectors of employment are concerned, the largest share of Ukrainian workers (on average in Poland) in 2014 was employed in private households (20.5 per cent of total permits), followed by construction (19.0 per cent), transport (10.0 per cent), trade (8.8 per cent), agriculture (7.3 per cent) and industry (5.4 per cent). Jobs in households as babysitters and domestic workers were mostly taken up by women. The demand for this type of work occurs mainly in large cities such as Warsaw and Cracow, which is why this type of employment is of little importance in Lublin voivodship (6.9 per cent) and of almost no importance in Podkarpackie voivodship (1.2 per cent). On the other hand, Lublin voivodship had the largest number of Ukrainian workers employed in transport (47.1 per cent) and trade (26.2 per cent), and Podkarpackie voivodship had the largest numbers in construction (30.1 per cent), transport (14.8 per cent) and trade (12.1 per cent). Quite a large percentage of Ukrainian academic personnel (mostly academic teachers) was recorded in Podkarpackie voivodship (9.0 per cent), especially at Rzeszow's universities and other centres of higher education in Podkarpackie voivodship.

Relatively few work permit applications for Ukrainians were rejected. In 2014 the percentage was 0.8 per cent at the national level and only 0.4 per cent in Lublin voivodship, but 2.0 per cent in Podkarpackie voivodship.

Since the beginning of 2008, a new simplified form of work legalization in Poland for citizens of Ukraine (as well as Armenia, Belarus, Georgia, Moldova and Russia) has been implemented, based on a statement of intention to employ a foreigner. Thus, citizens of Ukraine may work (if they have a valid visa or temporary residence permit) for a period not exceeding six months within the next 12 months, regardless of the number of entities employing them under a written contract. A written statement of an employer's intention to employ a foreigner should be registered by the employer in the district labour office. This statement should include the name of the occupation, the place of work, the starting date and period of employment, the type of employment contract, the gross remuneration, information on the inability of the local labour market to meet staffing needs and information on the employer's acquaintance with the law regarding the residence and work of foreigners. The procedures for employing a foreigner through means of a statement or work permit can be combined. An employer may employ a foreigner under a simplified procedure (based on a statement) and, after a few months, apply to the governor for a work permit. In this case, the employment of a foreigner based on a work permit can commence directly following his/her employment period based on a statement.

The liberalization of provisions relating to the simplified employment system for citizens of Ukraine and Armenia, Belarus, Georgia, Moldova and Russia were aimed at:

- reducing the volume of illegal employment among citizens of these countries (this does not mean, however, the complete elimination of the 'grey market'),
- a more flexible labour market, especially with regard to seasonal work,
- building international, including cross-border, socio-economic ties with neighbouring countries

The fact that at least some of these goals were achieved is shown by data for 2010–14. In 2010, under the statement of intention to employ a foreigner, 180,073 people were employed, including 169,490 from Ukraine (94.1 per cent of the total number of statements). In the case of Ukrainians, this is 13 times more than the number of people employed under work permits. On the other hand, in 2014 the number of statements increased to a total of 387,398 people, an increase of over 115 per cent compared to 2010, and in terms of Ukrainian employees to 372,946 (i.e. an increase of 120 per cent). The percentage of Ukrainian women employed in 2014 under statements amounted to 38.6 per cent of the total number of Ukrainian citizens employed. Ukrainian workers were most often aged 26–40 (43.3 per cent of total employed), unskilled (66.2 per cent), employed mainly in agriculture (47.4 per cent) and construction (14.1 per cent) for a period of three to six months (90.6 per cent). The largest concentrations of Ukrainian workers employed under statements were recorded in Mazowieckie (52.3 per cent), Dolnośląskie (9.7 per cent), Lublin (6.8 per cent), Wielkopolskie (5.6 per cent) and Małopolskie (5.2 per cent) voivodships. Against this background, Podkarpackie voivodship, located in the vicinity of the border with Ukraine, stands out in particular (2.1 per cent) (Figure 3.8).

The above deliberations show that growing numbers of Ukrainians are legally taking up employment. Work permits are mainly applied for by people with professional qualifications, for whom there is demand on the Polish labour market. Meanwhile, a much larger number of Ukrainians take up temporary work based on statements. This work usually does not require professional qualifications. The largest group of employees working both under permits and statements is found in economically well-developed voivodships with good communications (Mazowieckie, Wielkopolskie, Małopolskie, Dolnośląskie). The immediate vicinity of the Polish–Ukrainian border (Lubelskie, Podkarpackie) is of relatively less importance in this regard.

The issue of Ukrainians migrating to Poland in search of work can be viewed as compensatory migration, reducing labour shortages, especially in peripheral areas suffering from depopulation (Janicki 2015). Thus, the question arises: should Poland pursue a more active and flexible immigration policy towards Ukrainians, one not only limited to the two existing instruments, the work permit and the statement of intention to employ a foreigner.

Another important manifestation of cross-border social ties is student migration. It can represent the first step for students in settling down and starting work in the place (country) where they graduated from university. Studying abroad is a global phenomenon that applied, in 2014, to more than 4.5 million people around the world, and according to forecasts this number may double by 2020. Poland has not been among leading countries to accept foreign students. The percentage of foreign students in 2014 amounted to 3.1 per cent of all students – that is, 46,101 people from 158 countries – and although this was significantly higher than in 2010 – 1.2 per cent – it was and still is low, compared with the average of OECD countries, which is close to 9.0 per cent (*Study in Poland* 2015). The highest percentages of foreign students occurs in Lublin (6.7 per cent), Mazowieckie

(5.1 per cent) and Podkarpackie (4.3 per cent) voivodships (Figure 3.9). The high ranking of voivodships forming the Polish part of the Polish–Ukrainian borderland includes a certain 'Ukrainian-ization' of Polish universities. It appears that in the academic year 2014/15 as many as 50 per cent of foreign students in Poland were Ukrainians, while four years earlier the figure was approximately 20 per cent. The migrations of both students and workers are almost exclusively one-directional, with Ukrainian citizens migrating to Poland. Ukrainian students choose higher education in Poland because a degree awarded by a university located in the European Union increases their competitiveness on the labour market. The lack of significant cultural and language barriers between Poland and Ukraine is also not to be disregarded. In addition, university fees in Poland are relatively low, especially in comparison with universities in Western Europe, and do not contain any hidden formal and informal fees (as is the case in Ukraine). Some students, especially from western Ukraine, whose Polish origin can be documented and

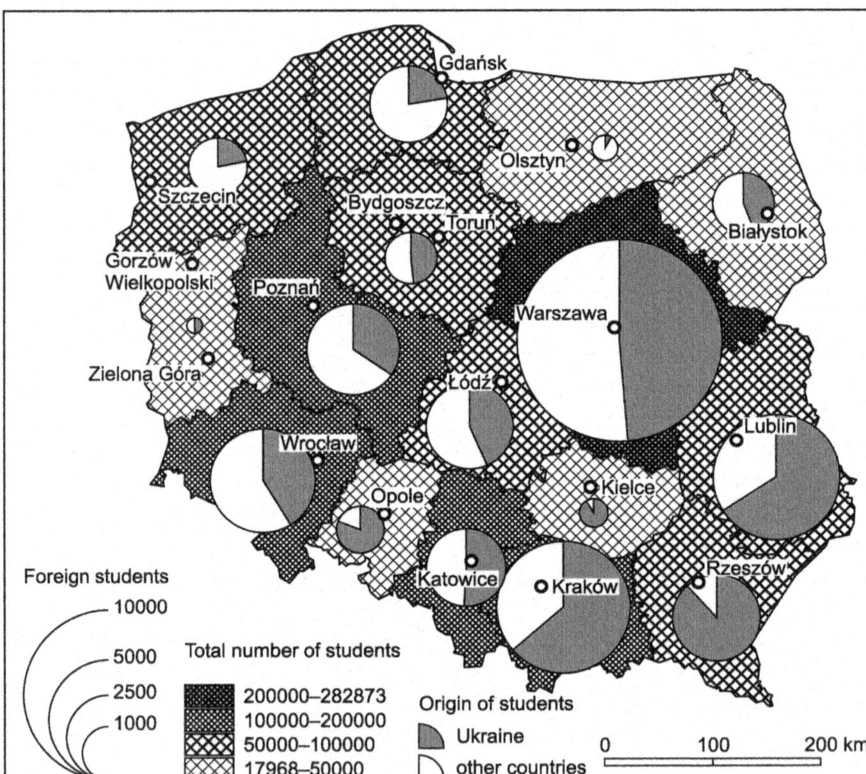

Figure 3.9 Students from Ukraine on background of total number of students in Poland in 2014

Source: Krzysztof Łoboda, on the basis of *Study in Poland* (2015).

who possess a so-called Polish Citizen's Card, can study free of charge. However, the incompatibility of primary and secondary education systems in Poland and Ukraine constitutes a problem. Ukrainian high school graduates are on average two years younger than Polish high school graduates. This means they do not always have sufficient knowledge to study in specialized technical or medical faculties.

Since the early 1990s the universities in the voivodships on Poland's eastern border (Lubelskie and Podkarpackie) have established closer cooperation with partners from Ukraine that has resulted in jointly organized conferences, seminars and summer schools. It is especially visible in the activities of the largest public universities in the area, the Maria Curie-Skłodowska University, Lublin (UMCS), the John Paul II Catholic University of Lublin (KUL) and the University of Rzeszów. Polish universities eagerly employ Ukrainian university professors, especially those with Polish language skills, offering them employment in Poland that is financially attractive compared with Ukrainian conditions. A unique form of cooperation with Poland's eastern neighbours was the establishment in 2000 in Lublin of the European College of Polish and Ukrainian Universities (ECPUU). This was a joint initiative of the UMCS and KUL in Lublin, the University of Taras Shevchenko, Kiev, the University of Ivan Franko, Lviv, the Kyiv-Mohyla Academy and the Lublin Institute of East-Central Europe. The originators of this new institution were Prof. Bohdan Osadczuk of the Free University in Berlin and Prof. Jerzy Kłoczowski of the Institute of East-Central Europe. Initially, its aim was to educate PhD students, and ultimately to establish a Polish–Ukrainian European university. Despite the willingness of subsequent representatives of Poland and Ukraine (Presidents Aleksander Kwaśniewski and Leonid Kuchma, Prime Ministers Donald Tusk and Yulia Tymoshenko), the Ukrainian authorities eventually withdrew from the project. As a result, ECPUU was wound up in 2011 and doctoral education was taken over by the Center for Central and Eastern Europe at UMCS and the Centre for Society and Culture of Eastern Europe at KUL. However, it would be worth applying previously gained experience and returning to the idea of the ECPUU, perhaps in a modified form, with reference to the Eastern Partnership and also involving a larger number of countries.

Table 3.5 contains the baseline data for the analysis of student migration in the Polish–Ukrainian borderland (on the Polish side). It should be noted that within the academic years 2010/11 and 2014/15 the number of students in Poland sharply decreased from 1,817,533 to 1,468,406 (19.2 per cent). A similar phenomenon was observed in Lublin voivodship (a decrease from 101,540 to 82,000 (19.2 per cent)) and Podkarpackie (a decrease from 73,336 to 59,321 (19.1 per cent)). This was caused by a significant long-term reduction in the rate of natural increase, and consequently in the volume of younger age groups, especially aged 19–24, and the increasing migration of students from Poland to universities in Western Europe. Thus, it might be said that the growing number of foreign students, including students from Ukraine, is a compensating factor for these losses at Polish universities. In Lublin

Table 3.5 Students from Ukraine studying in Lublin and Podkarpackie voivodships in the academic years 2010/11 and 2014/15

	Foreign students			
	Total		*From Ukraine*	
	Individuals	*% of total number of students*	*Individuals*	*% of total number of students*
Lublin				
Academic year 2010/11	2049	2.0	799	0.8
Academic year 2014/15	5428	6.6	3584	4.4
Podkarpackie				
Academic year 2010/11	1154	1.6	996	1.4
Academic year 2014/15	2574	4.3	2272	3.8
Polish–Ukrainian borderland (Polish part)				
Academic year 2010/11	3203	1.8	1795	1.0
Academic year 2014/15	8002	5.7	5856	4.1

Source: Own study, on the basis of data from the Central Statistical Office and *Study in Poland* (2015).

voivodship the number of foreigners entering universities/colleges in 2010–14 increased more than two and a half times, and the number of Ukrainians almost four and a half times. In the case of Podkarpackie voivodship the numbers more than doubled, in relation to both foreigners in general and Ukrainian students.

Students from Ukraine study at both public and private Polish universities. In the academic year 2010/11 in Lublin voivodship the largest number of Ukrainians studied at the State Vocational University of Szymon Szymonowic in Zamość (157 people), the University of International Relations and Social Communication in Chełm, a non-public university (133 persons), and the University of Management and Administration in Zamość, also a non-public university (128 people). The two largest universities of Lublin voivodship (UMCS and KUL) played a relatively less important role in this regard; the numbers of Ukrainian citizens studying there were 123 and 109, respectively. In the academic year 2014/15 the situation changed substantially. UMCS, with 954 Ukrainians (an eight-fold increase), ranked in first place, followed by the non-public Vincent Pol University of Social and Natural Sciences in Lublin (453 persons), the University of Economics and Innovation, another non-public university (430 persons), the State Vocational University of Szymon Szymonowic in Zamość (339 persons), Lublin University of Technology (333 persons), the non-public University of Enterprise and Administration in Lublin (285 people), the John Paul II Catholic University of Lublin (241 persons), the State Vocational University of Pope John Paul II in Biała Podlaska (162 people) and the non-public University of International Relations and Social Communication in Chełm (106 people). The most popular faculties among Ukrainians in Lublin voivodship are tourism and recreation, philology (including Slavic), political science, international relations, administration and computer science.

Meanwhile, in Podkarpackie voivodship in the academic year 2010/11 the first place in terms of numbers of Ukrainian students was taken by the non-public University of Computer Science and Management in Rzeszów (760 people). Four years later this university continues to lead in Podkarpackie voivodship, with 1,682 Ukrainians (an increase of over 120 per cent), in Poland surpassed only by the non-public Andrzej Frycz-Modrzewski Cracow University (1,776 people). Subsequent universities in the Podkarpackie voivodship ranking in the academic year 2014/15 were the public universities: the East European State Higher School in Przemyśl (251 Ukrainian students), the Bronisław Markiewicz State Higher School of Technology and Economics in Jarosław (123) and the University of Rzeszów (102). Most Ukrainians in Podkarpackie voivodship study computer science, economics, tourism and recreation, philology, logistics and international relations.

In summary, there are discernible patterns in the distribution of students from Ukraine in Poland. In the academic year 2010/11 an important role was played by the proximity of Polish academic centres to the state border. A significant number (approximately 50 per cent) of Ukrainians studying in Poland were admitted to state and private universities in both Podkarpackie and Lublin voivodships, located in the voivodship capitals (Rzeszow, Lublin) and in smaller centres (Chełm, Przemyśl, Zamość). The record holder in terms of student numbers from Ukraine continues to be the private University of Information Technology and Management in Rzeszów. In 2014/15 there was a rapid increase in the number of Ukrainian students in Poland, while at the same time, the relative importance of Lublin and Podkarpackie voivodships fell, with 25 per cent of the total number of students from Ukraine. Meanwhile, the importance of the two largest Polish academic centres as migration destinations for Ukrainian students – Warsaw and Cracow – significantly increased.

Economic relations

Poland's accession to the European Union resulted in an increase of trade not only with other member states but also with non-EU countries, including Ukraine. The territorial dimension of exchange with Ukraine has traditionally related to the main transport corridors (latitudinal from Germany via Krakow to Lviv and oblique from Kujawy and Warsaw via Lublin to Kiev and Lviv; Komornicki 2003). Since the early 1990s Poland's eastern borderland region has seen very intensive exports to immediate neighbours at least partly because of lower quality standards set by Russian, Ukrainian and Belarusian markets. Many small entrepreneurs from eastern Poland failed to compete in the EU market, but there was still a demand for less upmarket goods on the eastern market. Nevertheless, the importance of the Ukrainian market in the eastern voivodships (especially Lublin and Podkarpackie) fell after 2003. Meanwhile, a very large increase in exports to Ukraine occurred in other areas, primarily western and parts of northern Poland.

This demonstrates diversification of trading partners on the part of entrepreneurs from eastern Poland and their entrance into the Western European markets.

Over the past two years the spatial distribution of trade with Ukraine has changed once again. In 2013 (Figure 3.10) the trade relations of central Polish centres have continued to grow. Exports to Ukraine have increased from Warsaw, but also from Łódż and Płock (with fuel exports from Orlen refinery playing an important role). Meanwhile, the concentration of commercial contacts along the latitudinal A4 motorway corridor has clearly remained, especially in Podkarpackie voivodship. Currently, the Lviv–Warsaw corridor is less clearly defined. Companies in Lublin voivodship have penetrated the Ukrainian market less intensively than those of Podkarpackie voivodship. The formation of export centres in some smaller towns in western Poland (e.g. Gorzow Wielkopolski), where multinational

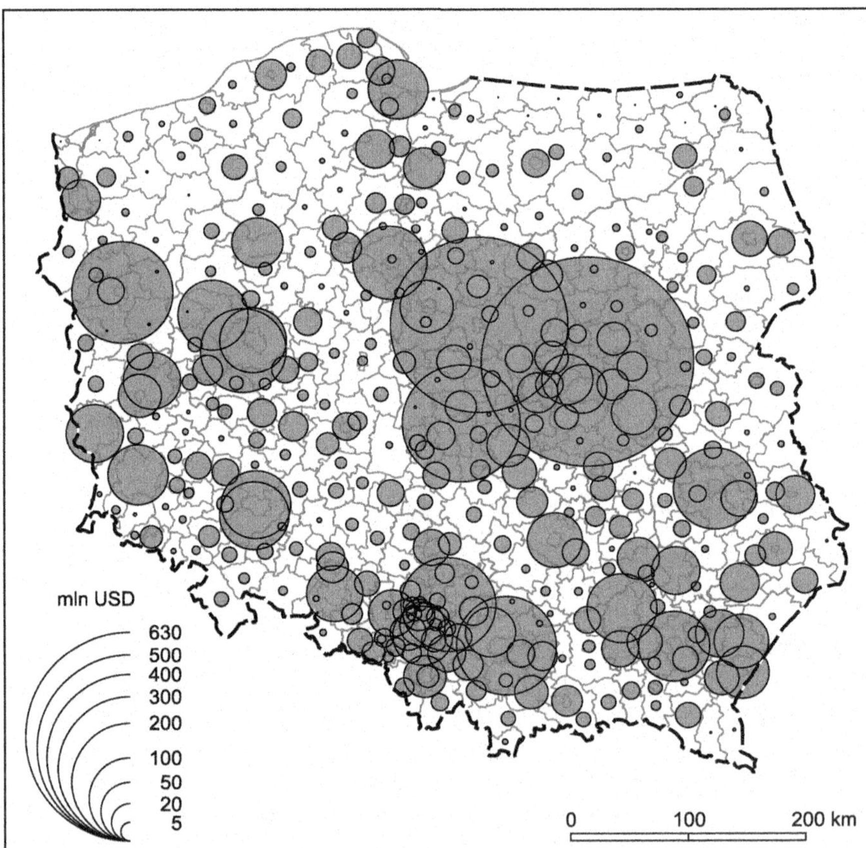

Figure 3.10 Total exports to Ukraine in 2013

Source: Krzysztof Łoboda, on the basis of Komornicki and Szejgiec (2011).

companies are located, can be assumed to be the result of the inclusion of Polish–Ukrainian trade into intra-industry and even intra-corporate turnover. Some urban centres (especially Przemyśl, but also Tomaszów Lubelski) in the borderland region have become places of export not by producers but by trading entities. This demonstrates the utilization of the border location by certain companies involved in the re-export to Ukraine of goods produced in Poland and other European Union countries. Nevertheless, Warsaw remains the biggest centre for this kind of re-export.

The role of official trade with Ukraine in the borderland area is better demonstrated by this partner's share in the total export value of districts (*powiats*) (Figure 3.11). In central and western Poland this share generally does not exceed 5 per cent. The situation is different in border voivodships. For several border

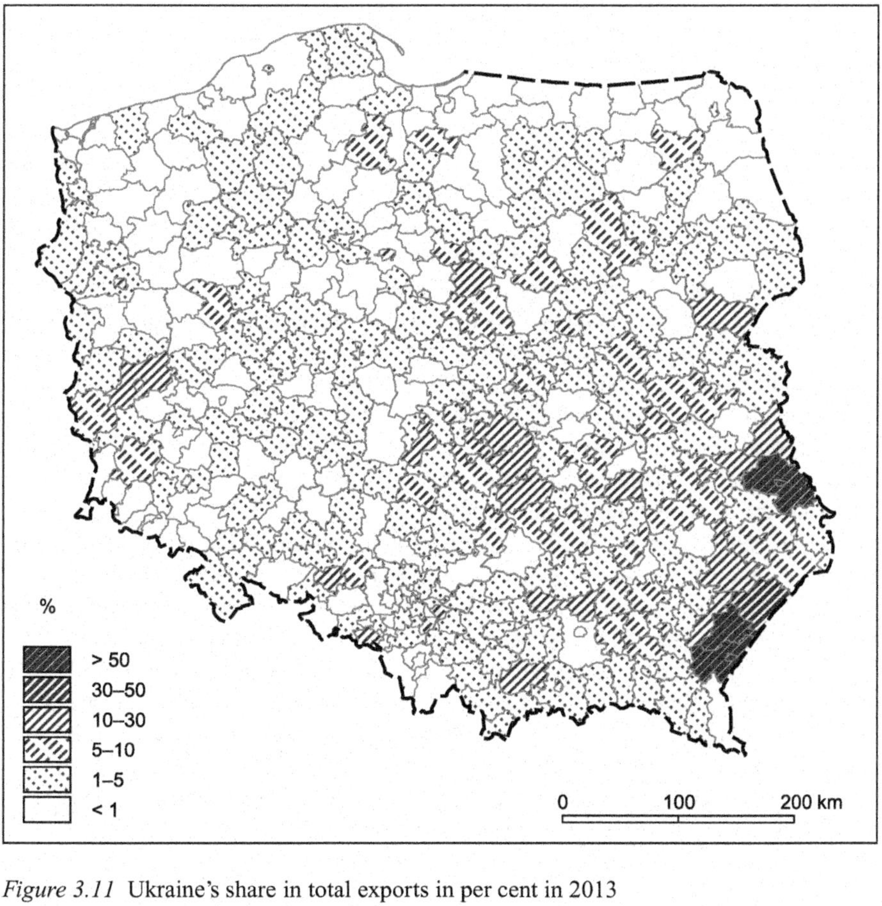

Figure 3.11 Ukraine's share in total exports in per cent in 2013

Source: Krzysztof Łoboda, on the basis of Komornicki and Szejgiec (2011).

districts – often, as mentioned above, trading areas – Ukraine remains the most important foreign purchaser of exported goods. Among these districts, Przemyśl (urban and rural), Lubaczów and Chełm are foremost. The picture obtained shows that the extent of economic relations with Ukraine in the border voivodships is spatially limited. These contacts form an operational base in only a few local economies.

Meanwhile, as previous research shows (Komornicki and Szejgiec 2011; Komornicki and Miszczuk 2011), the eastern Polish borderland is still a place of intensive export to the whole of Eastern Europe (not only to Ukraine). In 2009 zones were identified in which the concentration of total exports to Russia, Belarus and Ukraine exceeded 20 per cent. These were:

- The north-east of Lublin voivodship (Bialski, Włodawski, Chełmski districts; Chełm and Biała Podlaska city-districts);
- The east of Podkarpackie voivodship (Przemyśl district, Przemyśl city-district).

It was found, however, that the extent of these areas is decreasing. This process was already apparent in the period 2005–7 as a result of Poland's accession to the European Union and the subsequent increase in trade between eastern regions and EU partners (especially Germany). Research into the total share of export to eastern neighbouring countries has confirmed the earlier thesis that the role of border location as a factor stimulating above-average economic relations is diminishing (Komornicki and Szejgiec 2011). Later, under conditions of economic crisis and economic downturn (even in local market trade), only certain districts retained a strong position in terms of re-exports to Russia, Belarus and Ukraine. At the same time the share of these three partners in eastern Poland is still significantly higher than in other regions of the country, with levels of 10–15 per cent of the total value of exports compared with 1–5 per cent in western Poland. This reflects the real economic contacts maintained by producers of export goods.

Studies of the immunity of local economies to global economic problems (Komornicki et al. forthcoming) have shown that the territorial system of exchange with Ukraine demonstrates the susceptibility of mutual trade relations to economic cycles. Distance from the border was also found to be important for exports, but the significance of this factor has decreased in recent years (Komornicki 2003).

One of the first manifestations of economic links in the borderland when the state border was opened was spontaneous border trade, which became a source of income for, especially, many small businesses and private individuals. It was motivated by the lack of goods on one side of the border, or their lower prices, or by the specificity of tax systems. In the case of a totally unrestricted border, this type of demand usually decreases but does not completely disappear.[1] In its place a more lasting demand arises for services offered in the region (such as tourism or education) or for cooperation in the development and implementation of a product or technological innovation. However, on a border with limited permeability spontaneous cross-border trade has the chance of surviving because of artificially sustained differences in customs, tax and so on, thus securing the profitability of this type of undertaking. This phenomenon is well illustrated by trade in the Polish–Ukrainian borderland. In its first stage (1990–93) there was an influx of cheap, often poor-quality goods from Ukraine to Poland. Revenues from the sale of these goods were exchanged into dollars and taken back to Ukraine. The second stage (1994–8) was characterized by a reverse flow of money and goods. Shortages of goods on the Ukrainian market meant that Ukrainians came to Poland to buy them (popular groceries included fruit, vegetables and fish, and popular non-food items were clothing, furniture and building materials). The boom in border trade was felt by the municipalities where border checkpoints are located, as well as cities, especially larger ones, situated within a distance of 100 kilometres from the border. Since 1999, border trade has entered a third phase. Initially, its importance started to decrease, no doubt the consequence of increased economic activity on the Ukrainian side, which meant demand for goods and services was satisfied by local manufacturers or by foreign manufacturers developing their business in Ukraine, as well as of restrictions on the amount of imported goods introduced by the Ukrainian authorities. Nevertheless, Poland's accession to the EU in 2004 (Phase IV) opened new possibilities for cross-border trade. Ukrainians buy, *inter alia*, IT equipment, home appliances or construction materials and, in transporting them back to Ukraine, which lies outside the customs territory of the European Union, are entitled to a refund of VAT, which provides them with an income.

In analysing the size of cross-border trade on the Polish–Ukrainian border in 2010–14 it should be underlined that there are no accurate statistics, since the trade functions at least partially as a grey economy. Estimates of this phenomenon are based on surveys conducted by the Statistical Office in Rzeszów at border checkpoints. They show that in 2010 the main motivation for the arrival of foreigners from Ukraine was to buy goods in Poland. This concerned 85.5 per cent of people crossing the border – that is, 3,828,900 people. In 2014 the motivation to purchase goods was declared by 89.4 per cent, or 7,109,200 people.

The amount of expenditure incurred on the Polish side of the Polish–Ukrainian borderland is shown in Table 3.6. It shows the period 2010–14, when there was a more than two-fold increase in expenses incurred by Ukrainians in the Polish part of the borderland. They reached a level of 7.2 billion PLN in 2014, of which Lublin voivodship accounted for 55.6 per cent and Podkarpackie the remaining 44.4 per cent, while Podkarpackie was characterized by a significantly higher rate of growth in expenses compared with Lublin voivodship. In the expenditure structure in both 2010 and 2014, the purchase of goods dominated (over 90 per cent of expenditure), primarily non-food items (almost 90 per cent of the purchased goods value), particularly household appliances, electronics, computers, construction materials, vehicle parts and accessories.

Foreigners from Ukraine often cross the Polish–Ukrainian border. In the case of Lublin voivodship 43.5 per cent of them cross it several times a week and another 41.8 per cent cross several times a month. These proportions are slightly different in Podkarpackie voivodship, since 63.6 per cent of Ukrainians cross the border several times a week and 22.5 per cent cross several times a month. This difference

Table 3.6 Expenses incurred by foreigners from Ukraine in the Polish part of the Polish–Ukrainian borderland in 2010 and 2014

	2010	*2014*	*2010 = 100.0*
Lublin voivodship			
Total expenditure in thousand PLN	1866994.7	3988658.7	213.6
Total purchased goods in thousand PLN	1843401.9	3849010.9	208.8
– groceries	248019.0	575593.8	232.1
– non-food	1595382.9	3261666.3	204.4
Other expenses (services including accommodation and catering) in thousand PLN	23592.8	139647.8	591.9
Podkarpackie voivodship			
Total expenditure in thousand PLN	1115285.8	3179624.2	285.1
Total purchase of goods in thousand PLN	1097101.6	3131570.8	285.4
– groceries	104856.9	352485.3	336.2
– non-food	992244.7	2778400.9	280.0
Other expenses (services including accommodation and catering) in thousand PLN	18184.1	48053.4	264.3
Polish–Ukrainian borderland (Polish part)			
Total expenditure in thousand PLN	2982280.5	7168282.9	240.4
Total purchase of goods in thousand PLN	2940503.5	6980581.7	237.4
– groceries	352875.9	928079.1	263.0
– non-food	2587627.6	6040067.2	233.4
Other expenses (services including accommodation and catering) in thousand PLN	41776.9	187701.2	449.3

Source: Own study, on the basis of *Border traffic and flow of goods and services on the external border of the European Union in Poland in 2010* (2011). Warsaw, Rzeszów: Central Statistical Office–Statistical Office in Rzeszów, and *Border traffic and expenditure of foreigners in Poland and Poles abroad in 2014* (2015). Warsaw, Rzeszów: Central Statistical Office–Statistical Office in Rzeszów.

stems from the fact that the Medyka pedestrian border crossing operates in Podkarpackie voivodship (making it easier to cross the border), while in Lublin voivodship this type of border checkpoint did not exist until 2014. The vast majority of Ukrainian citizens crossing the Polish–Ukrainian border live within 50 kilometres of the border and purchase goods in Poland in the same vicinity (Table 3.7). The small spatial extent of this border trade stems from, among other factors, the delimitation of local border traffic (up to 30 kilometres from the border) with simplified procedures for crossing the border and the location of medium-sized cities such as Przemyśl, Chełm and Zamość in the vicinity of the border, which are able to meet Ukrainian demand, especially for the purchase of goods.

In the case of Poles travelling to Ukraine, the purchasing motivation was also dominant in both 2010 and 2014, concerning 89.9 per cent (1,858,500 persons) and 78.2 per cent (789,000 persons), respectively. It is worth noting, however, the declining number of Poles travelling to Ukraine and the growing importance of non-commercial motivations (among others, tourism). As a consequence of the declining number of Poles travelling to Ukraine from Lublin and Podkarpackie voivodships, the expenditure incurred by them fell by nearly one-third to a level of 260.5 million PLN in 2014 (Table 3.8) – that is, 28 times less than Ukrainians spend in these voivodships.

Table 3.7 Foreigners from Ukraine crossing the Polish–Ukrainian border by distance of residence and place of purchasing goods in 2014

	Foreigners from Ukraine crossing the Polish–Ukrainian border by distance of residence (%)				
	Total	*Distance*			
		Up to 50 km		*51–100 km*	*Over 100 km*
		Total	*Up to 30 km*		
Lublin voivodship	100.0	66.5	46.7	17.1	16.4
Podkarpackie voivodship	100.0	74.7	61.0	18.3	7.0
Polish–Ukrainian borderland	100.0	71.6	54.4	19.3	9.1
	Foreigners from Ukraine crossing the Polish–Ukrainian border by place of purchasing goods (%)				
	Total	*Distance*			
		Up to 50 km		*51–100 km*	*Over 100 km*
		Total	*Up to 30 km*		
Lublin voivodship	100.0	73.3	39.6	12.5	14.2
Podkarpackie voivodship	100.0	92.9	79.8	3.9	3.2
Polish–Ukrainian borderland	100.0	85.3	66.8	8.1	6.7

Source: See Table 3.6.

The only high growth rate (more than double) in 2010–14 was recorded in spending on services. Out of the total expenditure by Poles in Ukraine, Lublin voivodship accounted for 57.9 per cent and Podkarpackie the remaining 42.1 per cent. The expenditure structure is dominated by the purchase of goods (more than 80 per cent of value), particularly non-food products (over 60 per cent of the total value of purchased goods). Poles in Ukraine usually buy goods subject to excise duty, the prices of which are lower than in Poland, such as vehicle fuels, tobacco and alcohol.

Poles cross the Polish–Ukrainian border considerably less often than Ukrainians. In 2014 approximately two-thirds of Poles from Lublin voivodship crossed the border once a quarter, and approximately three-quarters from Podkarpackie voivodship. Just like Ukrainians, the vast majority of Poles crossing the Polish–Ukrainian border live and make purchases at a distance of 50 kilometres from the border (Table 3.9).

In summary, it can be said that trade in the Polish–Ukrainian borderland is significantly asymmetrical. It is dominated by Ukrainians who purchase goods, mainly non-food products, in Poland. This trend grew substantially in the period 2010–14. Border movements of people connected with trade are concentrated in a zone up to 50 kilometres from the border, in terms of both their place of residence and their place of purchase. The asymmetry of purchasing by Ukrainians in Poland in contrast to purchasing by Poles in Ukraine means that the balance of these

Table 3.8 Expenditure incurred by Poles from the Polish part of the borderland (Lublin, Podkarpackie voivodships) in Ukraine in 2010 and 2014

	2010	*2014*	*2010 = 100.0*
Lublin voivodship			
Total expenditure in thousand PLN	237898.3	150694.7	63.3
Total purchase of goods in thousand PLN	228064.7	134226.9	58.9
– groceries	32206.5	13292.4	41.3
– non-food	160262.6	86228.8	53.8
Other expenses (services including accommodation and catering) in thousand PLN	9833.6	16467.8	167.5
Podkarpackie voivodship			
Total expenditure in thousand PLN	144417.9	109775.8	76.0
Total purchase of goods in thousand PLN	135053.1	81335.9	60.2
– groceries	16405.2	10237.1	62.4
– non-food	94921.9	49430.4	52.1
Other expenses (services including accommodation and catering) in thousand PLN	9364.8	28439.9	303.7
Polish–Ukrainian borderland			
Total expenditure in thousand PLN	382316.2	260470.5	68.1
Total purchase of goods in thousand PLN	363117.8	215562.8	59.4
– groceries	48611.7	23529.5	48.4
– non-food	255184.5	135659.2	53.2
Other expenses (services including accommodation and catering) in thousand PLN	19198.4	44907.7	233.9

Source: See Table 3.6.

transactions was beneficial to the Polish part of the borderland and in 2014 amounted to +6,907,800 PLN – that is, an increase of more than 150 per cent on 2010 figures; in the case of Lublin voivodship the balance was +3,838,000 PLN (a more than two-fold increase) and in Podkarpackie voivodship it was +3,069,800 PLN (a more than three-fold increase).

Tourism relations

Both economic and social relations can be illustrated by the accommodation provided to Ukrainian citizens in Poland. The full scale of traffic is not included in the data because a large number of visitors do not stay overnight in Poland and many others stay in places where registration is not required. Commuters are not included in the statistics because they rent apartments or benefit from accommodation provided by their employer. In 2014 a total of only 274,000 Ukrainian citizens used accommodation in Poland for 560,000 overnight stays. These figures, compared with flows recorded on the border, show that the proportion of Ukrainians using accommodation in Poland does not exceed 5 per cent of the total number of Ukrainians crossing the Polish border. The differences in this regard with respect to previous years are small. Compared with 2013, the number of overnight stays slightly increased, with the number of people staying virtually

Table 3.9 Poles from the Polish part of the borderland (Lublin and Podkarpackie voivodships) crossing the Polish–Ukrainian border by distance of residence and place of purchasing goods in 2014

	Poles crossing the Polish–Ukrainian border by distance of residence (%)				
	Total	*Distance*			
		Up to 50 km		*51–100 km*	*Over 100 km*
		Total	*Up to 30 km*		
Lublin voivodship	100.0	68.0	43.7	14.0	18.0
Podkarpackie voivodship	100.0	77.7	62.3	9.5	12.9
Polish–Ukrainian borderland	100.0	70.0	55.1	14.5	15.5
	Poles crossing the Polish–Ukrainian border by place of purchasing goods (%)				
	Total	*Distance*			
		Up to 50 km		*51–100 km*	*Over 100 km*
		Total	*Up to 30 km*		
Lublin voivodship	100.0	81.2	78.7	4.6	14.2
Podkarpackie voivodship	100.0	84.8	83.3	2.9	12.3
Polish–Ukrainian borderland	100.0	82.7	80.7	4.6	12.8

Source: See Table 3.6.

unchanged. This indicates slightly longer average lengths of stay by tourists in Poland. In 2014, in the two borderland voivodships, a total of fewer than 60,000 people stayed overnight, with more than 36,000 in Podkarpackie voivodship.

The distribution of accommodation provided to tourists from Ukraine indicates the highest concentration of bilateral interaction to be in the largest Polish urban centres, mainly Warsaw, Cracow and Gdańsk, and in Wrocław. Among the most important destinations are also some of the Carpathian tourist centres, including, primarily, Zakopane and Krynica. In the border area the largest absolute numbers of overnight stays provided to Ukrainians were recorded in Rzeszów, Przemyśl and Lublin.

A high percentage of Ukrainians among the total number of foreigners staying overnight is recorded in many municipalities of Podkarpackie and Lublin voivodships. This situation is mainly due to the low development level of international tourism in the area. A relative increase in the absolute number (and percentage) of overnight stays provided to Ukrainians is recorded in areas along the German border (especially in Lubuskie voivodship). This is probably the result of the recent use of low-cost hotel services during transit journeys to Western Europe. The corridor pattern of accommodation provided to Ukrainians is especially significant along the A2 motorway (west of Poznań) and the A4 (west of Wrocław). A lack of such a distinct system in eastern Poland indicates that Poland's border area does not generally benefit from east–west transit. Thus, the beneficiaries are on the side of the border where prices of services remain lower. This suggests that a Ukrainian citizen travelling to Germany will generally make use of accommodation in Ukraine before crossing the Polish border, and will then in stay overnight in western Poland just before crossing the border into Germany.

Institutional relations

Cross-border institutional links in the Polish–Ukrainian borderland were mainly analysed in terms of local and regional authorities' activities in terms of formal partnerships, the development of cross-border structures and the initiation and implementation of cross-border projects. These projects were based on the experience gained from the Cross-Border Cooperation Program Poland–Belarus–Ukraine 2007–13, which was funded by the European Union.

The lack of institutional compatibility manifested in the varied terms of reference of local and regional authorities operating on either side of the state border, also known as 'institutional–organizational distance', is one of the main barriers – excepting geopolitical barriers – to cross-border cooperation (Miszczuk 2013). Indeed, it may be that the border areas are close in terms of geography, culture and language – as is the case in the Polish–Ukrainian borderland – but are institutionally very distant. Cross-border links develop more effectively between regions of decentralized states – that is, regions which are autonomous or have local self-government. If one of the states is centralized the situation is far more difficult. In this case, central government has to be involved in decision making, thus making cross-border cooperation complicated.

One of the main barriers to cross-border cooperation between Polish and Ukrainian public administrations at the local and regional levels is the institutional distance. As of 1 January 1999, the public administration system in Poland is based on three-tier local government: commune (*gmina*), district (*powiat*) and voivodship. Each level of public administration has clearly defined powers and financing, and their autonomy is subject to legal protection. It seems, therefore, that in terms of the territorial division of the country and the scope of powers of local government units, the fundamental structure of local and regional government in Poland does not require significant adjustment within the next 10–15 years. Matters are different in Ukraine, where the public administration system does not meet decentralized state standards and local government does not meet the standards specified in the European Charter of Local Government. This is the result of the ambiguously defined powers and finances of local and regional units, making them dependent on the central government administration. Organizational and functional changes in local and regional administrations in Ukraine would be conducive to reducing the institutional distance between them and Polish local government units and this, in turn, would stimulate the growth and scope of cross-border contacts.

One of the statutory tasks of local Polish voivodships is to determine priorities of international cooperation. In the case of Lublin and Podkarpackie voivodships the cross-border factor is significant, since Ukrainian regions dominate in official partner relations. These include the oblasts of Lviv, Luhansk, Odessa and Volhynia (Lublin voivodship) and Ivano-Frankivsk, Lviv, Odessa, Ternopil and Volhynia (Podkarpackie voivodship). Agreements concluded between these regions have created a favourable platform for cooperation between local authorities. Parallel to these 'eastern' priorities, local governments of the Polish–Ukrainian borderland also willingly cooperate with regions of the 'old' EU. Meanwhile, a new phenomenon is the increasingly dynamic relations with Chinese provinces.

In the case of district town relations (Figure 3.12), the impact of the cross-border factor is even more visible. Out of the total number of district towns in Lublin voivodship – 20 – 12 are in partnership with Ukrainian cities; in Podkarpackie, the figure is 17 out of 22 cities. The majority of Ukrainian cities are situated in the border oblasts – that is, Lviv and Volhynia. This does not preclude cities from contacts which are not of a cross-border nature, with Russian, Lithuanian, Ukrainian and Belarusian regions, of which the latter are least numerous. Close relations with Slovakian and Hungarian cities are recorded in Podkarpackie voivodship. Relations with German cities are also common.

The survey conducted by the Institute of Public Affairs on a national sample of 326 local government units (out of a total of 2,809) shows that more than 70 per cent have international contacts, primarily involving opportunities for the international exchange of residents (especially school students) and the promotion and exchange of good practices. The priority areas of cooperation are culture, tourism, sport, education and science. Joint activities in the field of economy and environmental protection are of decidedly less importance. The most common countries of cooperation for Polish local governments are Germany and Ukraine (Fuksiewicz et al. 2012).

Meanwhile, in a study conducted on a sample of 64 cities (including eight located in Lublin and Podkarpackie voivodships) by the Polish Institute of International Affairs, the level of cooperation activity was assessed and five categories were highlighted in this regard (Skorupska 2015):

- very active cooperation, involving the implementation of several joint projects annually,
- active cooperation, including one to two projects started in the last 18 months,
- beginnings of cooperation concerning planned joint activities,
- inactive cooperation, with no action taken for the past two years, but with scope for resuming it,
- end of cooperation by termination of a contract preceded by several years of inactivity, with poor prospects for renewed cooperation.

Table 3.10 lists types of local government cooperation between Polish, Ukrainian and (for comparison) German partners. This table shows that, among the analysed Polish towns, Germany is a more frequent cooperation partner than Ukraine.

Figure 3.12 Ukrainian partner cities of district towns in Lublin and Podkarpackie voivodships

Source: Krzysztof Łoboda, on the basis of the official websites of district town councils.

Table 3.10 Types of cooperation between Polish local governments and Ukrainian and German partners

	Forms of cooperation						
	Very active	*Active*	*Begun*	*Total active*	*Inactive*	*Ended*	*Total*
Ukraine	9	42	–	51	23	2	76
–Lviv oblast	1	4	–	5	8	–	13
–Volhynia oblast	3	3	–	6	1	–	7
Germany	28	60	2	90	2	2	94

Source: Skorupska (2015).

Polish–German cooperation is also much more active. While 96 per cent of relations with German partners are ongoing, one-third of links with Ukraine are inactive or have been terminated. Over 25 per cent of links in Polish towns concern the Ukrainian part of the Polish–Ukrainian borderland – that is, Lviv and Volhynia oblasts. The connections with Lviv are specifically due to its history and previous affiliation to Poland. However, in the case of Lviv oblast a worrying predominance of inactive cooperation over active has been recorded. This contrasts with Volhynia oblast, with fewer links, but which are, in the vast majority, active.

Another manifestation of local government cross-border links since the early 1990s is the development of Polish–Ukrainian euroregional structures in the Polish–Ukrainian borderland (Figure 3.13). These structures are mainly of a socio-cultural and, to a lesser extent, an economic nature.[2] Regardless of the official cooperation target, they have played a very positive role in overcoming negative stereotypes on both sides of the border in attitudes to cross-border cooperation, and have contributed to the creation of a favourable political climate – particularly important in post-soviet countries – for initiatives undertaken by local governments, businesses and non-governmental organizations.

The first Euroregion to be established in the Polish–Ukrainian borderland, on 14 February 1993, was the Carpathian Euroregion, and the second – and, so far, the last – was the Euroregion Bug, on 29 September 1995. The Carpathian Euroregion covers the border regions of five countries: Poland (including the communes of Podkarpackie voivodship and the territory of local government members of the Carpathian Euroregion Association Poland), Hungary (the regions of Borsod-Abauj-Zemplen, Hajdu-Bihar, Heves, Jasz-Nagykun-Szolnok and Szabolcs-Szatmar-Bereg and towns with district rights: Debrecen, Eger, Miskolc and Nyiregyhaza), Ukraine (Lviv, Transcarpathian, Ivano-Frankivs'k and Chernivtsi oblasts), Slovakia (the regions of Kosice and Presov and the area of local government units that are members of the Carpathian Region Association) and Romania (Bihor, Botosani, Maramures, Suceava, Satu Mare, Zilah and Harghita districts). The Euroregion covers an area of 161,200 square kilometres with a population of 15,770,400 people.[3] The aim of its establishment was 'to support joint local initiatives aimed at developing border regions, exercising advisory, consultation and coordination functions' (Euroregion Karpaty 1993). Meanwhile, the Euroregion Bug includes Lublin voivodship, Brest oblast in Belarus and Volhynia oblast, as well as the Zhovkva and

Figure 3.13 Euroregions on Polish borders

Source: *Euroregiony na granicach Polski* (2007).

Sokal districts[4] of Lviv oblast in Ukraine. It covers an area of 80,900 square kilometres, with a population of 4,853,600, and was established in order to 'create the conditions for socio-economic development and scientific-cultural cooperation in the border areas of neighbouring countries' (Euroregion Bug 1995).

The establishment of the Euroregions was an initiative of the regional state/ government administration. Local and supra-local self-governing units joined to these Euroregions later. The established Euroregions are very large in terms of area and population, and thus their cross-border cooperation is not very effective. Historical factors relating to resettlement of the population in border areas after World War II and a lack of any relations between the communities on both sides of the Polish–Soviet border were not conducive to cooperation. For over 40 years the border was impermeable.

One of the key financial instruments of Euroregion activities were European Union funds allocated for cross-border cooperation. Thus, in the years 1995–2003, Euroregions managed the pre-accession Small Projects Fund under the PHARE Cross Border Cooperation Programme (CBC), under the conditions of which the value of one project could not exceed €50,000. The funds were used to support non-investment projects implemented mainly by local governments and non-governmental organizations, such as:

- cultural exchanges between local border communities (arts activities, cultural and sports events, concerts, festivals, open-air painting, contests)
- local democracy development (NGO contacts, meetings, study visits)
- human resource development (training, vocational courses, language courses, exchange of professional experience)
- cross-border studies and development concepts (joint research projects, feasibility studies),
- economic development and border tourism (fairs, promotion, tourist trails).

In the period 1995–2003, within the Small Projects Fund of the PHARE CBC, 149 projects were implemented in the Carpathian Euroregion (3.6 per cent of all completed projects in all Polish borderlands) with a total value of €2,416,900 (7.0 per cent), and 140 projects in the Euroregion Bug (3.4 per cent), with a value of €1,941,600 (5.6 per cent). A similar role as administrators of EU funds allocated for cross-border cooperation via the INTERREG III A micro-projects was played by Euroregions in the first period of accession (2004–6). In the Carpathian Euroregion 120 projects were completed (7.6 per cent of the total number of projects completed in all Polish borderlands), amounting to €8,623,100 (13.4 per cent), and in the Euroregion Bug 119 projects (7.5 per cent) amounted to €8,684,600 (13.5 per cent). However, in the second period of accession (2007–13) Euroregions became merely one of various potential beneficiaries of EU funds, and this has significantly reduced their activity.

In the period 2004–6 Structural Funds, or more precisely the European Regional Development Fund under the Community Initiative INTERREG III A, became the main funding source for cross-border cooperation. Poland, as part of this initiative, implemented seven cross-border programmes (Figure 3.14) of which two were trilateral and one – the Neighbourhood Programme Poland–Belarus–Ukraine – was related to the Polish–Ukrainian borderland. The programme's allocated budget for the Polish side amounted to €37.8 million and for the Belarusian–Ukrainian participants was €8.0 million.[5] Investment projects were implemented exclusively on the Polish side. Figure 3.15 shows the spatial distribution of projects (including small projects). This distribution shows a low intensity of projects on the eastern Polish

Figure 3.14 Borderland cooperation programs INTERREG III A in 2004–6

Source: *Badanie ewaluacyjne ex-post efektow wspołpracy transgranicznej polskich regionow w okresie 2004–2006* (2011).

border (including the Polish–Ukrainian border), especially compared with the western Polish borderland. This situation has several causes. Firstly, the cross-border cooperation programmes implemented along the western border of Poland had a relatively larger budget in relation to both areas receiving support and programmes carried out on the eastern border. Secondly, in the case of investment projects, mainly relating to technical infrastructure, local governments from eastern Poland could obtain support from operational programmes (IRDOP, SOP Transport) applying simpler and better-known procedures. Thirdly, in the case of non-investment projects, eastern partners were necessary, including Ukrainians, but cooperation with these partners in terms of aspects such as reliability and punctuality could pose more problems than cooperation with partners from the EU member states.

The Neighbourhood Programme Poland–Belarus–Ukraine of 2004–6 shows characteristic asymmetry in leading partner locations to the disadvantage of Belarusian

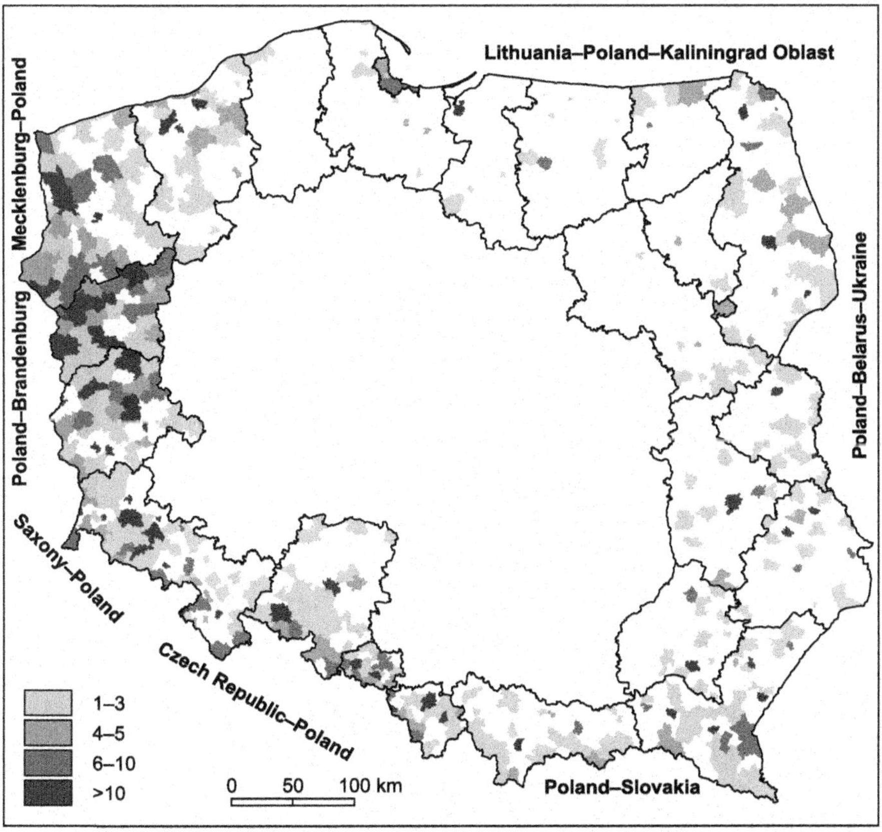

Figure 3.15 The number of projects (including small projects) in the communes included in the Polish part of the Community Initiative INTERREG III A 2004–6

Source: *Badanie ewaluacyjne ex-post efektow wspołpracy transgranicznej polskich regionow w okresie 2004–2006* (2011).

and Ukrainian partners. The leading partners for 59 projects in 18 cities/communes were situated in Lublin voivodship and for 36 projects in 19 cities/communes were in Podkarpackie voivodship. It is worth noting that the leading partners were located not only in large cities (Białystok, Lublin, Rzeszów), but also in medium-sized and small towns and also in rural communities. Meanwhile, for the Ukrainian participant, the leading partners for 10 projects were located in three major cities (Lviv, Lutsk and Uzhgorod). On the one hand, this asymmetry resulted from the funding methods, which were diversified in terms of amounts and sources to the disadvantage of Belarusian and Ukrainian participants. This was a sign of the EU's mistrust of countries that had no interest in integration with the EU, even at the level of association. On the other hand, this method of cross-border project implementation perpetuated the already large disparities occurring on both sides of the Polish eastern border.

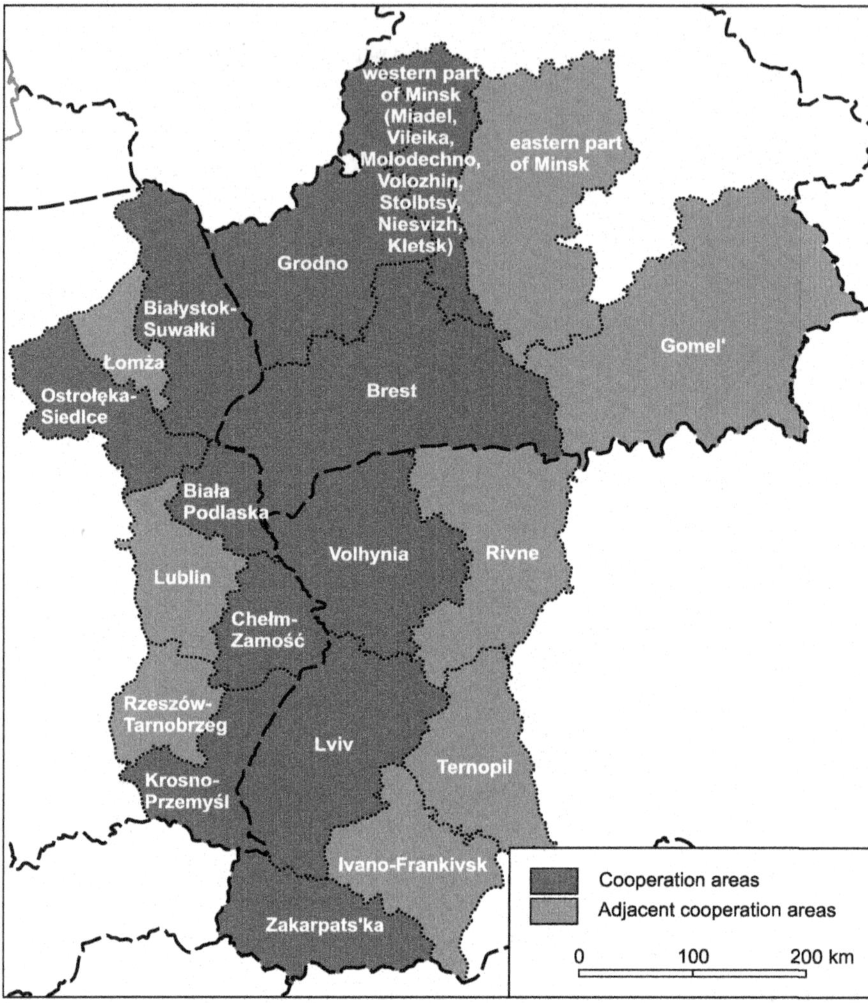

Figure 3.16 Area of Cross-Border Cooperation Programme Poland–Belarus–Ukraine in 2007–13

Source: *Book of Projects* (2015).

In 2007–13, within the European Neighbourhood and Partnership Instrument, the next edition of the Cross-Border Cooperation Programme Poland–Belarus–Ukraine was carried out with a budget of €186.2 million. The programme area (Figure 3.16) was divided into two unit categories: support regions and adjoining regions. The support regions included:

- in Poland, the following administrative sub-regions (NUTS-3): Białystok-Suwałki (Podlaskie voivodship), Biała Podlaska and Chełm-Zamość (Lublin voivodship),

Ostrołęka-Siedlce (Mazowieckie voivodship) and Krosno-Przemyśl (Podkarpackie Voivodship),

- in Belarus, the following oblasts: Brest, Grodno and the western part of Minsk,
- in Ukraine, the following oblasts: Lviv, Volhynia and Transcarpathian.

The adjacent regions included

- in Poland, the following sub-regions: Łomża (Podlaskie voivodship), Lublin (Lublin voivodship) and Rzeszów-Tarnobrzeg (Podkarpackie voivodship),
- in Belarus, the city of Minsk, the eastern part of Minsk Oblast and Gomel Oblast,
- in Ukraine, the following oblasts: Ternopil, Rivne and Ivano-Frankivsk.

Within the CBC Programme Poland–Belarus–Ukraine 2007–13, 117 projects were carried out, 74 of which (63.2 per cent) were within the Polish–Ukrainian partnership, 29 of which (24.8 per cent) were within the Polish–Belarusian partnership and the remaining 14 of which (12.0 per cent) were within the Polish–Belarusian–Ukrainian partnership (Table 3.11). As a priority, 40 projects amounting to €55.1 million were completed; subsequent waves saw 26 projects completed amounting to €76.5 million and 51 projects completed amounting to €42.5 million. In total, 177 public and private entities and non-governmental organizations from Poland, 144 from Ukraine and 54 from Belarus participated in the projects (Kawałko 2015).

Entities of Lublin voivodship were involved in the implementation of 56 projects and 18 micro-projects with a total value of €55 million (of which €49 million was EU funding). In Podkarpackie 34 projects and 29 micro-projects were carried out at a value of €42 million (€38 million from the EU). Meanwhile, in oblasts constituting the Ukrainian part of the Polish–Ukrainian borderland – that is, Lviv and Volyn – 45 projects with a total value of €65 million (€58.5 million

Table 3.11 Projects completed under the Cross-Border Cooperation Programme Poland–Belarus–Ukraine 2007–13 by activities and partnership countries

Actions	*Projects by state partnerships*			
	PL–UA	*PL–BY*	*PL–BY–UA*	*Total*
1.1. Better conditions for business	5	2	2	9
1.2. Tourism development	15	3	3	21
1.3. Improving access to the region	6	2	2	10
2.1. Natural environment protection in the borderland	11	5	–	16
2.2. Efficient and secure borders	7	3	–	10
3.1. Regional and local cross-border cooperation capacity building	26	13	6	45
3.2. Local community initiatives	4	1	1	6
Total	74	29	14	117

Source: Own summary, on the basis of *Book of Projects* (2015).

from the EU) and 29 projects and six micro-projects with a value of €36 million (€32.4 million from the EU) were carried out. Compared with the Neighbourhood Programme Poland–Belarus–Ukraine 2004–6, there is a distinct difference, not only in levels of financial resources but also in their fairly uniform allocation to both sides of the Polish–Ukrainian border. Figures 3.17, 3.18, 3.19 and 3.20 show the spatial distribution of partnerships established by entities from Lublin and Podkarpackie voivodships and Lviv and Volyn oblasts in the course of implementing projects under the Cross Border Cooperation Programme Poland–Belarus–Ukraine 2007–13.

As the result of programme implementation the road network, border-crossing infrastructure, and water and sewage infrastructure were expanded and modernized, rescue equipment was added to and improved, new tourist trails were marked out and cultural and scientific projects were financed. The next edition of the Cross-Border Cooperation Programme Poland–Belarus–Ukraine is being implemented under the European Neighbourhood Policy for the period 2014–20, with a slightly lower budget of €176 million. It is generally assumed that it will continue the activities of 2007–13, with slight modifications of priorities and the extent of the area receiving support (see Chapter 4).

Results of and barriers to Polish–Ukrainian cross-border relations

The above deliberations on cross-border ties in the Polish–Ukrainian borderland show a general trend resulting from differences in the level of development between Eastern and Western Europe, leading to the movement of the population towards the West. Poles seeking work and higher education migrate to the UK or Germany, while for Ukrainians Poland is an attractive destination, being a member of the European Union and fairly close in cultural terms. While the Polish part of the Polish–Ukrainian borderland cannot compete with the large urban centres of Poland's economic life, such as Warsaw, Cracow, Wrocław and Poznań, in terms of providing stable (not only seasonal) jobs, nevertheless in the field of higher education the borderland plays a very important role. Ukrainians are also far more active in border trade, expressed by the levels of expenditure they incur. Ukrainian citizens significantly dominate in border traffic on bilateral borders. Ukraine is by no means a transit country for journeys to Poland and further to other EU countries, although Poland, to some extent, performs these functions in the case of Germans, Czechs and citizens of other European Union countries travelling to Ukraine. The recorded surplus of arrivals over departures may indicate the hidden migration of Ukrainians to Poland and further to the West. Until 2014 the Polish–Ukrainian border was not burdened by the influx of refugees and migrants from the Middle East.

The development of official economic cooperation with Ukraine has been gradually moving away from the border area. The zone in which a Ukrainian partner is most important in international trade has become spatially restricted to a few units directly adjacent to the border checkpoints. Intermediaries are important in foreign

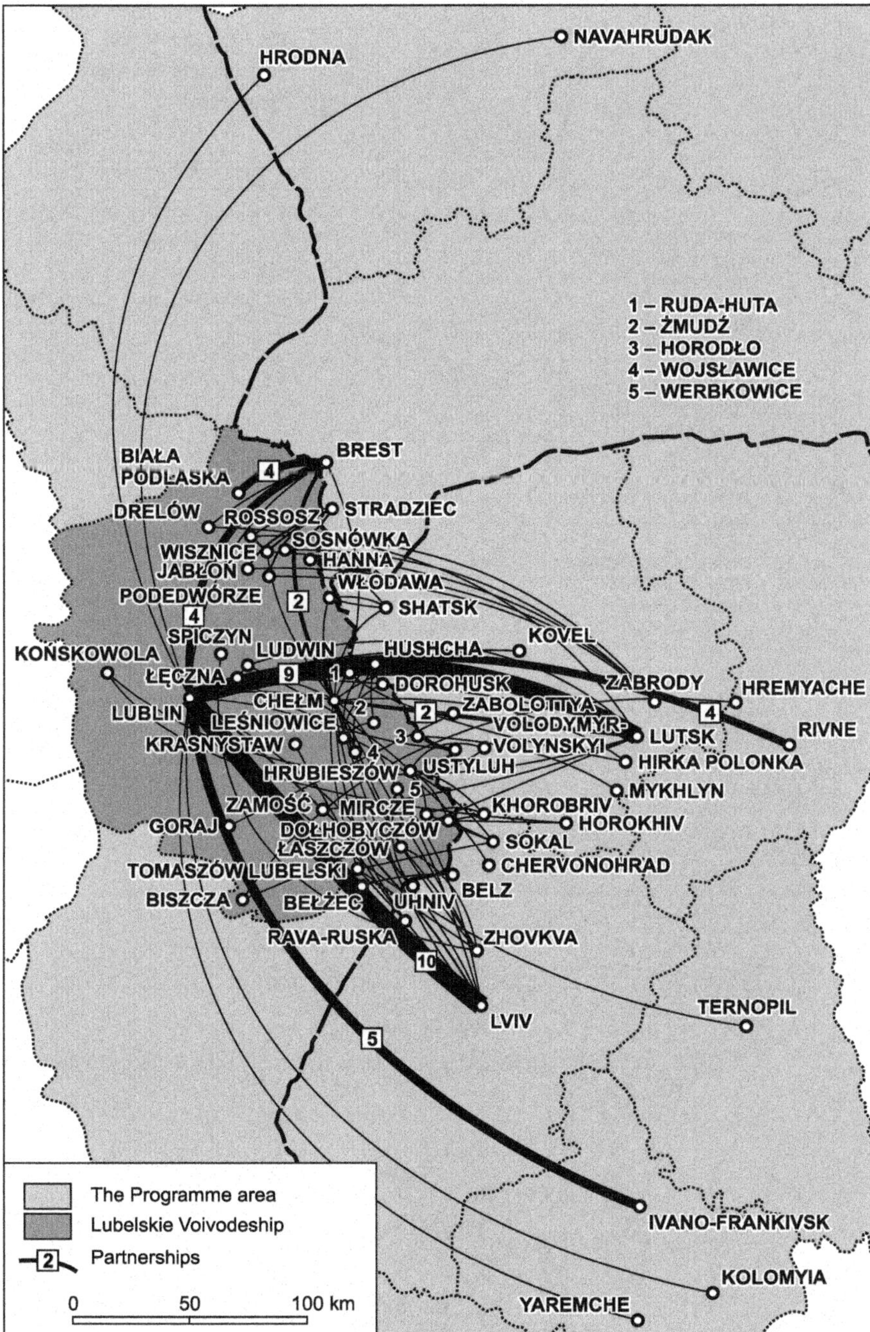

Figure 3.17 Distribution of partnerships established by entities from Lublin voivodship in the course of implementing projects under the Cross-Border Cooperation Programme Poland–Belarus–Ukraine 2007–13

Source: *Lubelskie Voivodeship* (2015).

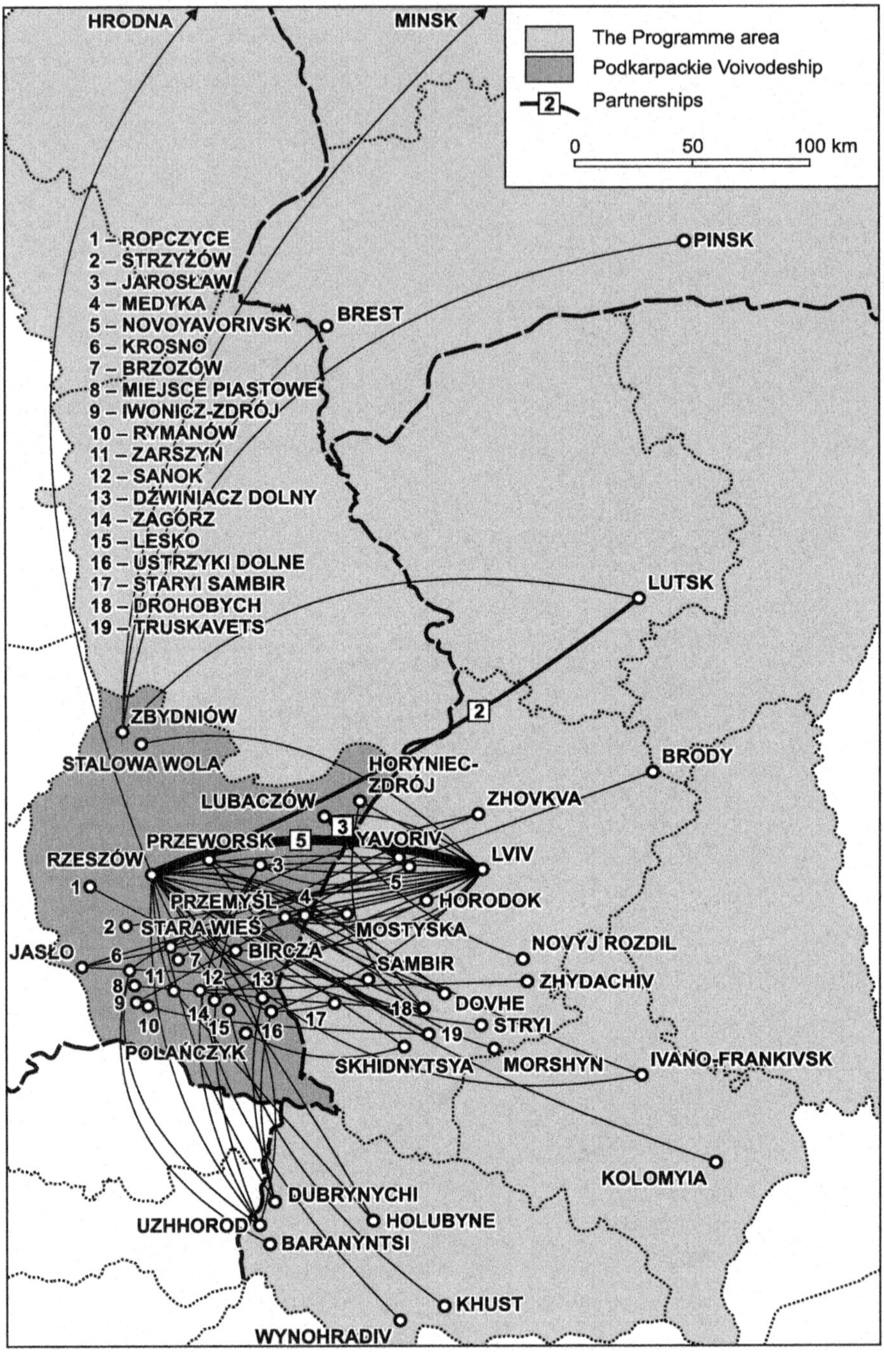

Figure 3.18 Distribution of partnerships established by entities from Podkarpackie voivodship in the course of implementing projects under the Cross-Border Cooperation Programme Poland–Belarus–Ukraine 2007–13

Source: *Podkarpackie Voivodeship* (2015).

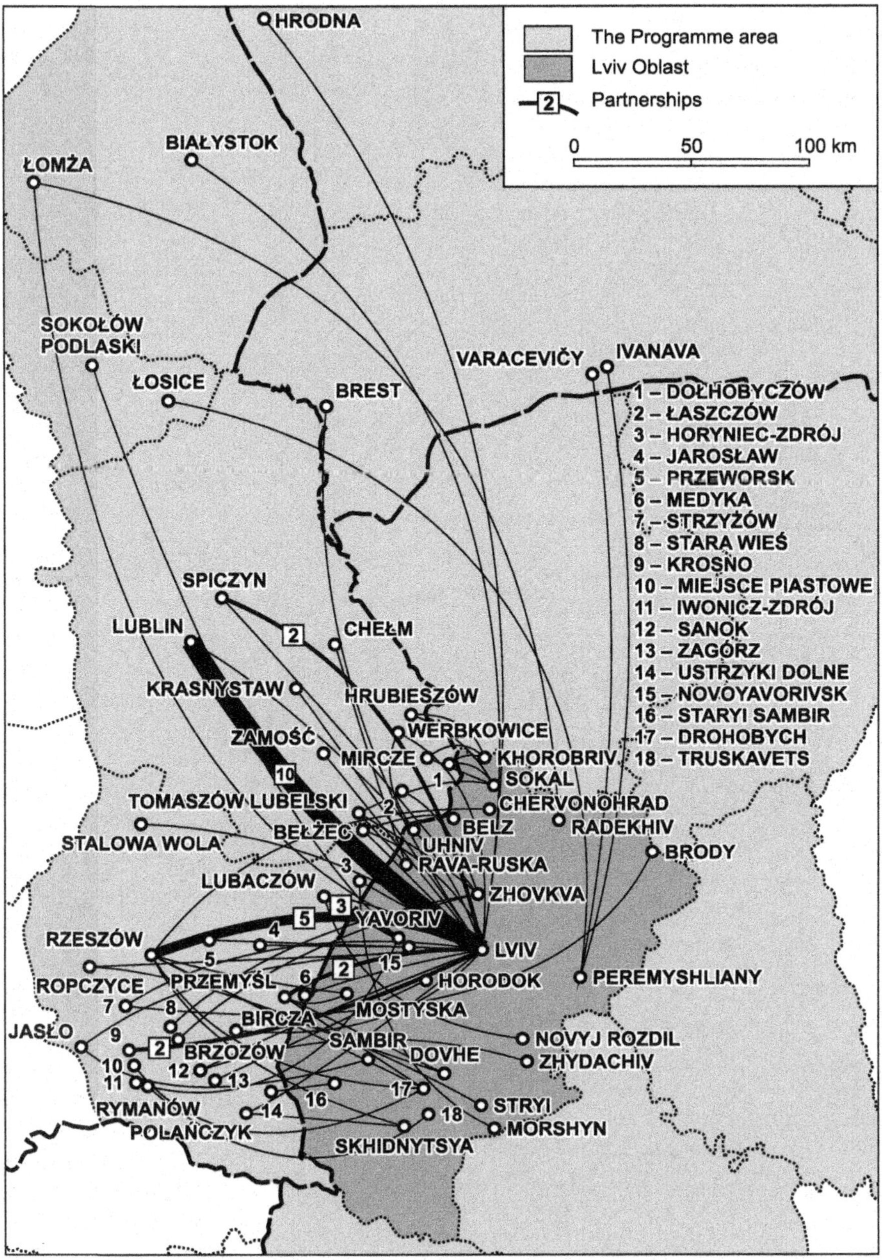

Figure 3.19 Distribution of partnerships established by entities from Lviv oblast in the course of implementing projects under the Cross-Border Cooperation Programme Poland–Belarus–Ukraine 2007–13

Source: *Lviv Oblast* (2015).

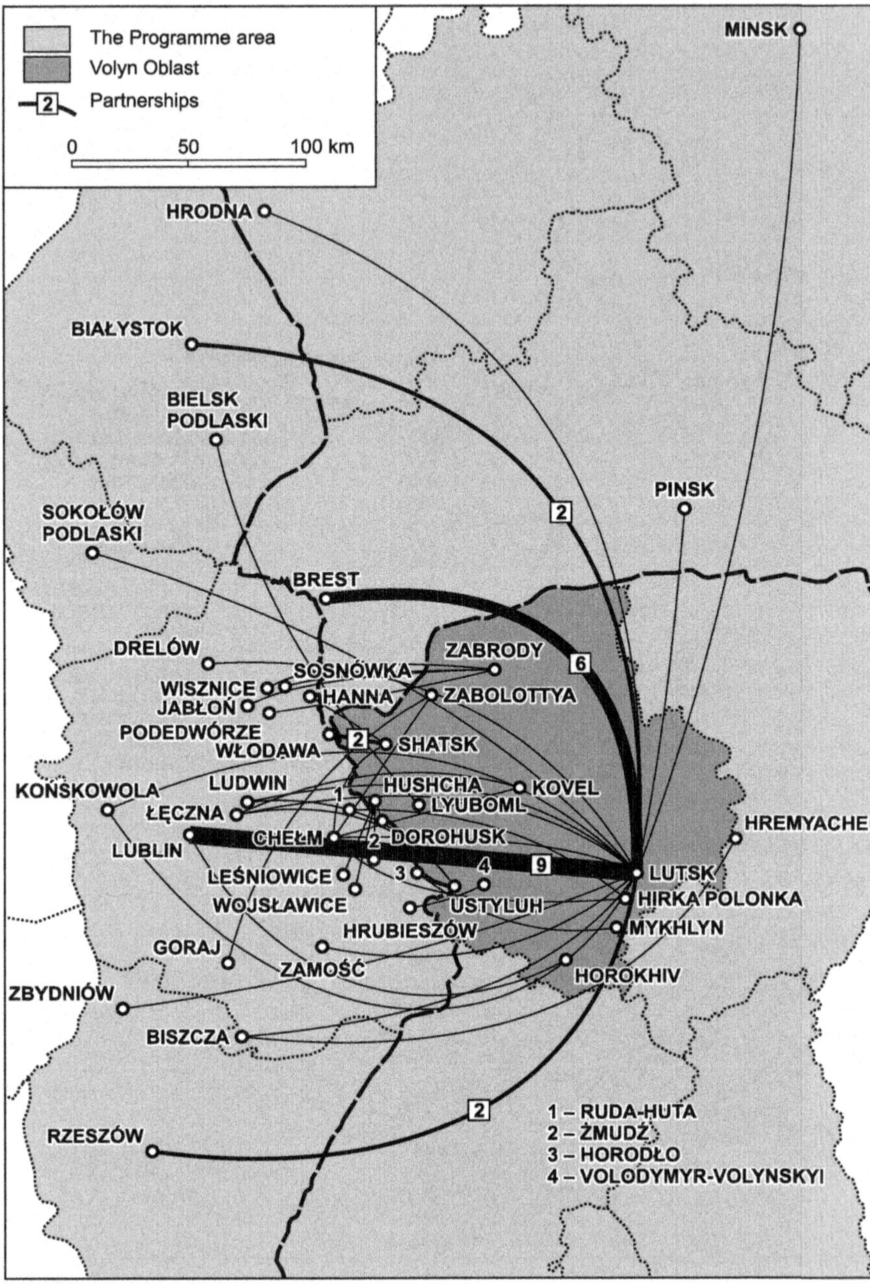

Figure 3.20 Distribution of partnerships established by entities from Volyn oblast in the course of implementing projects under the Cross-Border Cooperation Programme Poland–Belarus–Ukraine 2007–13

Source: *Volyn Oblast* (2015).

trade operations here. Meanwhile, the level of trade is heavily dependent on economic cycles. The borderland also benefits to only a limited extent from Ukrainian tourists: the local hotel facilities are used only by a small proportion of incoming travellers; most travel on to larger centres or use the facilities in western Poland on their way to third countries.

Representatives of local administrations from Lviv and Volhynia oblasts are important partners at the level of regional and local cooperation in Lublin and Podkarpackie voivodships. Ukrainian partners are not particularly active, but they are gradually becoming more reliable participants in projects under the EU Neighbourhood Policy, which are starting to be carried out more widely in the border regions of Ukraine.

By comparing these findings with the model transformations of cross-border cooperation development (see Martinez 1994; Ciok 2004) it is possible to identify phases of development in infrastructural and functional ties. These phases have been observed over the last 30 years on the Polish–Ukrainian border (Komornicki 2014). They are:

- **A highly formalized border** despite close official political and economic cooperation. There is a clear separation of economic functions (and a high intensity of cross-border transport) and social functions (a particularly hermetic spatial barrier). Infrastructure development in the first case is subordinated to economic factors, in the second case to geopolitics. Meanwhile, the mass scale of transport as a result of economies based on heavy industry means that demand for cross-border infrastructure is limited. Conventionally, this phase applies in the period until 1989.
- **A border in the period of spontaneous system transformation**. Initially, processes are similar to those at other borders. The geopolitical transition and the dynamic development of socio-economic relations cause pressure for the development of infrastructure (specifically, border crossings). Conventionally, this phase applies in the years 1990–95.
- **A border in the period of uneven system transformation**. Economic transformation is much faster in Poland, resulting in commercially unreasonable differences in consumer goods prices. Petty trade grows, eventually inhibiting infrastructure development. There is strong local pressure to construct new border checkpoints, while central governments in both countries are more sceptical (particularly in view of the then pending Polish membership of the European Union). The first signs of renewed formalization of the eastern border appear. Conventionally, this phase applies to the period 1996–2003.
- **An external border of the European Union**. The border is suddenly formalized once again. This does not cause ruptures in socio-economic relations, but causes them to 'move away' from the border. In local terms, the border becomes significantly less permeable. Meanwhile, trade is growing and large flows of passenger traffic are maintained (in part due to the fact that Poland has become an attractive labour market for Ukrainians, and eventually as the

result of the agreement on local border traffic). Geopolitical factors again limit the development of infrastructure. Conventionally, this phase applies in the years 2004–13.

- **A border with an internally unstable country**. Formal requirements for cross-border interactions do not change. At the same time, instability in Ukraine and the war with Russia influence the intensity and structure of cross-border links. This impact is stimulating in terms of migratory movements and petty trade, but destimulating in terms of macro-scale economic cooperation. Conventionally, the phase applies since 2014.

Notes

1 Examples of cross-border purchasing migration in the European Union are given by, among others, Spierings and Van der Velde 2008.
2 The legal basis for their creation was established thanks to the signing of:
 - The Treaty between the Republic of Poland and Ukraine on good neighbourhood, friendly relations and cooperation of 18 May 1992.
 - The Agreement between the government of the Republic of Poland and the government of Ukraine on inter-regional cooperation of 24 May 1993.

3 Data on Euroregions, where not otherwise stated, are taken from *Euroregiony na granicach Polski* 2007.
4 Two districts of Lviv oblast: Sokal and Zhovkva belong to two Euroregions, Carpathian and Bug.
5 Funding for the Belarusian and Ukrainian sides came from TACIS CBC 2004–6.

Bibliography

Badanie ewaluacyjne ex-post efektów współpracy transgranicznej polskich regionów w okresie 2004–2006 (2011). Warszawa: PSDB, CRSG.

Book of Projects (2015). *The Cross-Border Cooperation Programme Poland-Belarus-Ukraine 2007–2013*. Warsaw.

Breymeyer, A. (2011). Rezerwaty Biosfery i Polski Komitet UNESCO-MaB: przedstawienie aktualnej problematyki, in: A. Breymeyer (ed.) *Międzynarodowe sieci obszarów chronionych w Polsce: światowa sieć Rezerwatów Biosfery UNESCO-MaB i Europejska Sieć Natura 2000*. Warszawa: Komitet Narodowy UNESCO-MaB przy Prezydium Polskiej Akademii Nauk, Instytut Geografii i Przestrzennego Zagospodarowania PAN.

Ciok, S. (2004). *Pogranicze polsko-niemieckie. Problemy współpracy transgranicznej*. Wrocław: Wydawnictwo Uniwersytetu Wrocławskiego.

Euroregion Bug (1995). *Porozumienie z dnia 29 września 1995 r. o utworzeniu Związku Transgranicznego 'Euroregion Bug'*. Online. Available: http://www.euroregionbug.pl/index.php/zwiazek-transgraniczny-euroregion-bug/grupy-robocze/item/187-porozumienie-z-dnia-29-wrzesnia-1995-r (accessed: 28 January 2016).

Euroregion Karpaty (1993). *Porozumienie z dnia 14 lutego 1993 r. o utworzeniu Związku Międzyregionalnego 'Euroregion Karpacki'*.

Euroregiony na granicach Polski (2007). Wrocław: Urząd Statystyczny.

Fuksiewicz, A., Łada, A. and Wenerski, Ł. (2012). *Współpraca zagraniczna polskich samorządów. Wnioski z badań*. Warsawa: Instytut Spraw Publicznych.

Hartshorne, R. (1936). Suggestions on the terminology of political boundaries. *Annals of the Association of American Geographers*, 22, pp. 48–9.

Janicki, W. (2015). *Migracje kompensacyjne jako czynnik wzrostu obszarów peryferyjnych. Rola ukrytego kapitału ludzkiego*. Lublin: Wydawnictwo UMCS.

Kawałko, B. (2015). *Program Polska-Białoruś-Ukraina w polityce rozwoju regionów przygranicznych*, 'Barometr Regionalny', t. 13, nr 2, pp. 7–27.

Kawałko, B. and Miszczuk, A. (2008). Uwarunkowania rozwoju przestrzennego Polski wynikające z sąsiedztwa z Ukrainą, in: K. Saganowski, M. Zagrzejewska-Fiedorowicz and P. Żuber (eds) *Ekspertyzy do koncepcji przestrzennego zagospodarowania kraju 2008–2033*, t. III. Warszawa: Ministerstwo Rozwoju Regionalnego, pp. 175–232.

Komornicki, T. (1995). Polish eastern border under conditions of dynamic increase of international passenger and vehicle traffic, in: M. Rościszewski and M. Jakubowski (eds) *Polish eastern border. Past and present problems*, Conference Papers 22. Warsaw: IGiPZ PAN, pp. 67–81.

Komornicki, T. (1999). Granice Polski. Analiza zmian przenikalności w latach 1990–1996. *Geopolitical Studies*, 5. Warszawa: IGiPZ PAN.

Komornicki, T. (2003). Przestrzenne zróżnicowanie międzynarodowych powiązań społeczno-gospodarczych w Polsce. *Prace Geograficzne*, 190, pp. 255.

Komornicki, T. (2014). Spatial and social effects of infrastructural integration in the case of the Polish borders, in: M. Schiefelbusch and H. S. Dienel (eds) *Linking networks: The formation of common standards and visions for infrastructure development*. Dorchester: Ashgate, pp. 187–208.

Komornicki, T. (forthcoming). Zmiany w ruchu przez polską granicę wschodnią w roku 2014 na tle sytuacji geopolitycznej, *Prace i Studia Geograficzne*.

Komornicki, T. and Miszczuk, A. (2010). Eastern Poland as the borderland of the European Union. *Questiones Geographicae*, 29/2, pp. 55–70.

Komornicki, T. and Miszczuk, A. (2011). *Transgraniczne powiązania województw Polski wschodniej*. Warszawa: Ministerstwo Rozwoju Regionalnego.

Komornicki, T., Rosik, P., Szejgiec, B., Goliszek, S. and Kowalczyk, K. (2015). *Obszary funkcjonalne miast wojewódzkich Polski Wschodniej – stan rozwoju transportu i rekomendacje działań inwestycyjnych na lata 2014–2020*. Warszawa: Ministerstwo Rozwoju Regionalnego.

Komornicki, T. and Szejgiec, B. (2011). *Handel zagraniczny – znaczenie dla gospodarki Polski wschodniej*. Warszawa: Ministerstwo Rozwoju Regionalnego.

Komornicki, T. and Śleszyński, P. (2011). Changing accessibility of Polish airports on the course of demographic and Economic demand. *Geographia Polonica*, 84/2, pp. 47–63.

Komornicki, T., Śleszyński, P., Rosik, P. and Pomianowski, W. (2010). Dostępność przestrzenna jako przesłanka kształtowania polskiej polityki transportowej. *Biuletyn KPZK*, 241, pp. 167.

Komornicki, T., Śleszyński, P., Siłka, P. and Stępniak, M. (2008). Wariantowa analiza dostępności w transporcie lądowym, in: K. Saganowski, M. Zagrzejewska-Fiedorowicz and P. Żuber (eds) *Ekspertyzy do Koncepcji Przestrzennego Zagospodarowania Kraju*, t. II. Warszawa: Ministerstwo Rozwoju Regionalnego, pp. 133–334.

Komornicki, T., Zaucha, J., Szejgiec, B. and Wiśniewski, R. (forthcoming). Wpływ globalnych procesów ekonomicznych na rozwój lokalny. *Prace Geograficzne*, 250.

Lijewski, T. (1994). Infrastruktura komunikacyjna Polski wobec zmian politycznych i gospodarczych w Europie Środkowej i Wschodniej, *Zeszyty IGiPZ PAN*, Nr 23, p. 58.

Lubelskie Voivodeship (2015). *Regional Handbook. The Cross-Border Cooperation Programme Poland-Belarus-Ukraine 2007–2013*. Warsaw.

Lviv Oblast (2015). *Regional Handbook. The Cross-Border Cooperation Programme Poland-Belarus-Ukraine 2007–2013*. Lviv.

Martinez, O. J. (1994). The dynamics of border interactions. New approaches to border analysis, in: C. H. Schofield (ed.), *World boundaries, global boundaries*, 1. London: Routledge, pp. 1–15.

Miszczuk, A. (2013). *Uwarunkowania peryferyjności regionu przygranicznego*. Lublin: Norbertinum.

Podkarpackie Voivodeship (2015). *Regional Handbook. The Cross-Border Cooperation Programme Poland-Belarus-Ukraine 2007–2013*. Warsaw.

Praca nierejestrowana w Polsce w 2014 roku (2015). Warszawa: GUS.

Rąkowski, G. (2000). *Transboundary protected areas in the eastern border region of Poland: outline of the concept*. Warsaw: Institute of Environmental Protection.

Ricq, C. (2006). *Handbook on transfrontier co-operation for local and regional authorities in Europe*. Strasbourg: Council of Europe.

Rosik, P. (2012). Dostępność lądowa przestrzeni Polski w wymiarze europejskim. *Prace Geograficzne*, 233, p. 309.

Ruch graniczny oraz przepływ towarów i usług na zewnętrznej granicy Unii Europejskiej na terenie Polski w 2010 roku (2011). Warszawa, Rzeszów: GUS – Urząd Statystyczny w Rzeszowie.

Ruch graniczny oraz wydatki cudzoziemców w Polsce i Polaków za granicą w 2014 roku (2015). Warszawa, Rzeszów: GUS – Urząd Statystyczny w Rzeszowie.

Skorupska, A. (2015). *Dyplomacja samorządowa. Efektywność i perspektywy rozwoju*. Warszawa: Polski Instytut Spraw Międzynarodowych.

Spierings, B. and Van der Velde, M. (2008). Shopping, Borders and Unfamiliarity. Consumer Mobility in Europe. *Tijdschriftvoor Economische en Sociale Geografie*, 99/4, pp. 497–505.

Study in Poland (2015). *Studenci zagraniczni w Polsce 2015*. Warszawa: Fundacja Edukacyjna 'Perspektywy'.

Volyn Oblast (2015). *Regional Handbook. The Cross-Border Cooperation Programme Poland-Belarus-Ukraine 2007–2013*. Lviv.

4 Perspectives on and challenges of Polish–Ukrainian cross-border cooperation in the context of geopolitical changes in Central and Eastern Europe

Andrzej Jakubowski, Bogdan Kawałko, Andrzej Miszczuk and Roman Szul

Although cross-border cooperation occurs above all at local and regional level, its development relies on the conditions defined at national and international levels. The main aim of this chapter is to set the issue discussed in a broader context, encompassing the evolution of the European Cohesion Policy, the development of Polish–Ukrainian bilateral relations, the nature of the main assumptions of strategic documents at national and regional level and the dynamic changes in the international environment which are difficult to foresee. This will allow us to understand the factors influencing how Polish and Ukrainian actors develop two-way cross-border cooperation, adapting to changing external circumstances, including geopolitical changes, and responding to the challenges that these changes generate.

Experiences and perspectives of Polish–Ukrainian cross-border cooperation in the light of the European Neighbourhood Policy

The collapse of the Soviet Union presented the EU with the task of defining the nature of its relations with a number of so-called New Independent States, including Ukraine. Official relations were established on 2 December 1991, when the acting foreign affairs minister from the Netherlands (holding the presidency of the EU) recognized Ukraine's independence and called for open dialogue with the EU. The first bilateral agreement was signed in February 1992, and in September the same year an official meeting took place between the president of the European Commission, Jacques Delors, and the president of Ukraine, Leonid Kravchuk, while in October 1993 an EU delegation was opened in Kiev[1] (Legucka 2008).

Relations between the EU and Ukraine were established on a new institutional basis – the Partnership and Cooperation Agreement (PCA) (European Commission 1998), which was concluded on 16 June 1994 in Luxembourg. Ukraine was the first signatory of this document among post-soviet nations.[2] The PCA created a legal, political and economic basis for relations between the EU and Ukraine, defining the principles and priorities of bilateral cooperation. It included pursuing a new trading regime (with the aim of setting up a free-trade zone) and institutionalizing political relations, thus creating the right conditions for continuing dialogue. For this purpose the EU–Ukraine Cooperation Council was set up along with the Cooperation Committee and Parliamentary Cooperation Committee. At the same time the development of cooperation with and support from the EU depended on Ukraine's progress in implementing the necessary political and economic reforms (Zagorski 2004; European Commission 1998). Owing to the prolonged ratification process in EU member states (the PCA did not come into force until 1998), the Interim Agreement on trade and trade-related matters between the European Community, the European Coal and Steel Community, the European Atomic Energy Community and Ukraine was not signed until 1 June 1995; it enacted most of the economic clauses of the PCA and enabled the development of trade links (European Communities 1995).

This agreement created the basis for the development of relations between the EU and Ukraine, although it did not meet with Ukraine's expectations. The PCA was limited to provisions concerning the development of 'close political ties', the promotion of trade and investment and harmonious economic relations, promoting 'sustainable development'. A further aim of the PCA was to support Ukraine in its efforts to strengthen democracy and develop a market economy, yet in the document there was a lack of any mention of integration of Ukraine with the EU, or the conferring upon it of the status of an associated state (European Commission 1998). The limitations of the PCA signed with Ukraine stand out particularly in contrast with the provisions of the European Agreements that were signed several years earlier with Central European nations (including Poland), according to which the associate status established was intended to prepare the way towards full membership of the EU (Hillion 2005; Mayhew 2008).

Apart from developing political and economic cooperation, the EU extended certain support instruments to nations belonging to the Commonwealth of Independent States (CIS). The targets of the PCA were to be achieved above all through financial support in the form of the TACIS programme (Technical Assistance to the Commonwealth of Independent States), which was launched as early as 1991 under the management of the European Commission, with a total funding allocation of €7.57 billion in the period 1991–2006 (Raszkowski 2011). The main aim of the programme was to support the transition to a market economy and to strengthen democracy and the rule of law. These actions were designed to bring about the conditions for economic growth and to establish a real partnership with the EU, with the help of commonly agreed priorities. Ukraine became the second largest beneficiary (following Russia) of the TACIS programme, which consisted of distinct national and regional components. Under the national component alone, Ukraine received funds of around €1 billion (Raszkowski 2011). Although many varied projects were successfully carried out under the TACIS programme, it was not possible to exert greater system-wide influence on the course of reforms in post-soviet countries, including Ukraine (Zagorski 2004).

Considering the growing differences between the so-called New Independent States, as well as the diversification of EU goals relating to the post-soviet states, the EU began to gradually diversify its policies towards them. An example is the

Common Strategy on Ukraine, which was adopted during the European Council Summit in Helsinki on 11 December 1999. It was aimed at strengthening the 'strategic partnership between the EU and Ukraine, based on shared values and common interests', being 'a vital factor enhancing peace, stability and prosperity in Europe' (European Council 1999). The Strategy outlined an overall vision of partnership development, EU aims with respect to Ukraine and funds for realizing them. In the document it was stated that 'the EU acknowledges Ukraine's European aspirations and welcomes Ukraine's pro-European choice'. At the same time the EU confirmed its commitment to cooperation with Ukraine at national, regional and local levels in order to support successful political and economic transition, facilitating Ukraine's closer ties with the EU (European Council 1999). It is worth mentioning that, apart from Ukraine, a similar document was elaborated only with the Russian Federation. And although its adoption did not bring significant progress in mutual relations between the EU and Ukraine (Barburska 2006), the fact that it was elaborated implies that the EU ascribed Ukraine a specific role in building stability and security in Eastern Europe, while at the same time refraining from offering the perspective of membership (Baun 2000; Zagorski 2004).

The expansion of the EU to include ten new member states in 2004 marked a turning point in relations between the EU and Ukraine, making Ukraine a direct neighbour. The perspective of expansion forced EU member states to define their policy assumptions towards their new neighbours. These were presented in March 2003 in the document: *Wider Europe – Neighbourhood: A New Framework for Relations with our Eastern and Southern Neighbours*, which addressed southern Mediterranean nations as well as European post-soviet states. The aims contained within it were to deepen economic and political cooperation and to intensify actions to counter various types of cross-border threats. The document also talked about harmonizing law, lifting trade barriers, facilitating the flow of people, goods, services and capital (also known as the 'four freedoms') and developing science and research cooperation, as well as cultural exchange (Commission of the EC 2003b). The new approach was meant to lead to the establishment of a politically and economically stable zone covering the EU and its immediate surroundings, and thereby prevent the rise of a new divisions in Europe. In line with this philosophy, the EU worked towards shaping a friendly and prosperous neighbourhood around itself, a kind of 'ring of friends, with whom the EU enjoys close, peaceful and cooperative relations' (Liikanen 2013). Without doubt, this document was intended to define the limits of European integration by directing it exclusively to those nations for whom membership of the EU was not anticipated in the near future.

The final conception presenting the overall vision of the EU's relations with its neighbours was put before the European Commission on 12 May 2004 in the *European Neighbourhood Policy – Strategic Paper* (Commission of the EC 2004). Cooperation under the European Neighbourhood Policy (ENP) was based on the Action Plan, adopted in the same year (but replaced in subsequent years by the EU–Ukraine Association Agenda), which was a detailed description of the steps to realizing the ENP aims regarding Ukraine and the mechanisms of cooperation. It foresaw increased financial support for Ukraine, depending on progress in implementing internal reforms, including harmonizing law with the acquis communautaire. It is worth adding here that the proposals of the European Commission regarding the ENP were accepted by Ukraine with some disappointment. Above all, the ENP remained a one-sided EU initiative, and did not promote the development of partner-based relations. Moreover, the main assumption of the ENP was against Ukraine's interests in terms of the setting up of the neighbourhood policy as an alternative to expanding the EU and a lack of differentiation among European and non-European partners, particularly in reference to eventual aims and prospects for relations with the EU as well as the failure to consider introducing a mutual visa-free regime (Sydun 2010).

In the *European Neighbourhood Policy – Strategy Paper* a great deal of space is dedicated to issues of regional cooperation, including cross-border cooperation on the new eastern external border of the EU. Priority areas of cooperation were recognized as (Commission of the EC 2004):

- Reinforced cooperation on economy, business, employment and social policy, trade and infrastructure, including the adoption of European and international standards in order to encourage the sustainable socio-economic development of the countries in the region, as well as joint infrastructure and security projects of regional relevance in the sectors of energy and transport (including border crossings);
- Environmental problems such as water and air pollution, the management of spent nuclear fuel and the gradual harmonization of environmental standards and legislation;
- Justice and home affairs, in particular regional cooperation on border management, migration and asylum, the fight against organized crime, the trafficking of human beings, illegal immigration, terrorism, money laundering and drugs as well as police and judicial co-operation;
- People-to-people issues, including civil society development, activities in the fields of media and journalists' exchanges, promotion of good governance and respect for human rights, professional, academic and youth exchanges, visit schemes, cooperation in the sectors of education, training, science and culture, twinning between local and regional administrations and civil society organizations.

In order to realize these plans it was essential to provide the appropriate financing and technical support by modifying the existing programmes of cross-border cooperation and, if necessary, by using the New Neighbourhood Instrument (NNI), titled in the EC Commission statement *Paving the way for a New Neighbourhood Instrument* (Commission of the EC 2003a).

As a result of expanding the EU in 2004, ten new member states were incorporated into the third edition of the INTERREG III initiative, financed by the European Regional Development Fund (ERDF). Under the components of INTERREG IIIA relating to financing of cross-border cooperation, eight programmes were implemented along the Polish border in the years 2004–6, including the Neighbourhood Programme Poland–Belarus–Ukraine. This replaced the Phare Cross-Border Cooperation (CBC), being separated from the Phare programme in 1994 and directed towards supporting cross-border cooperation between Central and Eastern European countries and their neighbouring EU states.[3] Until 2004 support for cross-border cooperation on the eastern border of EU candidates took place under the Phare CBC National Programmes, which distinguished the Fund for Large Infrastructure Projects, the Fund for Small Infrastructure Projects and the Small Project Fund (SPF). The two first parts of the programme mostly concerned the development of border infrastructure and support and training for border guards, while SPF was directed mainly at developing 'soft' forms of cooperation, covering programmes supporting cultural exchanges, the development of local democracy, planning and development studies, economic development and environmental protection. Undoubtedly the priority of the Phare CBC programme was issues concerning increased security on borders with states that would not be members of the EU (i.e., the CIS). This was reflected in the division of allocated funds. For example, in the period 1997–2002 under the Poland Eastern Border programme €110.2 million was allocated to Poland for strengthening border security and €83.2 million for large border infrastructure projects, but only €9.6 million for the Small Project Fund (Sadowski 2004).

The situation resulting from the expansion of the EU also made it necessary to redefine support policies for new neighbours. A sign of this revised approach was the previously mentioned European Commission statement of 1 July 2003, *Paving the way for a New Neighbourhood Instrument*, in which perspectives on territorial cooperation with new neighbours were laid out. According to the assumptions presented at that time, the process of creating the New Neighbourhood Instrument (NNI) was divided into two stages (Commission of the EC 2003a).

In the first stage, covering the years 2004–6, the EU decided to create so-called Neighbourhood Programmes. The initiatives realized under these programmes were directed at increasing cohesion in borderland areas of the EU and between them and its new eastern neighbours. Funding was provided by two separate budgets – ERDF for activities in the EU area and the TACIS fund for neighbouring states. One of the Neighbourhood Programmes was the Neighbourhood Programme Poland–Belarus–Ukraine INTERREG IIIA/TACIS CBC (PBU), which aimed to support cross-border cooperation on the eastern border of Poland, which at the same time constituted the external border of the EU (Raszkowski 2011).

Here it is worth mentioning that the Neighbourhood Programmes were not the first initiatives of the EU directed at developing cross-border cooperation with CIS nations. The first activities of this nature took place in 1994, in the face of the increasingly real prospect of Central and Eastern European nations becoming members of the EU. The importance of cross-border cooperation was underlined in the Partnership and Cooperation Agreements signed with Russia and Ukraine as well as in the EU Common Strategies regarding Russia and Ukraine.

In order to intensify cross-border cooperation and accelerate political transformation, the TACIS CIS CBC programme was set up within the TACIS programme, concentrating on the Eastern European area as well as Russia, Ukraine, Belarus and Moldova. It was implemented in two stages: in the periods 1996–9 and 2000–2006. The anticipated budget for the first programme period was €110 million, of which 20 per cent went to Ukraine. For the realization of the second stage of the TACIS CBC programme, based on general assumptions set for 3–4 year periods and annually set priorities and action areas, a budget of €30 million was awarded annually. The projects implemented were divided into two types: large, relating to border crossings, environment and energy projects (with budgets of over €2 million), and small, directed at the development of cross-border cooperation among local authorities (with a value of €50,000–200,000) (Sadowski 2004).

The main goals for cross-border cooperation financed under the TACIS programme included (Liikanen 2013):

- assisting border regions in overcoming their specific development problems,
- encouraging the linking of networks on both sides of the border, e.g. border-crossing facilities,
- accelerating the transformation process in the partner states through their cooperation with border regions in the EU or Central and Eastern Europe,
- reducing trans-boundary environmental risks and pollution.

For example, the plan for the period 2000–2003 gave priority to developing the border infrastructure (40–50 per cent of the budget), while 10–25 per cent of funds were dedicated to small projects (Sadowski 2004). The TACIS programme became the main instrument of financial support for partner states from Eastern Europe, including Ukraine, until 2007, allowing the implementation of the assumptions of the European Neighbourhood Policy and the provisions of the Action Plan. A quota of €75 million was allocated for its implementation in the period 2004–6, while €700 million was earmarked for cross-border cooperation inside the EU (the INTERREG IIIA programme) (Commission of the EC 2004). From the above-mentioned funds €45.8 million was allocated to the Neighbourhood Programme Poland–Belarus–Ukraine INTERREG IIIA/TACIS CBC, including €37.8 million from the INTERREG fund and €8.0 million from the TACIS CBC.

Among all the cross-border cooperation programmes implemented on the borders of Poland, cooperation on the eastern border was of a specific nature. This was determined by the fact that, after Poland's accession to the EU, its border became the external border of the EU. This demanded additional instruments and various actions, often difficult to reconcile, which on the one hand would promote the development of social, economic and cultural cooperation but on the other would increase border security by sealing it and developing the border infrastructure. The specific nature of cross-border cooperation on the eastern border of Poland was also determined by the fact that in the past there had not been a separate Poland–Ukraine or Poland–Belarus Phare programme, and up to that time the cooperation had been undertaken on the basis of the 'Poland Eastern Border' Phare programme as well as funds from TACIS CBC (Ministry of Regional Development 2010a).

In order to make a broader analysis of the Neighbourhood Programme Poland–Belarus–Ukraine INTERREG IIIA/TACIS CBC it is necessary above all to bear in mind the scant funds allocated for its implementation.[4] Despite the unquestionably positive effects in terms of developing bilateral cooperation between Poland and Ukraine, developing links and building an atmosphere of trust, the cross-border cooperation realized under the programme met with all kinds of difficulties, resulting largely from the fact that in the period 2004–6 the Neighbourhood Programme PBU was financed from two uncoordinated sources – i.e. INTERREG IIIA and TACIS CBC – which in many cases even made it impossible to co-finance projects. The building of partner-based relations was also not helped by the distinct asymmetry of the two sides in terms of potential, experience and financial resources. In addition, technical problems connected with the centralized decision-making process and the high degree of formality in the administrative contacts of Ukrainian partners were further negative influences on the development of cooperation. Meanwhile, too wide an area of support in relation to the limited funds brought about a 'watering-down' of cross-border projects (Ministry of Regional Development 2010a). In the view of M. Guz-Vetter, the Neighbourhood Programme Poland–Belarus–Ukraine was well prepared in terms of conforming to the procedures and formal recommendations of the European Commission, but not in terms of conforming to the priorities of Polish foreign and economic policy regarding its eastern neighbours, with the aim of supporting real, beyond-border civil and economic cooperation. Attention was also paid to the marginal treatment of opportunities for cooperation between small and medium-sized businesses, particularly in view of the considerable interest of businesses in the east of Poland in economic cooperation with eastern partners (Guz-Vetter 2004).

Without doubt, the implementation of the Neighbourhood Programme Poland–Belarus–Ukraine in the first stage of the European Neighbourhood Policy allowed new forms of Poland–Ukraine cross-border cooperation and the development of bilateral links. However, the scale of impact of the Neighbourhood Programme PBU in the period 2004–6 was too small to have a beneficial effect on the progress of functional integration in areas located on either side of the border, including better use of common developmental potential. Neither was it able to impact significantly on limiting the developmental barrier relating to the borderland location and reducing the peripheral nature of the borderland areas.

In the second stage of creating the NNI, covering the period 2007–13, a new financial instrument of the European Neighbourhood Policy, the European Neighbourhood and Partnership Instrument (ENPI), was created based on the experiences of the previous stage. It provided co-funding for processes supporting the management and equitable development of the economy and society. The ENPI also supported cross-border and cross-regional cooperation as well as the gradual economic integration of beneficiary states with the EU. The programme focused on the four key objectives identified in July 2003 (Commission of the EC 2003a):

- Promoting sustainable development in regions on both sides of common borders;
- Working together through joint actions to address common challenges in fields such as environment, public health and the prevention of and fight against organized crime;
- Ensuring efficient and secure common borders through joint actions;
- Promoting local cross-border 'people-to-people' type action.

According to the Regulation (EC) no. 1638/2006 of the European Parliament and Council of 24 October 2006 setting out general guidelines regarding the enactment of the ENPI, this instrument supported, in particular (European Commission 2006):

- Political reforms, including utilizing and adapting institutional and administrative potential, building the rule of law, respecting human rights, engaging civil society, facilitating international dialogue and fighting corruption, organized crime and terrorism;
- Economic reforms, including economic development, the development of a market economy, the intensification of trade and economic integration with the EU market;
- Social reforms, including integration, employment, fighting discrimination, fighting poverty;
- Sectoral cooperation, particularly in sectors of common interest such as environmental protection, sustainable development, energy, transport, telecommunications, health, food safety, education, research and innovation;
- Regional and local development as well as regional and sub-regional integration;
- Participation in the programmes and work of EU agencies.

Under the ENPI, national and international programmes were planned for implementation in each partner country in addition to cross-border cooperation programmes between partners and EU member states neighbouring each other on land or across the sea. The ENPI budget for the period 2007–13 amounted to €11.2 billion, of which 95 per cent was allocated to national and international programmes and 5 per cent to cross-border cooperation programmes (European Commission 2006). This second component was put towards financing the Cross-border Cooperation Programme – Poland–Belarus–Ukraine (PBU) 2007–13, as one of ten cross-border cooperation programmes implemented on the Polish borders, including one of two relating to cross-border cooperation on the eastern external border of the EU.[5]

The Cross-border Cooperation Programme Poland–Belarus–Ukraine 2007–13 provided for continued at the same time as more extensive cooperation in borderland areas in the three countries covered by the Neighbourhood Programme Poland–Belarus–Ukraine INTERREG IIIA/TACIS CBC. The basic aim of the programme was to support cross-border development processes by implementing joint projects of a non-commercial nature. The area covered by the programme included the main regions of support as well as adjoining regions. In the Polish–Ukrainian borderland the range of main support regions covered the sub-regions of Krosno-Przemyśl (in Podkarpackie voivodship), Biała Podlaska and Chełm-Zamość (in Lublin voivodship), as well as the whole territory of Lviv and Volhynia oblasts, while adjoining regions included the sub-region of Rzeszów-Tarnobrzeg (Podkarpackie voivodship) and Lublin (Lublin voivodship).

The programme assumptions were elaborated by a joint working team constituting representatives of central and regional governments from the three affected nations. In this work they took account of the achievements of the Neighbourhood Programme PBU in terms of infrastructure development, tourism, culture, environmental protection, human resources and people-to-people projects, which established new links between border regions and helped to break down the barriers in cross-border relationships. At the same time, efforts were made to decentralize management and simplify procedures, particularly with respect to micro-projects (projects up to €50,000) in order to speed up and improve the implementation of the ENPI. Making the idea of partnership a reality was to be aided by the inclusion of a wider range of beneficiaries from Belarus and Ukraine along with provision of adequate funding.

Along with the assumptions, the Cross-border Cooperation Programme PBU was directed at creating stable and lasting mechanisms for cooperation among administrative bodies, inhabitants, institutions and organizations and businesses and local communities in order to better utilize the endogenous potential of borderland regions. The main aim of the programme, to support cross-border development processes, was realized under three priorities:

1 Growth in competitiveness in cross-border areas focused on actions promoting and supporting better conditions for doing business, developing tourism and improving the accessibility of the region by developing transport links, although infrastructural investment projects were financed only in the main regions of support.
2 Improving quality of life, with consideration given to environmental protection in borderland areas, management of environmental threats and the development of renewable sources of energy, improved efficiency of infrastructure, better border procedures and greater border security.
3 Network cooperation and local community initiatives focused on actions promoting and supporting cross-border cooperation, including local community initiatives.

The main beneficiaries and participants of the projects implemented under the Poland–Belarus–Ukraine programme were central and local government institutions, business entities and non-government organizations. In the course of implementing the programme three calls for proposals were made, in 2009, 2011 and 2012. In this process a total of 824 projects was proposed, including 307 project in the first call and 505 in the second, while in the third round, dedicated to umbrella projects, 22 projects consisting of a total of 226 micro-projects were proposed. The most projects, 553, were proposed in the Poland–Ukraine partnership; in the Poland–Belarus partnership 145 were proposed; while in the trilateral partnership 127 were proposed. Finally, in the course of all the calls, 117 projects were contracted and implemented, including 74 in the Poland–Ukraine partnership and 14 in the three-way partnership. Besides projects selected in the competition procedure, the programme also envisaged the non-competitive selection and financing of large strategic projects linked to building, modernizing and providing technical equipment to border crossings. In this mode, nine projects were financed, with a total quota of €45 million. The total value of contracted projects under the whole programme amounted to over €174 million out of a total available allocation of €186.2 million (Kawałko 2015).

A full and final assessment of the outcomes achieved and their impact on the development of the cross-border region will be possible only after implementation of the programme is completed and an evaluation is made; yet, even today, certain conclusions can be drawn in this respect. Above all, the increased allocation of funds is worth underlining, as well as their greater accessibility to partners from Ukraine and Belarus by the replacement of the two budget lines with one common source of funding, the ENPI. At the same time, the increased size of grants has allowed the implementation of large investment projects, while the greater pool of funds dedicated to micro-projects has had a positive effect on the resilience of the whole programme. A positive assessment can also be given to the programme strategy for implementing project ideas based on applying partnership principles to all levels and ranks of joint activity. Thanks to this approach, even in cases where individual projects have not indicated a significant cross-border effect in their assumptions, the joint process of constructing, preparing and implementing the projects has, in itself, led to a new quality of cross-border cooperation between entities participating in a given project (Kawałko 2015). However, an important problem has remained the complicated procedures for transferring funds to partners in Ukraine as well as accounting for them (Ministry of Regional Development 2010a).

The extent of the change that the ENP underwent after three years of operation (2004–6) was wider, and was not limited to creating the ENPI. In December 2007 the European Commission presented a statement entitled *A Strong European Neighbourhood Policy* that proposed new solutions to reinforce and extend the scope of cooperation between the EU and its neighbouring countries (European Commission 2007). On 18 February 2008 the EU Council accepted the findings regarding the ENP. As a result new elements appeared in the ENP, including, among others (Council of the EU 2008):

- Scope for entering into far-reaching agreements that would replace the current PCA;
- The creation of a so-called free trade zone as the main tool of economic cooperation, including the trade of goods and services, open to nations that have joined the WTO. In the long term, scope for establishing a Neighbourhood Economic Community between the EU and countries covered by the ENP;

- Numerous means for facilitating the movement of people, including manpower, along with a recognition of the need to facilitate visas for ENP partners and make agreements on local border traffic;
- Scope for non-member states to participate in EU programmes.

These provisions were reflected in further activities of the EU relating to Ukraine, including the initiation of work on concluding the Association Agreement, which was intended to replace the expiring PCA. Following Ukraine's accession to the WTO in May 2008, the negotiations also covered the issue of creating a Deep and Comprehensive Free Trade Area with the EU.

However, the first measurable effect of the strengthened ENP was the introduction of the local border traffic (LBT) regime on the Poland–Ukraine border on the basis of the international agreement of 28 March 2008 concluded in line with the provisions of the Regulation (EC) no. 1931/2006 of the European Parliament and Council of 20 December 2006, laying down rules for local border traffic at the external land borders of the member states and amending the provisions of the Schengen Convention. This regulation enabled regular crossing of the border between the Republic of Poland and Ukraine (that is, the external border of the EU) by inhabitants of the borderland zone of Poland and Ukraine for social, cultural, family reasons or justified economic reasons excepting gainful activity. The borderland zone was recognized as the area of administrative units of Poland and Ukraine extending, in principle, no further than 30 kilometres from the common border[6] (Figure 4.1). A single stay in the borderland zone of the Republic of Poland was initially defined as 60 days from the moment of crossing the border, later extended to 90 days.

With the aim of developing the ENP in the East a special programme was designed for the nations of Eastern Europe and the South Caucasus entitled the Eastern Partnership (EP). It was presented at the meeting of EU foreign ministers in Brussels in May 2008 by representatives from Poland and Sweden and was finally set up in May 2009 during the summit in Prague. It included in its scope Armenia, Azerbaijan, Belarus, Georgia, Moldavia and Ukraine (Council of the EU 2009). This was the second initiative, alongside the Black Sea Synergy regional initiative of 2007 (Commission of the EU 2007), to incorporate Ukraine.

The main aim of the EP was to 'accelerate political association and deepen economic integration' between the EU and its eastern partners, with the level of integration and cooperation being proportional to the degree to which individual partner countries observed European values, standards and structures, as well as to their progress in making reforms. The partnership was intended to support democracy and good government, improve energy security, stimulate sectoral reforms (including in the area of environmental protection), promote people-to-people contacts, support economic and social development and provide additional financial resources for projects aimed at reducing socio-economic inequalities and improving stability. The multi-track process of the EP rests on four thematic platforms encompassing democracy, good governance and stability, economic integration and convergence with EU political activities, energy

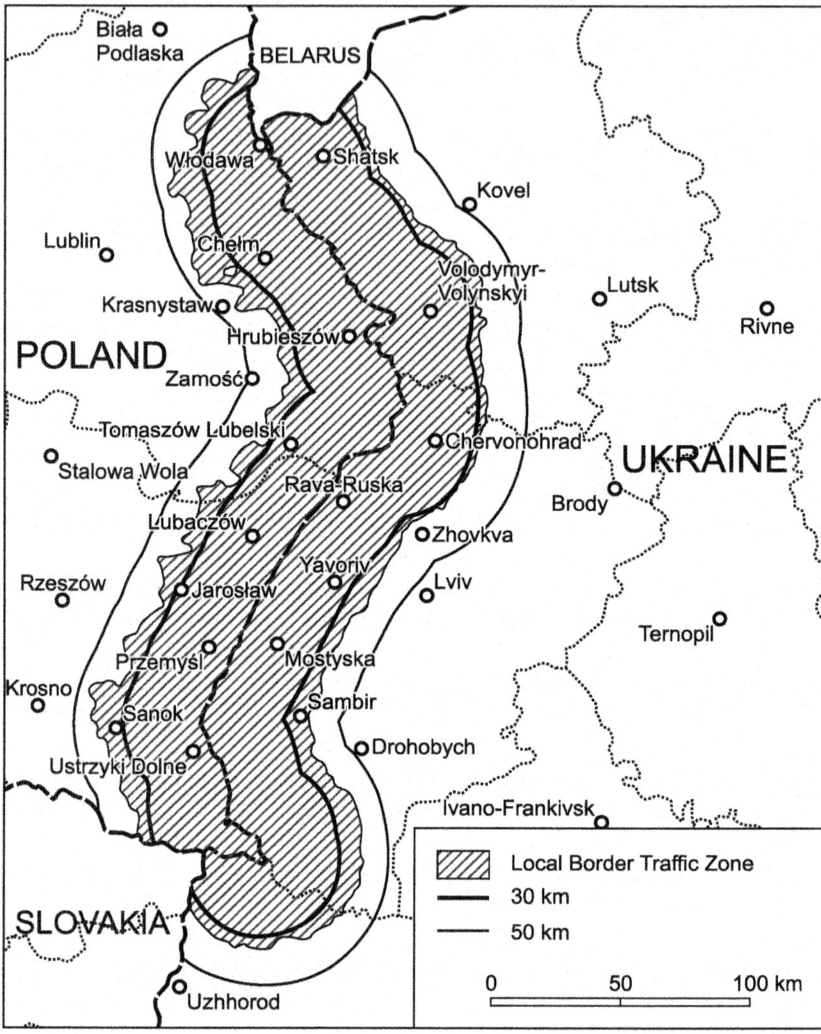

Figure 4.1 Zone of local border traffic

Source: Krzysztof Łoboda, on the basis of Mandryk and Novak (2012).

security and people-to-people contacts. Flagship initiatives were also launched, including an integrated programme of border management, an instrument for financing small and medium-sized enterprises, regional energy markets and actions for improving energy efficiency, the greater use of renewable energy, support for appropriate management of the natural environment, the prevention of natural and manmade disasters and preparation for and response to these events. Of particular importance from the Ukrainian perspective was the support for citizen mobility and simplified visa procedures with a view to fully liberalizing the visa regime (Council of the EU 2009). In order to implement the EP the European Commission allocated a budget of €600 million, in addition to the pool of funds provided in the 2007–13 budget for bilateral cooperation between the EU and its neighbours under the ENP.

Initially, the idea of the EP was received with enthusiasm, in the hope of reviving and modifying the negatively assessed ENP. However, conforming to the logic of ENP, the partnership programme did not open the way for Ukraine to join the EU, which was met with evident dissatisfaction on the Ukrainian side. The Ukrainian authorities placed much greater hopes in the Association Agreement, although in this case it became clear that EU and Ukrainian politicians had quite different perceptions of this document. According to the new formula elaborated by Ukrainian authorities – 'Partnership–Association–Membership' – this arrangement was intended to be a milestone on the road to Ukraine's full integration with European structures. This approach did not take heed of the signals issuing from Brussels indicating that the EU was not inclined to define the development of its relations with Ukraine in the more distant future, nor to make any firm declaration in this respect (Malyhina 2009).

Work on the content of the Association Agreement and on the EU–Ukraine Deep and Comprehensive Free Trade Area was completed in the second half of 2011, and their texts were initialled on 30 March 2012 in Brussels. The ratification process was suspended, however, owing to the marked worsening of standards of democracy and rule of law in Ukraine manifested in, among other things, the sentencing of Yulia Timoshenko and Yuriy Lutsenko. At the same time Ukraine began talks on the subject of preparing an 'appropriate model' of relations with the Customs Union created by Russia, Belarus and Kazakhstan. Simultaneous pressure from the EU, directed at bringing back the standards of the rule of law, and from Russia led to Ukraine withdrawing from preparations to sign the Association Agreement. This decision brought on a major political and social crisis in the country, leading to the overthrow of president Viktor Yanukovych and the announcement of early presidential and parliamentary elections. Finally, the political part of the Association Agreement between the EU and Ukraine was signed on 21 March 2014 and the economic part on 27 June 2014, while the agreement on the Deep and Comprehensive Free Trade Area (DCFTA) was enacted on 1 January 2016.

The Association Agreement concluded between the EU and Ukraine is an extensive document consisting of 2,135 pages together with appendices, defining the shape and scope of future bilateral relations. On the strength of the Agreement the parties are obliged to cooperate and converge policy, legislation and regulation across a broad range of areas, taking account of, among other factors, equal rights for workers, the gradual implementation of movement without visas, the modernization of the Ukrainian energy infrastructure, access to the European Investment Bank and broad cooperation in terms of foreign policy and security. At the same time, the Agreement committed Ukraine to introducing a whole range of economic, financial and legislative reforms leading to the gradual alignment of its legislation to that of the EU. In return, the EU committed itself to providing political and financial support to Ukraine and giving it preferential access to EU markets (*Association between the European Union and its Member States, of the one part, and Ukraine, of the other part* 2014).

An integral part of the Association Agreement is the commitment to creating the EU–Ukraine Deep and Comprehensive Free Trade Area, which came into force on a temporary basis on 1 January 2016. According to the European Commission,

> The DCFTA will offer Ukraine a framework for modernizing its trade relations and for economic development by the opening of markets via the progressive removal of customs tariffs and quotas, and by an extensive harmonisation of laws, norms and regulations in various trade-related sectors, creating the conditions for aligning key sectors of the Ukrainian economy to EU standards [. . .] Unlike classical FTAs, it provides for both the freedom of establishment in services and non-services sectors, subject to limited reservations, and the expansion of the internal market for a set of key services sectors once Ukraine effectively implements the EU-acquis.
>
> (European Commission 2015)

As G. Van Der Loo points out, although the EU–Ukraine Association Agreement is considered to be the most ambitious agreement that the EU has ever proposed to any non-member state, the real outcomes of the Agreement remain to a large degree unknown (Van Der Loo 2016). Without doubt, the implementation of the main provisions of the Agreement, and in particular its parts concerning DCFTA (including lifting the 99.1 per cent customs tariff on the Ukrainian side and the 98.1 per cent tariff on the EU side, as well as unifying the majority of regulations), allow intensified economic cooperation and trade, making it possible to obtain new potential goods and services suppliers and better investment opportunities. At the same time it must be remembered that many of the benefits foreseen in the Agreement depend on the implementation of long and complicated processes of harmonizing legislation in Ukraine (Ministry of Development 2016).

The signing of the Association Agreement should lead to the gradual improvement in the functioning of state institutions, including greater transparency, reduced corruption and better standards of public service, while access to the largest free trade zone in the world should in the long term lead to the greater competitiveness of the Ukrainian economy. While effective reforms in the institutional and legislative sphere can bring about relatively fast positive effects, there are many signs that in the short term the impact of the Association Agreement on the conditions of the Ukrainian economy will be unfavourable, above all because of the low competitiveness of Ukrainian enterprises on the European market. It is certain that the social costs of implementing reforms will be painful, if only with respect to the necessity of rationalizing employment.

The Association Agreement should also be seen in terms of the prospects that it opens up for cross-border cooperation between entities from Polish and Ukrainian borderland regions. There is no question that great potential benefits should ensue from the liberalization of visa laws for Ukrainian citizens. In the short term this could influence, above all, the growth of turnover from borderland trade and increased economic immigration of Ukrainians to Poland. In the longer term, the lifting of visas could lead to enhanced social, business and cultural links, resulting in a multi-faceted functional relationship. Furthermore, the transfer of the Acquis to the Ukrainian legislative system and the harmonization of customs and plant-health laws, as well as the adoption by Ukraine of European norms and standards, should have a positive impact on the scale of cross-border business ties. In this area, much will depend, however, on the pace of reforms in Ukraine and the activities of business people themselves.

Without doubt, the basis for developing cross-border cooperation on the Poland–Ukraine border over the next few years will be funding from the European Neighbourhood Instrument (ENI), the main financial instrument of the ENP in the years 2014–20, with a total allocation of €15.4 billion, replacing the existing ENPI[7] (European Parliament and Council 2014). Financed from the ENI, the Cross-border Cooperation Programme (CCP) Poland–Belarus–Ukraine 2014–20 assumes the continuity and expansion of cooperation in the borderland areas of the three engaged nations. The PBU budget for the period 2014–20, at over €176 million, is lower than in the previous programme perspective (Table 4.1). At the same time important changes were adopted in the implementation principles in relation to the 2007–13 version (Kawałko 2015), as follows:

- The implementation of infrastructure projects will be possible in the whole programme area and not only in the main area, as was previously the case;
- Important changes making it easier for beneficiaries to implement projects, including resignation from the application of rather complicated procedures for contracts contained in the Practical Guide to Contract Procedures for EU External Action (PRAC);
- A departure from implementing 'umbrella' projects in favour of implementing projects with a value of €20,000–60,000.

Table 4.1 Cohesion policy and ENI budget for the period 2014–20 compared to the period 2007–13

Specification	*2007–13*	*2014–20*
ETC budget (million €)	7,500.0	9,000.0
Cross-border cooperation (%)	73.86	73.24
Transnational cooperation (%)	20.95	20.78
Inter-regional cooperation(%)	5.19	5.98
ENPI/ENI budget (million €)	11,181.0	15,400.0
PBU Programme budget (million €)	186.2	176.0

Source: Kawałko (2015).

As previously, the programme area covers the main support regions and adjoining regions; in the Polish–Ukrainian borderland area it includes:

- in Poland, main sub-regions: Krosno-Przemyśl (in Podkarpackie voivodship) and Biała Podlaska and Chełm-Zamość (in Lublin voivoship); adjoining sub-regions: Rzeszów-Tarnobrzeg (in Podkarpackie voivodship) and Puławy and Lublin (in Lublin voivodship);
- in Ukraine, main oblasts: Lviv and Volhynia.

Despite the division of the area into main regions and adjoining regions, the programme anticipates that institutions from both these parts applying for funding from the programme will be treated identically. The financing of projects implemented partly outside the programme area will be possible providing that the applicants show that the projects are necessary for achieving the aims of the programme and bring benefits to the programme area, and that the total sum located under the programme for actions outside the programme area does not exceed 20 per cent of the EU contribution at the level of the whole programme.

The Cross-border Cooperation Programme Poland–Belarus–Ukraine 2014–20 is largely based on the cooperation experiences of previous years between the local, regional and national institutions of Poland, Belarus and Ukraine, and is a continuation of them. The programme was devised with the direct participation of representatives from the programme regions; it was preceded by an in-depth analysis of the PBU programme implementation in the period 2007–13, as well as an assessment and diagnosis of the situation in the programme regions in the new perspective to 2020. The thematic aims of the programme conform to the Programme Document for ENI support of Cross-border Cooperation (2014–20), anticipating three strategic goals:

- the promotion of economic and social development in regions on both sides of the common border,
- solutions to shared challenges regarding the environment, public health and security,
- better conditions and principles enabling movement of people, goods and capital.

Emphasis is placed on strengthening integration in cross-border regions while at the same time supporting and conserving cultural, historical and natural heritage, improving communication access, solving common problems in the area of safety and security and promoting border management. The main aim of the Cross-border Cooperation Programme Poland–Belarus–Ukraine 2014–20 is to support cross-border development processes on the borders of Poland, Belarus and Ukraine. The PBU programme is leading to the realization of all the above strategic goals and is responding to the identified regional needs by financing non-commercial projects relating to the following four jointly prepared thematic aims and dedicated priorities (Kawałko 2015):

1 The promotion of local culture and the conservation of historical heritage;
   - Priority 1.1 Promotion of local culture and history;
   - Priority 2.2 Promotion and conservation of natural heritage;
2 Improved access to regions, development of transport networks and communication systems that are durable and able to withstand the climate;
   - Priority 2.1 Improvement and development of transport services and infrastructure;
   - Priority 2.2 Development of ICT infrastructure;
3 Joint challenges in safety and security;
   - Priority 3.1 Support for developing health protection and social services;
   - Priority 3.2 Tackling shared challenges relating to security;
4 The promotion of border management and the management of security, mobility and migration;
   - Priority 4.1 Support for border efficiency and security;
   - Priority 4.2 Improvement of border management operations, customs and visa procedures.

It should be stressed that these thematic aims and priorities are complementary to the development priorities of the states whose territories lie in the support area, as will be discussed in a subsequent part of this chapter.

Cross-border cooperation is one of the most important instruments in breaking down barriers, reducing the peripheral character of cross-border regions and tempering the negative effects of the border's existence. This is particularly significant in the case of the Polish–Ukrainian border, which became partially impenetrable in 2004 and has been even more so from 2007. However, it should be borne in mind that the funds allocated represent only a meagre portion of the European Cohesion Policy and ENPI/ENI and, as a result, the possibilities are limited. In this context, the reduction in the pool of funds allocated to implementing the Cross-border Cooperation Programme Poland–Belarus–Ukraine 2014–20 compared with the previous programming period is particularly jarring, especially in view of the overall increase in the ENI budget of nearly 40 per cent compared with ENPI allocation for the period 2007–13. This decision must be seen as a step backwards and contrary to the frequently stressed rhetoric of EU representatives regarding the development of bilateral cooperation with Ukraine and the building of partner-based relations. It also means that, in the case of Polish–Ukrainian borderland regions, the chances of narrowing the development gap resulting from their peripheral location depend above all on the effective implementation of regional policies on the national and regional level. Actions undertaken under the

ENI can only be of a supplementary nature, stimulating the development of cross-border cooperation and lessening the negative impact of border obstacles on socio-economic development.

Perspectives on Polish–Ukrainian cooperation in the light of national and regional strategic planning

Cross-border cooperation between the borderland regions of Poland and Ukraine was established in 1992. In formal terms, two main areas can be identified resulting from the legal and political conditions: government and government–local self-government cooperation.[8] The first relates to the general functioning of government administrations, while the second is mainly connected with the activities of local self-government units. The existence of these systems, often interdependent (particularly on the Ukrainian side), is conditioned by the competencies of the partners. These two elements are combined at regional level. On the Poland–Ukraine border, the four institutionalized forms of cooperation are the Poland–Ukraine Inter-government Coordination Council for Interregional Cooperation, Euroregions, the Association Agreement and cross-border agreements.

The basis for bilateral relations is the Treaty between The Republic of Poland and Ukraine on Neighbourhood, Friendship and Cooperation, which was drawn up in Warsaw on 18 May 1992.[9] This sets out that the parties of the Treaty will promote the establishment and development of direct contacts and cooperation between regions, territorial–administrative units and cities of the Republic of Poland and Ukraine. According to the Treaty, particular attention should be devoted to cooperation in borderland areas, including in relation to development planning perspectives. The most important task for implementation is seen as increasing the number of border crossings and streamlining customs and border controls. The implementation of arrangements to activate cooperation between regions is served by the Inter-government Coordination Council for Interregional Cooperation and the Commission for Cross-border Cooperation.

The main aim of the Council is to coordinate and guide the course of cross-border and interregional cooperation in the areas of utilizing EU funds, developing infrastructure on the Polish–Ukrainian state border, widening interregional cooperation, activating joint action in spatial planning, and humanitarian issues. Six inter-governmental commissions operate within the Council:

- *The commission on border crossings and infrastructure* – undertakes and synchronizes work on infrastructure development and other action necessary for the future introduction of joint border and customs controls at Polish–Ukrainian border crossings;
- *The commission on utilizing EU funds* – takes action to obtain EU funds from the Cross-border Cooperation Programme Poland–Belarus–Ukraine and other external funds allocated to the eastern border;

- *The commission on humanitarian cooperation* – coordinates and evaluates work regarding the legal employment of citizens from both nations, according to the agreement between Poland and Ukraine;
- *The commission on borderland cooperation* – coordinates and evaluates activities relating to joint work in the field of environmental protection, including the creation of an information exchange system on ecological threats and the establishment of a state of emergency of a cross-border nature.
- *The commission on spatial planning* – covering cross-border cooperation in spatial planning, in particular transport infrastructure planning, environmental protection and the economic development of the Polish–Ukrainian borderland.
- *The commission on interregional cooperation* – dealing with the synchronization of transport networks in borderland regions, cooperation in tourism and the promotion of cultural heritage.

Besides the above-mentioned Treaty between the Republic of Poland and Ukraine on Neighbourhood, Friendship and Cooperation, the basic system of bilateral agreements regulating issues of cross-border cooperation also includes:

- *The Agreement between the Government of the Republic of Poland and the Government of Ukraine on Border Crossings*, drawn up in Warsaw on 18 May 1992,[10] containing provisions on the possibility of creating conditions for joint controls, wide-reaching cooperation for simplifying border traffic, optimal use of existing border crossings and the opening of new border crossings in convenient locations;
- *The Agreement between the Government of the Republic of Poland and the Cabinet of Ministers of Ukraine on the Principles of Passenger Traffic* of 30 July 2003 was aimed at simplifying the journeys of citizens from Poland and Ukraine, according to internal legislation and international obligations, in conformance to the laws of the EU, and contained provisions for visa-free travel of Polish and Ukrainian citizens and the free issue of visas to Ukrainian citizens by Polish consuls.

The 1992 Treaty of the Republic of Poland and Ukraine on Neighbourhood, Friendship and Cooperation identified the need to enter into cooperation in borderland areas. As an outcome of cross-border cooperation up to 2000 the document 'A study of land use in the area along the Polish–Ukrainian border – part I' (Part I – 1997, updated in 2000) was prepared. From that time until the end of 2008 this cooperation practically ceased; only the session of the Inter-governmental Council took place, with no particular outcome. The situation changed during the seventh meeting in March 2009, during which the commission for spatial planning was reactivated. The commission on borderland, inter-governmental and humanitarian cooperation was combined with a newly created commission on cross-border cooperation. The commission on border crossings and infrastructure was also in involved the work of this commission.

The signing of a 'Road Map of Cooperation for Poland and Ukraine in the period 2009–2010' by the presidents of the Republic of Poland and Ukraine in September 2009 meant that at the eighth session of the Polish–Ukrainian Inter-governmental Coordinating Council on Interregional Cooperation in October 2009 the need to finish the inventory and exchange of documents relating to land use covering the borderland area was identified. The responsibility for coordinating cooperation during work on the 'Study on spatial planning in the area along the Polish–Ukrainian border' (updated) was given to the Earth Sciences Institute of the Biology and Earth Sciences Faculty at UMCS University in Lublin and the Ukrainian State Scientific Research Institute for Urban Design 'Dipromisto' in Kiev.[11] During the ninth session of the Polish–Ukrainian Inter-governmental Coordination Council it was deemed necessary to prepare the document 'Map of intended investments in the Polish territory of the Polish–Ukrainian borderland'. This document was created by the Institute of Earth Sciences at the UMCS University in Lublin in February 2011. In reference to the work of the commission on border crossings, it was considered vital to perform a review of existing border crossings in terms of their full utilization and to analyse the scope for increasing their permeability. The 'Road Map of Cooperation for Poland and Ukraine in the period 2011–2012' led to the continuance of cross-border cooperation at the tenth (March 2012) and eleventh (June 2013) sessions of the Polish–Ukrainian Inter-governmental Coordination Council on Interregional Cooperation, concerning particularly the need to continue work on creating the Roztocze Cross-border Biosphere Reserve on the Polish side and further development under the Operational Programme on European Territorial Cooperation 2014–20. In addition, the need for a common Polish–Ukrainian planning document, to be entitled 'The concept of spatial development in regions lying along the border of Poland and Ukraine', was indicated. In reference to border crossings and infrastructure, there will be renewed discussion regarding the opening of new border crossings at Budynin-Belz; Zbereże-Adamczuki; and Kryłów-Krechiv. Until now, there have been twelve sessions of the Polish–Ukrainian Inter-governmental Coordination Council on Interregional Coordination, the last of which took place on 31 March 2015 in Rzeszów. At the session, discussion concerned the agreement leading to the exchange of diplomatic notes regarding the opening of a new border crossing at Dołhobyczów-Uhryniv, as well as plans and the state of work on the modernization of existing border crossings, including that at Zosin-Ustyluh.

Without doubt the choice of concrete actions under the regional policy in borderland regions should be made according to the principle of simultaneous, synergistic impact on the territories lying on either side of the border. Thus it is important to devise an efficient system for selecting and implementing undertakings resulting from the joint cross-border agreements and preparations, including those relating to land use programmes and joint development strategies in borderland areas. The choice and character of actions should be mutually adapted to the specific needs of given areas, taking into account their level of development. In this context, in areas lying along the external borders of the EU, regional policy aims should first concentrate on providing greater mutual socio-economic access. The main and most important plane of cooperation should relate to increasing economic exchanges, realizing joint projects for the protection and touristic use of the natural environment and shared cultural heritage, and the development of the cross-border system of public services. Actions in this area may be eligible for financial support both from EU programmes and territorial cooperation and from regional programmes and budgets.[12]

Of key significance for development policy are the mechanisms and instruments for financing it. The use of funds from the EU budget is conditioned by the degree to which the aims and directions of national development policy align with EU policy, as laid out in the *Partnership Agreement* (Ministry of Development 2015). This document replaced the National Strategic Reference Framework, which was binding in the programming period 2007–13. The Partnership Agreement is a document which defines the strategy of European fund intervention under three EU policies – cohesion policy, the common agricultural policy (CAP) and the common fisheries policy (CFP) – in Poland in the years 2014–20. In Poland European funds for the period 2014–20 are treated as the main, though not the only, source of financing investments that ensure rapid, lasting and sustainable development (MR 2015). The logic of planning and programming development is based on linking European expectations regarding the aims of the *Europe 2020 Strategy for Smart, Sustainable and Inclusive Growth* for smart, sustainable and inclusive growth with the aims set out in national strategic documents.

An assumption of EU policy to 2020 is the reduction of the degree of peripherality in borderland areas, achieved by, among other things, increasing their accessibility nationally and internationally. This should be bring about increased integration and mutual ties between areas lying on either side of the border and gradually shape cross-border functional areas with effective economic, social and communication links. In the case of Lublin voivodship and its neighbouring areas, use should be made of the existing good neighbourliness and tradition of cooperation in order to develop economic, scientific and cultural ties at both regional and local levels, especially in those fields which influence the growth of competitiveness and the development of key potential in these areas, such as ICT, education, culture, environmental protection, tourism, border and transport infrastructure and enterprise. This may be assisted by the fact that one of the main cohesion policy aims of the EU is to build territorial cohesion and counteract marginalization in problem areas (Ministry of Regional Development 2012a). This is essential, bearing in mind that the developmental situation of regions along the EU border in comparison with European regions has been unfavourable for many years.

Undertaking, coordinating and implementing the developmental plans in Poland relies on a coherent model of the system of national and regional strategic documents. Development policy is carried out by the Council of Ministers, local government (voivodships), metropolitan unions and district and commune authorities (*powiat* and *gmina*) on the basis of development strategies and programmes.

According to the adopted model, the system for managing development includes categories of strategic documents at national and regional level. These include:

- at national level: long-term national development strategy, medium-term national development strategy, national strategy for regional development, national spatial development concept,
- at regional level: voivodship development strategy, voivodship spatial development plans,
- at local level: development strategy, study of conditions and directions of spatial development, local spatial development plans.

The range of cross-border cooperation issues and other national development strategies is conditioned above all by the keeping of a coherent hierarchy of aims and directions of intervention and, in the case of regional strategy, by the geographic position of the voivodships and their diversified location relative to the state border. In formulating the development strategy for voivodships and implementing development policy, the voivodship authority can cooperate with international organizations and regions of other nations, especially those neighbouring it.[13] One aspect belonging exclusively to the voivodship assembly in this respect includes the resolution 'Voivodship foreign cooperation priorities' and the adoption of the resolution on participating in international regional associations and other forms of regional cooperation.[14]

The decisions in the *National Spatial Development Concept 2030* concerning cross-border cooperation result mainly from the competency of the relevant minister of regional development, and include cross-border and borderland cooperation in spatial planning and land use management.[15] The national spatial development concept defines the conditions, aims and directions of sustainable development for the country as well as the action necessary for achieving it, including:[16]

- the distribution of social infrastructure of international and national significance;
- the distribution of technical and transport infrastructure, strategic water resources and water management structures with international and national significance;
- functional areas with supra-regional significance, including borderland functional areas.

In referring to aspects of cross-border cooperation at the regional level, the adopted regulations indicate the basic scope of land-use plans for voivodships, including definitions of:[17]

- the basic elements of the settlement networks in voivodships and their communication and infrastructure links, including directions of cross-border links;
- the limits and principles of managing functional areas with supra-regional significance as well as, depending on needs, the limits and principles of managing functional areas of regional significance.

The next strategic document at the national level is the *Long-term Development Strategy for the Polish Nation 2030 – Third Wave of Modernity*. This document sets out the development vision for Poland in the 2030 perspective. According to its content, sustainable territorial development requires a developmental synergy effect resulting from a growth in the significance and positive impact of cities on their regions and peripheral areas and the exchange between territories at differing levels of socio-economic development. These processes are of key significance not only within the country but also in cross-border relations, especially in areas with significant asymmetry in their development potential.

The Long-term Development Strategy indicates the need to closely relate decisions at a national level to strengthening the future development of regions in eastern Poland. In the National Spatial Development Concept this area is identified and treated as the target for actions supporting utilization of the qualified (also politically) potential offered by its borderland location. The main urban centres in the area are desirable locations for the concentration of metropolitan functions and businesses as well as for developing functional ties both in internal and external systems towards the east. Besides actions directed at increasing the level of integration in the region with other parts of the country, it is necessary to build lasting economic foundations for using these areas as the gateway to economic cooperation and trade with the whole of Central and Eastern Europe. In the context of developing cross-border cooperation, the greatest significance lies in implementing the nine strategy aims, which demand an increase in Poland's territorial accessibility. This should occur through the development of sustainable, coherent and user-friendly transport systems as well as the carrying out of the desired range of state interventions, including (Ministry of Administration and Digitization 2013):

- improvements in the quality of public services in terms of rail transport via the modernization, revitalization, building, reconstruction and development of railway lines and infrastructure (including stations), the complex modernization and/or replacement of rolling stock and the improvement of the organization and management of the rail sector;
- the modernization and development of roads, mainly within the basic and complex TEN-T networks, and the maintenance of the whole national road system.

An important aspect of planning development in the long-term strategy, which should also be seen from a cross-border perspective, is contained in Objective 7. This defines the vital need to provide energy security as well as to protect and improve the environment. Among the directions of intervention indicated in the cross-border dimension, this document recommends:

- implementing and financing modernization projects for electric, oil and gas power infrastructure;
- increasing the quantity of two-way cross-border gas pipeline distribution systems.

The main strategic document for Polish regions, defining the aims and strategic tasks for Poland in the medium-term perspective, is the *National Development Strategy 2020*. This strategy's vision incorporates the European policy aims set out in the Europe 2020 strategy and takes into account the diagnosed conditions for development as well as the priorities defined in the long-term national development strategy. In the context of the conditions for development in borderland regions of eastern Poland and cross-border cooperation, the parts of the vision which assume the provision of social and territorial cohesion are of particular importance.

The main courses of action adopted by the National Development Strategy concerning borderland areas are as follows (Ministry of Regional Development 2012b):

- counteracting marginalization processes on a national scale by reinforcing existing city networks and aiding urbanization;
- impacting on borderland areas in order to break down the development barrier and release their potential (with particular consideration for the border of the Schengen area);
- developing border infrastructure, including that of local significance;
- building infrastructure allowing crude oil transport from various regions of the world, including the Caspian Sea under the Eurasian Oil Transport Corridor, and developing the transmission, transhipment and storage infrastructure for crude oil and liquid fuels;
- extending external and internal (inter-regional and local) territorial access through realizing investments with a two-tier structure incorporating a base network (nodes and connections of key national significance) and supplementary networks, and with consideration for the key role of the TEN-T network in creating a coherent transport infrastructure network for the EU.

The next key document from the perspective of implementing regional policy in Poland, including in terms of cross-border cooperation, is the *National Strategy for Regional Development 2010–2020: Regions, Cities, Rural Areas*. The aims of this strategy and the set of actions indicated under them point to international cooperation as an important instrument in supporting the competitiveness of regions, tackling the persisting peripherality of borderland areas, reinforcing territorial cohesion and counteracting the marginalization of problem areas.

The National Strategy for Regional Development points to districts (*powiat*) whose capitals lie within 50 kilometres of the Schengen border as areas of intensive regional policy action regarding borderland cooperation; it also indicates areas beyond the Polish borders, to which actions of a cross-border nature are applied.

Regarding cross-border issues, the National Strategy for Regional Development recommends frameworks for actions that are essential for the borderland regional development strategy, including (Ministry of Regional Development 2010b):

- improving national and regional energy security, taking into account aspects relating to climate change;

- ensuring an integral national system of protected areas by protecting migration corridors and ensuring the integrity of important cross-border conservation areas (including the creation of international biosphere reserves);
- helping eastern regions to take advantage of their location and long-lasting tradition of cooperation with eastern neighbours to develop economic, scientific and cultural ties which influence the development of their potential in areas such as ICT infrastructure, education, energy, health, culture, selected public utilities, transport infrastructure and competitiveness;
- strengthening metropolitan functions and promoting cooperation between the largest centres, both within the nation and internationally;
- improving national and continental communication links between all the main economic centres of the country.

One of the key documents aimed at spatially reflecting the adopted policies in national strategic documents is the *National Spatial Development Concept 2030*. This document adopted an integrated approach to development in which the national space is seen as an area of diversified socio-economic, environmental and cultural processes, and the proposed developmental vision stresses the significance of spatial conditions for optimal use of the endogenous potential perceived both at national and regional levels. With respect to the regions of eastern Poland, the document points to the potentially large pro-development significance of Poland's juxtaposition with countries remaining outside the EU: that is, Russia, Belarus and Ukraine.

However, diagnosis of the problems and risk indicates that these opportunities cannot be fully taken advantage of without the deeper economic and political integration of these countries with the EU (Ministry of Regional Development 2012a). The existing potential of these areas is influenced by the relatively weak and unstable economic and social links with borderland regions on the eastern side of the Polish border. An additional factor exacerbating the difficulties in development is the weakness of urban centres located in these territories, the unfavourable socio-economic situation, low levels of innovation and competitiveness in the economy and poor access to regional growth centres. The National Spatial Development Concept indicates quite clearly that the border with Belarus, Ukraine and Russia still remains a development barrier, mainly for political reasons but also because of the pronounced asymmetry in systems of government, law, administration, programming and planning. The forms of cooperation entered into, which tend to have insufficient support from the European Territorial Cooperation programme, seldom go beyond cultural, tourism or educational activities. The scale of their impact is too small to have a significant influence on progress in the functional integration of areas situated on either of the border, including better use of common development potential.

One element of Poland's spatial development vision defined in the National Spatial Development Concept 2030 is the integrated and reinforced spatial cohesion of Poland both internally and externally (Ministry of Regional Development 2012a). The basis for reinforcing spatial cohesion is seen to lie in developing and building new international functional ties, mainly between links in metropolitan networks. This document assumes that international functional ties will be developed mainly through cross-border cooperation in terms of economic, R&D sector, social, educational, symbolic and cultural matters. The intensity and character of these functional ties depends partly on the economic strength of urban centres and the economic alignment of nations, and partly on affiliation to EU structures. This means that the National Spatial Planning Concept 2030 sees greater difficulty in achieving socio-economic integration with Eastern European countries – that is, Russian, Belarus and Ukraine. The document recognizes that the reinforcement of functional ties between eastern regions of Poland and western regions of Ukraine should be based on scientific, cultural and natural resources. With respect to cross-border cooperation within the framework of implementing national spatial development policy, the reinforcement of eastern regional centres is recommended, including, above all, Lublin and Rzeszów, as well as of sub-regional and local centres in borderland regions located near the external EU border by means of the following (Ministry of Regional Development 2012a):

- the transfer of benefits resulting from the spread of development factors from main regional centres to sub-regional towns (including Biała Podlaska, Chełm, Zamość, Przemyśl);
- increased access to medium- or higher-order public services especially relating to education and health;
- support for activities relating to new economic investments;
- placing important institutions connected with cross-border bilateral and European cooperation in the area;
- situating important management functions of the public sector with regional range in the area;
- raising the standards of secondary and tertiary schooling in fields which complement development in neighbouring countries;
- implementing joint projects in areas of culture, health resort tourism and recreational tourism.

The territorial approach adopted in the National Spatial Development Concept 2030 also involves realizing spatial development aims relating to particular functional–spatial structures. In the case of the Polish–Ukrainian border the following structures can be singled out (Ministry of Regional Development 2012a):

- the network of areas providing natural continuity and requiring coordinated conservation action on both sides of the border, including the Bug Valley corridor along with the Bug Gorge Landscape Park, the West Polesia Trilateral Biosphere Reserve and the Roztocze International Biosphere Reserve;
- the Bug River basin and catchment, as an area liable to flooding and subject to protection and management of water resources; recommendations for this area involve increasing retention capacity in the river valley, increasing the

buffering role of wildlife structures and achieving the required norms for the ecological status of surface water;
- the cross-border area, for which cooperation is recommended, connected with increasing transport access from borderland areas to the centre of the country as well as access from over the border to new border crossings. The implementation of border crossings will take into account the border procedures demanded by political conditions, relating for example to the EU external border, including visa, customs, plant health and veterinary and migration controls. In this context, there is a requirement to prepare common strategy and development plans for areas on both sides of the border.

An important aspect of cross-border cooperation, for which the National Spatial Planning Concept 2030 identifies specific courses of action, is to ensure the continuity of infrastructural systems, including:

- construction of the Odessa–Brody–Płock oil pipeline;
- development of road links in the system of motorways and expressways;
- development of rail links based on the railway lines running on the Berlin–Warsaw–Moscow and Warsaw–Dorohusk–Kiev routes and the Broad-gauge Steelworks Line, which forms an element of the trade route between Central Europe and Asia.

Among the most important strategic documents in Ukraine, the *State Strategy for Regional Development*, adopted in 2014, deserves particular attention. It devotes great attention to the cross-border dimension by defining and implementing the following aims (KMU 2014):

- the development of cross-border cooperation promoting the deepening of economic, social, scientific–technical, ecological, cultural and other relations between local communities, their representative bodies, local government executive bodies and territorial administration units along with the relevant government organs of other nations;
- the creation of the conditions for utilizing the organizational, financial and institutional skills of participants in cross-border cooperation in order to realize programmed cross-border cooperation projects;
- joint action on developing cross-border cooperation, continuation, activation and development of cooperation within the framework of Euroregions, eliminating infrastructure barriers and supporting joint economic activities in cross-border regions by small and medium-sized enterprises;
- more effective use of external aid under the ENP and other available programmes;
- the implementation of projects aimed at socio-economic development in borderland areas, the improvement of their ecological state and the development of border infrastructure and of cooperation between local communities in the neighbouring countries via the implementation of joint cross-border projects of a socio-humanitarian, economic, cultural or ecological nature;

- support of the acceleration of processes to align the living standards of borderland inhabitants with wider European levels and to facilitate both the flow of people, goods and capital across the border and joint actions in cross-border cooperation aimed at solving common problems in borderland regions;
- the provision of financial support for regional development programmes under international cooperation programmes, including EU funds from the ENP, cross-border cooperation programmes and other international programmes and funds.

The question of cross-border cooperation is also reflected in regional strategic documents. *The Lublin Voivodship Spatial Development Plan*, within the framework of areas of development and concentrated socio-economic function, distinguishes (BPP 2015):

- the basic elements of the settlement network, including Lublin, as a centre requiring the reinforcement and development of functional ties with national metropolises, as well as internationally with Kiev, Lviv and Vilnius;
- towns that are important points serving international transport (Małaszewicze, Okopy, Zawada, Hrebenne, Zosin, Koroszczyn).

Meanwhile, in the area of strengthening communication links, the document identifies those elements of the road and rail infrastructure which are particularly significant for maintaining and developing international relations, above all (BPP 2015):

- the Via Intermare transport corridor;
- II Pan-European transport corridor network TEN-T;
- the Via Carpatia transport corridor.

Also, owing to the increasing significance of Far Eastern markets, the need is identified to better use the potential offered by the Broad-gauge Steelworks Line (see Figure 2.7). The transport possibilities of this line have attracted the interest of large shipping and transport companies that take advantage of trade between east and west. The potential of the Broad-gauge Steelworks Line amounts to 10–12 million tonnes of cargo annually. Use of the line could be a factor in economic growth in regions in its immediate vicinity (Kawałko 2011a).

To achieve regional integration within the national and European space in terms of wildlife and natural landscapes, the voivodship plan indicates the need to take action in the framework of supra-regional as well as international cooperation, including in the following areas (BPP 2015):

- the West Polesia Cross-border Biosphere Reserve, the Bug Gorge CPA and the Roztocze CPA (planned as the Roztocze Cross-border Biosphere Reserve);
- the Bug River catchment area;
- the Pan-European ecological corridor of the Bug Valley.

A further element of the voivodship spatial development plans are functional areas. These are the outcome of using the typology defined in the National Spatial Development Concept 2030 as well as the spatial focus of strategic intervention areas identified in the Development Strategy for Lublin Voivodship. In terms of cross-border cooperation, the Lublin Voivodship Spatial Development Plan indicates (BPP 2015):

- areas of supra-regional significance with importance for national spatial policy referred to as Borderland Functional Areas with distinct frontier zones[18] and external zones;
- functional areas with significance for voivodship spatial policy, including:
  - *the Bug River Functional Area*, for which the development priority is to utilize its touristic value to bring about socio-economic revitalization in the area, while the main management targets are given as: implementing border crossings for local tourist traffic and utilizing natural and cultural assets for the developing tourism (including the educational assets of the River Bug in developing river tourism);
  - *the Polesia Functional Area* with the Wieprz–Krzna canal impact zone, for which the development priorities are to activate the economy through utilizing its agricultural and touristic potential, particularly in the central parts encompassing the border of the Polish section of the West Polesia Cross-border Biosphere Reserve;
  - *the Roztocze-Wilderness Functional Area*, for which the development pritority is to activate the economy by utilizing its health resort, forest and tourism potential and – of special significance in terms of cross-border cooperation in this part of the voivodship – by the creation of the Roztocze Cross-border Biosphere Reserve.

A key instrument of Lublin voivodship regional policy is the declaration of intent by the public authority which sets out the key directions for the development of the whole region in the *Lublin Voivodship Development Strategy for 2014–20 (with a Perspective to 2030)*. This document forms the basis for formulating programmes co-financed by the EU and other sources. One of the key principles of regional policy, defined in the National Strategy for Regional Development and adopted in the document, is thematic and geographical emphases resulting from a new paradigm indicating, among others, a diversified approach to different types of territory (understood in functional terms as problem areas and centres of growth).

Cross-border cooperation in the Lublin Voivodship Development Strategy is one of the most important issues of the entire development policy of Lublin voivodship. It is reflected both in the regional development vision for 2020, with a perspective to 2030, as well as in the operational objectives. One element of the development vision defines the relations of the voivodship with neighbouring regions of Ukraine and Belarus, indicating that:

> Accelerated development will occur in the most important regional towns, with Lublin at the fore, with a growing importance of supra-regional and

> international functions, including as a result of increased scientific, academic, cultural and economic links with centres in Belarus and particularly in Ukraine. Sub-regional towns will strengthen and improve their economic, cultural and educational functions, which – also thanks to better communication with their surroundings – will be widely used by inhabitants of surrounding areas.
>
> (UMWL 2014)

The strategic aims contained in the Lublin regional strategy[19] result from identifying the most important developmental challenges faced by the region. These are directed at innovation, strengthening cities, modernizing rural areas, enterprise and the use of scientific potential and regional integration to improve cohesion. Of particular significance in the context of cross-border cooperation is the operational objective 4.4 'to overcome the adverse effects of the region's borderland location', defined under four strategic aims. This stems from the need to identify actions in response to the diagnosed weaknesses of the region, which are (UMWL 2014):

- its peripheral location in relation to the country and the EU;
- weak incentives for development from foreign neighbours and negligible benefits arising from its borderland location;
- the lack of modern and efficient communication links between Lublin and other strategically important towns (Warsaw, Rzeszów, Kielce, Lviv, Lutsk).

Overcoming these limitations could be accomplished by taking advantage of the most important aspects of Lublin voivodship's potential, as follows (UMWL 2014):

- the considerable significance of Lublin as an academic, scientific and cultural centre as well as the main Polish centre for contacts with eastern neighbours, reinforced by the scientific, academic and economic potential of several sub-regional centres;
- the relative abundance of natural assets (energy and agricultural resources that are not fully capitalized on) and landscape value, which – along with cultural heritage – can serve to develop tourism.

A perpetual factor influencing the region's level of competitiveness is its location on the external border of the EU. This conclusion, drawn from in-depth diagnosis, demands the search for a means of breaking down this developmental barrier. For this purpose, the Strategy sets out the following main directions for action and intervention: the support of action and cooperation in building, developing and modernizing border crossings (rail and road); the creation of conditions and support for developing infrastructure to serve border traffic; the selective support of economic functions, including export and the development of logistic centres and trade centres. One course of action included in the Lublin Voivodship

Development Strategy is: 'to draw up a comprehensive development policy for the borderland areas of Lublin voivodship in cooperation with borderland regions of Ukraine and Belarus' (UMWL 2014).

In realizing the remaining strategic aims, the following courses of action and intervention focusing on cross-border cooperation are important (UMWL 2014):

- inspiring and supporting actions aimed at the functional integration of metropolitan areas, such as developing a low-emission urban transport system (including a commuter railway), complex revitalization and more efficient management of the Lublin Metropolitan Area;
- cooperation with the relevant government departments to enhance Lublin city and regional ties with eastern neighbours;
- cooperation with the appropriate entities and departments (including international) responsible for developing transport infrastructure.

One of the instruments for implementing the aims of the Lublin Voivodship Development Strategy, directed at utilizing the potential of its borderland location, is the designation of borderland areas as Areas of Strategic Intervention.[20] The delimitation of this type of area under the Strategy, owing to its importance for the development of the whole of Lublin voivodship, involves giving preferential treatment in the implementation of regional development policy. It envisages that intervention relating to Areas of Strategic Intervention – borderland areas – can be carried out by various means, instruments and mechanisms which are aimed at:

- the socio-economic development of borderland areas in the region;
- utilizing the endogenous potential of this area;
- strengthening transport and communication links
- building functions serving the EU and building logistics infrastructure;
- reinforcing the role of cities and building social and economic functions;
- modernization and support for the development and utilization of human resources as well as enterprise development;
- building new border crossings, modernizing and developing existing border crossings;
- opening seasonal (tourist) crossings;
- improving security in the region and borderland area.

While the cross-border dimension is not considered in the *Podkarpackie Voivodship Development Strategy for 2020* (Samorząd Województwa Podkarpackiego 2013), in the *Spatial Development Plan for Podkarpackie Voivodship 2030 Perspective* the following management principles are defined for borderland areas (UMWP 2014):

- counteracting peripherality by improving national and international access to these areas, developing transport infrastructure, modernizing and opening new border crossings and simplifying visa procedures from Ukraine;

- strengthening sub-regional and local centres (Jasło, Krosno, Lubaczów, Przemyśl and Ustrzyki Dolne) by supporting the development of new functions and extending the range of services of a supra-local nature provided;
- improving access to public services located in cities and in rural areas;
- developing the tourism function in harmony with conservation principles for areas of natural and cultural value;
- strengthening cross-border cooperation in terms of spatial and socio-economic planning by implementing and coordinating joint action and projects to ensure integrated planning in environmental protection, water resource management and cross-border infrastructure.

The specific conditions and perspective of the border location are also acknowledged in the strategic documents of both Ukrainian borderland regions. According to the draft *Lviv Oblast Development Strategy for the Period to 2020*, presented at the beginning of 2016, cooperation issues are dealt with in the third strategic aim, entitled 'Open borders', in which three operational objectives are set out (LODA 2016):

- international cooperation, including the requirement to: utilize the possibilities for international technical help, strengthen/improve the effectiveness of inter-regional cooperation, expand the network of offices of international institutions in the region, promote the region internationally and support and develop communication networks with the Ukrainian diaspora;
- cross-border cooperation, including the development of enterprise, organizations and institutions under the operational programmes of the European Neighbourhood Instrument 2014–2020, the development of cross-border logistics and trade centres, and institutional support in creating cross-border cooperation networks;
- border infrastructure, including the need to develop international border crossings, develop transport infrastructure, implement approved infrastructure projects, develop Lviv international airport as a European regional centre and modernize rail links in borderland areas.

Cross-border issues are also taken into account, although to a much lesser degree, in the *Volhynia Oblast Development Strategy for the Period to 2020*, which, under its strategic Objective 2 'Touristic Volhynia', points to the necessity of supporting the development of incoming and domestic tourism, including via the creation of national and cross-border tourist routes (VOR 2015).

The directions for cross-border cooperation indicated in the Lublin Voivodship Development Strategy for 2014–20 (with a perspective to 2030), the Lviv Oblast Development Strategy for the period to 2020 and the Volhynia Development Strategy for the period to 2020 are fully elaborated with their operational details in a separate document, the *Cross-border Cooperation Strategy of Lublin Voivodship, Volhynia Oblast, Lviv Oblast and Brest Oblast for the Years 2014–20*. This is an important system element in the process of building integration and deepening cross-border cooperation in the so-called 'sensitive' external eastern border of the EU. The adopted strategy, owing to the fact that it encompasses regions situated on either side of the eastern external border of the EU, has a unique, even exemplary, character from the point of view of conducting the ENP. The main premises of the strategy for cross-border cooperation within the four regions included:

- seeking solutions and promoting European integration processes in difficult geopolitical circumstances;
- system and programme engagement in realizing the Eastern Partnership Programme as a major priority for Poland and one of the priorities of EU policy;
- working out aims and priorities as well as systemizing the long-term strategic cooperation of Lublin voivodship with regions situated on the external border of the EU.

An assumption of EU policy to 2020 is the reduction of the degree of peripherality in borderland areas via, among other methods, increasing their accessibility nationally and internationally. This should lead to increased integration and growing mutual ties of areas lying on either side of the border, and the gradual shaping of cross-border functional areas which are effectively linked economically, socially and in terms of communication. In the case of Lublin voivodship and its neighbouring areas, the existing neighbourly relations and tradition of cooperation should be utilized for developing economic, scientific and cultural links at both regional and local level, especially in those fields that have an impact on growth in competitiveness and the development of key areas of potential, such as ICT infrastructure, education, culture, environmental protection, tourism, border infrastructure, transport and enterprise. This may be encouraged by the fact that one of the main aims of the EU cohesion policy is to build territorial cohesion and counteract the marginalization of problem areas (Ministry of Regional Development 2012a; Ministry of Regional Development 2010b). This is important in as much as the development position of the regions along the eastern border of the EU has been unfavourable for years.

The main aim of the strategy is to increase the socio-economic competitiveness of borderland areas by effectively utilizing the strategic endogenous potential identified in analysis and to mitigate the limitations resulting from the functioning of the external eastern customs border of the EU. The Cross-border Cooperation Strategy document was elaborated in partnership, using the methods recommended by national and EU institutions in preparing local, regional, national and European strategic documents.[21]

In accordance with the adopted methodological approach, the cross-border cooperation strategy has a functional character. The time horizon covers a seven-year programming period in line with the EU financial perspective for 2014–20, while the spatial range encompasses Lublin voivodship and the bordering oblasts of Lviv and Volhynia in Ukraine, as well as Brest in Belarus. It is worth underlining that this delimitation in the strategic document means that the subject of programming is the whole area of the four regions included in the strategy, for which diagnoses were conducted, SWOT analyses prepared, mission statements and strategic and operational aims defined and an indicative list of desired key projects drawn up. Therefore, the Cross-border Cooperation Strategy of Lublin Voivodship, Volhynia Oblast, Lviv Oblast and Brest Oblast for the years 2014–20 is not prepared for the four regional administrations separately; rather, they are treated as a single cross-border region. Despite the fact that the area covered by the Strategy includes three functioning borders (Polish–Belarusian, Polish–Ukrainian and Belarusian–Ukrainian) only two of these (Polish–Belarusian and Polish–Ukrainian) are the subject of consideration, as they form sections of the external EU border. The concept of cross-border cooperation is also limited to these two border sections.

The directional section includes the general aims of the Strategy, strategic analyses in specific fields and the detailed aims, directions and outcomes of actions. A system of indicators is also identified to help monitor the implementation of the Strategy and an outline of the implementation system and its sources of funding is presented. Based on analyses conducted on the potential of the cross-border area, SWOT analyses and identification of strategic fields of action by Polish, Belarusian and Ukrainian experts, the general aims of the Cross-border Strategy was formulated as: 'Raising the socio-economic competitiveness of cross-border area in European, national, regional and local dimensions by effective use of its endogenous potential as well as mitigating limitations resulting from the functioning of the external EU customs border' (UMWL 2013). Meanwhile, common strategic targets were defined as (UMWL 2013; see Figure 4.3):

- economic cooperation;
- natural environment, culture and tourism;
- communication infrastructure;
- science and higher education.

The first target area involves the creation of favourable conditions for enterprise development and foreign capital investment. The effect of actions taken to achieve this should be improved economic competitiveness in the cross-border region. The main obstacles to economic cooperation include the lack of information on conditions for doing business in each part of the cross-border region, the very diversified and unclear laws, the customs barrier and the difficulties in finding reliable partners. In this context, in order to achieve the desired aims and outcomes of economic cooperation in cross-border areas, the following courses of action were adopted:

- the delivery of complete and up-to-date information on conditions for doing business and economic entities of the cross-border region;
- the creation of further incentives to do business;
- support for the specialization of existing institutions linked to business in serving firms interested in cross-border cooperation;
- the integrated economic promotion of the cross-border area.

The second target area involves enhancing natural and cultural potential and utilizing it for the development of tourism. The effects of action taken to achieve this should include an increase in the attractiveness of the cross-border region for tourism in the national and European dimension through the preservation of its biodiversity and culture heritage assets. Weaknesses include the lack of a modern tourist infrastructure or an integrated information system, varying standards of tourist products and poor access to tourist attractions. In order to achieve the set aims and outcomes in the natural environment, culture and tourism, the following courses of action were adopted:

- cross-border cooperation of crisis management services and in the field of health protection;
- the development of cross-border cooperation in the sphere of the health service;
- the stimulation of action aimed at establishing and coordinating the functioning of cross-border protected areas;
- the stimulation of cross-border action aimed at water purity in the Bug River basin;
- the support and coordination of cross-border cultural events and sporting events;
- the creation of cross-border cooperation networks among institutions and organizations dealing with the natural environment, culture, tourism and sport;
- the design and implementation of a system promoting renewable energy sources.

The third target area involves supporting actions aimed at improving external and internal communication access. The assumed outcome of action in this area should be the improved coherence of communication in cross-border regions, demonstrated by significantly shorter and easier border crossings between Poland and Belarus and between Poland and Ukraine. Without question, the external border of the EU presents a real spatial barrier with low permeability, both in physical and technical terms (the border crossing itself) and in formal and legal terms (visas), thus representing one of the more serious limitations blocking the development of cross-border cooperation. It also holds back improvements in communication access to borderland areas, being a constituent element of cross-border regions. In order to mitigate and eventually change this situation, the following courses of action were adopted:

- increasing the permeability of the Polish–Belarusian and Polish–Ukrainian border by opening new border crossings and modernizing those already in existence, including crossings for pedestrians and tourists (Figure 4.2);
- improving the road access to border crossings;
- increasing the number of cross-border communication links;
- widening the zone of local border traffic;
- revitalizing the cross-border railway infrastructure (Figure 4.2);

- supporting the development and range of airports in view of opening new connections, including cross-border services.

In a knowledge-based economy, a particular role in activating development potential is played by colleges of higher education and science and research institutions, both in the sphere of generating and absorbing innovation and in creative

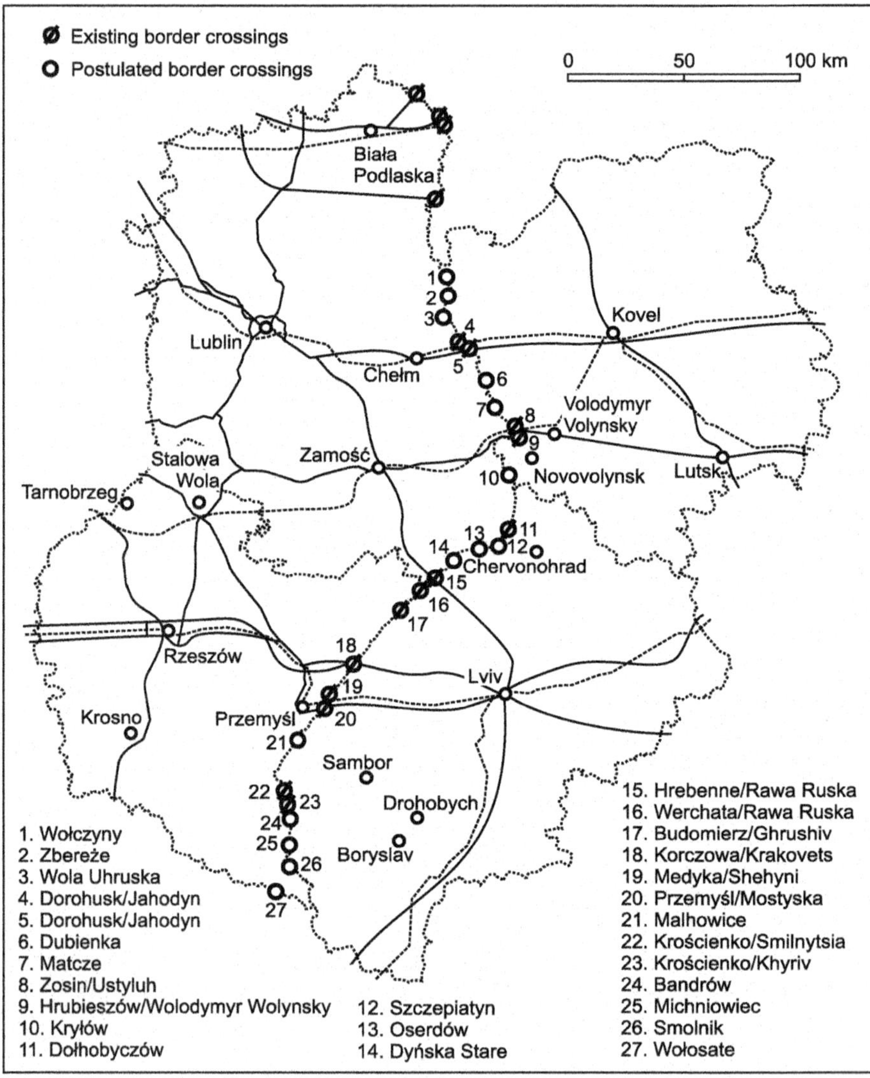

Figure 4.2 Border crossings

Source: Andrzej Jakubowski and Krzysztof Łoboda, on the basis of Kawałko (2011a).

staff training. Owing to the weight of this issue in the new paradigm of regional development contained in, among others, the EU strategy Europe 2020, matters relating to it are recognized as being of high significance. Therefore, the fourth target area concerns building a knowledge-based economy by supporting cooperation among colleges of higher education and scientific research institutions (Figure 4.3). The assumed outcome is the raising of education standards, the internationalization of academia and inter-collegiate research teams, the development of scientific cooperation and the exchange and education of students. To achieve this aim, the following courses of action were adopted:

- extending the Bologna System to all colleges of higher education in the cross-border region,
- adapting the educational offerings of colleges to the changing economic demands based on knowledge, with particular consideration for the cross-border economy,
- creating inter-collegiate partnerships aimed at absorbing external funds for scientific research.

Owing to their concentration of scientific research and educational potential, cities, and particularly regional capitals, will play a leading role in improving the standards of education and internationalizing the academic offer and scientific research in the cross-border region.

The location of Lublin and Podkarpackie voivodships on the eastern external customs border of the EU, as well as the length of this border, mean that they perform an important function not only in regional but also in national and European terms. The borderland regions of Ukraine – that is, Lviv and Volhynia oblasts – are of key significance with respect to the scope and form of cross-border cooperation as well as its social, economic and political benefits. These Ukrainian areas are more poorly developed economically, and are also equipped with much weaker institutions for supporting the development of a market economy, a civil society and non-government organizations supporting local and regional development. The degree of autonomy, powers and decision-making competences of local and regional authorities are incomparably lower than in Poland, which is one of the most important barriers to the development of cross-border cooperation. It also prevents greater and more rational use of the existing potential and scope for development in cross-border regions. For this reason the current benefits of the borderland location are insignificant and for the most part – in the economic sphere – are limited to trading within the areas positioned along the borderland belt.

In the context of the current political situation and weak economy in Ukraine it must be accepted that, in all probability, there will be no new development impulses from the eastern regions to Lublin and Podkarpackie voivodships. Despite some views that significant benefits may flow into the region owing to its position, its situation on the external EU border, adjoining more poorly developed regions, has not brought the anticipated benefits.

General aim of the Strategy			
Increase the socio-economic competitiveness of the cross-border area in the European, national, regional and local dimension, by effective use of endogenous potential and by mitigating limitations resulting from the functioning of the external EU border			
Target areas for strategic action			
1. Economic cooperation	**2. Natural environment, culture and tourism**	**3. Communication and border infrastructure**	**4. Science and higher education**
Aims and directions of strategic action			
1.1 provide complete and up-to-date information on conditions for doing business and economic entities in the cross-border region 1.2 create more business incentives 1.3 support the specialization of existing institutions linked to business in serving firms interested in cross-border cooperation 1.4 integrated economic promotion of the cross-border area	2.1 cross-border cooperation of crisis-management forces and in the field of health protection 2.2 develop cross-border cooperation in the health service sphere 2.3 stimulate actions aimed at establishing and coordinating cross-border protected areas 2.4 stimulating actions aimed at water purity in the Bug river basin 2.5 designing cross-border tourist products 2.6 cross-border action aimed at protecting world cultural heritage 2.7 support and coordinate cross-border cultural and sporting events 2.8 create cross-border cooperation networks of institutions and organizations dealing with the natural environment, culture, tourism and sport 2.9 design and implement a system of promoting renewable energy sources	3.1 increase the permeability of the Polish–Belarusian and Polish–Ukrainian border by opening new border crossings and modernizing existing ones, including pedestrian and tourist crossings 3.2 improve road access to border crossings 3.3 increase the number of cross-border communication links 3.4 widen the zone of local border traffic 3.5 revitalize the cross-border railway infrastructure 3.6 support airports in opening new connections, including cross-border services	4.1 spread the Bologna System to all colleges of higher education in the region 4.2 adapt the educational offer of colleges to the changing demands of a knowledge-based economy, with particular consideration for the cross-border economy 4.3 create inter-collegiate partnerships aimed at absorbing external funds for scientific research

Figure 4.3 The design and layout of aims in the Cross-border Cooperation Strategy for the years 2014–20

Source: UMWL (2013).

Possible scenarios for the future of Polish–Ukrainian relations in the context of geopolitical changes in Central and Eastern Europe

The collapse of the bipolar world in the 1980s and 1990s led to far-reaching geopolitical change, on both global and regional scales. As a result of the dissolution of COMECON and the Warsaw Pact, the countries of Central and Eastern Europe – including Poland – found themselves in a zone of 'tenuous security', but nonetheless they gained the chance of independently defining their geopolitical position. The road which Poland went down in this respect was presented in Chapter 1. However, here it is worth emphasizing once again that Poland definitively set its long-term integrational aim as early as 1992, giving priority in its foreign policy to future membership of NATO and the European Community. Rejecting numerous concepts, such as Lech Wałęsa's NATO-2 idea, the 'Brest Triangle' (covering Poland, Belarus and Ukraine), the proposal of Leonid Krawchuk for establishing Zones of Stability and Security in Europe, or the proposal put forward by Russia of 'cross-security guarantees' for countries of Central and Eastern Europe (Łastawski 2011), they began cooperation within the Visegrad Group (1991) and Central European Free Trade Agreement CEFTA (1992) in preparation for European integration processes. It was recognized then that only this road could help make up for the many years of backwardness and allow Poland to become an equal partner of western European nations. The explicit nature of this course is also testified by the fact Poland submitted an official application for EU membership as early as 1994, and three years later adopted the *National Integration Strategy*, marking the road to Poland's accession to the EU in 2004, while even earlier, in 1999, it became a member of NATO.

Poland's accession to NATO and the EU had a decisive impact in changing its geopolitical position. For centuries Poland had been functioning between Russia and Germany, and from the end of the eighteenth century to the end of World War I it existed merely as a space belonging to foreign nations – Russia, Germany and Austria. For this reason some politicians and researchers were apt to say that Poland's EU and NATO membership had finally brought an end to its historical–geopolitical vulnerability to both east and west (Łastawski 2011). However, the Russian–Ukrainian conflict clearly showed that the international order of this part of Europe is by no means set, but quite the contrary – geopolitical relations remain turbulent.

Currently, Polish interests and foreign policy objectives on the global and continental scale to a large extent align with those of the EU, although they are not identical. Poland is trying, however, to exert greater influence on the shape and direction of Europe's eastern policy, a tangible example of which is the Polish–Swedish Eastern Partnership initiative. A policy such as this is a natural consequence of Poland's position on the external border of both the EU and NATO. On the one hand, this puts Poland in a vulnerable position if the situation in Eastern Europe were to become further destabilized, but on the other hand it places Poland in a specific role with reference to Eastern European states, including Ukraine.

This role has been termed 'the regional exporter of stability', 'the keystone of Europe', 'the gates to the East', 'mediator', as well as 'the bridge between East and West' (Łastawski 2011). This policy dates back to the pre-war era (e.g. the Promethean movement, the main representative of which was the regional governor Henryk Józewski, mentioned in Chapter 1), and was based largely on the consensus of the political elite. Owing to this, Poland's eastern policy consisted of clear priorities, including support for the sovereignty of Central and Eastern European nations (understood as independence from Russia) and support for processes of political and economic transformation, as well as for the move towards European integration. For a long time Poland was one (or one of two, with Lithuania) nation reminding the EU of the existence of Ukraine and the need to support its independence. Without doubt, the accession of Ukraine to the EU would be of particular geopolitical significance to Poland, as it would move the external boundary of this group further to the east. It should be pointed out, however, that Poland's influence on the situation in Ukraine and on EU and NATO policy towards Ukraine is limited. Although Poland and Sweden managed to bring about the adoption of the above-mentioned Eastern Partnership, the resources which this initiative has at its disposal are too modest to effect a real impact on the economic and social situation of the EU's eastern neighbours. Polish diplomats, represented by President Kwaśniewski, acting with EU support, managed to achieve an end to the crisis in Ukraine in 2005 (the Orange Revolution), but in resolving the Ukrainian–Russian crisis of 2014 and beyond (the Minsk agreement) Poland was excluded in a unanimous vote by Russia, Germany, France and Ukraine. The latest events – the governmental crisis in Ukraine in February 2016 mediated by foreign affairs ministers from Germany and France – once more demonstrated the 'ousting' of Poland from the group establishing EU policy towards Ukraine. These events show, on the one hand, Poland's relative weakness and, on the other, a divergence of Polish interests and those of the main EU powers – Germany and France – on the question of Ukraine. The strategic goal of Poland is a sovereign Ukraine to potentially counterbalance the imperial ambitions of Russia, while for the main EU powers the strategic goal is to stabilize Ukraine without compromising their interests with Russia.

Meanwhile, the geopolitical situation in Ukraine was much more complicated than in Poland, and its geopolitical choices rather unclear. Although after 1991 almost every Ukrainian government emphasized the 'road to Europe' and its intentions of integrating with European structures, its activities remained ambivalent, incoherent, changeable and at times even in opposition to the declarations made. However, it should be recognized that this situation was the result of specific circumstances. First, Ukraine has been internally divided in its aspirations from the outset. The occidental group, looking to develop cooperation with nations in the West, was offset by an equally large or even larger group supporting historical ties with Russia. Second, Ukraine is strongly linked to Russia in economic terms, and is almost fully dependent on Russia in terms of energy. Third, political ties between both nations were strong. While Poland broke off most of its geopolitical ties with its former patron (except for its dependence on energy supplies) as a result of the dissolution of the Warsaw Pact and COMECON as well as the withdrawal of Russian forces from its territory in 1993, Ukraine became one of states that in 1991 founded the CIS on the ruins of the USSR and played an important role in many integrational initiatives within this organization. There is no doubt that Russia was able to place military pressure on Ukraine (although for a long time this was not made explicit), and instruments such as the Black Sea Fleet naval base in Crimea and the deep penetration of Ukrainian military structures and intelligence services could be used (and, as it turned out, was used) to counteract the unfavourable (in Russia's view) reorientation of Ukraine. Moreover, in contrast to Poland, Ukraine has never received a guarantee or even a promise of EU membership. Current initiatives of the EU towards Ukraine have been met with disappointment and have provided insufficient motivation to bring about far-reaching political and economic reforms. On the other hand, it should be recognized that the lack of a clear declaration on the part of the EU towards Ukraine stems largely from a lack of progress in state reforms, which is due partly to the above-mentioned circumstances but also to indolence and a lack of determination on the part of Ukrainian decision-makers.

As Andrew Wilson points out, for the first few years of independence the Ukrainian elite did not even attempt to define Ukraine's place in the international community. By doing so, it could have persuaded the West that Ukraine did not pose a threat to fragile European security and assured Russia that Ukraine's turn towards the West did not undermine the international position of the Russian nation. At the same time, this political indecision had considerable significance for internal relations, tempering the mood of both the occidental group and those with pro-Russian inclinations (Wilson 2002). Although the government of the independent Ukraine continually underlined its 'European choice' and its affiliation to the 'European family' (reflecting 'European-ness' as an important element of the Ukrainian 'national idea'), these declarations were not always followed up with real action. Both Leonid Kravchuk and Leonid Kuchma tried, above all, to even out the east–west feeling, pursuing eastern (pro-Russian) and western (pro-European) policies simultaneously.[22] This multi-vector (or, rather, dichotomous) foreign policy reflects the deep-set geopolitical divide that has accompanied Ukraine for at least 350 years (see the Treaty of Pereyaslav of 1654 and the Treaty of Hadiach of 1658[23]), resulting from its position on the crossroads between East and West. However, this multi-vector policy has brought Ukraine negligible benefits. While it has remained dependent on Russia in many respects, the intensity of its relations with the West has weakened over time and the nature of these relations has worsened. This unproductive policy was clearly opposed by Bohdan Ghavrylyshyn, the long-time economic advisor to several heads of state in Ukraine, who stated that Ukraine must make a geopolitical choice, and the only choice that exists is between the East (not so much the CIS, but rather the Eastern Slavic Union incorporating Russia, Ukraine and Belarus) and the West (integration with the EU). In each of these options he perceived numerous benefits and drawbacks (Ghavrylyshyn 2000).

To a certain degree, an alternative to this dichotomy was to be another geopolitical course, the Eurasian one, alluding to the works of prominent Ukrainian thinkers such as Mykhailo Hrushevsky, Stepan Rudnytsky and Yurii Lypa, and put forward by the political supporters of Leonid Kuchma. According to this course, instead of wasting its effort on European integration, Ukraine should strengthen its position in the region and then perform as an equal partner in the international arena. However, this vision of Eurasia was developed in opposition to Russia's Eurasian strategy. According to this vision, Ukraine should create its own sphere of influence between the EU and Russia, becoming the heart of an alternative Eurasia, uniting Europe (Ukraine), the Caucus (Azerbaijan and Georgia) and Central Asia (Kazakhstan and Uzbekistan). This was to be aided by the opening of the geo-economic corridor TRACECA.[24] In the same way Ukraine wanted to focus on putting economic and political relations in order in this strategic area neighbouring Europe (Wilson 2002). In a sense, this concept was embodied by the creation, at Ukraine's instigation, of the GUAM organization.[25] This idea was also supported by Viktor Yushchenko, as shown by his engagement after 2005 in resolving existing problems in the Black Sea area, including in Moldova and Georgia. It should be pointed out, however, that initiatives such as TRACEA and GUAM were of a virtual nature, existing as intellectual ideas of politicians and political scientists without exerting real influence on the political and economic existence of the states involved or the relations between them.

In 2004, as discussed in Chapter 1, the 'Orange Revolution' occurred; subsequently, the newly chosen heads of state – the president, Viktor Yushchenko, and the prime minister, Yulia Tymoshenko, for the first time in history clearly and unequivocally stressed the Euro-Atlantic aspirations of Ukraine, which were directed at full membership of the EU and NATO. However, the dissent rapidly expressed among leaders of the Orange Revolution and the lack of realistic reforms (Kuzio 2009) led to only slight intensification of work on the 'Association Agreement', which – in not considering the perspective of membership – only partly met Ukraine's political and economic priorities.

The pro-European course of Ukrainian politics was supported by Viktor Yanukovych, who regarded EU membership as a strategic aim of his country. This rhetoric mainly resulted from the desire to strip his predecessor of the monopoly on the 'European choice' and to reflect the mood of a major part of the population (Moshes 2006). Meanwhile (also as a result of the preferences of a majority of Ukrainians), in 2010 he withdrew from the process of integration with NATO, which was soon confirmed by the Supreme Council, and removed the corresponding entry from the Ukrainian National Security Strategy.[26] In reality, he returned to the previous 'balanced policy'. On the one hand, it aimed to developed cooperation with the EU via work on the text of the Association Agreement as well as the Deep and Comprehensive Free Trade Agreement (DCFTA); on the other hand, it negotiated conditions for cooperation with the Customs Union of the Republic of Belarus, the Republic of Kazakhstan and the Russian Federation.

Further events, including the suspension of preparations to the Association Agreement, the outbreak of the 'Revolution of Dignity' and the overthrow of

President Yanukovych have been described in Chapter 1. However, it should be pointed out here that in 2014 – 10 years after the Orange Revolution – Ukraine for the second time in its history made a clear geopolitical turn towards the West. The policy section of the Association Agreement between the EU and Ukraine was signed on 21 March 2014 and the economics section on 27 June 2014, and on 1 January 2016 the Deep and Comprehensive Free Trade Agreement (DCFTA) came into force. It seems that Ukraine, after nearly a quarter of a century of vacillating and balancing between East and West, has taken up a definite course towards integration both with European (EU) and Euro-Atlantic (NATO) structures.

Towards the end of the twentieth century Andrew Wilson (2002) wrote that Ukraine occupies a special place on the borders of two great geopolitical concepts – the 'European' and 'Eurasian' ideas – and its future is defined to a decisive extent by how these two concepts are comprehended at the beginning of the new millennium. It would seem that these words are more true today than ever before. Currently, in the conditions of transformation initiated in Ukraine by the so-called 'Euromaidan Revolution' and the civil war in the east of Ukraine (referred to by Ukrainians themselves as 'ATO' – the Anti-Terrorist Operation), the situation may lead to a decisive delimitation of European and Eurasian space (Wallerstein 2014; Snyder 2014; Wozniak 2014).

Here, the question arises as to whether the European choice of Ukraine can be considered as definitive and final. For a long time it was thought that the pro-European aspirations of Ukraine were the choice of a small political elite in the country, and not the majority of society. In recent years this situation has certainly undergone dramatic change. According to the findings of the survey conducted by the Il'ko Kucheriv Fund 'Democratic Initiatives' and the Kiev International Institute of Sociology, the idea of Ukraine's membership of the EU is currently supported by around half the population of Ukraine (Table 4.2). There are still visible regional variations as regards Ukraine's 'European choice': it is supported by 78.1 per cent of inhabitants in west Ukraine, but by merely 26.9 per cent of inhabitants in east Ukraine (KIIS 2016). Furthermore, the support of Ukrainians for the European integration process can be regarded as only moderate. For comparison, acceptance of Poland's EU membership was and still is almost ubiquitous – during the referendum on accession in 2004, 77.5 per cent of voters were in support, while in March 2014 (and thus 10 years from the moment of EU accession) support for Poland's EU membership amounted to 89.0 per cent (CBOS 2014).

At the same time, from 2014 Ukraine has witnessed considerable growth in support for NATO membership (Table 4.3), which is connected with the unprecedented events that saw the annexing of Crimea by the Russian Federation, the outbreak of conflict in Donbas and the constant threat to Ukrainian security from Russia. In this context, the tardiness of Ukrainian authorities in reforming the state, the high social costs of the changes which they were able to implement, the lack of tangible benefits connected with the signing of the Association Agreement, the fall in support for the highest state authorities and the ever more visible conflict between Petro Poroshenko and prime minister Arseniy Yatseniuk may all lead to diminishing support for European integration.

Table 4.2 Attitudes of Ukrainians to integration with the UE and the EACU 2011–15

Question: What course of integration should Ukraine pursue?	*Oct. 2011*	*Feb. 2012*	*Dec. 2012*	*Feb. 2013*	*May 2013*	*Mar. 2014*	*May 2014*	*Feb. 2015*	*Sept. 2015*	*Dec. 2015*
	responses (%)									
Join the EU	43.7	38.6	42.4	36.6	41.7	45.3	50.5	47.2	44.1	52.0
Join the Customs Union of Russia, Belarus and Kazakhstan/the Eurasian Customs Union	30.5	29.7	32.1	37.5	31.0	21.6	21.4	12.3	17.3	14.6
Join neither the EU nor the Eurasian Customs Union	9.3	11.7	10.5	10.7	13.5	19.6	17.4	27.3	27.5	21.3
Difficult to say	16.4	20.0	15.0	15.2	13.7	13.4	10.6	13.1	11.1	12.0

Source: FDI (2014); KIIS (2016).

Table 4.3 Attitudes of Ukrainians towards integration with NATO 2012–15

Question: In your opinion, which option would be the best guarantee of security for Ukraine?	*Apr. 2012*	*May 2014*	*Sep. 2014*	*Dec. 2014*	*Jul. 2015*	*Nov. 2015*
	responses (%)					
Joining NATO	13.0	32.6	43.6	46.4	35.9	45.7
A military alliance with Russia and other CIS nations	26.2	13.0	14.8	10.1	7.8	8.2
A military alliance with the USA	–	1.5	–	–	3.2	3.4
Non-bloc status of Ukraine	42.1	28.3	22.2	20.9	28.9	22.6
Other	0.9	1.0	0.4	1.0	1.6	2.4
Difficult to say	17.8	23.7	19.0	21.7	22.6	17.6

Source: FDI (2015).

However, of great importance in this respect will be the position which the EU itself takes, including its engagement in resolving the military, political and economic crisis in Ukraine and eventually presenting a real prospect of membership. Meanwhile, the growing threat from Russia may influence further growth in support for Ukraine's membership of NATO. It is worth adding that the 'eastern course', as a geopolitical vision of Ukraine's place in the world, has lost public support. Less than 15 per cent of Ukrainian inhabitants are in favour of integration with the Eurasian Customs Union, while less than 10 per cent are in favour of a military alliance with Russian and other CIS nations. For many people, the optimal solution would be non-bloc status, this being advocated by one in four inhabitants of the country.

The EU's relationship with Ukraine has been discussed in detail at the beginning of this chapter. However, in order to analyse Polish–Ukrainian relations in the context of modern geopolitical transformations in Central and Eastern Europe it is necessary to consider and describe the position and role of the Russian Federation in the region. Above all, Russia's relations with Ukraine are influenced by the issue of their 'common heritage'. In the nineteenth century Russian historiography perpetuated the view that all Eastern Slavs shared common roots, the cradle of which, the first state organization, was supposed to be the Kiev Rus. This idea was taken up by Soviet historiography, providing the foundation for the idea of brotherhood among eastern Slavic nations (Szeptycki 2013). This idea is still alive in contemporary Russia, underlining the continuity of the Rus and Russian nations.

A second key element affecting Russia's attitude to Ukraine is the issue of borders and zones of influence. For over 200 years the western extremity of the Russian Empire, and subsequently the USSR, lay in Central Europe. In the period of the Soviet Union – and particularly after the end of World War II – this border was reinforced and closed, taking the form of a clear geographical, political and ideological barrier in the highly polarized world of the Cold War. It should be remembered, however, that this border separated Russia from socialist countries that were officially allies and friends of the USSR. The collapse of the Soviet Union led to the clear shift to the east of the boundary of areas controlled by Russia, opening its south-western extremity to the influence of other actors – above all, the United States and the EU. In the Russian view, the threat to its interests is not the appearance of a certain kind of 'security vacuum' in this region, but the establishment of order in this area dictated by nations of the West. Without doubt the Russian Federation represents an important power in the region, and Ukraine belongs to the zone of its strategic interests (so-called 'near abroad'). Loss of influence in the region has far-reaching negative effects for Russia in terms of national security, its international position, and the economic sphere. In the opinion of Zbigniew Brzeziński, a former advisor of American president Jimmy Carter, Ukraine is a geopolitical pivot, determining the balance of powers on the 'Eurasian chessboard', and its significance depends specifically on the influence that it can exert on Russia, defining its strategic position. According to Brzeziński, Russia, along with Ukraine, has the chance of becoming a Eurasian Empire. Without it, Russia can maintain its empire status, but only as an Asian Empire (Brzeziński 1998). For this reason, along with a growth in the engagement of EU states and the USA, Ukraine has increasingly become an area of conflicting interests between Russia and the West.

The first short-term stage in shaping Russian foreign policy involved resigning from military force and severing the imperial legacy. According to Andrey Kozyrev, the hegemony was replaced by an attempt to base mutual relations with Ukraine and other post-soviet countries on the CIS, which was established at the end of 1991. In a fairly short time, however, the Russian Federation reoriented its policy towards the 'near abroad' states, which had begun to articulate their national interests, giving itself a specific role and mission in this respect. This change was reflected in the adoption in 1993 of the document 'Principle assumptions of the Russian Federation's foreign policy', according to which the whole territory of the former USSR was to be a zone of special Russian interest. By the same token, Russian foreign policy gave primacy to the defence of its own interests as well as the recovery and maintenance of the influence it had enjoyed in the soviet era. This policy was given particular impetus by the presidency of Vladimir Putin who, benefiting from favourable economic conditions (thanks to a rise in fuel prices on the world market), began to create a new vision of Russia as a world power, able to outface the United States. This course of foreign policy – alluding to Russia's position in both imperial eras (Russian and the Soviet), has met with the general acceptance of Russian society (Rutland 2015).

The series of 'colourful revolutions' at the beginning of the new millennium, which Russia saw as being orchestrated by nations of the West, led to the pro-western turn in the policies of Ukraine and Georgia. Starting from 2004, the significance of the EU also began to grow in the region. This related, among other factors, to the implementation of the ENP, which was another initiative viewed by Russia as a threat to its own interests. Meanwhile, Ukraine and Georgia became more closely tied to NATO under the 'Partnership for Peace' programme, with the prospect of membership becoming ever more clearly defined (both nations were to be presented with a Roadmap during the NATO summit in Bucharest in 2008). While Russia was able to tolerate the EU's increased engagement, it could not and cannot accept any action leading to the expansion of the North Atlantic Treaty in the area of Russia's 'near abroad'. In attempting to keep the post-soviet states within a zone of exclusively Russian influence and to prevent an increased presence of the United States and NATO in the region, the Russian authorities decided on armed intervention in Georgia in August 2008 (Asmus 2010), using the opportunity which the Georgian president Mikheil Saakashvili created in attacking the rebel Georgian province of South Ossetia.

The next important threat to Russia's regional position and its plans for reintegrating the post-soviet area under the wings of the Russian Federation by creating a Eurasian Economic Union on the model of the EU (until 2014 the Eurasian Economic Community), as well as the Eurasian Customs Union (until 2015 the Customs Union of the Republic of Belarus, the Republic of Kazakhstan and the Russian Federation), was the prospect of Ukraine signing the Association Agreement with the EU and its entry to the European free trade zone. The loss of Ukraine significantly weakened the geopolitical and economic position of both Russian initiatives, which until then it had only managed to sell to Belarus, Kazakhstan, Armenia and Kyrgyzstan. Towards Ukraine, in contrast to Georgia, Russia initially attempted to use 'soft power' means, testified by Putin's offering a loan of $3 billion as well as preferential gas prices, while at the same time exerting political pressure on Ukrainian authorities regarding their loss of a huge Russian market. However, the opposition of people in western and central Ukraine towards the pro-Russian course of national policy (the Euromaidan revolution) led to the demise of this policy. Therefore, the Russian Federation resorted to instruments of 'hard power', by annexing Crimea and unofficially supporting the pro-Russian rebellion in

Donetsk and Luhansk oblast. Here it should be pointed out that the annexation of Crimea was officially carried out in accordance with the wishes of the people of Crimea for self-determination and unity with Russia. Irrespective of the level of honesty of the referendum conducted in Crimea, there is no doubt that most people of this peninsula, which is inhabited mainly by Russians, were in favour of separating from Ukraine and joining Russia. In the international arena Russia justified its decision to annex Crimea by the right of nations to self-determination and the Kosovo precedent – the region of Serbia which, under the military protection of NATO and outside Serbia's control, announced independence, which was recognized by most nations in the West. Without doubt, the nature of Russia's actions regarding Crimea and the so-called Donetsk and Luhansk People's Republic was encouraged by the lack of a firm response from the West to Russia's previous invasion of Georgia. Therefore, the conflict in eastern Ukraine should be treated as an element of the 'great game' between Russia and the West, marking the border of international influence. It is in Russia's interests to maintain this border in an unsettled state, which would permanently weaken Ukraine and slow down its integration with European and Euro-Atlantic structures. At the same time, it should be emphasized that, in Russia's eyes, it is not they who present a threat to the international order, but the hostile policies of the western world that do not take account of Russian interests.

Russia's attitude to Ukraine in the space of the last quarter century can be said to have been ambivalent. For a long time Russia seemed to treat Ukraine as a Saisonstaat, testified by the fact that the state duma treaty on friendship, cooperation and partnership was not ratified until 1999. Almost from the beginning of Ukraine's independence an 'energy war' has been waged between these two nations and the failure to recognize the Russian language in Ukraine and allow dual citizenship has been seen as discriminating against the Russian minority. At the same time, Russia has constantly developed its relations with Ukraine, aiming at keeping it within its own sphere of influence and seeing it as having an important role in the process of reintegration in the post-soviet area, tightening the already strong economic ties.

In assessing Russia's international policy it is impossible not to allude to the concept of the Heartland of Halford Mackinder, on which Russian authorities largely base the geopolitical vision of their state. Alexandr Dugin also alludes to this concept in his deliberations, according to which Russia's most important task is to control the northern part of the Eurasian continent (i.e. the Heartland), allowing the effective rivalry of continental Russia (the Eurasian civilization) with the Atlantic world (the western civilization) under the leadership of the United States. And, although Dugin's geopolitical concept is extremist in nature, it seems to reflect the mood of Russian society and the Russian political elite, and is reflected in global Russian geopolitics. It is worth mentioning that, within this conception, Poland is counted as belonging to the German sphere of influence (with which Russia does not intend to compete), while Ukraine is to undergo 'geopolitical disintegration', in which the greater part (without west Ukraine) is integrated with the Russian nation (Eberhardt 2010). Alluding to this idea, Vladimir Zhirinovsky (the leader of the Russian nationalists) 'offered', in the course of the Maidan Revolution, west Ukraine to Poland, presenting his vision of partitioning (i.e. the 'disintegration' of) Ukraine.

In discussing the geopolitical circumstances of the current transformation in Eastern and Central Europe it is necessary to return once again to the question of energy security and fuel transfer. As already indicated, the Ukrainian–Russian 'energy war' has continued essentially without pause since 1991, culminating in Russia cutting off supplies in 2006, 2009 and 2014, each time owing to political events in Ukraine. On the one hand, Ukrainians aim to free themselves from dependence on Russian fuels, for which they have to pay a considerable sum, and, on the other, Russia has accused Ukraine for many years of defaulting on payment or 'stealing' Russian gas piped through Ukrainian territory to western Europe. There is no doubt that fuels, and the dependence of Eastern European nations on them, form an instrument of Russian foreign policy, although its frequent accusations of Ukraine in many cases have been justifiable (Wilson 2002). Currently, Ukraine has almost completely freed itself from dependence on gas bought directly from Russia by using gas (also Russian) pumped via so-called reverse flows from nations of Western and Central Europe.

In the context of cross-border energy security it is necessary to mention the Odessa–Brody pipeline, completed in 2002, which stretches for 700 kilometres between the Black Sea and the 'Friendship' pipeline near the Polish border.[27] From the outset there were plans to extend the pipeline to Płock, allowing the transport of Caspian oil from Azerbaijan, Kazakhstan and Turkmenistan to the Baltic Sea (Gdańsk). The agreement on this matter was signed in 2008 in the presence of the Polish and Ukrainian presidents, Lech Kaczyński and Victor Yushchenko. Until the present time work on building the pipeline has not been able to start, although the project was fully approved by the European Commission.[28] It is worth pointing out that this section of the pipeline is the only missing element of the so-called Eurasian Oil Transport Corridor. For this reason, too, the pipeline itself was used for a long time for the opposite purpose – that is, to transport Russian oil to the Black Sea (Figure 4.4).

The success of this and other projects may significantly improve Ukraine's geopolitical position as a transit country, turning it into an important player in this part of Europe. However, particularly in view of Russia's mistrust towards Ukraine, the implementation of construction plans and wider use of the existing corridors that bypass Ukraine (as well as Poland), such as Nord Stream, Nord Stream 2, South Stream, Blue Stream and the pipelines allowing transport of Caspian fuel bypassing Ukraine (Baku–Tbilisi–Ceyhan and Nabucco), could reduce its geopolitical significance as an important transit country. An example of this would be the agreement signed in September 2015 between Gazprom and the heads of BASF and E.ON (both German), ENGIE (France), OMV (Austria) and Royal Dutch Shell (Great Britain/the Netherlands), foreseeing the construction of two offshore gas pipelines leading from Russia to Germany via the Baltic Sea (Nord Stream 2). The Russian authorities do not hide the fact that their main aim is to exclude Ukraine from the transport of gas. However, the agreement is in itself

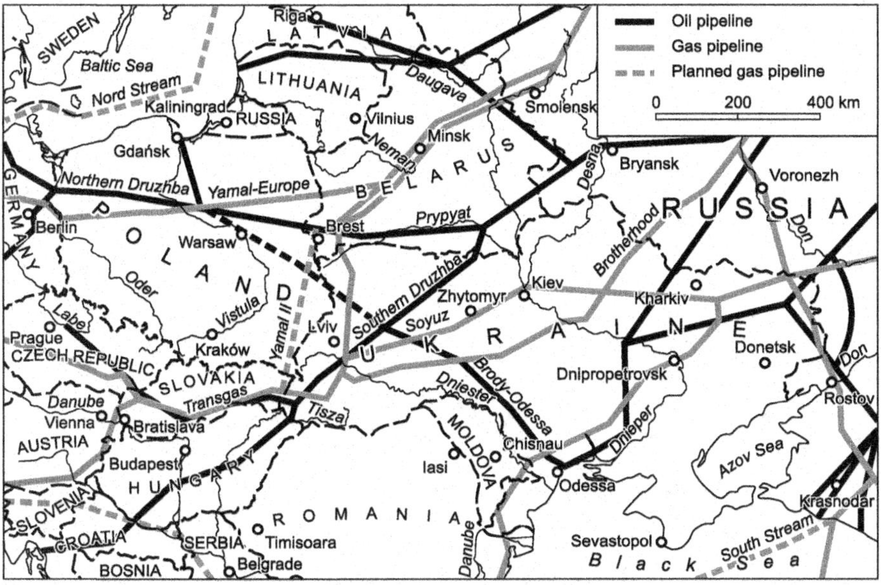

Figure 4.4 Existing and planned energy corridors in Central and Eastern Europe in 2016

Source: Andrzej Jakubowski and Krzysztof Łoboda.

highly controversial. Although it does not violate the sanctions imposed on Russia (in any case, they concern the oil market, rather than gas) it infringes on European energy solidarity and is aimed at stifling both Poland and Ukraine, having far-reaching consequences for the energy security of both nations.

The matter of forecasting future relations between Ukraine and the EU, as well as Poland, has been the subject of several studies. In 1999 a team of experts from the Ukrainian National Security and Defense Council drew up a set of seven evolutionary scenarios for the international position of Ukraine, including the scenarios of the slow demise of the nation and of successful integration with European structures (Belov et al. 1999). In 2002 a study was published in Poland presenting a catalogue of scenarios for future relations between Ukraine and Poland in the context of EU–Russian relations, based on the principles of game theory (Surmacz 2002). Recently, the findings were also published from a study by a group of Ukrainian experts which considered four different development scenarios for relations between Ukraine and the EU (FES 2014). However, given the dynamic transformations that are taking place in the international environment, the two first proposals soon became vastly out of date, while the last focuses exclusively on the realization of the pro-European variant in Ukraine's foreign policy. The aim of the authors in this chapter is to once again verify and define the possible development trajectories of Polish–Ukrainian relations in the context of geopolitical transformation in Central and Eastern Europe, taking into account the roles played by the EU and the Russian Federation (Figure 4.5).

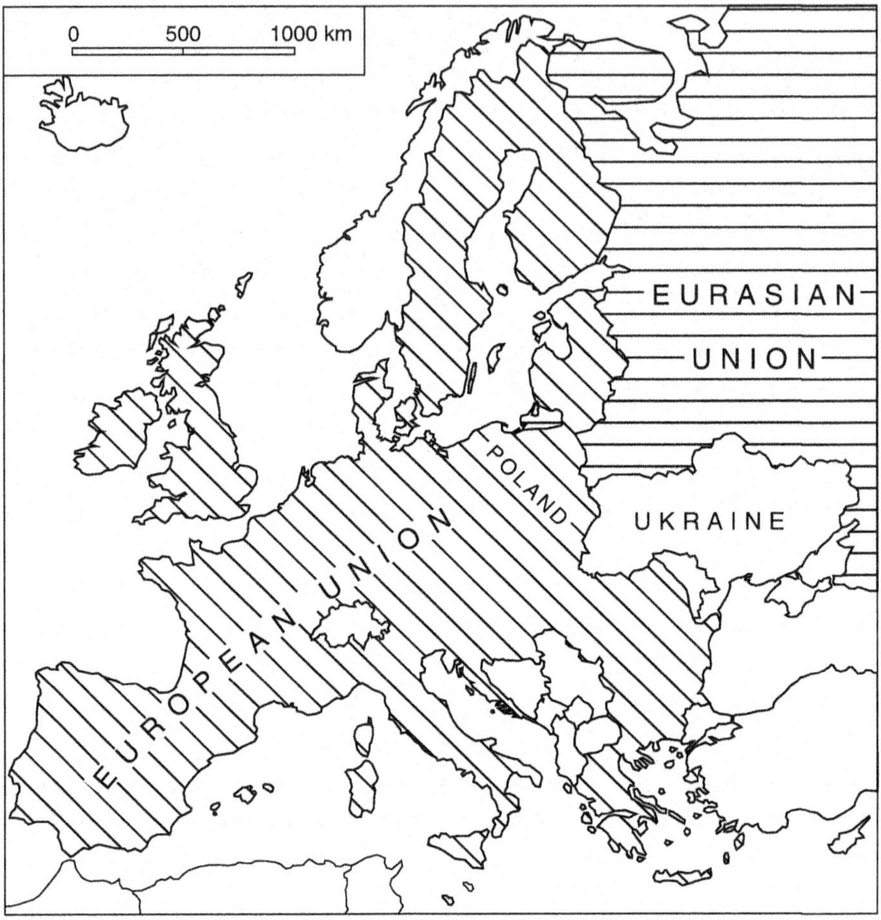

Figure 4.5 The geopolitical division of Europe in 2016

Source: Andrzej Jakubowski.

In our projection a scenario is understood according to the definition of Kosow and Gaßner: 'the description of a possible future situation (conceptual future), including paths of development which may lead to that future situation' (Kosow and Gaßner 2008). In order to predict future relations between Poland and Ukraine in the context of geopolitical transformation in Central and Eastern Europe it is necessary to make certain initial assumptions based on an assessment of current relations in the region as well as the degree of their stability. These are presented in Table 4.4. At the same time it is essential to define the most important aims of the analysed international entities in relation to the future of Ukraine, viewing them in the context of geopolitical changes occurring in Central and Eastern Europe. These are set out in Table 4.5.

Table 4.4 The current state of relations in the central and eastern European area

	Poland	*Ukraine*	*European Union*	*Russian Federation*
Poland	x	Good and stable	Good and stable	Bad and stable
Ukraine	Good and stable	x	Rather good and unstable	Very bad and unstable
European Union	Good and stable	Rather good and unstable	x	Bad and rather unstable
Russian Federation	Bad and stable	Very bad and unstable	Bad and rather unstable	x

Source: Own study.

Table 4.5 The interests of Ukraine, Poland, EU and Russia

	Ukraine	*Poland*	*European Union*	*Russian Federation*
Maintaining the integrity of Ukrainian territory	++	++	++	+–
Decentralization of Ukraine	–	+	++	+
Federalization of Ukraine	—	–	–	++
Development of a security zone/belt of stability in Europe	++	++	++	—
Ukraine's membership of the EU	++	+	–	—
Implementation of the DCFTA and full opening of the Ukrainian market	++	++	++	—
Ukraine's membership of NATO	++	++	—	—
Ukraine's membership of the Eurasian Customs Union	—	—	—	++
Political stability in Ukraine	++	++	++	—
Economic and financial stability in Ukraine in terms of repaying liabilities	++	+	++	++
Civilizational development and modernisation of Ukraine	++	+	++	+–
Ukraine's adoption of acquis communautaire	+	++	++	—
Improved living conditions of the population	++	+	++	+–
The opening of a security buffer zone (cordon sanitaire) in central and eastern Europe	—	++	+	+
Support for Ukraine using EU Structural Funds	++	–/+–	–	+–
Establishment of a sealed 'Westphalian' type border on the current Polish–Ukrainian border	—	–	+	+–
Control of Ukrainian transmission networks	++	+–	+	++
Transit of Russian fuels through Ukrainian territory	++	++	+	—
Transit of Caspian fuels through Ukrainian territory	++	++	+	—

Key: ++ totally compatible, + rather compatible, +– neutral, – rather incompatible, — totally incompatible

Source: Own study.

On this basis, it can be concluded that the most convergent interests are held by Poland and Ukraine, which makes them natural strategic partners. A relatively close convergence of interests is held by Poland and the EU as well as by the EU and Ukraine. However, the interests of Ukraine, Poland and the EU are in conflict with the interests of the Russian Federation on almost every issue analysed.

Meanwhile, in terms of a prognosis, it is worth describing the stability of the political systems of the analysed entities, which can testify to the relative constancy of their chosen course of foreign policy, and also to assess the level of support for political systems' execution on the part of the governing elite, as well as of society, which can also impact on the course of foreign policy both through pressure of public opinion and in election cycles (Table 4.6).

In order to make a prognosis it is also necessary to adopt certain assumptions concerning the whole macro-system, which can define the level of stability of the external environment, thereby determining the behaviour of the analysed participants in international relations. These basic assumptions are as follows:

1 the EU remains one of the most important entities in the international arena, and its position is not threatened by the challenges relating to the immigration of refugees, possible Brexit, or the crisis in the Eurozone. This assumption does not imply a lack of awareness of the risks faced by the EU, and later discussion will take into account an alternative assumption concerning the EU and the resulting alternative scenario;
2 the strategic alliance between the United States and nations of the EU is maintained;
3 the Russian Federation remains an important regional power.

At the same time, alternative assumptions can be made according to which the EU becomes weakened, its cohesion is reduced, national egoism grows, the Schengen zone collapses, and structural and cohesion funds are limited. As a result, the EU is less attractive to countries both inside and outside its borders, and its ability to impact on the international scene is also reduced. In relation to the international

Table 4.6 The stability of the political systems in Poland, Ukraine, EU and Russia

	Stability of the political system	*Decisiveness of the political system*	*Support of the political elite for the current course of foreign policy regarding Ukraine*	*Public support for the current course of foreign policy regarding Ukraine*
Poland	Stable	Fairly high	High	Moderate
Ukraine	Unstable	Fairly high	High	Moderate
European Union	Rather stable	Low	Moderate	Low
Russian Federation	Stable	Very high	Very high	High

Source: Own study.

environment, certain countries pursue independent policies. In relation to the post-soviet area, the most important role is played by Germany, which is guided primarily by the need for economic cooperation with Russia.

In adopting the basic assumptions it is also necessary to define the factors which could impact on the principal changes (in terms of geopolitical reorientation) in the activities of each entity. The factors which can determine the behaviour of participants to the greatest extent are considered to be:

1 The implementation of reforms directed at integrating Ukraine with the EU. Visible progress in this area will promote closer ties between Ukraine and the EU, opening the way, sooner or later, to EU membership. Conversely, a lack of reforms could lead to reduced interest in Ukraine on the part of the EU, and therefore contribute to the weakening of integration processes as well as negatively impacting on the public mood, leading to the victory of the pro-Russian option or a radical (far-right) pro-western option in the internal sphere.
2 The dynamics of the conflict in east Ukraine – a 'freezing' of the conflict or its escalation – will have major negative consequences for the international system, cementing the bad relations between the EU and the Russian Federation. In the case of the conflict ending (as a result of Russian withdrawing its unofficial support for pro-Russian separatists and actively and constructively engaging in the rebuilding of Ukraine's territorial integrity), relations between the EU and Russian will improve, and this would be in the economic interests of many western European nations. Meanwhile, in terms of Ukraine's internal policies, an end to the conflict could – as a result of a lack of reform, the high social costs of reform and public antipathy towards Ukraine's European integration processes without the real prospect of EU membership – lead to renewed pro-Russian leanings in Ukrainian politics.

The first of the selected factors concerns variables on the level of the micro-system (the political system of Ukraine), which we diagnosed as being the least stable, and therefore the most susceptible to change. The second selected factor concerns the macro-system (i.e. the international environment), with the variable likely to have the greatest impact on changes in the behaviour of individual participants being identified as the dynamics of the conflict in east Ukraine. Of course, the chosen factors do not represent an exhaustive list. There may be more factors relating to both the micro-system and the macro-system. However, a larger number of parameters would imply a larger number of scenarios, with the differences between each scenario becoming less distinct.

Taking these factors into account, future relations within Central and Eastern Europe may develop into one of six alternative scenarios (Table 4.7). Profiles of the basic scenarios are:

1 **Western European scenario 1 (*The European Choice Scenario*)** – according to which Ukraine successively implements reforms aimed at full transposition of the acquis communautaire, opening the way to EU membership.

Table 4.7 A morphological table of alternative scenarios for future relations in Central and Eastern Europe

Variable 1: Implementing reforms directed at EU integration (micro-system level)	*Variable 2: Dynamics of conflict in east Ukraine (macro-system level)*	*Name of scenario*	*Relations between:*					
			PL–EU	*UA–EU*	*RU–EU*	*RU–UA*	*PL–RU*	*PL–UA*
Implementation of reform	Frozen	Western European I (*The European Choice Scenario*)	++	+/++	+–	–/––	–/––	++
	Escalating	Western European II (*New Cold War Scenario*)	++	+	–/––	–/––	–/––	++
	Resolved	Complimentary (*Pan-European Scenario/ New European Order Scenario*)	++	+/++	+	+	+	++
Lack of reform	Frozen	Central European I (*Intermare Scenario*)	+/+–	–/+–	+/+–	–/+–	–/+–	+/++
	Escalating	Central European II (*Antemurale Scenario*)	+	–/+–	–/+–	––	–/+–	+
	Resolved	Easterçn European (*Eurasian Scenario*)	+/+–	–/+–	–/+–	+/++	–/+–	–/+–

Key: ++ very good, + good, +– neutral, – bad, –– very bad.

Source: Own study.

Meanwhile, relative stabilization of the situation in east Ukraine (i.e., the freezing of the conflict in Donbas) means that, over time, sanctions imposed on the Russian Federation by the EU are reduced. EU–Russian relations remain cool, and Russia remains an isolated state in the European space. Nevertheless, for pragmatic reasons, western nations develop economic cooperation with Russia in chosen spheres.

2 **Western European scenario II (*New Cold War Scenario*)** – according to this scenario, the successful implantation of reforms in Ukraine brings positive effects in socio-economic and political terms and leads to closer ties between Ukraine and the EU, including full implementation of DCFTA. However, escalating conflict in east Ukraine discourages EU nations from offering Ukraine full membership. At the same time, the existing divide between the EU and Russia is cemented, with mutual reinforcement of the sanctions regime. This antagonism leads to a New Cold War in Europe, in which Ukraine performs the role of a 'security buffer' or 'cordon sanitaire', protecting Europe from Russian threat.

3 **Complementary scenario (*Pan-European Scenario/New European Order Scenario*)** – according to this third scenario, a successful process of reform directed at transposing the acquis communautaire as well as European integration opens the way for Ukraine's membership of the EU. Meanwhile, the democratic and pro-western turn in policy of the Russian Federation (relinquishing their Eurasian orientation in favour of occidental orientation, i.e. *zapadnichestva*) leads to closer ties between the EU and Russia as well as the engagement of Russia in devising a constructive resolution to the conflict in east Ukraine. In this situation, relations between the EU and Russia would be based on a modified ENP and Eastern Partnership, or on a new instrument taking account of the specific status and position of Russia, leading to the shaping of a New European Order.

4 **Central European scenario I (*Intermare Scenario*)** – the fourth scenario envisages passivity on the part of the Ukrainian authorities in implementing political and economic reforms, leading to reduced interest in Ukraine on the part of decision-making nations of the EU and disillusionment in Ukrainian society with European integration processes. Meanwhile, continuing conflict in East Ukraine prevents significant improvement in relations with the Russian Federation. The governments of EU member states, under pressure from the business environment, which is orientated towards economic cooperation with Russia, allows the lifting of sanctions and relations between the EU and Russia gradually become increasingly pragmatic. In this situation Ukraine develops cooperation in the political and security sphere with Poland. This leads to the implementation of the pre-war 'Intermare' concept in Central and Eastern Europe.

5 **Central European scenario II (*Antemurale Scenario*)** – according to the fifth scenario, the escalation of the conflict in east Ukraine combined with a lack of reform leads to regression in both EU–Russian relations and EU–Ukrainian relations. In this situation Poland (with its own security in mind) would decide on adapting EU policy and taking on the role of an 'bulwark', protecting EU nations from the unstable position in Eastern Europe.

6 **Eastern European scenario (*Eurasian Scenario*)** – this scenario envisages the halting of reforms and resulting disillusionment both on the part of the EU towards Ukraine and on the part of Ukrainian society towards European integration processes. The possible constructive engagement of the Russian Federation in helping Ukraine implement beneficial solutions to the conflict could lead to gradual improvement in relations between Ukraine and Russia as well as growth in support for pro-Russian parties. This reorientation in Ukrainian politics would certainly result in a cooling of relations between Ukraine and Poland.

According to the alternative scenario, the EU becomes less attractive to Ukraine and its scope for impacting on Ukraine's situation is reduced. Ukraine, bereft of a role model and stimulus, as well as the funds for implementing necessary changes in the economic and social system, descends into an ever greater socio-economic, political and identity crisis. This is followed by disintegration of the country: individual regions pursue *de facto* independent policies to cope with the crisis, having at their disposal armed forces in the form of voluntary militia and the private armies of oligarchs.

Each of the above-mentioned scenarios would have different consequences for the future of the Polish–Ukrainian borderland region:

1 In the case of the **Western European cohesion scenario 1 (*The European Choice Scenario*)**, the Polish–Ukrainian state border (and simultaneously the external EU border) would gradually open up, and there would be a real possibility of lifting the visa regime, which, along with the introduction of the DCFTA, would allow rapid development of contacts and the establishment of new social and economic functions. The open border would create opportunities for growth in terms of cross-border links in technology and capital, the flow of workers and the initiation of joint enterprise partnerships, which would be an important development factor for the regions on each side of the border. In the same way, the peripheral nature of the borderland regions could undergo change, assuming the character of an important geopolitical keystone. Their significance for the transit of goods, including Caspian fuels, would also grow. Whether these opportunities are taken advantage of would depend on mutual Polish–Ukrainian relations at central, regional and local level, and also on the potential of each borderland region. The scenario in which good relations at the central level are accompanied by less favourable relations at regional and local levels (caused, for example, by the resurgence of historical animosity and predjudice), leading to a so-called 'tunnel vision' effect (i.e. the borderlands are 'missed out' in international dealings), cannot be excluded.

2 In the case of the **Western European cohesion scenario II (*New Cold War Scenario*)**, the Polish–Ukrainian border would be partly sealed, or its permeability would remain unchanged (i.e. the visa regime would be maintained in addition to a possibly modified principle of local border traffic). This would

lead to the development of limited contacts and socio-economic ties; however, it would not provide significant development stimulus for Polish and Ukrainian borderland regions.

3 The consequences for the future of the borderland regions of the **Complementary scenario (*Pan-European Scenario/New European Order Scenario*)** would be almost identical to the first scenario, with the difference that the Polish–Ukrainian cross-border area would perform a transit role on the intercontinental scale.
4 In the case of the **Central European scenario I (*Intermare Scenario*)** Polish–Ukrainian relations would develop on a political and security level, but there would be less progress in socio-economic terms. The Polish–Ukrainian border would probably remain a formal and legal barrier with moderate levels of permeability.
5 As a result of the **Central European scenario II (*Antemurale Scenario*)** the Polish–Ukrainian border would become a strong formal and legal barrier with low or very low permeability, established for the purpose of protecting the EU territory from threats issuing from Eastern Europe. In this case the peripheral nature of the Polish–Ukrainian borderland regions would be cemented and they would become marginalized.
6 Finally, as a result of the Eastern European scenario (***Eurasian Scenario***), the Polish–Ukrainian borderland could become a border area between two great economic and political unions, namely the EU and the Eurasian Union, and its role would depend on the bilateral relations between these two groupings.

In the case of Ukraine's 'disintegration', the Polish–Ukrainian border would primarily perform the function of a protective barrier, which would be crossed above all by refugees and economic emigrants, and the Polish territory would be a buffer zone protecting Germany and other western European nations against a wave of emigration from Ukraine.

Without doubt, the most advantageous scenario, from the perspective of Polish–Ukrainian relations as well as the future of the Polish–Ukrainian borderland, would be a situation conforming to Scenarios 1 and 3, while the least beneficial would be Scenarios 5 and 6. Meanwhile, the alternative scenario involving the 'disintegration' of Ukraine would be disastrous. It would seem that the current situation in Ukraine is evolving in line with Scenario 1, which bodes well for the future position of regions in the Polish–Ukrainian borderland area as an important geopolitical keystone on the continental scale. Nevertheless, the possibility of alternative scenarios should not be disregarded. As implied by the assumptions of this scenario, it depends largely on the EU and its opportunities and willingness to make a positive impact on the situation in Ukraine.

Without doubt EU programmes, such as the Neighbourhood Programme and the Programme Poland–Belarus–Ukraine, are important and have definite significance for supporting development on both sides of the border. Even more important is their impact on building the bases for cross-border cooperation in the macro-region. However, owing to the inadequate scale of intervention in relation to needs, the ENP is an insufficient instrument to bring about rapid structural change in this area. It does not provide adequate support for reinforcing and stimulating development and economic processes, including the development of border infrastructure, tourism and transport, and environmental protection, as well as the improvement of the social mobility of inhabitants in borderland areas. This situation means that the objectives adopted under the ETC and Eastern Partnership will be difficult to achieve.

Despite the difficult circumstances and many limitations, placing the problems of cross-border cooperation within the main developmental aims in national and regional strategic documents demonstrates a long-term vision of cooperation and a pragmatic approach to creating development using the opportunities, resources and potential of the borderland regions. This is supported by the document that was jointly prepared and implemented by four regions: the Strategy for Cross-border Cooperation of Lublin Voivodship, Lviv Oblast, Volhynia Oblast and Brest Oblast 2014–20. This document is also unique and exemplary in terms of realizing the aims of the ENP.

The future of Polish–Ukrainian cross-border cooperation will nevertheless depend largely on the evolution of Ukraine's internal situation as well as on changes in the international environment, including relations between the West and the Russian Federation. At the present time we find ourselves at the point of far-reaching transformation thanks to which there are, on the one hand, new hopes of Ukraine taking up a long-term pro-western course of foreign policy, implementing essential internal reforms and forming closer ties with the EU. However, on the other hand, numerous fears have arisen regarding the security and future of this nation.

Notes

1 In July 1995 a Ukrainian delegation was opened by the European Community in Brussels.

2 Apart from Lithuania, Latvia and Estonia, with whom a different type of agreement was signed.

3 This was created back in 1989 with the aim of supporting political and economic transformation in Poland and Hungary (hence its name – an abbreviation of *Poland and Hungary Assistance for Restructuring their Economies*). In time, the programme incorporated further countries of Central and Eastern Europe, and in 1997 it was reconstrued as an instrument of pre-accession aid. In the years 1990–2003, and thus while the programme was in force, Poland received €3.9 billion, the most among all the benefactors (US Wrocław 2007).

4 Financial expenditure under INTERREG IIIA in the period 2004–8 represented 0.91 per cent of the total expenditure of all operational programmes implemented in Lublin voivodship and 0.73 per cent of expenditure in Podkarpackie voivodship.

5 On the external border of the EU cross-border cooperation with partner countries was supported by funds from the European Instrument of Neighbourhood and Partnership, while on the internal borders of the EU cross-border cooperation was funded by means of European Territorial Cooperation (ETC), including three types of programme: cross-border cooperation, trans-national cooperation and inter-regional cooperation, for which a total sum of €7.75 billion was anticipated.

6 If part of an administrative unit is situated between 30 and 50 kilometres from the border, it is nevertheless taken to be part of the borderland area.
7 In order to finance the ENP other instruments and programmes are also used, such as the Instrument for Civil Society in Neighbourhood Countries. Moreover, the Commission provided financial support in the form of subsidies for partners, and the European Investment Bank and the European Bank for Reconstruction and Development supplement this aid by providing loans.
8 These forms of cooperation are anticipated in the Madrid Convention.
9 *Journal of Laws* 125/573 (1993).
10 *Polish Official Gazette* (M.P.) 37/530 (24 July 2003).
11 As yet (March 2016), this document has not yet been prepared.
12 See Kawałko 2011b.
13 Art. 12. 2. of the Act dated 5 June 1998 on voivodship self-government.
14 Art. 18 of the Act dated 5 June 1998 on voivodship self-government.
15 Art. 46 of the Act dated 27 March 2003 on spatial planning and management (*Journal of Laws*, 199 (2015), with later amendments).
16 Art. 47.2 of the Act dated 27 March 2003 on spatial planning and management (*Journal of Laws*, 199 (2015), with later amendments).
17 Art. 39.3 of the Act dated 27 March 2003 on spatial planning and management (*Journal of Laws*, 199 (2015), with later amendments).
18 Act dated 12 October 1990 on protection of state borders (*Journal of Laws*, 12/67 (2009) with later amendments), Regulation of the Ministry of the Interior dated 29 August 2005 on the schedule of communes and other basic territorial units situated in the border zone and tables defining the range of these zones (*Journal of Laws*, 188/1580 (2005)).
19 The strategic aims of development are not ranked hierarchically, as they are of equal importance.
20 Strategic Areas of Intervention are areas to which regional policy is specifically addressed; areas where government intervention is required owing to a burden which the region itself is unable to bear; areas which, for social, economic or environmental reasons, may have an impact in the future on the development of the country (Ministry of Regional Development 2010).
21 Work on the cross-border strategy was funded by the Ministry of Foreign Affairs of the Republic of Poland within the programme 'Polish Aid' by implementing the project 'Building partnership for executing the Cross-border Strategy 2014–2020' as part of the competition 'Support for the civil and local government dimension of Polish foreign policy 2013'. The project was implemented between June and November 2013.
22 At the turn of the twenty-first century the aims of Ukrainian foreign policy and national security included: 1) the revival of a European identity and integration into European and Euro-Atlantic political and social structures; 2) the policy of active neutrality; 3) development of a strategic partnership with the USA; 4) development of equal and mutually beneficial relations with the Russian Federation; 5) strong regional policy toward alternative leadership in the former USSR and active cooperation with those states that regard Ukraine as a reliable equal partner; 6) the strengthening and consolidation of special relations with strategically important neighbours; 7) the formation of a strategic Polish–Ukrainian–Turkish triangle; 8) active participation in the creation of European and Eurasian transportation corridors; 9) the support and enlargement of the economic (including military–economic) and political presence of Ukraine in Middle Eastern, Central and South Asian and APR states (Belov et al. 1999).
23 As was mentioned in Chapter 1, on the strength of the Pereyaslav Agreement of 1654 Ukraine (de facto its eastern part) was subject to the rule of the Tsar of Russia, while the Treaty of Hadiach four years later envisaged the reshaping of the Republic of Two Nations into a union of three equal entities – crowns (i.e. Polish, the Great Kingdom of Lithuania and the Duchy of Ruthenia). However, this Union remained only a political declaration without geopolitical effects.

24 Transport Corridor Europe–Caucasus–Asia.

25 An acronym of the names of member states: Georgia, Ukraine, Azerbaijan and Moldova. In the years 1999–2005 the organization was called GUUAM because of the membership of Uzbekistan.

26 According to the findings of studies conducted by the Gallup Institute in 2009, support of Ukrainian inhabitants for NATO membership was negligible. Only 17 per cent of those surveyed saw membership of NATO as a chance to increase security, while 40 per cent saw NATO as a threat (Ray and Esipova 2010).

27 The city of Brody is situated in the north-east of Lviv oblast.

28 The planned extension of the Odessa–Brody oil pipeline to Płock (the Adamowo–Brody pipeline) was included in the list of priority infrastructural projects PCI (List of Projects of Common Interest) that are to be financed by the European Commission (European Commission 2013).

Bibliography

Asmus, R. (2010). *A Little War that Shook the World. Georgia, Russia, and the Future of the West*. New York: Palgrave MacMillan.

Association Agreement between the European Union and its Member States, of the one part, and Ukraine, of the other part (2014). Online. Available: http://eur-lex.europa.eu/legal-content/EN/TXT/?uri=CELEX per cent3A22014A0529(01) (accessed: 19 February 2016).

Barburska, O. (2006). Polska wobec europejskich aspiracji Ukrainy, in: J. Borkowski (ed.) *Rola Polski w kształtowaniu polityki wschodniej Unii Europejskiej na przykładzie Ukrainy*. Warszawa: Centrum Europejskie Uniwersytetu Warszawskiego, pp. 51–64.

Baun, M. (2000). *A Wider Europe. A Process and Politics of European Union Enlargement*. Oxford: Rowman & Littlefield Publishers, Inc.

Belov, O., Honcharenko, O., Marchenko, N., Parakhonsky, B., Rubanets, M. and Yanishevsky, O. (1999). *Ukraine 2000 and beyond: Geopolitical Priorities and Scenarios of Development*. Kiev: National Institute for Strategic Studies and National Institute for Ukrainian-Russian Relations.

Book of Projects (2015). *The Cross-Border Cooperation Programme Poland-Belarus-Ukraine 2007–2013*. Warsaw.

BPP (2015). *Plan Zagospodarowania Przestrzennego Województwa Lubelskiego*. Lublin: Biuro Planowania Przestrzennego Wojewodztwa Lubelskiego.

Brzeziński, Z. (1998). *The Grand Chessboard: American Primacy And Its Geostrategic Imperatives*. New York: Basic Books.

CBOS (2014). *10 lat członkostwa Polski w Unii Europejskiej. Komunikat z badań Centrum Badań Opinii Społecznej*. Online. Available: http://www.cbos.pl/SPISKOM.POL/2014/K_052_14.PDF (accessed: 22 February 2016).

Commission of the EC (2003a). *Paving the way for a New Neighbourhood Instrument*. Online. Available: http://ec.europa.eu/regional_policy/sources/docoffic/official/communic/wider/wider_en.pdf (accessed: 12 February 2016).

Commission of the EC (2003b). *Wider Europe – Neighbourhood: A New Framework for Relations with our Eastern and Southern Neighbours*. Online. Available: http://eeas.europa.eu/enp/pdf/pdf/com03_104_en.pdf (accessed: 17 February 2016).

Commission of the EC (2004). *European Neighbourhood Policy – Strategy Paper*. Online. Available: http://eur-lex.europa.eu/legal-content/EN/TXT/PDF/?uri=CELEX:52004DC0373&from=EN (accessed: 23 February 2016).

Commission of the EU (2007). *Black Sea Synergy - A New Regional Cooperation Initiative*. Online. Available: http://eeas.europa.eu/enp/pdf/pdf/com07_160_en.pdf (accessed: 22 February 2016).

Council of the EU (2008). *Council Conclusions on European Neighbourhood Policy*. Online. Available: http://www.consilium.europa.eu/ueDocs/cms_Data/docs/pressData/en/gena/98790.pdf (accessed: 24 February 2016).

Council of the EU (2009). *Joint Declaration of the Prague Eastern Partnership Summit*. Online. Available: http://www.consilium.europa.eu/uedocs/cms_data/docs/pressdata/en/er/107589.pdf (accessed: 24 February 2016).

Eberhardt, P. (2010). Koncepcje geopolityczne Aleksandra Dugina. *Przegląd Geograficzny*, 82/2, pp. 221–40.

European Commission (1998). *Partnership and Co-Operation Agreement between the European Communities and their Member States and Ukraine*. Online. Available: http://trade.ec.europa.eu/doclib/docs/2003/october/tradoc_111612.pdf (accessed: 22 February 2016).

European Commission (2006). *European Neighbourhood and Partnership Instrument (2007–2013)*. Online. Available: http://eur-lex.europa.eu/legal-content/EN/TXT/?uri=URISERV:r17101 (accessed: 2 March 2016).

European Commission (2007). *A Strong European Neighbourhood Policy – further efforts are needed*. Online. Available: http://europa.eu/rapid/press-release_IP-07–1843_en.htm?locale=en (accessed: 16 February 2016).

European Commission (2013). *Energy: Commission unveils list of 250 infrastructure projects that may qualify for €5,85 billion of funding*. Online. Available: http://europa.eu/rapid/press-release_IP-13–932_en.htm (accessed: 16 February 2016).

European Commission (2015). *EU-Ukraine Deep and Comprehensive Free Trade Area*. Online. Available: http://trade.ec.europa.eu/doclib/docs/2013/april/tradoc_150981.pdf (accessed: 11 February 2016).

European Communities (1995). *Interim Agreement on trade and trade-related matters between the European Community, the European Coal and Steel Community and the European Atomic Energy Community, of the one part, and Ukraine, of the other part*. Online. Available: http://eur-lex.europa.eu/legal-content/EN/ALL/?uri=OJ:L:1995:311:TOC (accessed: 15 February 2016).

European Council (1999). *European Council Common Strategy of 11 December 1999 on Ukraine*. Online. Available: https://www.consilium.europa.eu/uedocs/cmsUpload/ukEN.pdf (accessed: 12 February 2016).

European Parliament and Council (2014). *Regulation (EU) No 232/2014 of the European Parliament and of the Council of 11 March 2014 establishing a European Neighbourhood Instrument*. Online. Available: http://eur-lex.europa.eu/legal-content/N/TXT/?qid=1457526270706&uri=CELEX:32014R0232 (accessed: 21 February 2016).

FDI (2014). *Zovnishnopolitychni orientacii naselennia Ukrainy: reghional'nyi, vikovyi, elektoral'nyi rozpodil ta dynamika*. Fond Demokratychni Iniciatyvy im. Il'ka Kucheriva. Online. Available: http://www.dif.org.ua/ua/events/evropeiska-integracija–ukraini-sogodni–problemi_-vikliki_-zavdannja—dumka-gromadskosti-ta-ekspertiv.htm (accessed: 23 February 2016).

FDI (2015). *Chy khochut ukrainci vstupu do NATO – zaghal'nonacional'ne opytuvannia*. Fond Demokratychni Iniciatyvy im. Il'ka Kucheriva. Online. Available: http://www.dif.org.ua/en/polls/2015a/chi-hochut-ukrainci-vstupu-do-nato—zagalnonacionalne-opituvannja-.htm (accessed: 23 February 2016).

FES (2014). *The Future of EU–Ukraine Relations. Four Scenarios*. Online. Available: http://library.fes.de/pdf-files/id-moe/10608.pdf (accessed: 16 February 2016).

Ghavrylyshyn, B. (2000). *Ukraina mizh Shodom ta Zahodom, Pivnichchiu ta Pivdnem: geopolitychni mozhlyvosti ta obmezhennia*. Instytut Naukowykh Dozlidzhen' ta Politychnykh Konsul'tacij v Ukraini. Online. Available: http://www.ier.com.ua/ua/publications/working_paper?pid=1737 (accessed: 2 February 2016).

Guz-Vetter, M. (2004). *Nowe granice UE: Polska-Ukraina-Białoruś. jak wykorzystać doświadczenia polsko-niemieckiej współpracy transgranicznej?* Warszawa: Instytut Spraw Publicznych.

Hillion, C. (2005). *The Evolving System of European Union External Relations as Evidenced in the EU Partnerships with Russia and Ukraine*. Leiden: Leiden University.

Kawałko, B. (2011a). Wybrane problemy polsko-ukraińskiej współpracy transgranicznej. *Barometr Regionalny*, 2/24, pp. 35–60.

Kawałko, B. (2011b). Wybrane problemy współpracy transgranicznej, in: W. Janicki (ed.), *Województwo Lubelskie. Środowisko–społeczeństwo–gospodarka*, Lublin: Norbertinum, pp. 213–28.

Kawałko, B. (2015). Program Polska–Białoruś–Ukraina w polityce rozwoju regionów przygranicznych. *Barometr Regionalny*, 13/2, pp. 7–27.

KIIS (2016). *Yakym integhraciinym napriamkom mae ity Ukraina: Evropeis'kyi Soiuz, Mytnyi Sojuz (ghruden' 2015)*. Kyivs'kyi Mizhnarodnyi Instytut Sociologhii. Online. Available: http://kiis.com.ua/?lang=ukr&cat=reports&id=584&page=1 (accessed: 10 February 2016).

KMU (2014). *Derzhavna strategiia reghional'nogho rozvytku na period do 2020 roku*. Kiev: Kabinet Ministriv Ukrainy.

Kosow, H. and Gaßner, R. (2008). *Methods of Future and Scenarios Analysis. Overview, Assesment, and Selection Criteria*. Bonn: Deutsches Institut für Entwicklungspolitik.

Kuzio, T. (2009). Viktor Yushchenko's Foreign Policy Agenda. *Eurasia Daily Monitor*, 6/230. Online. Available: http://www.jamestown.org/programs/edm/single/?tx_ttnews[tt_news]=35840&tx_ttnews[backPid]=485&no_cache=1#.VsjzM0Bw_gY (accessed: 1 March 2016).

Legucka, A. (2008). Ewolucja polityki Unii Europejskiej wobec Ukrainy. *Doctrina. Studia Społeczno-Polityczne*, 5, pp. 113–22.

Liikanen, I. (2013). EU Common Foreign Policies in Wider Europe, in: A. Ergun and H. Isaxanli (eds) *Security and Cross-Border Cooperation in the EU, the Black Sea Region and Southern Caucasus*. Amsterdam: IOS Press BV, pp. 58–69.

LODA (2016). *Proekt Strateghii rozvytku L'vivs'koi oblasti na period do 2020 roku*. L'viv: L'vivs'ka Oblasna Derzhavna Administraciia.

Łastawski, K. (2011). Sytuacja geopolityczna Polski po przemianach ustrojowych i wstąpieniu do Unii Europejskiej. *Studia Europejskie*, 1, pp. 19–40.

Malyhina, K. (2009). EU Membership ambitions: What alternative approaches exist and how is the European foreign policy perceived in Ukraine? In: S. Schäffer and D. Tolksdorf (eds) *The EU member states and the Eastern Neighbourhood – From composite to consistent EU foreign policy?* Munich: Centrum für angewandte Politikforschung, pp. 24–8.

Mandryk, I. P. and Novak, I. I. (2012). Malyi prykordonnyi rukh iak instrument liberalizacii vizovoi polityky ta intensyfikacji torghivli mizh Ukrainoiu ta Polscheiu. *Naukovyi visnyk Volynskogho nacionalnogho uniwersytetu in. Lesi Ukrainky: Geografichni nauky*, 9/234, pp. 120–28. Online. Available: http://esnuir.eenu.edu.ua/handle/123456789/782 (accessed: 11 March 2016).

Mayhew, A. (2008). *Ukraine and the European Union: financing accelerating integration*. Warszawa: Office of the Committee for European Integration.

Ministry of Administration and Digitization (2013). *Długookresowa Strategia Rozwoju Kraju Polska 2030 – Trzecia Fala Nowoczesności*. Warszawa: Ministerstwo Administracji i Cyfryzacji.

Ministry of Development (2016). *Umowa o strefie wolnego handlu Unia Europejska – Ukraina*. Ministry of Development. Online. Available: https://www.mr.gov.pl/strony/aktualnosci/wpisz-tytul-1–3/ (accessed: 12 February 2016).

Moshes, A. (2006). *Ukraine Between a Multivector Foreign Policy and Euro-Atlantic Integration. Has It Made Its Choice?* PONARS Policy Memo No. 426. Online. Available: http://csis.org/files/media/csis/pubs/pm_0426.pdf (accessed: 17 February 2016).

Ministry of Development (2015). *Umowa partnerstwa*. Warszawa: Ministerstwo Rozwoju.

Ministry of Regional Development (2010a). *Badanie ewaluacyjne ex-post efektów transgranicznej współpracy polskich regionów w okresie 2004–2006*. Warszawa: Ministerstwo Rozwoju Regionalnego.

Ministry of Regional Development (2010b). *Krajowa Strategia Rozwoju Regionalnego 2010–2020: Regiony, Miasta, Obszary wiejskie*. Warszawa: Ministerstwo Rozwoju Regionalnego.

Ministry of Regional Development (2012a). *Koncepcja Przestrzennego Zagospodarowania Kraju 2030*. Warszawa: Ministerstwo Rozwoju Regionalnego.

Ministry of Regional Development (2012b). *Strategia Rozwoju Kraju 2020*. Warszawa: Ministerstwo Rozwoju Regionalnego.

Raszkowski, A. (2011). Program TACIS w państwach postsowieckich. *EKONOMIA*, 4/16, pp. 436–45.

Ray, J. and Esipova, N. (2010). *Ukrainians Likely Support Move Away From NATO*. GALLUP. Online. Available: http://www.gallup.com/poll/127094/ukrainians-likely-support-move-away-nato.aspx (accessed: 21 February 2016).

Rutland, P. (2015). An unnecessary war: the geopolitical roots of the Ukraine crisis, in: A. Pikulicka and R. Sakwa (eds) *Ukraine and Russia: People, Politics, Propaganda and Perspectives*. Bristol: E-International Relations, pp. 129–40.

Sadowski, R. (2004). *Współpraca transgraniczna na nowej granicy wschodniej Unii Europejskiej*. Warszawa: Ośrodek Studiów Wschodnich.

Samorząd Województwa Podkarpackiego (2013). *Strategia rozwoju województwa - podkarpackie 2020*. Rzeszów: Samorząd Województwa Podkarpackiego.

Snyder, T. (2014). Ukrainian crisis is not about Ukraine, it's about Europe. *Lt Daily*. Online. Available: http://m.en.delfi.lt/article.php?id=66368672 (accessed: 9 February 2016).

Study in Poland (2015). *Studenci zagraniczni w Polsce 2015*. Warszawa: Fundacja Edukacyjna 'Perspektywy'.

Surmacz, B. (2002). *Współczesne stosunki polsko-ukraińskie. Politologiczna analiza traktatu o dobrym sąsiedztwie*. Lublin: Wydawnictwo Uniwersytetu Marii Curie-Skłodowskiej.

Sydun, S. (2010). Ewolucja stosunków pomiędzy Ukrainą i UE. *Środkowoeuropejskie Studia Polityczne*, 3, pp. 201–16.

Szeptycki, A. (2013). *Rusi starczy dla wszystkich*. Nowa Europa Wschodnia. Online. Available: http://www.new.org.pl/1405,post.html (accessed: 2 February 2016).

UMWL (2013). *Strategia Współpracy Transgranicznej Województwa Lubelskiego, Obwodu Lwowskiego, Obwodu Wołyńskiego i Obwodu Brzeskiego na lata 2014–2020*. Lublin: Urząd Marszałkowski Województwa Lubelskiego.

UMWL (2014). *Strategia Rozwoju Województwa Lubelskiego na lata 2014–2020 (z perspektywą do 2030 roku)*. Lublin: Urząd Marszałkowski Województwa Lubelskiego.

UMWP (2014). *Plan Zagospodarowania Przestrzennego Województwa Podkarpackiego – Perspektywa 2030*. Rzeszów: Urząd Marszałkowski Województwa Podkarpackiego.

US Wrocław (2007). *Euroregiony na granicach Polski 2007*. Wrocław: Urząd Statystyczny we Wrocławiu.

Van Der Loo, G. (2016). *The EU–Ukraine Association Agreement and Deep and Comprehensive Free Trade Area. A New Legal Instrument for the EU Integration Without Membership*. Leiden, Boston: Brill Nijhoff.

VOR (2015). *Strateghiia rozvytku Volyns'koi oblasti na period do 2020 roku*. Lutsk: Volyns'ka Oblasna Rada.

Wallerstein, I. (2014). *The Geopolitics of Ukraine's Schism*. Common Dreams. Online. Available: http://www.commondreams.org/views/2014/02/15/geopolitics-ukraines-schism (accessed: 21 February 2016).

Wilson, A. (2002). *Ukraińcy*. Warsaw: Świat Książki.

Wozniak, T. (2014). *Ukraina jak pole zitknennia svitovykh geopolitychnykh ghravciv*. Ukrains'ka Pravda. Online. Available: http://blogs.pravda.com.ua/authors/voznyak/531ebe7732e70/ (accessed: 19 February 2016).

Zagorski, A. (2004). Policies towards Russia, Ukraine, Moldova and Belarus, in: R. Dannreuther (ed.) *European Union Foreign and Security Policy. Towards a Neighbourhood Policy*. London: Routledge, pp. 79–97.

Conclusion

Andrzej Jakubowski, Bogdan Kawałko, Tomasz Komornicki, Andrzej Miszczuk, and Roman Szul

The Polish–Ukrainian borderland, incorporating Lublin and Podkarpackie voivodships on the Polish side and Lviv and Volhynia oblasts on the Ukrainian side, is a relatively young borderland, since the state boundary that forms its axis was delimited in 1945 and took on its current shape following adjustments in 1951. The present border of Poland and Ukraine has experienced fluctuating levels of permeability. In the period 1945–91, when it divided Poland and the Soviet Union, to which the Ukrainian Soviet Socialist Republic belonged, it was a sealed 'hostile' border, isolating the border regions from each other. This resulted in the disproportional development of these areas, in both intrastate and cross-border dimensions.

The relations between Poland and Ukraine as two sovereign states date from 1991, when the Ukrainian nation arose from the collapsing Soviet Union and Poland, formerly a soviet 'satellite' state, regained full autonomy. Before this came about, Polish–Ukrainian relations had had a long and intricate history. The beginnings date back to the tenth century, when two nations arose which contemporary Poles and Ukrainians regard as the root of their national identity. These were the nations of the Piast dynasty (Poland) and Kiev Rus (Ukraine). The Kiev Rus crisis and Poland's expansion to the east in the fourteenth to sixteenth centuries meant that the greater part of present-day Ukraine then lay within Polish borders. The contacts and conflicts of the native Rus people with Poland and the Polish people generated specific traits and the emergence of a Ukrainian national identity. The nineteenth century saw the rise of the Ukrainian national movement aimed at creating a Ukrainian nation. However, attempts to do so during World War I and II, and in the aftermath, were unsuccessful, and were accompanied by harsh conflict with the Polish national movement. This movement managed to create a Polish nation following World War I and defend its existence in the war against the Russian Bolsheviks, as well as occupy territory in the present-day western Ukraine. As a result of World War II, the Polish–Soviet (Polish–Ukrainian) border was shifted several hundred kilometres to the west. Ethnic cleansing during the war, as well as voluntary and forced resettlement of the population, meant that both sides of the border became ethnically uniform. The border itself became an impenetrable barrier up until the end of the Soviet Union's existence.

When Ukraine regained independence in 1991 and Polish–Ukrainian relations improved there followed a period of intensive and spontaneous cross-border contact. However, the Polish–Ukrainian border did not become fully open; it worked as a filter, which was reinforced in 2004 and 2007 when Poland joined the European Union and the Schengen zone. In this way the Polish–Ukrainian border became the external boundary of the EU.

It is worth emphasizing that, in Poland, the course of transformation ran fairly smoothly, rapidly overcoming the fall in production and GDP (1992) and building a stable democratic system and market economy. Soon Poland joined the Euro-Atlantic structures: NATO (1999) and the EU (2004). An important role was played by the unanimity of Polish society in pursuing unification with the West, the prospect of membership in Euro-Atlantic structures and help and incentives from the EU. Meanwhile, in Ukraine the transformation met with set-backs. The decline in production and GDP continued throughout the 1990s, reforms were inconsistent, and those that were implemented led to corruption and the emergence of a tier of so-called oligarchs who negatively influenced the state of democracy in the country. The ideological and cultural diversification of Ukrainian society, pressure from Russia and a lack of concrete support from western nations meant that Ukraine neither wanted nor could not count on membership of Euro-Atlantic structures, but neither did it seek full unity with Eurasian structures created by Russia. The economic hardships and dissonant views of Ukrainian society regarding Ukraine's political system and place in the international setting, particularly the differing attitudes between the east and west of the country, became the cause of frustration and frequent political crises. The most severe crisis – in the years 2013–14 – led *de facto* to civil war, the annexation of Crimea by Russia (supported by the majority of the inhabitants of the peninsula) and revolt in two regions of eastern Ukraine, aided by Russia. At the present time, after diplomatic efforts and international pressure from all sides involved, fighting in the east of the country has ceased to escalate, but the conflict has still not been resolved.

Currently (at the beginning of 2016), the perspectives for the internal development of Ukraine and its place in the international system are very uncertain. In extreme scenarios Ukraine will either: 1) overcome its internal crisis, successfully implement economic and political reforms and establish close ties with the European Union, or 2) suffer an erosion of state structures and the seizure of real power by regional oligarchs wielding money, political influence and private armies. In between these two extremes, various intermediate scenarios apply. The European Union presents another source of uncertainty as regards its ability and willingness to influence the situation in Ukraine. Nor are Polish–Ukrainian relations entirely firm. On the one hand, Poland continues to support the independence and territorial integrity of Ukraine, and for this reason enjoys popularity there. On the other hand, public opinion and some political forces in Poland are troubled by symptoms of what they call a growth in nationalist feeling, including the glorification of figures and organizations which in Poland are regarded as hostile, having been responsible for the murder of Poles in World War II. The financial cost of helping Ukraine is another cause for concern, including the sanctions imposed on trade with Russia and Russia's contra-sanctions, particularly the embargo on Polish food imports.

Over the last few decades, on a European scale, the significance of cooperation between borderland regions has grown, with the aim of mitigating the negative effects of the border's existence, improving the living conditions of the borderland region's inhabitants and utilizing the scope for development by, for example, smoothing out the variations in economic development levels resulting from the peripheral location of borderland zone, improving the transport infrastructure, enhancing the region's attractiveness for investment and increasing competitiveness. However, while the functioning of the borderland regions of internal EU borders is aided by their permeability, resulting from a reduction in formal and legal barriers, cooperation along external EU borders remains problematic.

The fact that problems relating to cross-border cooperation are included in the main developmental aims of national and regional strategic documents confirms the intent to overcome existing barriers and limitations of cooperation and to spur development by using the scope, resources and potential of the borderland regions. This is further supported by the joint preparation and implementation by the four regions of the Strategy for Cross-border cooperation of Lublin Voivodship, Lviv Oblast, Volhynia Oblast and Brest Oblast 2014–20, which represents the first document of this type prepared for a cross-border area situated along the external border of the European Union. The strategy presents an interesting example of action aimed at effectively utilizing the cross-border development potential of neighbouring regions and the scope offered by the European cohesion policy. At the same time, the fact that this is the first document of this type concerning a cross-border area along the external border of the EU lends it a unique and exemplary character.

The Polish–Ukrainian borderland is among the least developed areas in Europe, displaying clear peripheral traits in both geographical and economic aspects. Moreover, the level of development in the regions on either side of the analysed section of the external EU boundary is marked by considerable asymmetry, to the disadvantage of the Ukrainian side. This, in consideration of geopolitical circumstances to date, only further impedes the development of advanced forms of cross-border cooperation and improved cohesion between Polish and Ukrainian borderland regions. Furthermore, the strong economic ties (through trade) are largely generated by major economic centres far removed from the border (central Poland, Kiev, eastern Ukraine). Meanwhile, social relations and those relating to the labour market and education remain focused within the borderland. Official economic cooperation with Ukraine has gradually moved away, in spatial terms, from the borderland area. The zone for which a Ukrainian partner is most important in international trade has become limited to the few units directly neighbouring the border crossings. Intermediaries dealing in foreign trade are of major importance here. The scale of borderland trade relies heavily on economic cycles and is sensitive to signals from the global economy.

The peripheralization of the Polish–Ukrainian borderland has been exacerbated by the poor transport access to the area, both on a European scale as well as within the respective countries. A breakthrough in this situation is the completion of the Polish A4 motorway in 2016, running the whole stretch from the German border to the Ukrainian border. Other investments in Poland, implemented using EU structural funds, have also made a difference.

The permeability of the Polish–Ukrainian border is currently fairly low, primarily owing to the existence of formal and legal barriers. The role of infrastructural barriers is of secondary significance, and it is unlikely that a growth in the number of check-points will improve permeability. The possibility of launching tourist check-points (similar to the border crossings existing on the Polish–Belarusian border), particularly in the Bieszczady region, remains an open question.

Social relations in the borderland are currently dominated by Ukrainian citizens. They are the main participants in borderland trade and temporary migration for work or educational purposes. Inhabitants of the Polish side of the border take part in petty trade, mainly importing excise goods (fuel, alcohol, tobacco). Data on Ukrainian arrivals indirectly indicate the existence of unregistered migration from Ukraine to Poland and the European Union. They also prove that Poland is a transit country for a large group of those arriving. A relatively small number of third-country citizens cross the Polish–Ukrainian border en route to the European Union. Until the end of 2015 there was no sign of migration pressure from Middle Eastern nations. There is also little transit traffic from Romania and Bulgaria, despite its being the shortest geographical route. Meanwhile, transit traffic from Russia broke off as a result of the events of 2014–15.

The geopolitical crisis in Ukraine resulted in a fall in the number of crossings by heavy goods vehicles, while passenger traffic increased. The direction of HGV border traffic has been influenced by the gradual improvement in the road infrastructure in Poland. As a result, we can observe renewed concentrations of traffic on the main road corridors (earlier on, at the beginning of transition, the traffic tended to spread out to make use of newly opened border crossings).

Records of overnight accommodation offered to Ukrainian citizens in Poland show that the borderland benefits only to a limited extent from longer stays of visitors from across the border (they mostly head for large towns or to certain tourist resorts). Nor does the borderland benefit much from transit traffic, which generally favours the Polish–German border area.

The above-mentioned conditions and processes have led to a deepening of the economic asymmetry which works to the disadvantage of Ukraine, including its borderland regions at the external EU boundary. As long as there is no significant tightening of economic cooperation between the EU and Ukraine, this situation is set to persist in the long term.

Index